PECULIAR PEOPLE

PECULIAR PEOPLE

MORMONS AND SAME-SEX ORIENTATION

EDITED BY

Ron Schow, Wayne Schow & Marybeth Raynes

FOREWORD BY

Lowell L. Bennion

SIGNATURE BOOKS   SALT LAKE CITY

1991

Jacket illustration by Trevor Southey, Betrothed, *pen and ink, 1991*
Jacket design by Ron Stucki

© 1991 by Signature Books, Inc. All rights reserved.
Signature Books is a registered trademark of Signature Books, Inc.
Printed in the United States of America.

∞ Printed on acid-free paper.

95   94   93   6   5   4   3

LIBRARY OF CONGRESS CATALOGING-IN-PUBLICATION DATA
Peculiar People: Mormons and Same-Sex Orientation
edited by Ron Schow, Wayne Schow, Marybeth Raynes
p.   cm.
Includes bibliographical references.
ISBN 1-56085-012-4, cloth
ISBN 1-56085-046-9, paper
1. Homosexuality—Religious aspects—Mormon church.
2. Mormon church—Doctrines. 3. Mormon gays.
I. Schow, Ron II. Schow, Wayne III. Raynes, Marybeth
BX8643.H65P43   1991
261.8'35766'088283—dc20
91-31162

for Brad

who challenged our complacency
and enlarged our vision of
human potential

Contents

II. PROFESSIONAL AND CHRISTIAN PERSPECTIVES

Foreword

Lowell L. Bennion

Among many members of the Church of Jesus Christ of Latter-day Saints homosexuality is regarded as disgraceful, and those engaging in homosexual acts who do not repent have often been excommunicated.

It can be a jarring experience for LDS persons to have a son or daughter, a spouse, a sibling, or a friend, one who has been active in their church and who seems to be living a normal life, confess to them that he or she is homosexual and has been throughout life. The confessing person may further tell them of trying in every way to overcome his or her homosexuality through prayers, counseling, and sometimes even more drastic treatments, such as electric shock therapy, all to no avail. Such revelations may be all the more surprising if as so often happens his or her life has been characterized by exemplary religious faith and service.

This book came into being because Ron Schow, Wayne Schow, and Marybeth Raynes had witnessed either in friends or offspring or clients the dilemma of the Mormon homosexual in our midst. They recognized their own lack of understanding and need for more information. They sought not merely a theoretical, scientific view, but especially a human perspective—how Mormon homosexuals feel about themselves, how they get along with their families and associates both in the church and in society. Above all they were interested in the challenge of creating a better climate of understanding and tolerance for homosexual people.

Peculiar People: Mormons and Same-Sex Orientation begins with personal accounts of homosexuality, how individuals have reacted to this condition, how they have tried unsuccessfully to change,

---

Lowell L. Bennion holds a Ph.D. from the University of Strasbourg, France. He served as director of the LDS Institute of Religion adjacent to the University of Utah for twenty-six years and as a professor of sociology at the university. He is a founder and past director of Salt Lake City's charitable Community Services Council.

how they have sought desperately to make troubled marriages work, how they have struggled to maintain their religious faith. These personal accounts are followed by the experiences of family members and friends in their relationships with homosexuals. The book concludes with the findings of professionals interested in the scientific study of human sexuality. They are convinced that homosexuality is complex in origin. Some of them believe that there is evidence to support the conclusion that a genetic or biological basis contributes to the sexual orientation of an individual. If this is true, it explains why homosexuals find change so difficult, and it obliges us to evaluate anew our attitudes towards gays and lesbians.

The editors are to be commended for their labors and their willingness to share their feelings and information.

Editors' Introduction

For some readers an explanation of the title of this book may be needed. In the Bible the phrase "peculiar people" describes favorably the Hebrews as special children of God with distinctive traits. Latter-day Saints use the phrase to refer to themselves in this sense. We adopted it for our title because of its irony in relation to homosexuals, whom society has frequently chosen to label as "peculiar." We think it captures well the ambiguous position of homosexuals in our midst, loved of God surely, with perhaps a special status, and at the same time misunderstood and held in contempt by many.

As the editors of *Peculiar People: Mormons and Same-Sex Orientation*, we do not ourselves agree on all the complex questions relating to homosexuality. But we share the following persuasions:

First, homosexuality touches the lives, directly and indirectly, of far more Latter-day Saints than is generally recognized. There is no reason to believe that there are fewer Mormon homosexuals proportionately than in the general populace. Assuming a worldwide Mormon population of nearly 8 million, and that 10 percent of these men, women, and children are homosexual, this means there are almost 800,000 homosexual Mormons. Each one of them comes with parents, with grandparents, usually with siblings, aunts, uncles, cousins, sometimes with a spouse, sometimes with children. From this perspective, one can easily grasp how much larger than 10 percent is the number of Mormons affected by the phenomenon of homosexuality.

Second, because of the condemnation of homosexuality by their church, most Mormons are ill-prepared, emotionally and intellectually, to confront this fact of life. When young Latter-day Saints begin to realize that they are "different," they almost inevitably conclude that they are perversely out of harmony with what one ought to be. This is a culturally-conditioned response, typically attended by guilt and shame. Thereafter follow predictably the anxious—even desperate—efforts to reorient those sexual feelings, for to be homosexual is contrary to all the scenarios for a happy life that the dominant religious culture has sanctioned.

As for Latter-day Saint (LDS) parents, their hopes and dreams for their children typically rest on a foundation of marriage and family increase. When a son or daughter then comes to believe that his or her homosexuality is not deliberately chosen but a condition to which one is born, a condition that significantly alters one's life path, how are the parents to deal with the flood of emotions which result, how are they to resolve the contradictions generated by love and loyalty and faith?

In varying degrees these feelings of shame, bewilderment, disapproval, or anger may be felt by other family members and friends. Even those called on to minister to the homosexual person—religious or professional counselors—must confront the ambivalence created by views which deny the legitimacy of an insistent divergent sexual orientation.

Third, Latter-day Saints who encounter homosexuality—personally or through a family member—face practical problems. Frequently they need someone to talk with, someone who they believe will be both knowledgeable and understanding. And they need information. Unfortunately for many Mormons it is difficult to find either. The stigma attached to homosexuality both in the church and in the culture generally makes them reluctant to "confess" their personal or family problem, especially if they feel that the friends or ecclesiastical leaders to whom they would normally turn are unlikely to have informed and noncondemnatory views. At the same time, while there is no dearth of helpful published material relating to homosexuality, many Mormons feel cut off from it for one of two reasons. First, the shame they feel about homosexuality at home is sufficient to inhibit their seeking out information in libraries and bookstores. Second, even if one is bold enough to ask for it, most of what has been written about homosexuality originated with persons whose views and experience lie outside the Mormon world. They desire information which takes their Mormon connection into account.

Fourth, much of the suffering endured by gays and lesbians in the church is not the result of their own doing but rather caused by an inadequate Christian response on the part of many in the

heterosexual majority. To the extent that the latter hold a mista-
kenly narrow—even bigoted—view of homosexuality, they help to
perpetuate the climate of scorn, fear, and hatred in which gays
and lesbians must live. They undermine in this way the attempts
of homosexuals to realize their potential. We think all Latter-day
Saints should respond to their homosexual brothers and sisters
in an open-minded, compassionate way and should inform themselves adequately in order to do so.

Peculiar People: Mormons and Same-Sex Orientation has grown
from an awareness of these conditions and the needs they create.
We reasoned that a conveniently available collection of relevant
materials, drawn largely from the experiences of Latter-day Saints,
would fill a pressing need. It could help those first confronting
homosexuality to overcome the obstacles described above. It could
assure them that they are not alone and that there are resources
available to help them. Not least, we hoped that such a collection
would encourage church members generally to become better
informed about the realities in the lives of many around them and
thus become better able to respond with acceptance and love.

Latter-day Saints who attempt to discover "the certain truth"
about homosexuality are likely to be frustrated. For while some
individuals believe they have the last word, there is not at this time
a generally accepted, wholly consistent set of explanations. The
best one can do is to consider thoughtfully the experiential assessments made by homosexuals and others, the scientific data, incomplete as they are, and the theological evaluations, evolving as they
are. One must then sift out from this complex mix those elements
that seem mutually consistent.

The selections in this volume were chosen to provide an
opportunity for such sifting. From LDS church documents we have
included only official statements on homosexuality. (Other LDS
documents having quasi-offical status have been published elsewhere and circulated widely.) We have attempted to gather the
most thoughtful responses on the subject that we could find. We
were not necessarily seeking polished, professionally-written
pieces. What we recognized from our own reading is that one
learns much about homosexuality from those who have confronted it themselves, and so we wanted to present their voices, with
authenticity being the foremost criterion for inclusion. We wanted

to present varying constructive views (we have allowed some personal bias, but clearly bigoted statements have been avoided), and while we acknowledge that our own views of the subject have inevitably influenced the selection process, readers will discover here a considerable heterogeneity and even at times outright contradiction. (For example, on the question of "change" and the degree to which it is possible, many of the essays take a position but each author speaks for himself or herself.) Readers will observe that some of the same points are stressed repeatedly. We chose not to eliminate this repetition because it emphasizes prevalent facets of the homosexual experience, if not final "truth."

In addition to excerpts from published books, essays have been drawn from such diverse sources as *Dialogue: A Journal of Mormon Thought; Sunstone* or annual Sunstone conferences; *Exponent II;* proceedings of a Conference of the Association of Mormon Counselors and Psychotherapists; publications by Parents and Friends of Lesbians and Gays (P-FLAG); and *Affinity,* the newsletter of Affirmation, a Mormon organization for gays and lesbians. Finally several accounts not previously published or formally presented are included.

These materials are divided into two sections: Personal Perspectives and Professional/Christian Perspectives. Among the personal voices are accounts by gays and lesbians, married partners, and family members and friends. Both "church approved" and "nonapproved" perspectives are represented. In all of them readers will find evidence of honest attempts to confront the challenges of homosexuality. The professionals represented in the latter half of the book include on the one hand researchers, therapists, medical doctors, and psychologists and on the other theologians and church members who confront Christian and moral issues.

Eight of the contributors to this anthology have declined to identify themselves by name. Their reasons for not doing so are understandable, given the prejudice that exists in our culture and the disadvantages often attending such disclosure. That so much anonymity should be necessary is a sad comment on the level of tolerance found in our midst.

In compiling this volume, we have sought the advice of many individuals. They included persons of varied persuasions and positions, from representatives of the establishment to those alienated from it. Some helped us secure material, some read the manuscript at various stages, some challenged us in our conception of our task. We have benefitted from their suggestions, and we believe the book is richer and better balanced as a result. We regret that concerns relating to anonymity prevent us from acknowledging them individually. To all of them, we express our sincere appreciation.

Terminology, Misconceptions, and "Sealed Premises"

A major difficulty in discussing homosexuality and heterosexuality derives from misapplying the terms themselves through oversimplifying their implications. These words are often used to suggest that all of humankind can be divided into two mutually exclusive categories. The extensive gathering of sexual histories from about 18,000 people by Alfred Kinsey and his associates revealed that no such strict division exists, that in fact there is a continuum between two extremes of sexual orientation (Kinsey et al. 1948, 1953). Kinsey used a 7-point scale to distinguish the strictly heterosexual person (0) from the strictly homosexual person (6). But between these extremes, a large number of people were distributed. Kinsey also distinguished between homosexual behavior and homosexual feelings. Persons do not necessarily act on their feelings. Sometimes persons with a heterosexual orientation become drawn into homosexual activities and vice versa. The Kinsey study stressed the importance of distinguishing carefully the nature of homosexual/heterosexual feelings *and* experience. Kinsey and his associates reported that between one-fourth and one-third of all males surveyed had some degree of homosexual feeling and a similar number had been involved in homosexual behavior. For women they found a somewhat lower prevalence.

Two conclusions emerge from Kinsey's findings. First, we need to acknowledge how relatively common homosexual feeling and behavior are; and second, we need to see that homosexual behavior may or may not correspond to a strongly persistent homosexual orientation. Some of Kinsey's work is included in the appendices to this anthology and may be studied by the interested reader.

We wish to make clear from the outset that most of the essays compiled here describe people who would be assigned 5 or 6 on

Kinsey's scale. Thus, they deal with people who are very strong and persistent in their homosexual orientation, whether or not they have acted upon such feelings. Only a few of the essays address bisexuality, a condition wherein sexual attraction is substantial toward both the opposite and the same sex (2, 3, and 4 on the Kinsey scale). Bisexual people will likely identify to some degree with what is written here about homosexual orientation. Because of their intermediate position they may find it easier to conform to church behavior standards (many are married and as a result avoid ostracism and censure). Nevertheless, they too experience difficulties. Perhaps some future publication will more fully explore their concerns.

The sometimes bitter controversy over whether homosexuality is "curable"—whether individuals can change not only homosexual behavior but, more crucially, homosexual orientation—might be clarified if all parties recognized the implications of the sexual continuum described by Kinsey. If those who claim to have "cured" homosexuals by helping them to exercise their heterosexual potential and to ignore their homosexual feelings have actually treated those rating 2, 3, or 4 on Kinsey's scale, such adaptability may not be expected in people rating 5 and 6, and their success may not be as widespread as alleged. On the other hand, those who argue that homosexuals can never "change" must beware of the opposite oversimplification which ignores the bisexuality of those in the middle range of the continuum.

Some of the controversy surrounding homosexuality can be eliminated at the outset by recognizing several widely believed misconceptions about the psychology and behavior of homosexuals. Homosexuality is often seen as a condition dealing primarily with sexuality: sexual impulses, feelings, and behavior. Since the word "sexual" appears in the word "homosexual," this idea is easily promulgated. However, both gays and lesbians affirm that their sense of self is not rooted mainly in their sexual impulses. Rather this sense of self is tied to those with whom they are bonded, with whom they feel trust and delight, with whom they primarily want to spend their life. They assert that their sexual interest and response are tied to the basic feeling of deep connection with the same sex. Most homosexuals say that they felt a stronger friendship, interest, or bond with people of the same sex long before sexual interest emerged. We do not want to discard the idea of sexuality; it simply needs to be placed in correct context (Blumstein and Schwartz 1983). The best way to do that is to ask readers to bring to mind what they think is the central concern in life for a heterosexual person. Are heterosexual relationships only sexually inclined or do they have roots in a much broader range of connections, with sexuality only a part of it?

Linked with the stereotype of homosexuals being primarily sexual is the common belief that homosexuals are hypersexual (Moses and Hawkins 1982). Those who hold this view would say, "Of course homosexuals are sexually active every day, maybe several times, maybe with different partners. The whole lifestyle revolves around dangerous and immoral promiscuity. No lasting relationships, no family, no children are available to gays." Admittedly any group which is stereotyped—including Mormons—will have some members fitting the stereotype almost perfectly. Those people often are most visible and most publicized, and as a result the broader reality is distorted. It is true that some homosexuals fit the above stereotype. But in fact most homosexuals are like other members of the community. Desires for continuity, fidelity, family, and true caring abound among homosexuals just as they do among heterosexuals. The national movement by gays toward affirming marital union and its privileges confirms that the values which support committed love run deep (Berzon 1988).

Lesbians take particular exception to the hypersexual label. Sexual interest occurs of course, but most would say that it follows the pattern of women in general: sexual response occurs in the context of feeling loved and safe, not the other way around. In fact, the research on sexual frequency among various types of couples shows that lesbian couples have the lowest frequency of sexual interaction in long-term relationships (Blumstein and Schwartz 1983).

Additionally, more and more lesbian and gay couples are having children (Barrett 1989). Many of these children are from former marriages, but increasingly many are born in unions, often through artificial insemination or surrogate mothers. The prejudice toward children being raised in gay families is great, and the dynamics are difficult to work through, though heterosexuals also face unique challenges in raising children.

Another common error is the belief that sexually-active homosexuals are addictively sexual. Again, some homosexuals are sexually addicted. But this topic is separate from homosexuality. Sexual addictions (i.e., obsessive fantasies over which one has little control, seeking sexual satiation often to avoid other issues in one's life, or a repeated entrenched cycle of excitement and release that interferes with normal functioning) are common among heterosexuals as among homosexuals. The topic of sexual addiction is coming more to the fore, and treatments of it in current books and articles are primarily focused on heterosexual interaction (Carnes 1983). The comparative addiction or compulsion rates of heterosexuals and homosexuals are simply not known, and we have chosen not to address this topic because we do not consider it unique to the homosexual experience.

An appendage of the hypersexual stereotype is the conviction that homosexuals are more unfaithful, more sneaky, more secretive than heterosexuals. Similar beliefs about blacks have also been held in the past: they are less intelligent, less achievement-oriented, and so on. Both groups acquired this stereotype because they were forced to stay in an underground culture in order to function. Both blacks and homosexuals have suffered for wanting to enjoy the same rights to a self-determined life as white heterosexuals take for granted. Within Mormonism we have the history of the underground society of polygamy with its tortured rules of conduct when both families and the church were threatened or damaged. From the diaries and records of these families emerged tales of pain and loneliness which echo feelings expressed in homosexual discourse.

It is true that homosexual unions are more fragile than heterosexual unions (Berzon 1988). But it may be that the prejudice against them and the backlash occurring when they become public contribute greatly to that relative instability. In the research on stability in heterosexual marriage, several facts have emerged. Those couples who marry within a church, who have good relationships with their families, and who are embedded within an approving network of friends and community are most likely to have marriages that last. Since none of these conditions easily exist for gay and lesbian couples, the dissolution rate is understandably much higher.

It may be that some of the hypersexuality that occurs in both homosexual and heterosexual cultures occurs because of the need to hide part of one's true nature. John Money in his book *Gay, Straight or In-between* (1988) sees addictive or highly variant compulsive sexual behavior occurring far more often in people who are raised to believe their good self is non-sexual and their sexual self is bad or evil. Since all people are sexual and many have a naturally occurring high degree of sexual interest, the split occurs and widens as sexual behavior and other parts of the self grow farther and farther apart.

One final misconception. Homosexuals are not pedophiles, persons whose sexual fantasies, feelings, and behavior are directed toward children (Money 1988). Pedophiles are generally heterosexual. As with sexual addictions, pedophilia is not a topic for this book.

In his book *How Real is Real?* Paul Watzlawick (1977) introduces the idea of a "sealed premise." When a person has a firm belief which is not open to revision, *any* new information or experience, pro or con, validates that idea or premise. For example, life's experiences may be regarded as blessings from God. If those experiences are favorable, if they are desired, they are seen as direct blessings. If an event is negative or unwanted, it will be seen as teaching an important lesson or principle and regarded as a blessing in disguise.

The concept of a sealed premise, often rooted in a deeper life orientation, may help to explain why people hold such varied views on homosexuality. For example, a person who believes that science is the most valid means to determine what is real will be impressed by what biological or psychological researchers say about homosexuality and will discount ways of knowing that fall outside that premise. Those who believe that final truth is revealed spiritually will be certain that homosexuality is sinful if those they regard as God's agents claim such is the case. They will evaluate scientific research according to its compatibility with their sealed premise. Those who rely principally on their own direct experience as the final test of what is real relative to homosexuality also have a sealed premise, in relation to which they relegate scientific or spiritual authority to an inferior status.

These sealed-premise postures illustrate in part why as a culture we will not easily achieve congruent understanding of such phenomena as homosexuality. Implicitly they suggest the need for a more open, more comprehensive premise. Such a premise would help us understand why we have different views and enable us to live more easily with each other. Under the umbrella of a more expansive premise our arguments could be tempered and less damaging to those who differ from our views. Above all, a comprehensive, open premise would regard all humans as God's children, and it would encourage us to find what can be loved in each individual. It would bring us to a wider understanding of life and to the recognition that diverse, even paradoxical experience is helpful to learning.

For most of us, sealed premises limit our ability to expand our horizons. But if we are willing (and others are willing to allow us) to seek accommodation and reconciliation, if we can broaden or remold our premises to recognize the compatibilities in new information and experience, and if at the same time we refrain from attempting to persuade others on the basis of one viewpoint or one isolated set of data only, we will move towards wholeness as individuals and as members of communities. The application of these principles to the debate over sexual orientation and behavior seems obvious.

Historical Overview

For the benefit of readers whose awareness of the history of homosexuality is slight, we offer here a brief overview to explain how the current cultural situation developed. Lengthy treatises have been devoted to this subject, and readers may wish to consult some of them. Our purpose in the several pages that follow is simply to highlight a few significant historical facts, especially those relevant to Latter-day Saints.

While homosexuality has been present in all cultures, ancient and modern, acceptance of homosexual behavior has varied (Crooks and Baur 1987). Some nonwestern societies have shown a high level of tolerance for it, and in the West such early Greeks as Homer, Sappho, and Plato idealized homosexual relationships as ennobling. Despite evidence that homosexual behavior was found among the Hebrews, homosexuality has generally been condemned in the Judeo-Christian tradition. Jesus was silent on the subject, but church fathers such as Paul, Augustine (353-430), and Thomas Aquinas (1225-74) spoke against homosexual behavior, consistent with their view that sexual feelings are sinful and that any sexual act not intended for procreation should be forbidden.

Because of this strong condemnation of sexual expression outside of marriage in the Christian West, homosexuals have generally kept to themselves until recently to avoid persecution and prosecution. During repressive periods such as the colonial American era, homosexuals were variously punished by execution, castration, whipping, branding, imprisonment, and lobotomy. In relatively more tolerant periods, such as the Renaissance and the modern era, homosexual inclinations of prominent individuals were acknowledged. Such people include Leonardo Da Vinci, Michelangelo, and Sir Francis Bacon. Recent examples include George Sand, Walt Whitman, Peter Tchaikovsky, Oscar Wilde, Gertrude Stein, Somerset Maugham, E. M. Forster, Willa Cather, Langston Hughes, Tennessee Williams, Truman Capote, and Adrienne Rich.

In the late nineteenth century, physicians took an interest in homosexuality as something they could reverse. They categorized it not as crime but as illness. At the same time, the medical profession made other prescriptions for sexual health such as advising that sexual activity be pursued only in moderation. In 1886 an influential work by German neurologist Richard Kraft-Ebbing argued that homosexuals had an unchangeable, congenital condition. A few years later, however, Sigmund Freud challenged this theory, proposing that homosexuals were stuck in an early stage of their development. He viewed homosexuals as regressed but not sick. He once said about homosexuality, "It is nothing to be ashamed of, no vice, no degradation, it cannot be classified as an illness." But most of the psychiatric profession subsequent to Freud ignored this caveat and prescribed long-term therapies, shock treatments, and even brain surgery.

In the 1940s and 1950s Alfred Kinsey and his associates (1948, 1953) published major surveys of male and female sexuality. They included assessments of homosexual feelings and behavior, which they found to be more common than had previously been assumed. Based on their data, Kinsey and his associates viewed homosexuality as within the range of normal sexual behavior. In 1957 the Wolfenden Report commissioned by the British Parliament concluded that homosexuality should be decriminalized since it was not harmful, not a disease, and not a therapeutic problem. Studies by psychologists Evelyn Hooker and Mark Freedman found no differences in the psychological profiles of healthy homosexual men and women compared to heterosexuals. Such findings subsequently led the American Psychological Association and the American Psychiatric Association to conclude that homosexuality is neither illness nor cause for medical intervention. These professional reassessments led directly to the rescinding of laws aimed at homosexuals. In addition to Great Britain, such nations as Canada, France, the Netherlands, and Sweden no longer prohibit sexual acts involving consenting adults. In Holland and Denmark, same-sex marriages were legalized in 1989. A number of American states have abolished anti-homosexual laws, beginning with Illinois in 1961. The Stonewall Riots of 1969 in New York City, which mark the beginning of the lesbian and gay liberation movement, drew attention to persecution and discrimination directed against homosexuals. However, since the Stonewall Riots only a few municipalities have passed laws banning discrimination against homosexuals in employment, insurance, housing, and so on (Crooks and Baur 1987).

In the early history of the LDS church, the subject of homosexuality was not addressed in revelations and only very rarely in speeches, diaries, ecclesiastical court transcripts, and other contemporary records (see, for example, *The Wasp*, 22 July 1842; Taylor 1971, 146). Male church officers sometimes voiced strong emotional ties to fellow priesthood leaders, and both men and women manifested considerable affection toward members of the same sex (see JD 5:99, 22:365; Kenney 1983, 2:510-16, 540; Faulring 1987, 366). By and large, this homosocial expression was culturally based and changed within Mormonism as the broader society became increasingly influenced by Victorian mores. Joseph Smith made no recorded statements on the subject of homosexuality, nor did it figure prominently in pronouncements by subsequent prophets until the middle of the twentieth century. A few ecclesiastical and secular sources commencing in the 1840s indicate anti-gay attitudes within the Mormon community, reflecting mainstream Christian rejection of homosexuals and homosexuality (Archives

GLHSU).

The recent history of homosexuality in the Mormon church includes the expulsion of homosexuals from Brigham Young University and the excommunication policy which developed out of the recommendations of apostles Spencer W. Kimball and Mark E. Petersen. Elders Kimball and Petersen were assigned in 1959 to be in charge of sexual cases (Kimball and Kimball 1977). During the following decade they counseled many homosexuals referred from BYU and throughout the church. These people usually underwent counseling over a period of time and were given an opportunity to "repent" before dismissal and excommunication occurred. Beginning at the time of his assignment in 1959, Elder Kimball also began working on a book, *The Miracle of Forgiveness,* which was published ten years later. By then he had formulated ideas about homosexuality which have dominated church policy since that time.

Elder Kimball's view of homosexuality was also translated into a church publication called *Hope for Transgressors* (1970). This nine-page manual concluded with 73 scriptural references ostensibly relating to homosexuality and listed Elders Kimball and Peterson as people to contact on homosexual cases. This manual was followed by a publication, *New Horizons for Homosexuals,* written in the form of a "letter to a dear friend" printed by the LDS church and signed by Spencer W. Kimball (1971). In 1973 a statement on homosexuality by the First Presidency was published in the *Priesthood Bulletin.* In part it declared that "homosexuality in men and women runs counter to . . . divine objectives and, therefore, is to be avoided and forsaken. . . . Failure to work closely with one's bishop or stake president in cases involving homosexual behavior will require prompt Church court action." This declaration was followed immediately by an LDS Welfare Services publication entitled *Homosexuality* (1973).

By the mid- to late 1970s church policy had prompted vigorous efforts to "help" homosexuals at BYU. A program utilizing negative reinforcement (shock therapy) was established, and homosexual students were sometimes followed to gay establishments by BYU security police and referred to school administrators as violators of BYU rules (McBride 1976). In 1978 *New Horizons for Homosexuals* was published in a slightly revised form as *A Letter to a Friend,* and that same year Apostle Boyd K. Packer gave a special address entitled *To the One* at a BYU Sunday devotional. With one exception only, he referred to homosexuality as "perversion." The church position was modified slightly with a second edition of *Homosexuality* (1981). That same year a new LDS Social Services manual incorporated testimonials from people claiming to have been cured of homosexual orientation.

As developed by apostles Kimball, Petersen, and Packer and described in these publications, church policy in the 1960s and 1970s seemed to rest on the following premises concerning homosexuality: (1) it is inherently sinful and proscribed by the scriptures as such; and (2) it is incompatible with the doctrinal concepts of marriage, family, and procreation. Little if any distinction was made between homosexual feelings and homosexual behavior: both were condemned. Based on these premises, homosexuality was denied authenticity, and vigorous efforts were implemented to change the "mistaken" sexual "choice" of those with homosexual feelings. These efforts took the form of therapy and counseling which stressed prayer and fasting, mind control, gospel goals of mission-marriage-children, avoidance of "sinful" behavior such as masturbation and association with other homosexuals, and—as a last resort—electric shock and vomiting aversion therapies to "reorient" erotic feeling (McBride 1976). According to most reports, these therapies did little to change the orientation of those to whom they were applied.

The 1970s also saw the first efforts by individuals to question openly official church policy and procedures regarding homosexuality. In an article in *The Advocate*, a national gay-oriented magazine, managing editor Robert McQueen (1975), himself a former Mormon missionary, described critically the church's policy toward gays. In 1977 a support group for lesbian and gay Mormons called Affirmation was formed in Los Angeles and soon spread to other metropolitan areas, including Salt Lake City a year later. The next year Cloy Jenkins, a student at BYU, collaborated on a treatise evaluating church policy and doctrine on homosexuality. Published anonymously under the title, *Prologue* (1978), it was sold in booklet form and also appeared in *The Advocate*. At about the same time Mark E. Petersen (1977-78) wrote six editorials for the *Church News* attacking the gay liberation movement as "a menace to the population at large."

Several articles which appeared on the BYU campus in 1982 in the independent student-run *Seventh East Press* encouraged a more tolerant attitude toward homosexuality. Carol Lynn Pearson's *Goodbye, I Love You* (1986) described the difficulties in a loving marital relationship when one of the partners (in this case her husband) has dominant homosexual feelings. Appearing at a juncture when publicity about AIDS seemed near its zenith, the book did much to foster dialogue about homosexuality among church members. However, in an interview published in the *Church News*, Apostle Dallin Oaks (1987) stated that the church's position would not be softened due to AIDS. The *Church News* summed up his message with the phrases, "Love the sinner; condemn the sin." An official First Presidency statement on AIDS (1988) also made this clear. More recently, a semi-annual world conference address by Elder Packer (1990) indicated that he intended to hold to a strict standard for those with homosexual orientation, even though he acknowledged that the answers are not simple and that perhaps "leaders in the Church do not really understand these problems." But they understand temptation, he asserted. To those speaking in favor of tolerance for homosexuals he said, "What one is may deserve unlimited tolerance, what one does only a measured amount."

In the late 1980s, articles relating to homosexuality appeared more regularly in Mormon-oriented publications such as *Sunstone*, *Dialogue: A Journal of Mormon Thought*, and *Exponent II*, including an important treatise by Jan Stout (1987), past president of the Utah Psychiatric Association and professor of clinical psychology at the University of Utah. Such writings continued to raise concerns about the effect of church policy on the lives of lesbians and gays. Some addressed the apparent incompatibility between doctrine and experience; others challenged the value of counseling and therapeutic approaches advocated by the church.

In the midst of such dialogue, the LDS *Bishop's Handbook* was revised to condemn not "homosexuality" but "homosexual relations" and to allow a more tolerant attitude toward celibate homosexuals. Some church officials currently support therapy promising less than a full "cure" and emphasizing celibacy rather than heterosexual conversion. Church policies have been softened

(Ferre, et al. 1989; Pritt and Pritt 1987). Excommunication for homosexuality is now discouraged, and there seems to be more recognition in LDS Social Services that homosexuality is not chosen. In 1988 the Mormon church appointed a special assistant to the director of LDS Social Services to study the issues and provide individual and group counseling for church members and their families. His presence and involvement in homosexual concerns has initiated a period of review and a more tolerant and compassionate environment. Viewed against the background of the past thirty years, these changes offer hope of a significant transition.

References

Anonymous. *Prologue: An Examination of the Mormon Attitude Towards Homosexuality.* Los Angeles: Affirmation, 1978.

Archives, GLHSU—Gay and Lesbian Historical Society of Utah, Salt Lake City.

Barrett, Martha Barron. *Invisible Lives: The Truth About Millions of Women Loving Women.* New York: William Morrow, 1989.

Berzon, Betty. *Permanent Partners: Building Gay and Lesbian Relationships That Last.* New York: E.P. Dutton, 1988.

Blumstein, P. and P. Schwartz. *American Couples: Money, Work, Sex.* New York: William Morrow, 1983.

Brodie, Fawn M. *No Man Knows My History: The Life of Joseph Smith.* New York: Alfred A. Knopf, 1976.

Carnes, Patrick. *Out of the Shadows: Understanding Sexual Addiction.* Minneapolis: CompCare Publications, 1983.

Crooks, Robert and Karla Baur. *Our Sexuality.* 3d ed. Menlo Park, CA: The Benjamin/Cummings Publishing Co., 1987.

Faulring, Scott H., ed. *An American Prophet's Record: The Diaries and Journals of Joseph Smith.* Salt Lake City: Signature Books in association with Smith Research Associates, 1987.

Ferre, Richard C., Clyde Sullivan, Thomas Pritt, and Gary Day. "LDS and Other Christian Approaches to Homosexuality." Panel at Sunstone Symposium, Salt Lake City, Aug. 1989.

First Presidency. "Statement on AIDS." Salt Lake City: Church of Jesus Christ of Latter-day Saints, *Ensign* 18 (July 1988): 79. Reissued by the Public Communications Department, April 1991.

———. "Statement on Homosexuality." In *Priesthood Bulletin,* Feb. 1973, 2-3. Reissued by the Public Communications Department of the Church of Jesus Christ of Latter-day Saints, July 1977; April 1991.

Homosexuality. "LDS Welfare Services Packet 1." Salt Lake City: Church of Jesus Christ of Latter-day Saints, 1973.

Homosexuality: Understanding and Changing Homosexual Orientation Problems, 2d ed. Salt Lake City: Church of Jesus Christ of Latter-day Saints, 1981.

Hope for Transgressors. Salt Lake City: Church of Jesus Christ of Latter-day Saints, 1970.

JD. *Journal of Discourses,* 26 vols. (Liverpool: Latter-day Saints Book Depot, 1855-86).

Kenney, Scott G., ed. *Wilford Woodruff's Journal.* 9 vols. Midvale, UT: Signature Books; 1983-85.

Kimball, Edward and Andrew E. Kimball, Jr. *Spencer W. Kimball.* Salt Lake City: Bookcraft, 1977.

Kimball, Spencer W. *The Miracle of Forgiveness.* Salt Lake City: Bookcraft, 1969.

————. *New Horizons for Homosexuals.* Salt Lake City: Church of Jesus Christ of Latter-day Saints, 1971.

Kinsey, A., W. Pomeroy, and C. Martin. "Homosexual Outlet." In *Sexual Behavior in the Human Male.* Philadelphia: W. B. Saunders, 1948.

Kinsey, A., W. Pomeroy, C. Martin, and P. Gebhard. "Homosexual Responses and Contacts." In *Sexual Behavior in the Human Female.* Philadelphia: W. B. Saunders, 1953.

A Letter to a Friend. Salt Lake City: Church of Jesus Christ of Latter-day Saints, 1978.

McBride, Max Ford. "Effect of Visual Stimuli in Electric Shock Therapy." Ph.d. diss., Brigham Young University, 1976.

McQueen, Robert. In *The Advocate,* 13 Aug. 1975.

Money, John. *Gay, Straight, or In-Between: The Sexology of Erotic Orientation.* New York: Oxford University Press, 1988.

Moses, A. Elfin and Robert O. Hawkins, Jr. *Counseling Lesbian Women and Gay Men: A Life-Issues Approach.* St. Louis: C. V. Mosby Co., 1982.

Oaks, Dallin. "Apostle Reaffirms Church's Position on Homo-sexuality." In *Church News,* 14 Feb. 1987.

Packer, Boyd. *To the One.* Salt Lake City: Church of Jesus Christ of Latter-day Saints, 1978.

————. "Covenants." In *Ensign* 20 (Nov. 1990): 84-86.

Pearson, Carol Lynn. *Goodbye, I Love You.* New York: Random House, 1986.

Petersen, Mark. "Editorials." In *Church News,* 9 July 1977, 16; 14 Jan. 1978, 16; 4 Feb. 1978, 16; 18 Mar. 1978, 16; 29 July 1978, 16; 16 Dec. 1978, 16.

Pritt, Thomas and Ann Pritt. "Homosexuality: Getting Beyond the Therapeutic Impasse." In *Association of Mormon Counselors and Psychotherapists (AMCAP) Journal* 13 (1987): 37-65.

Stout, Jan. "Sin and Sexuality: Psychobiology and the Development of Homosexuality." In *Dialogue: A Journal of Mormon Thought* 20 (Fall 1987): 29-41.

Taylor, Samuel W. *Nightfall at Nauvoo.* New York: Avon Books, 1971.

Watzlawick, Paul. *How Real is Real?* New York: Vintage Books, 1977.

I.

PERSONAL

PERSPECTIVES

Gay and

Lesbian

Voices

ONE

Solus

▼

Anonymous

It was October general conference, and I was sitting in the tabernacle with several friends attending the priesthood session. The
meeting had been especially good, and I was where I most wanted
to be, surrounded by close friends, sitting in that sacred building
listening to a prophet's voice. President Harold B. Lee spoke as he
always did, seemingly off-the-cuff and from the heart, a speech
which would become famous throughout the church. The subject
was marriage. Why are there those in the priesthood who are
postponing this sacred obligation? Why do some, even among the
active brethren, refuse to follow counsel? Such unmarried priesthood bearers are outside of God's house. My friends nudged me
good-naturedly. It had become one of the rituals of our association.
I wiped mock beads of sweat from my brow and said, "Ouch!"

Looking back on my childhood, I cannot remember how it felt
not to be haunted by homosexuality. Not that I would ever have
used the word! I was well into middle age before I would bring

---

"Solus" originally appeared in *Dialogue: A Journal of Mormon Thought* 10
(Autumn 1976).

myself to say "homosexual" even in private prayers—which always concluded with a plea for help in "overcoming my problems." . . .

Maleness and sexuality became so terrifying to me that I began a long—and successful—flight from my own manhood. As a child I chose girls as playmates, but when adolescence arrived, I could no longer remain exclusively in their company, so I turned back to boys. I soon began "admiring from afar" the masculine qualities I couldn't find in myself.

My junior high school years were an unending nightmare. I was too much of a "sissy" to be accepted by the boys, and my own confusion about sex kept me an arm's length from girls. I took refuge in church activity. Once a girl in my class asked me to a "preference dance." I bought a corsage, shined my shoes, and reluctantly started off on my first real date. After the dance we went to an ancient apartment near the business district where all her friends were meeting for a party. After the lights went off, couples started kissing and petting in the dark. After a few moments I fled in panic.

My high school years were anxiety-filled but tolerable. I dated infrequently—only enough to avoid suspicion—and I developed my first "crush" on another young man. He was dating the girl who lived across the street. During one whole summer I peered out of the window in a darkened room trying to see him across the street. My feelings of disgust and revulsion at my own actions were exceeded only by my compulsion to watch him. When he made the school basketball team, I went to every game, safely hiding in the anonymity of the crowd. I was always careful not to appear too interested in his scoring.

In college I usually dated only girls with whom I had established a platonic relationship, but once a friend in my young adult priests' quorum invited me to double date with him. We drove to the canyon and parked. He and his date kissed and petted in the front seat for what seemed an eternity while my date and I sat in the back seat trying to make small talk. I was miserable. Obviously more was expected of me than I was producing. It was a hellish night.

College was interrupted by a draft notice which raised unimaginable anxieties. How would I survive in a totally male environment? Could I mask my "problem"? What if I talked in my sleep? To my great relief, I managed quite well. After basic training I was

I was called on a part-time mission and went out proselyting three nights a week. It got me out of the bawdiness of the barracks, and bunkmates always assumed that the suit and tie meant I was going off on a date. I said nothing to correct their misinterpretation. After two years I was honorably discharged. I felt great: I had held my own in a male society; had not given myself away; had survived group showering even among those I was physically attracted to; and had survived two years without a date and without anyone asking why.

Returning to college was another matter. Parents and friends, whether knowingly or not, were escalating their subtle suggestions that I start dating more frequently. I didn't date often, but when I did I got a lot of mileage out of it, making certain everyone knew I had gone out. It was now impossible to avoid kissing without really being suspect, so I tried my best. The whole evening was often ruined by my anxiety about that good-night kiss. There were times when I was certain the girl was deliberately trying to arouse me. What if I failed? All the world would know the truth. Sometimes I pretended she was a boy.

I was rescued by a mission call. To my great relief none of the interviews raised the question of masturbation, and aside from that I was worthy to go. When I was set apart for my mission the General Authority said, "Those things in your life which have been amiss have been forgiven." There it was. God knew after all but was willing to let me serve as his emissary. Tears ran down my face as I promised not to disappoint him. My mission was a beautiful religious experience. I grew very close to the gospel. My resolve to put homosexual thoughts behind me worked most of the time, and the garments eliminated much of the sensuality of sleeping with my companion.

The next several years are a blur of parents and bishops and friends and neighbors and former missionary companions and total strangers all asking me the same question: "Isn't it time you were getting married?" I always answered with good humor (part of the "cover"), but the question always cut me to the quick. I certainly had not written off the possibility of marriage, but I knew something would have to change. While completing my work at the university, I attended LDS Institute of Religion regularly. One Sunday I heard Elder Joseph Fielding Smith say that homosexuality was so filthy and abhorrent that he would rather see his sons dead than homosexual. In growing confusion I tried to analyze my problem. Was I forever lost? . . . Was I given homosexuality as a test to mold or strengthen me? Was there any meaning in my suffering? Would my infirmity be corrected in the resurrection? Was marriage an absolute requirement for everyone in life? If I married should I tell my wife? Could I hide it from her? Would Joseph Fielding Smith want me in his family? Would anyone else? Was I better off dead?

For all my pondering, I found only more questions. I decided to ask my stake patriarch for a special blessing. He lived in our ward and knew our family well. While I could not tell him my problem, I could rely on his inspiration for whatever counsel God had for me. I fasted and prayed and went to his home for the blessing. The patriarch gave me a beautiful blessing concerned mainly with choosing a proper career, but he said nothing about marriage or dating.

I decided to try another fast and go to the temple, seeking an answer through prayer and "good works." After asking a temple worker where I might go for private prayer, I was directed to a tiny hall closet. There was no room to kneel, but I offered a lengthy prayer pleading for some direction. I went home and lay awake most of the night, anticipating some message. None came.

The pressure to marry increased almost to my breaking point. It seemed everyone wanted to line me up with "a friend." Even total strangers called and said they had heard of me and wanted to introduce me to somebody special. I started dating with more regularity, hoping that somehow the magic would strike. But a man can go out with the same woman only so many times before the relationship must either end in marriage or be broken off. Somehow we always broke off. The young woman would want to marry, and I could not do it.

About this time the bishop asked me to start teaching the priests quorum each Sunday. The request brought a new crisis. I was physically attracted to every boy in the quorum. I knew I could do a good job—I had taught classes for years. I felt I could reach some boys who needed strengthening in the gospel. But what if I slipped? The question was larger than just one teaching assignment for a group of older adolescents. I had to know if there were any place in the church for people "with problems" like mine. Does a homosexual have the right to participate? Was I worthy of a temple recommend? Could I continue to attend all my meetings, teach classes, pay tithing, and accept leadership positions without being a hypocrite? I felt that only a General Authority could tell me.

After tremendous soul-searching I went to the Church Office Building, but it took over an hour to get up enough courage to enter the front door. There were so many imponderables. Whom should I ask to see? I certainly didn't want to be told I'd be better off dead. On the other hand, was I being honest if I avoided anyone who might criticize me? Should I use a phony name? My father was well-known enough that someone might connect my name to his. I finally walked into the lobby, scanned the roster of names, and decided on the one who had set me apart as a missionary; perhaps he could help me now.

The secretary said I could not get in without an appointment. Perhaps I could come back another time. My face must have shown my inner turmoil, for she invited me to stay. She took my name and asked the purpose of my visit. I replied "personal counsel" and nervously sat down and waited. Finally just before 5:00 I was told I could see him. He said he was tired and anxious to spend some time with his family, but he graciously consented to hear me out. I briefly stated my problem, putting it in the best possible light. He seemed to understand and encouraged me to take the priests quorum assignment and any other assignment I was asked to fill. He mentioned a prominent citizen with a similar problem who had recently died and said much good could be done by those with such problems. As a final thought he suggested that I might aim for more masculine activities in my life, such as playing basketball. The advice was given in good faith and was appreciated. But I wondered if he saw the dilemma. Had I confessed to heterosexual problems, would he have prescribed more physical contact with girls, culminating in the showers?

He concluded by writing an address on a card and directing me to the top floor of the Union Pacific building across from Temple Square. There a kindly gentleman greeted me and asked me to hear his story about the beauty of physical love between a man and a woman. He went into explicit detail in great humility and candor. He asked me to picture myself capable of such love-making. I really tried. He felt I should marry but counseled me definitely not to tell my wife I was a homosexual as it would strain the relationship too severely.

I left determined to take whatever church callings came my way. I would live all the commandments possible and live as normal an existence as possible. But I felt certain that a marriage built upon such a deception could never succeed.

Upon graduation from the university I moved into my own apartment and began teaching high school. My teaching has brought tremendous satisfaction to me. I have developed a reputation for being able to communicate with students no one else could reach. I identify totally with them and am willing to work with them long after most adults have lost all patience.

Like many singles I fled the marriage pressure in my resident ward and joined a singles ward at the university. Things got better. My parents were pleased just knowing that I was surrounded by all those eligible girls. I appreciated the freedom from interference by neighbors and family, but student wards also exact a price. Marriage is the name of the game, and few church meetings went by without strong reminders of that fact. I was swept up in the new ward activities which weren't exactly dates but served as good substitutes. I was also named president of the elders quorum.

My new position forced me to look at the other quorum members more carefully, and I began to wonder if many of them were just like me. Were some dating so frenetically just to remove all doubt about their virility? One that I felt confident shared my problem managed to be seen with a copy of *Playboy* in his briefcase at priesthood meeting. Better to be thought a lecher than a homosexual.

Through this period, my parents, especially my mother, began a not-so gentle chastising of me, urging me to find the right girl and settle down. My close friends, long since married, started inviting me to their homes where unescorted girls seemed always to be waiting. In my teaching job, I was always being named to the prom committee, along with eligible faculty members.

Before age thirty I could reasonably carry off the charade of being eager to find "the right one." After thirty it got much harder. Any interest in a thirtyish female led inevitably to a tremendous push. I really couldn't blame the woman. However unsatisfactory

I might be as a marriage partner, I was male and an active priesthood bearer. Marriage would end for my partners the same kind of nightmarish pressure I was experiencing.

By age thirty-five I decided that dating was terribly unfair to my partners. I was using women only as a convenience, a smoke screen for conformity's sake. I had no right to raise someone's hopes about marriage when my intentions were otherwise, so I quit taking partners to proms, dinners, and social gatherings. If people didn't want me along, they soon learned not to invite me.

Outwardly my new resolve was a tremendous relief. Inwardly it was no answer at all. I learned for myself that it is not good for man to be alone. For the first time in my life loneliness became a gnawing concern. During the winter I had my work, my students, and activities I was expected to attend with or without a partner, but during the summers I could literally go days at a time without speaking a word to anyone. Sometimes the loneliness was so unbearable that I drove up and down the streets hoping to find a hitchhiker with whom I could strike up a brief conversation. My actions were totally circumspect if my thoughts were not. The worst time of the year was always New Year's Eve. There is simply nothing a single, active Latter-day Saint can do on a New Year's Eve without a partner. Every ward or stake in the church holds a dance. You either sit at home alone and brood about the passing of the years or you get a date. On one such occasion I joined the crowd in the traditional kiss at the stroke of midnight. On the way home my date slid over in the seat and started kissing me again. At her apartment I made a concerted effort at nominal petting. I tried everything, including the old ploy of thinking of boys. It was awful. I found myself growing physically ill. It was so shoddy I could no longer stand myself. Breaking things off, I left and started home. Soon I was crying so hard I had to pull myself off the road. What does a person do who knows the gospel is true, who believes fervently in marriage for time and all eternity, who sustains the president of the church as a prophet of God, and yet is so warped that even kissing a girl can be accomplished only by cheap and demeaning subterfuge?

I arrived at home, undressed for bed, and started to say my prayers. Soon I was sobbing uncontrollably, stifling the sounds in the covers. I knew I couldn't go on without some resolution. For the first time, some thirty years after the fact, I told God I was a homosexual and begged for help. My initial "Thou knowest of my problem" gave way to "Please, God, you've got to help me deal with my homosexuality; you are the only one I can talk to." I prayed more intimately and familiarly than I have ever done before or since. For about an hour, I poured out my soul and then went to bed and stared at the ceiling until almost dawn. When I awoke I felt a tremendous peace. God would not require marriage of me in this life. For all the dark corners of my heart, I was still a child of God. I would live as exemplary a life as possible and give all I had to the building up of the kingdom, but I would never marry.

My friends at the tabernacle continued poking me all through President Lee's talk. My mother later clipped it out of the Sunday paper and had it waiting for me when I arrived for a visit. Another copy arrived anonymously in the mail. Both my bishop and my stake president called me in to talk with me about it. Couldn't I see my mistake? Didn't I sustain the prophet? What was wrong with me?

During this time I was having trouble with my eyes. I had consulted several physicians who were unable to find the cause. Finally one asked me bluntly, "Is there anything in your life that might be creating undue anxiety?" To my own surprise I found myself answering, "Well I'm forty and still a bachelor." Then I added, "The reason I'm still a bachelor is because males interest me more than females, and I can't very well marry a male."

I couldn't believe myself. There it was, the great secret of my life, the secret around which my whole life had been structured, blurted out to a near stranger. The doctor was as nonchalant as if I had commented about the weather. He asked if I wanted to leave things as they were or if I wanted to work on them. I replied that if my problems were creating enough turmoil inside to affect me physically, maybe I had better do something about them.

He recommended to me a psychiatrist, "very discreet" and new to the area, who would not be apt to have any ties with anyone I knew. The prospect scared me to death. It was finally arranged that the psychiatrist would come to my home every Sunday right after church. These sessions were extremely helpful and allowed me to understand myself better. But then the psychiatrist advised me that the only way I could end my male fixation was to experience male sex. He reasoned that I might discover that it was not all I had fantasized it to be. While that advice carried a certain logic and the intellectual side of my nature responded affirmatively, my spiritual side was horrified. Where would I draw the line? If male sex proved unsatisfactory, should I experiment heterosexually?

To whom then should I turn for an answer to my excruciating dilemma? In a lifetime of church activity I have yet to hear a single word of compassion or understanding for homosexuals spoken from the pulpit. We are more than a family-oriented church. Our auxiliaries and priesthood quorums presuppose marriage. A single, much less a homosexual, simply does not fit in. Even the Special Interest program, which is excellent for those eager to marry, is just one more humiliation in a whole lifetime of humiliations for people like myself. High council members now seek out partners for me or tell me how to make myself more attractive to the opposite sex. The temple interview has questions about masturbation and homosexuality. I must either lie and continue a life of "Let's Pretend," or come out of the closet, proclaim my homosexuality openly and pay whatever price must be exacted. I doubt that my community is ready to accept a self-proclaimed homosexual teacher, and it is highly unlikely that the church will accept a declared homosexual into fellowship.

Still I have a strong testimony of the gospel. I know the church is true and I want to remain loyal and active. I can only hope that he who welcomed to his side sinners, publicans, and harlots will grant the same grace to me—and that his church will also.

TWO

Suffering Into Truth

▼

"Anna Hurston"

"It's up to you," the professor was telling the class, "to write the tragedies. We don't have enough good Mormon tragedy."

I sat in class, mute. Could the man mean what he was saying? As a lifelong Mormon, I knew I was silent about my struggles—you just didn't hear church members candidly talk of their conflicts. Despite Joseph Smith's definition of truth as "knowledge of things as they are, as they were, and as they are to come" (D&C 93:24), there didn't seem to be an audience for honesty about hard things in the church. We felt free to share only those shards of reality that we thought others would accept without judging us as derelict, less than worthy.

"I could write such a tragedy," I replied mentally, "but no Mormon would be willing to read it. They don't want to know about any part of reality, any suffering, that challenges their souls to explore. All they want is safety—saying that the church is true is the end of all discussion."

For this Brigham Young University class, I wrote a long paper comparing favorable cultural attitudes toward suicide in Japanese and Greek societies. At that point I wished fervently that our own culture could see suicide as an honorable choice. I needed an alternative that would allow me to be remembered lovingly in the only world I had ever known—Mormonism—and also leave behind the impossible demands that living as Mormon made on me. Death seemed the only way out.

As I think back now, physical death would have been simpler and less rewarding than the painful rebirth I have undergone, making my way into a universe where I now understand and claim my birthright—living completely as a loving and vibrant woman.

From the time I first recognized that my attraction to women was stronger than my interest in men, I knew instinctively that there was no place for me in the Mormon scheme of things. I absorbed the taboos as completely as I did other church teachings, believing all I was taught and working with my whole soul to comply so God would love me. Still my genetic inheritance could not be shed like an unwanted coat.

Over the years I've found individual Mormons who have offered me strong and unfailing friendship, a gift I treasure still. The church's policies, however, showed an utter lack of awareness of the challenges that faced me, ultimately excluding me from the community I trusted as a family.

I remember writing my first "love" letter to a girl when I was in third grade. I was honestly expressing the true feelings of my heart and thought nothing of it. A few years later another girl showed a similar note from me to her friends, and I was ridiculed unmercifully. Already I was learning that life can be treacherous for one with a sensitive heart.

All this time I eagerly followed the church's teachings. As a teenager I was an exemplary Mormon, always at the head of the seminary class, sharing the gospel with friends and teachers, ready to accept any calling and give it my best efforts. Rebellion? The word wasn't in my vocabulary.

Growing up female and Mormon was confusing to me. Often I wished for the certainty of another birthright. I didn't envy boys the priesthood. I wanted the ability to plan my future, go on a mission, choose a profession, earn the same respect given the men in my culture as I demonstrated my talents and my worth.

Instead there was always the obligation that took precedence over all others—marriage. Not even serving God was more important. I couldn't go on a mission if marriage were offered first. I could go on to college but must be ready, unconditionally, to abandon my pursuits at a moment's notice if a man should happen along and ask that paramount question.

Throughout my developing years, I was marginally interested in boys, but the real drama recorded in my journals centered on my female friends. My emotional life in eighth grade revolved around a Mormon girl I had met at girls' camp the previous summer and a classmate who had told me she didn't want to be best friends. My very happiness was bound up in these friends.

None of my high school teachers were Mormon, but I tried to convert one unmercifully. She was an intelligent, thoughtful woman who took a personal interest in her students' success. I drew inspiration from her example.

Now years later I know what I didn't consciously acknowledge then—she too was lesbian. I know she recognized our similarities, but she never said or did anything that might have made me aware of that, providing only an example of calm maturity, impeccable character, and inner strength.

Referring to this teacher, my father warned me, "There's something wrong with a woman who never marries." Today I am a living witness that we unmarried women are not emotionally, mentally, or spiritually deficient.

Although I had always felt different from my friends, I never wanted to name what made me so. Still when a girlfriend and I expressed interest in the same guy, time after time I would let my friend have him. Keeping my friends meant more to me.

During these years I dated and had several steady boyfriends, looking for the one who would take me to the temple. I had a strong desire to have children and raise them under the temple covenant—a yearning which wasn't accompanied by that overwhelming attraction to the opposite sex that most people feel and follow into marriage.

During young adulthood when my closeness to a particular friend grew, a familiar pattern emerged: I'd flirt with the idea of marrying her brother. Such wishful thinking, however, never yielded any promise. I'd discover that I felt merely sisterly toward him—there was absolutely no electricity.

The conflict between the church's teachings about sexuality

and the reality of my own experience had begun in earnest for me. I had been taught to dislike and fear my own body; what if men looked at my breasts and desired me? I would be to blame somehow for their thoughts, and I hadn't done anything. The assumptions that (1) the sexual impulse is evil and (2) women are to blame for men's sexual thoughts and feelings were explicit in the teachings I received about sexuality from my parents and the church.

I recalled my own childhood intuition that God, in making everyone male or female, had really botched the whole deal. If being sexual is so bad, why give us sexual parts? There must be another, better way for humans to create families, a safer mechanism not so loaded with guilt and self-abhorrence. Surely an all-powerful God could manage that, since "he" loves "his" children and wants us to succeed.

Finally the moment came that I had coveted all my life. I turned twenty-one and could go on a mission as well as enter the temple. When I went through the endowment ceremony, I marveled at the peace I felt and took the covenants with full-hearted desire to live each one always. I was confident I could.

I avidly prepared myself for the mission field, which proved to be a welcome challenge. I was productive and hard-working, so I was given senior companion responsibilities early. My mission president later lamented I hadn't been born male. What an invaluable assistant to the president I could have been, he said, with the example I set and my enthusiasm for the work.

In the mission field I also learned that the miracle of a changed nature had not been granted to me though I daily gave my all as advised by priesthood leaders. Throughout my mission I felt attracted to most of my companions, although I never acted on these feelings. I was considerate, served them every way I could think of, told them I loved them daily as the Missionary Handbook told me to, listened to them. But I never crossed any line of propriety, even when I was assigned a companion who was also attracted to me. I was bewildered. I'd been promised that serving God wipes the slate clean and would change our souls. How could this happen?

Months later I began teaching Bridgette, and she eventually joined the church. We corresponded, reams upon reams, but I always kept my letter-writing to Preparation Day. She never wanted to distract me from my work and would go tracting and teaching with me when she could.

Thoughts of her infused my life and work with meaning. As the end of my mission approached, I didn't want to go home. Bridgette meant everything to me. How could I face a life devoid of her presence with an ocean between us? I put off thinking about it until my last day there when she came to help me pack. Everything we did that day was permeated with sorrow.

She stayed that night, an emotional and sleepless one as we stared into each other's eyes. As morning began to lighten the sky ever so slightly, her lips brushed mine, and we kissed. I left the bed, crying as I frantically went about my packing. The love we felt for each other was stronger than anything we'd ever known, but I hated myself so blackly for those few moments that no words could have conveyed my despair.

I confessed to my mission president, who learning that the indiscretion was a mere kiss admonished me not to let this mar my memory of a mission honorably completed.

I flew home, living for the day when her first letter would come. I was so depressed that I didn't unpack my suitcases for weeks. All I wanted was to be on my way back to the only home I'd ever known—her heart.

Letters, rich with shared experiences, bridged the miles between us. A year after our first meeting, Bridgette arrived in my hometown for a visit. My mother told me before Bridgette's arrival, "You've always looked to find with your friends what you'll only have with your husband." Mom knew I was born lesbian but could not speak the word, as I couldn't then. My parents, who meant well in their ignorance, worked to separate us.

It's strange how family and church officials don't want to accept that a person's hereditary nature will not vanish once outsiders break up existing gay relationships. I guess it stems from their assumption that deep down everyone must be attracted to the opposite sex. That must be why they think we'll miraculously change, once the gay relationship dissolves. The majority of humans are born with romantic attraction for the opposite sex. Deciding which partner you'll love is a conscious choice, but the instinctual attraction is not. I can choose which woman I will love, but my attraction to women is as involuntary as my impulse to breath.

The month that followed was turbulent for us. I could no longer deny the power of my feelings. I would have married her, but there was no such option, no way for our love to be honored and accepted by families and friends like my brothers' and sisters' unions were. Like many other young adults, Bridgette and I wanted to share our lives together, but I could not bear the clash between my feelings and the self-hatred my upbringing had taught me. I confessed to my bishop. He called a court. It was humiliating beyond conception, although I bore it in the belief that it would save me, as they said. I sat before those married men, who hadn't a clue of how I felt or why, answered their prying questions as best I could and listened as they violated the sacredness of our relationship. I knew we had shared, over the year we'd been close, so much more than desire. I knew for a fact that Bridgette had certainly been more sensitive to my emotions and less preoccupied with her own pleasure than any man would have been in the same situation.

Still I gave those men power over my future and accepted their judgment, wanting only to bear it and make my way back into the fold. After some discussion, they commuted my sentence to disfellowshipment on condition that I never see Bridgette, talk to her, or write her again. Why must we not even write? She had left me voluntarily, unselfishly wanting only my happiness regardless of what it cost her. But I did as required and began regular sessions with a counselor at LDS Social Services to rearrange my violated psyche.

If it hadn't been for my counselor I probably would have gone completely out of my mind. Here at least I could voice my despair freely, give vent to my agony and frustration. The silence that surrounded the most vital feelings of my soul could end and with it my isolation. I still feel affection for my counselor. I know he genuinely cared and gave so much. Still it provided me with temporary relief only. Some people, born with equal attraction to both sexes, may be able to make a permanent transition to heterosexuality—I was not so gifted. But I put all my energy into making it come true for me, believing that God would accept this hardest sacrifice and make me over. I was giving everything I had. Certainly that would be good enough and I would find the miracle they said was there. I poured all my faith into the sincere, intense fasting and prayer I'd been taught creates permanent change.

It was excruciating. I kept trying to convince myself I loved men I met at Young Adult activities. It didn't work. My bishop had warned me never to tell any man about my past. I was a piece of merchandise on the auction block. I must hide any flaw or human characteristic to be considered a possible purchase. For young Mormon men, with perhaps a glorious exception or two, don't really believe that their future wife is washed clean in the blood of Christ. They want flawless property.

Although I couldn't help but sense that, I denied its truth. I had almost married before my mission. I chose not to because I knew I didn't love him but couldn't help questioning now if that decision had been right. Still wouldn't lack of love make the marriage unbearable as the years wore on? I returned to BYU to finish my education, hoping my prayers had worked the miracle.

But I kept falling in love with women, to my bewilderment and distress. The first involvement plunged me into an abyss. Feeling utterly abandoned by my God and all the church teachings that did not work, I daydreamed of suicide as freedom.

My bishop put me on probation. Struggling and bone-weary, I managed to avoid excommunication. The bishop advised me that I should live a productive celibate life, devoid of intimacy. Two years later as I was about to graduate, I fell in love with another woman. I fled Provo but put my fate in the hands of a new bishop, who delayed excommunicating me until months later when I had an affair with a non-Mormon man.

I tried going through the motions of love, but in my heart I knew I didn't feel what I should for him. I couldn't convince myself to live out the lie, so I stopped seeing him. Eventually I decided to share my life with the woman I love.

It took me about a year to gather enough courage to tell my family after I found a woman to share my life with. My family had been very supportive when I went through the first church court, but I thought that was because I was doing what the church wanted. I feared they would reject me when they learned I was committed to a relationship. I'm grateful I underestimated them. Their love means so much to me. My father and siblings are encouraging, and my mother, although she doesn't want my partner coming home with me for visits, continues to tell me she loves me. She thinks God must have a reason for making me as I am—I see it as a test of my fundamental honesty.

I've thought a lot about why gay marriages sometimes don't seem to have the longevity some conventional marriages do. The burden is often upon us to deny that we're committed to a gay relationship and pretend we're just friends or roommates. We don't get the same support from family, friends, church and social groups of all kinds that anyone entering into a straight marriage receives. When problems crop up, to whom can we turn for the emotional support that helps us hold on until the difficulties can be worked out? Despite these pressures, many gay couples enjoy lifelong marriages—I hope I am joining their ranks.

I have also thought about the strain in work and social settings for gay individuals. While others confide freely about their personal lives, I usually remain silent. When I unexpectedly find a friend, it's a great relief to know I am being judged mainly on my character, not solely on my choice of a life partner. Few states include gays in civil rights legislation that protects them from discrimination, so silence still seems the most prudent choice.

But I have learned that no human institution can ever separate me from the love of God, which abides in me as Christ taught and gives me wisdom when I open my heart. I have also had to accept that our ways as mortals who fear others' differences are not God's ways. I was created lesbian because I had much to learn, and it is my God-given responsibility to move beyond fear of persecution and live a full and happy life, making my way with a life partner who shares the joys and challenges with me.

I am fortunate to have a wonderful partner. When we exchanged rings and vows of fidelity, we didn't send out wedding announcements. My parents may not understand and wish we could be different. But we're making a go of it. I still believe love and monogamy can work.

Through spiritual searching and developing the unselfishness that we learn best in marriage, I have achieved a unity with God and confidence in my own divine nature which sustain me in daily challenges. My spouse and I continue to find enlightenment, and I feel blessed that our relationship embraces every aspect of a good marriage—spiritual, emotional, and temporal growth.

I've learned through my own experience and much searching that God has not created me to be lonely and miserable but led me to women like myself so we can help bear one another's burdens and find peace and fulfillment. It isn't good for anyone to be alone, regardless of the challenges life sets before her.

THREE

With All Thy Getting, Get Understanding

▼

Don D. Harryman

I was not raised in the church but was introduced to it in high school by friends. Around the same time my parents were divorced and I went to live with a Mormon family who had taken an interest in my life. Not necessarily because of this association but because of my own personal conviction that Mormonism was divine, I was baptized at age sixteen.

In my life prior to baptism, I always had a feeling that I was different, and in my interview for baptism, I was asked about something I always vaguely suspected but never fully understood about myself—that I might be homosexual. The question was moot since I had had no sexual experience of any kind that made me unworthy for baptism, and I dismissed it from my mind.

"With All Thy Getting, Get Understanding," by Don D. Harryman, was originally presented at the annual Sunstone Symposium in Salt Lake City in August 1986. Mr. Harryman graduated from Brigham Young University in 1980 where he majored in Japanese language and Asian studies. Currently residing in Honolulu, Hawaii, he is a travel and financial counselor for American Express and is involved in gay civil rights issues.

I had had no previous religious training or involvement before joining the Mormon church, and I embraced my new-found faith with energy. I found great satisfaction in participating in church meetings, youth activities, and early-morning seminary. My intense involvement with church and my lack of sexual experience prior to joining the church precluded me from fully answering the nagging suspicion which surfaced again—indeed, I did not even understand the question, since I was not really sure what a homosexual was. I was relieved when I confessed my fear to my bishop. He assured me that what I needed to do was continue to date girls, participate fully in church activity, and follow the commandments.

With that assurance I poured renewed energy into my church activities, schoolwork, and social life, which included friendships with both boys and girls. Liking or disliking women was not the issue—I liked girls and had many friendships with them in school and church. Probably my best friends were my sisters. Living in the Mormon subculture as I did, the only acceptable social interaction with other boys or girls that I had was non-sexual. It was easy under those circumstances for me to ignore the sexual feelings I had for men and to interpret the friendships I felt for women as sexual attraction.

In the fall of 1969 I graduated with honors from high school, and I set out for BYU, the only university I considered or applied for. It felt right to me—surely it was the best place for me to prepare for the kind of life I wanted, and for that first year, it was. I enjoyed my classes, my social activities, and involvement with my student ward. If I ever thought about any homosexual feelings, it was only fleetingly—I was certain that I would go on a mission, return to BYU, and marry.

My mission call to Japan came in the fall of 1970. During the week I spent in the old mission home in Salt Lake City, we heard among the many inspiring messages given to us by various General Authorities of the church some terrifying ones about the evils of unrepentant sexual sin. The word which I could barely say to myself was repeated several times. Homosexuality, we were warned, was consummate evil, and any unrepentant person was doomed to a mission filled with spiritual darkness and failure. I was certain they were right, and with my heart pounding, I requested to speak to the Mission Home president. Upon hearing my confession, he assured me that I was involved in the darkest of sins. But after questioning me about specific instances and people I had been involved with, he determined that since I had only sexual feelings but no experience, I was clean and worthy to go on my mission. Relieved, I left Salt Lake City for the Language Training Mission in Hawaii determined to be the best missionary that I could be.

I loved my mission. I excelled in the language, enjoyed most of my companions, and developed a real love for the Japanese people and their beautiful and fascinating country. I found some aspects of mission life competitive in a way which seemed more like what I imagined boot camp would be than what a mission should be, and sometimes the endless rules seemed harsh. But my mission was a profound religious and cultural experience.

Still at times terrifying feelings came over me with hot, undeniable certainty. At times I felt intense, compelling, and definitely sexual feelings for some men—especially for certain church members and for certain companions with whom I also had strong emotional ties. Certain nights during the summer stand out in my memory. I awoke from sleep, drenched with sweat from the heat of the stifling Japanese summer, from the erotic dream I was having, and from the passions I felt for my companion who slept next to me. I followed what was by now a familiar pattern and confessed my feelings to my mission president. He listened patiently and seemed unable to comprehend what I was telling him. Then he did the wisest thing a person in his position could do: since I had not acted on my feelings, there could be no punishment. He withheld both judgment and punishment and told me he loved me and appreciated my efforts as a missionary. The love and support of my mission president and his wife helped me to finish my mission.

In November 1972 I finished my mission and returned home to California with a growing certainty that I was homosexual and no one could help me know what to do. After working at home for six months, I decided to return to BYU—I worked in Provo that summer and formulated a plan. My repeated interviews with church leaders had yielded nothing. I knew I had to find another solution.

I decided that for the first time in my life I would talk to a psychiatrist or psychologist. I didn't understand the difference nor did I have any idea what such a person did, but my growing terror forced me to what seemed my only course of action. I thought I was the only person with this problem—I felt completely alone with it. Having read somewhere about the BYU Psychology Clinic, I sought out the anonymity of a telephone booth and, after several tries ending with my hanging up, I completed the call.

The person on the line tried in vain to get me to say what my problem was, but I simply could not say it. In a few weeks the fall semester would begin, I was told, and if I would call back, I could make an appointment to see a counselor. I subsequently made the call—and waited through the following anxious days for the appointment.

In an old "lower campus" building, I sat paralyzed with fear waiting for my appointment and was finally greeted by a pleasant and attractive man. Once in the session, he explained that he was a graduate student in psychology and that counseling experience in the clinic was part of the requirements in his doctoral program. Both in that session and in the following sessions, we talked comfortably on general topics and I gradually overcame some of the resistance I had to talking in detail about my sexual feelings. Hypnosis was used to facilitate this process, and I began to gain some confidence that perhaps I was really going to be helped with what I had always feared, never experienced, and learned to hate so perfectly about myself.

As the sessions progressed, we reached a point where my counselor indicated we had spent enough time in an analysis phase and now needed to move into a treatment phase. My purpose there was to change from a homosexual into a heterosexual. That premise was never discussed as one of many alternatives by my counselor, nor would it have occurred to me that there were other alternatives—like accepting myself as I was. He explained a new treatment called aversion therapy which had shown "promising results" and which involved the use of electric shock and sexually explicit slides. I did not even briefly consider the possibility of emotional, physical, or spiritual damage to myself in the treatment—I was determined to change. Without hesitation I signed the forms which released the Psychology Clinic and BYU from any liability.

My counselor explained that it would be necessary for me to obtain sexually erotic, preferably nude, photographs of men—the shock would be applied while I was viewing the slides. It was never indicated where I might find such photographs—perhaps he assumed that I knew. Having no car and no one with a car in whom I could confide my secret, I hitchhiked to Salt Lake—it was the only place I figured I could find such photographs. Up and down the streets of Salt Lake I walked, until at length I discovered a bookstore that looked seedy enough to have pornography. I entered, terrified that I might see someone I knew and examined every book and magazine in the store, until I finally made my way to the shelf where pornographic magazines were displayed. I stuffed a few copies of *Playgirl* in between some other magazines I had selected hoping that the *Playgirl* might seem a last minute casual selection for a wife or girlfriend. Purchasing those magazines was not casual by any means, and it was the first time in my life that I had ever seen, let alone purchased, any such publication. I felt out of place, alone and frightened.

My next assignment was to view the photographs and to take the ones I found most erotic to a local camera store, where I was told an arrangement had been made through the Psychology Clinic to have the photographs made into slides. All was approved, I was told, and only the owner of the store knew about the arrangement. Of course I would also have to pay for the slides. I took the photographs in a plain manila envelope to this store and, summoning my courage, went to the counter and stated that I had photographs to be made into slides for a program supervised by a BYU professor. I had been told his name was the key to complete anonymity. No sooner were the words out of my mouth than it seemed the eyes of every employee left their immediate task and stared. It was humiliating and embarrassing. I felt as though all of those strangers knew my most private business.

The actual sessions of aversion therapy began after that, and with the exception of about a two-month break, I had sessions twice a week for the next year. Beginning with the first call to the Psychology Clinic and continuing on with the weekly visits, the trip to Salt Lake and to the camera store, I started to lead a double life. I was secretive about my whereabouts and timed my sessions to precede or follow other activities so that no one would know. I would go to a room in the Smith Family Living Center where an electrode was attached to my arm and I was asked to ruminate or otherwise fantasize about sexual activity with men—no small task since I had never had the experience and was not too sure what two men did with each other. During the viewing, random and painful electric shocks would be sent through my arm. Later the procedure was modified. When shock was being introduced during the viewing of a male slide, I could stop the shock by pressing a plunger, which would cause a slide of a clothed woman to appear on the screen. Even now other details of the therapy are too embarrassing for me to write about. (A detailed description of this therapy can be found in M. F. McBride, "Effect of Visual Stimuli in Electric Shock Therapy," Ph.D. dissertation, Brigham Young University, 1976.) This treatment was augmented by counseling, in which I was encouraged to be "physical" with women, and by more hypnosis, wherein suggestion was made that I would become uncontrollably nauseated if I thought about men in an erotic way.

I cannot say that I ever became nauseated thinking about men—but I certainly became very skilled at looking away and thinking about something else at the first sign of any sexual feelings. Likewise I never became "physical" with women. I liked the women I dated but became even more anxious than I previously had been about holding hands or kissing them. Besides I was never certain how "physical" I was supposed to be.

The counselor with whom I had started my treatment graduated part way through my treatment, and his replacement was another graduate student who was working on the aversion therapy as part of his dissertation. Since I had signed the release at the beginning of the treatment which freed BYU or any person involved with this experiment from any liability for any ill effects that I might suffer, the burns on my arms and the emotional trauma I experienced seemed to me the price that I had to pay for change. The countless talks I had heard about knocking on the door until your hands were bloody rang in my ears, and in my desperation I began to feel that my suffering and hence my being a martyr was additional proof that what I was doing was right.

In the spring of 1975, I finished the treatment. The criteria used by my counselor to determine whether I was cured of homosexuality were not clear to me, but in the final few sessions he talked optimistically about my "progress" and the woman, soon to come into my life, whom I would marry. I also believed that would happen.

The following summer I remained in Provo and worked at my job in the Cannon Center cafeteria. Some women whom I worked with told me about their friend who was coming from Seattle to attend school that fall. Knowing I needed a roommate to share the expenses of my small apartment, they asked me about accepting their friend as a roommate. It seemed perfect.

A week prior to the beginning of the semester in the fall of 1975, I walked across campus to meet my new roommate at Heritage Halls where he was waiting, having driven to Provo with a woman friend. When I first saw him, my heart jumped. He was handsome, and as we walked the distance back to my apartment, I discovered that he had an engaging personality and a quick wit. We talked easily, and after dinner and arranging some of his belongings, we retired.

Small, almost imperceptible things in his conversation had raised a vague suspicion, and in the few moments after I turned out the single light, my new friend reached out and touched my arm. That single, innocent touch was electrically erotic and terrifying. The feelings I had worked so hard to suppress came crazily, uncontrollably to the surface. What I had always feared and hated about myself became searingly and unavoidably a part of my consciousness. I was falling in love.

My carefully constructed defenses crumbling, I lay awake all night, and when the first light of morning began to fill the room, I made a desperate decision. When my friend, whom I will call Steve, awoke, I confronted him with my suspicion that he was homosexual. I could not afford to focus on my own feelings. In self-defense, for what was to be the last time, I declared absolutely that I was not homosexual. Contrary to my expectations, he felt no need to deny my accusation. He had long ago accepted his homosexuality and was still determined to finish his year at BYU and to serve a mission for the church.

In the days and weeks which followed that first day, I began to feel the weight and the terror of my dilemma. I was not cured, nor did the relationship which was developing between Steve and me feel sordid and awful as I had been led to believe it would. Falling in love was a roller coaster mix of emotions I had never experienced. Having once felt them, I knew that I could not and would not ever be the same again. Another new set of emotions grew—a rage that I began to feel towards the church. Why after all that I had been through was I still homosexual? There was never any doubt in my mind and in my heart that I not only had done what I had been told would make me a heterosexual but much, much more. Had I been lied to? Had I lied to myself? My anger grew and grew, and although Steve tried to help me clarify the issues that sometimes flooded my mind and emotions, he also began to feel overwhelmed by my confusion. The most troublesome aspect of my dilemma was that what I had always been told in the church about my sexuality and what I was now learning from my own experience were very, very different.

It was then that I met by telephone Steve's friend, Howard. Howard had been a role model for Steve and was the person who had helped him resolve the crisis that I was now having. An excommunicated Mormon, Howard spent many hours on the phone over the next many months helping me to sort out the complex issues of homosexuality and the church. Many nights I would take long walks in the snow and think and cry.

In the spring of 1976, Steve left for a mission in Europe, and I moved to northern California to Howard's home. Waking up that May morning in Howard's home on the banks of the Russian River among the redwoods was like having been transported to another world. It was in that supportive and loving environment with Howard and the many friends who visited that I began to stabilize. There came interesting people of all kinds—Howard knew everybody. Heterosexual people who were married with children, single heterosexual people, homosexual people in couples, and those who were single came in and out that summer and fall. I began to understand that my homosexuality need not be the only issue in my life. Howard's friends accepted his homosexuality and mine, and they seemed more interested in what I thought and what kind of a human being I was. What also became clear to me was that accepting my homosexuality did not preclude me from having a life filled with useful work and rich, loving friendships. Slowly I could see that I was homophobic and filled with self-hatred and that the key to my happiness was in accepting myself.

Howard gave me back my life. He taught by precept and by example many things which have helped me to develop my own personal framework for sexual morality. These things have become more clear and more valuable to me with the passage of time and with experience. Unlike my relationship with Steve, which was romantic and had a sexual expression, my relationship with Howard was more like a relationship with a parent. I began to see that in any relationship, love was the most important element.

At Howard's insistence, I went back to BYU in January 1977 to finish my degree and to face the problems that I had bolted from the year before. The following June, while standing on the banks of the beautiful river and while playing with his beloved dogs, Howard collapsed and died of a massive heart attack. Back in Provo I was devastated by the news, and several days later after attending the funeral in Springville where Howard was from, I made the long trip across the desert to California and back to Howard's home in Guerneville.

In the days that I spent there and in the following months back in Provo, I was depressed and could not imagine a world without Howard in it. He was my best friend and the greatest man I ever knew. Time has eased the pain of losing him, but I have never stopped missing him or being grateful that he touched my life so significantly.

With Howard gone and Steve still in Europe for another year, I was lonely but felt the comfort of friends and found renewed satisfaction in my school work. Howard had insisted that I come back to finish my degree, and I set about that task with dedication and energy.

Steve completed his mission in 1978. When he returned to Provo, our relationship went the way of so many adolescent loves and ended. He missed Howard terribly and could not endure the oppressive atmosphere which had become the norm for homosexual people at BYU during the 1970s. At the end of that fall semester, he moved to Salt Lake City with a new circle of friends he had made at a newly-formed group called Affirmation/Gay and Lesbian Mormons.

I had attended Affirmation a few times with Steve, but Steve's presence there and my own uncertainty about Affirmation made association with the group impossible after Steve moved to Salt

Lake. With Howard and now Steve gone, my isolation felt complete. I had many friends but not a single one who knew about my homosexuality. The darkest depression and loneliness I had ever experienced set in.

That Christmas I visited a friend in the San Francisco Bay area. On the last day of my visit, she drove into San Francisco to work, and I decided to spend the day looking for a job. Most of that day I walked the streets, sometimes crying and sometimes just trying to pray in my heart that I might understand what to do. My life in Provo had become unbearable, and I could not face going back. Perhaps I might find a job and come here, I thought, and I actually did a few interviews. At the end of that winter day, I made my last stop the San Francisco City Hall. For a moment I forgot my troubles as I gazed at the rococo splendor of that building and then made my way to the basement personnel office. As I reached the bottom of the stairs, I was overcome with a feeling of warmth and well-being, and I knew what I was to do. The impression was unmistakable that I was to return to Provo and accept the job I had previously applied for at the Language Training Mission, now called the Missionary Training Center (MTC). I knew my friends in Provo cared about me, the missionaries needed me, and I needed them. That impression proved to be true. My friends did not understand because I could not tell them, but they loved anyway. Also during fourteen months teaching Japanese at the MTC, I was able to share my mission experience and my language expertise with the missionaries. Being able to give of myself was the most important medicine I could take. It helped me through that difficult time.

In the fall of 1979, with one more year left of school, I faced my final crisis at BYU. A former roommate figured out my relationship with Steve and turned me in, because in his words I posed a "danger" to the missionaries I was teaching. That Sunday morning as I faced my bishop, I became nearly hysterical. I knew too well about the lists of suspected homosexuals maintained by BYU security, about the decoys and the possible entrapments. I was terrified.

As I related to him my entire story, my bishop was dumfounded. He couldn't believe what he was hearing, nor could he believe that the person who sat before him was homosexual. I fit none of his stereotypes or preconceptions. His reaction was loving, and he assured me that my situation was between him, the stake president, and me only.

In the days that followed, he and the stake president determined that since it had been so long since my sexual involvement with Steve and since I did not fit into the category of "rebellious homosexual" as defined by the Bishop's Handbook, I could remain at BYU and no action would be taken against my church membership. At first both the bishop and stake president were determined to send me to a counselor. Given my prior experience I was scared. However, during the next several weeks, the bishop seemed to drop that idea and seemed to become more and more confused and concerned. In one of our many interviews, he confessed that he did not know how to help me and that he now had several more cases of homosexuality in his ward to deal with. Furthermore, his desire to go directly to the General Authorities to gain more understanding had been firmly opposed by the stake president.

At that point, I took the first real step towards taking responsibility for my own life. I felt as if everyone was making decisions about my life but me. I made an appointment with the stake president, whom I had not yet met. Our meeting began cordially, but he seemed surprised that I was well-read and conversant on the subject of psychological theory as it related to homosexuality. Indeed, he seemed surprised that I could also be a credible witness for my own experience. My frustration began to grow as did my anger when he confessed that as a professional—he had a Ph.D. in educational psychology—he knew that homosexuality was not a curable or changeable state. But in his position as a church leader, he felt compelled to support the official church position. Besides, he said, the brethren did not really mean that one could be cured, just that a homosexual should not act on his or her feelings.

I was outraged. It was finally clear to me that the church's position on this was not clear-cut. What I had been told previously and what I was now being told were quite different indeed. Finally I knew that I had to get my own answers.

During the previous weeks I had agreed with my bishop to abide by all church and BYU standards during my remaining time there. Now I informed the stake president that I had requirements of my own. The previous year, someone in Affirmation who had heard about my aversion therapy experience had given my name to the public television station in Salt Lake City because they were interested in producing a program on homosexuality at BYU. Although I had declined to be interviewed, I now told the stake president that if I even suspected any harassment from security, I would go public with my story on public television or to the newspapers or anyone who would listen.

The color drained from his face. He stammered that I just couldn't do that. He asked, "What about BYU?" I finally understood that BYU's public image was more important to this man than I was.

I asked, "What about me?" That was it, the end, I was finished. I would complete my degree and leave BYU and Provo. Maybe I would even leave the church. My last interview with my bishop is something I can never forget. With tears in his eyes, he told me that he was sorry that he had failed me and that the church had failed me. My answer to him was and still is that no one could have treated me with greater Christian concern and love than he had. He apologized that his desire to get more understanding directly from the brethren had been blocked by the stake president. I replied that while I felt the stake president's course of action was more an example of administrative expediency than of Christian love, I really did not blame him. In his position I might have done likewise.

And thus I finished my term, got my degree, and left. It was clear to me that I had to find my own life and that I could not find it where I was. I moved in September 1980 to the San Francisco Bay area. In 1983 I reconnected with Affirmation, and although I attended church at first, I eventually became inactive. Perhaps there is greater spiritual safety within the congregation of the Saints, but my choice to leave reflects my desire to live my life free of lies, denial, and self-hatred and my desire to accept responsibility for my own life. Ultimately I cannot and will not go where I am made to feel unworthy or unwanted.

I have found with my friends in Affirmation and with many other friends and family a profound sense of community, and by accepting myself a greater sense of belonging to the human family which includes all people—black and white, male and female, old and young, the righteous and the not-so righteous, those who believe, those who do not, those who are homosexual, those who are heterosexual, those who fit into the church and into society and those who are merely different.

In June I marched with my Affirmation family in the San Francisco Gay Freedom Day Parade. I felt pride to be there with those who have been my friends and family in our Affirmation group and to be there with that vast and varied throng of humanity—to see the acceptance we have among the community of gay and lesbian people and among the larger community of the San Francisco Bay area and to feel pride in my identity as a homosexual person and in my heritage as a Mormon.

It is to my heritage in the church that I look for my greatest source of strength. It is to the example of Joseph Smith, who as a young boy asked God directly to guide him, that I look for inspiration. It is also to the Latter-day Saints, with whom I sometimes feel enormous frustration, that I look for a better example than I now see. I know that in the Saints there is an enormous reservoir of honesty, Christian love and compassion, understanding, intelligence, and good will.

Finally, I find comfort and understanding in the scriptures, especially the Book of Mormon. One particular reference speaks most clearly to me of the Book of Mormon's power as a witness of Jesus Christ because it defines most beautifully and clearly the central message of the gospel: "And charity suffereth long, and is kind, and envieth not and is not puffed up, seeketh not her own, is not easily provoked, thinketh no evil, and rejoiceth not in iniquity but rejoiceth in the truth, beareth all things, believeth all things, hopeth all things, endureth all things. Wherefore my beloved brethren, if ye have not charity, ye are nothing, for charity never faileth. Wherefore, cleave unto charity, which is the greatest of all, for all things must fail. But charity is the pure love of Christ, and it endureth forever; and whoso is found possessed of it at the last day, it shall be well with him" (Moroni 8:45-47).

FOUR

Lesbian and Mormon

▼

Ina Mae Murri

Picture the typical small Mormon town of the 1940s and 1950s. In Idaho and Utah such towns were over 90 percent Mormon. Families were large, usually with six or more children. Mothers stayed home and reared their offspring in a sheltered environment. The awareness of pioneer heritage was strong, and many were from polygamous backgrounds. Education was favored, and almost everyone graduated from high school. Those who could went on to Ricks College or Brigham Young University. A few ventured even "farther away" to study or work in Salt Lake City or California. Teenage marriages were common, and the cycle continued.

Like many others I came from just such a background. However, I did not come out of the experience like most others. I am lesbian. In order to explain how I came to an understanding of my homosexuality, I must tell you something about myself. I am the eighth of nine children. My parents were of pioneer stock. They

Ina Mae Murri lives in San Leandro, California. She is Coordinator for Women's Concerns in Affirmation. She also edits a newsletter for lesbian Mormons.

were married in the Mormon temple. I consider my upbringing to be in no significant way different from the others in my family. As I recall my childhood and teenage years, I wanted what my peers did, and I had the same role models. If anything, my family emphasized the church rules more than did many of my friends' families. I daydreamed of boys, dating, and marriage. I dated some, but on a deeper level I realized years later that my strongest feelings were for my female friends. These were close relationships, and although they were never overtly erotic, I became jealous when my girlfriends had other close friends.

After high school I lacked the inclination to go on to college, and no one else pushed me to do it. I drifted along, helping out with older brothers' and sisters' families and on their farms. I was fortunate to spend a year as a mother's helper to a Latter-day Saint family in Washington, D.C. Still being unsure of myself, I spent most of my time there still in a very protected LDS environment. I did not think I was capable of seeking employment with the government agencies in that area.

I would call my religious upbringing practical Mormonism. Our religion was part of our everyday life, but we were not scholarly. We had family prayer but were not especially devout. I liked pioneer stories, Mormon folklore, and the stories in the church magazines. We read the scriptures but learned more from Sunday school class than from personal study. Even in Washington at that time (1954-55), most of the LDS people were transplants from rural Utah and Idaho and were only a bit more sophisticated. In more recent years I have studied Mormonism along with other religions and philosophies. To this day I am more a doer than a thinker.

So how do I reconcile my religious training with my life as it has been for the past thirty years? I was always taught to go to church, listen to church leaders, study, pray, listen to the still small voice, and then "do what is right." Translated that meant—as far as my mother and the church leaders were concerned—"do as we say." Yet we were always admonished to follow our own personal revelations. In discovering my sexuality, I did this, and I have never felt wrong or guilty about it.

In 1955 I enlisted in the Air Force. Still unsure of my abilities to go to school or find a job, I was in effect opting for the military patriarchal system to take care of me. In an environment where there were at least ten men to every woman, for the first time in my life lots of men were asking for dates. But life is full of surprises, and I fell in love with a woman. That first lesbian experience was a mixed bag of euphoria at being in love and fear of Air Force rules against homosexuality. Since I was a student at the base and scheduled for transfer, the relationship did not fully develop before I left, but as a result of that homosexual friendship I was discharged after fourteen months' service.

I was left with a lot of ambiguous feelings, and so after finding . a job in Los Angeles, I began to attend church regularly and to date men. I had had only a brief look at homosexual life, and not knowing where to meet anyone outside of a chance encounter at work (or possibly at church), I did not actively seek out other women. I had close women friends both at church and work but was not otherwise attracted to them. I did not talk to any of the priesthood leaders about this, as I did not consider that I any longer had a problem.

In 1960 I met Jim at work. I dreaded the possibility of a temple recommend interview if I married an active LDS man (I intended to be honest with my future husband). But Jim was an inactive Mormon. He was not terribly upset when I told him about my Air Force experience. We married after a somewhat tumultuous court-ship—we were basically reluctant but still had some desire to marry. Eventually we became parents of a son. Jim remained inactive in the church, and at his request I became inactive after about three years of marriage. Following several moves we settled in the San Francisco East Bay area in 1966. During the years of our marriage, as we both sensed that it didn't fit, the thoughts staying with me were of women. By an odd coincidence I again met the woman I had known in the Air Force. I found that my feelings had not changed, and knowing the marriage was over, I began living actively as a lesbian (though not with her).

At about that time the women's movement was claiming the attention of women everywhere. Women were exploring their roles as wives, mothers, housewives, and men's sexual partners. In many cases it was as though we had awakened from a slumber to reach out into the real world, to recognize our real selves, to shed layers of socialization, and to reject the expectations of our upbringing. My partner and I became active in the women's movement and its sub-movement, the gay women's liberation groups. We attended consciousness raising groups, helped organize women's centers and bookstores, and created a new and stimulating life for ourselves.

Out of this exploration came a way to define myself as a lesbian. I am a woman whose primary social, psychological, emotional, and erotic interest is with another woman. I do not dislike men, I prefer women. I think there is something in my genes, my nature that makes me this way. I do not think it is from the way my parents raised me (why me out of nine siblings?). As far as I can discern, my upbringing was essentially the same as the rest of my family and friends.

I do not know how I came to be this way. If God has some scheme for me, I do not understand it. I only know I am happy with my life and am not sorry for the decisions I have made. Except for our intimate relationships, most lesbians' lives are indistinguishable from those of straight women. Many of us have been married and have children. So we work, raise our families, buy homes, pay taxes, take vacations, have hobbies, and so on. Many of us are still active church members.

During all this I still retained my ties to the Mormon church. I was not active but kept an interest in the daily workings of the church. I came to recognize that a great deal of my oppression came from my upbringing in a patriarchal church. Women are the neglected and exploited majority in the church. With more women members than men, the emphasis is still on the men, since they hold the priesthood. The church's programs for working with homosexuals are directed toward gay men. Lesbians are even more invisible than gays, hardly rating a line in the manuals bishops use for counseling homosexuals. We are largely unrecognized in our relationships with other women. I am sure if you look you will find us in your wards and stakes, many in leadership positions. If we stay in the church, we often do not have children and so have more time to devote to these positions.

In 1979 I heard about two groups, Mormons for ERA and Affirmation/Gay and Lesbian Mormons. I became active in both and especially in Affirmation, where I have held many leadership positions, including two years as international coordinator. We fill a need for many members of the church. Why? Because gay and lesbian members approach the church troubled and anxious and in search of compassion and understanding. Instead, we find a refusal to listen to our feelings at all levels, from apostles and church Social Services personnel and BYU professors to stake presidents and bishops. We find tunnel vision, people refusing to look beyond "sinful" behavior to see the tremendous loss of uncounted souls who would be active, contributing members if allowed to be ourselves and not forced to hide a most important facet of our personal lives.

Affirmation functions as a place for us to be. There we are allowed to express our innermost selves, to function as complete human beings. I could speculate on the blind acceptance by church leaders of the mainstream Judeo-Christian definition of homosexuality and the failure of LDS scriptures to mention the subject. Church officials and members seem to depend on personal prejudices and to brush off the "problem" because the "answer" is in the Bible and in some relatively recent writings by Spencer W. Kimball and others.

The church does not recognize scientific assessments of homosexuality nor the personal experiences of its own members. Talks have been given in conferences and church-wide firesides and pamphlets written which blame a poor family life. These talks must drive daggers into the hearts of parents who know this is not true but have a lovely son or daughter who was an exemplary member until his/her unconventional love surfaced. Little compassion or understanding for those parents or that person comes from untrained bishops, poorly trained counselors at church Social Services, or officials at church schools.

So in recent years the only place to turn to has been Affirmation. We are a self-help support and social group. We do not try or intend to take the place of the church. In the past eight years we have been a lifeline for thousands seeking understanding and caring from others like themselves. I pray for the day when Affirmation is not needed, when we have an understanding of the plan of salvation that could include a recognition of our love, and when we have better informed and better trained church officials and members to help us sort through the pieces of the puzzles of our lives.

FIVE

To Thine Own Self Be True

▼

Gordon Johnston

I was born in 1952 into a strong LDS family. As I grew up, the church was always a central part of my life. Through the children's Primary organization, the Young Men's Mutual Improvement Association, and the various priesthood quorums, I was a leader—president of my class, senior Boy Scout patrol leader, and so on.

At an early age I showed a particular interest in music, and my parents used to take turns driving me to lessons and recitals. We were a happy family and were very close. Mom and Dad were always affectionate with each other and with us kids, and this trait has become a part of each of us children now as adults. Our family has remained close in spite of physical distances and individual changes

"To Thine Own Self Be True," by Gordon Johnston, was originally presented at the annual meeting of the Association of Mormon Counselors and Psychotherapists, 1 October 1987, in Salt Lake City. Mr. Johnston holds an M.A. degree in music from Brigham Young University (1979). He lives in Ottawa, Ontario, where he is a professional organist for an Anglican parish and is a free-lance organist and harpist. He is also conductor of the Ottawa Men's Chorus and is involved with the international Gay and Lesbian Association of Choruses.

and growth.

Throughout my growing up years, I had many good friends, including as a teenager the requisite series of girlfriends and heartbreaks. Although I enjoyed the company of my girlfriends, I had little problem keeping the church's standard of morality, since I was never sexually attracted to women. From my earliest stirrings of sexual awareness, my feelings have always been homosexual. I learned at an early age that sexual feelings were private and homosexual feelings were especially private. I accepted the church's teaching that homosexuality was an unnatural and wicked temptation.

In 1974 following a mission to England, I enrolled at Brigham Young University. While pursuing my academic and spiritual goals, I hoped to find there the woman the Lord had in mind for me. Although my feelings toward women were friendly and never sexual, I was not worried. I believed in a God of miracles. A God who could part the Red Sea could surely find a woman who would appeal to me and with whom I could form a lasting relationship of love, including sexual love.

But it did not happen. Five years later I left BYU with a master's degree but no wife and moved to a new home. I soon made new friends in the church there. Over the years one by one my friends got married. I prayed and prayed for my time to come. During this period I dated girls and had many good friends, both male and female. I ignored my homosexual feelings and prayed that they would go away.

In the spring of 1984, I began dating our bishop's daughter, who was recently divorced. She was beautiful. Although we were extremely different, I liked her very much, and I proposed to her. I was sure my number was up.

We were a terrible mismatch. The story of our engagement is a nightmare of internal conflict for me. Ten days before our wedding we had a bitter, explosive fight, and I called it all off. My friends were concerned for me but so relieved that the marriage was off. Inside my head I felt as if I had cracked. I was unable to cope, and I knew I needed help. Two days later I was on a plane to Salt Lake City.

I stayed that summer with my mother in Salt Lake City and arranged to see an LDS psychologist, a friend of a friend. It was important to me that my counselor be a member of the church because there was so much cultural baggage tied up with being thirty-two and single and engaged to the bishop's daughter in a small town. I wanted someone who would understand all those things. I had an excellent counselor who helped me regain a great deal of self-confidence, but I could not bring myself at that time to tell him of my homosexuality, although I knew deep inside that it was THE issue.

At the end of the summer, I moved back home, ready to face the world again. However, I soon discovered that I needed more than a quick fix for what was troubling me. On the recommendation of a friend, I went to a Christian counselling center. I wanted someone to guide me through the process of working out my religious and cultural issues without a particular bias one way or the other. It was also important to me that my counselor be essentially nondirective. I didn't want someone to tell me what to do or how to feel: I wanted a counselor who would help guide my thinking and encourage me to find the right answers for me.

My counselor's name was Fred, and over the next few months we worked through a number of problems. After four or five months, things were going much better, but I knew that inside I still wanted to tell Fred I had these homosexual feelings. Eventually I did tell him what was troubling me. It was such a relief. Fred asked what I wanted to do about my feelings, and I said that I wanted to know more about them before doing anything.

The first place I looked to for guidance and information was the Mormon church. I consulted its guidelines for bishops on homosexuality. As I read through the church's statement, it struck me as simplistic and naive. It kept insisting that my homosexuality was a chosen, learned behavior, and I knew that was not true. I never chose to feel this way.

I remember years before having heard Elder Boyd K. Packer's talk, *To the One*. Ironically, I was the organist at the BYU Marriott Center the evening he gave that talk. He had advised homosexuals to suppress, and I had followed his advice. By so doing I learned that Steven Covey was right when he said that "unexpressed feelings never die, they just lie in wait to be resurrected later." Elder Packer said that homosexuality was a form of selfishness, and I had tried to make that description fit me. At the time I was a counselor in a branch presidency, attending the temple two or three days a week, living by choice with three handicapped roommates, and involved in numerous volunteer projects. But when Elder Packer suggested that my homosexual feelings were because I was selfish, I redoubled my efforts to give more of myself. Now as I reread his talk, I admire his courage in approaching such a sensitive subject, but I know from experience that his conclusions are not correct. I am not gay because I am selfish and self-centered.

So my search for knowledge continued. I went to the university library and Christian bookstores and read all kinds of books on sexuality and homosexuality. It was amazing—I, who read an average of a book a year, became a voracious reader, staying up until all hours reading and learning about homosexuality.

And I prayed. I prayed fervently from the bottom of my heart for insight. I had new questions that I couldn't find answers to, and I needed Heavenly Father's guidance. I learned to trust him in a whole new way.

Again and again I returned to the church's statement on homosexuality. I was determined to wring every possible truth out of it. Like the Book of Mormon prophet Nephi I tried to liken this statement to me. There was a long section on the cause of homosexuality, but the likening just didn't work. I didn't have an overbearing mother, my father wasn't distant, I hadn't been raped as a child or exposed to homosexuality as a youth. Having arrived at the age of thirty-two, I hadn't had sex with either a man or a woman. I knew that whatever feelings I had, I had not learned my basic sexual drive from anyone. The church's insistence that homosexual feelings were chosen was devastating for me. There are simply not words to describe the feeling of being let down by my church at the most critical time of my life. I couldn't believe that the church was so unenlightened on this subject yet judged so harshly.

As my search for knowledge progressed, I decided that I wanted to meet some real live gay people—but where to go? As an organist I was used to going to other churches, so I decided to attend a service at the Metropolitan Community Church, a Christian church with a special ministry to the gay and lesbian community. I was afraid that if I went to a club or something like that, I might get propositioned for sex, but neither was I sure what to expect from a gay-oriented church. What a surprise! It was just a regular church with men and women singing and praying. Afterwards I met them, a lawyer, a doctor, a politician, a French teacher, just nice normal people who happen to be gay.

I studied the concept of "homosexual change." The literature in this area is distressingly biased and simplistic. Most advocates of "homosexual change" emphasize the social unacceptability of homosexuality and dwell on all the problems that gay people face. I found this thinking irrelevant. I could find no documented study showing that homosexuals who claimed to be "changed" had in fact become heterosexual and that the "change" was sustained over a significant number of years.

The literature advocating change was without exception based on a "Pollyannaish" view of human sexuality. The goal of "change" is never clearly defined. One author described it as "a kind, humane, overall enjoyment of warmth and affection with both men and women, without erotic undertones." The world is full of both gay and straight people who have kind, nonerotic feelings toward men and women, but that has nothing to do with their sexual orientation. The only acceptable goal of "change" is complete heterosexuality, and I am convinced by my study, prayer, and personal experience that that is not possible.

Once I understood that my homosexuality was unchosen and unchangeable, I was faced with a whole new set of questions. How can I live a life that is congruent, moral, and fulfilling? I categorically reject the world's image of homosexuality and incidentally much of the world's image of heterosexuality. If I were straight I could work toward marriage and a family. So I asked myself, as a gay person how can I fulfill the measure of my own unique creation? How can I live to the fullest the life that God has given me?

Today, I am more convinced than ever that homosexuality is both unchosen and unchangeable. When one accepts these twin premises, however, he or she is confronted with an entirely new set of questions. These are questions that gay people are constantly faced with, and we need the brightest minds and the best thinking to help us in making our moral decisions. As long as church authorities believe that our sexuality is born out of selfishness and rebellion, they will not seek for new answers. As long as they think that counselling can change us into heterosexuals, they will have no reason to seek for further light and knowledge.

I believe we are all engaged in the same cause, the cause of truth. As gay people, we seek only to be known as we truly are, to be allowed and even encouraged to live congruent, honest, and full lives.

SIX

One Mormon's Lesbian Experiences

▼

Anonymous

... When I got involved in the lesbian lifestyle before, I convinced myself that it was okay to deviate somewhat from the gospel teachings because I was hurt and hurting and I longed for companionship . . . It was these feelings that prompted my marriage. I wanted so much to be important to one person. I wanted to plan and work with that person and to give of myself to him in whatever way I was able. I longed for the companionship and the tenderness of another. But I didn't find that kind of relationship in my marriage, and in the many months since then, I have wondered if I can have that with a man.

I know that I can have that kind of relationship with a woman because I have experienced it. Letting go of that security caused me great confusion and pain, but there are certain eternal realities (eternal marriage, family, and exaltation) that never change. I know that I can never give another woman the blessing of an eternal family, nor can I bless her life with the priesthood—a power I know

---

"One Mormon's Lesbian Experiences" originally appeared in *Exponent II*, Winter 1987.

so well and could never deny. I cannot stand with another woman before God and say, "Here we are—a family unit." That is blasphemy. I must accept the reality that I could never kneel with another woman at the altar in the temple of God and make vows for time and all eternity. That just doesn't happen. And yet I have to wonder why I insist on living a religion that robs me of a lifestyle where I have sought and found much peace and love—a lifestyle where all my needs were met and fulfilled with great tenderness. Why is it more comfortable for me to talk to and relate with other women than it is for me to be with men?

There is another side of all this that I must look at if I am to be totally fair and honest with myself. I remember all of the mornings when I woke up after the night befores feeling sick to my stomach because I had chosen to sleep with another woman and make love to her. I did not intend to end up in that situation. All I wanted was for someone to love me and hold me close to them and make me a part of their life . . . . I only had sexual relationships with two women, and both of those relationships went on over months and years in actual time spent together. In each relationship we shared an apartment and lived a moderately gay lifestyle in which we kept it hidden and did not seek outside reinforcement. I attempted to live the life of a good LDS woman because I found much good in the church. I also found so much good in my life as a lesbian. It somehow filled the gaps in my life. But I never felt totally at peace. My struggle was based in the fact that I knew within myself that my having physical relations with another was against the morals and the principles I had been taught all my life.

Why did I continue living a lesbian lifestyle? The relationships were meeting and filling so many of my needs that the pain and guilt consuming me were worth the sacrifice at the time. I hungered for companionship, and it was there for me. I didn't have to beg for love, and I didn't have to walk on eggs around the women I loved. Throughout my short marriage, I looked for the same tenderness, warmth, and communication from my husband, but I never found it with him. I never enjoyed having sex with my husband. He showed no concern for my feelings, and several times he hurt me in his haste to satisfy his own desires. I got to where I dreaded going to bed with him. He made me feel dirty. . . .

It has been a little over five years since my rebaptism. I have had my temple blessings restored, but my life has not been free from temptation nor free from past desires and thoughts. The process of repentance was the most difficult time I have ever gone through. It forced me to find out what I really wanted and what I was willing to do to have it. Somehow I had the unrealistic idea that as soon as I was baptized, all my troubles would be over. In truth it's been even more difficult at times—battling with thoughts and recurring flashbacks. I have come through what was probably the most important test in my life—to be straight or gay. It was as if everything that I held close to me was put up on the auction block. Would I sell out or would I keep my priceless treasures? These treasures that I speak of are of an eternal nature.

When I think of Christ's love for me, I realize that I have much to learn about love. I realize that I thought I knew love so many times in my life, but it was so much a self-fulfilling or selfish love then. My need to be a part of someone's life is very real, and I know that I have gone about filling that need in ways which have isolated me from the very form of love that I crave most—the love that brings peace of mind and heart. I know that I am not abnormal. The Lord would never have created me with a flaw that deviates from his eternal law of chastity. I know he would never tempt me with that as a weakness. It is okay to love another woman deeply and share with her. I think that women share something with each other that they do not share with men. It is not evil or wrong, but it is an eternal bonding of hearts which creates a deep sense of willingness to serve and cherish each other.

I have wondered whether or not I shall remarry. I know that there is a good chance that I won't. I know too that God will not let my heart dry up and produce juices of hatred, bitterness, and jealousy. I will not become a bitter old maid. I might be an old maid, but I will not end up being a victim of Satan's deadly poisons. If I grow old without children of my own, I shall not be alone. I will be surrounded with loving friends. Even if they precede me in death, I shall not be left alone. They will minister to me in times of my need for them. I shall not regret my choice to be straight, and I shall love both those who are not and those who are.

SEVEN

I Love My Mormon Family

▼

Linda May Peterson

My first response to seriously thinking I might be lesbian was to run away. Between the ages of seventeen and twenty-seven I struggled with the church, with feminist thinking, and with my growing awareness that I might be lesbian. At twenty-seven I ran away from the Mormon world I was struggling with and came to Japan. I never dreamed at that time I would still be living here more than ten years later. At that time I really was running away. I needed a complete change of scene. I was angry and hurt and afraid. I felt confused and pressured and misunderstood and uncomfortable. I loved my large Mormon family and spent lots of time with them, and I couldn't make the explorations I felt I needed to make in the middle of them and in the middle of Mormon culture. I was not sure at the time that I was a lesbian. I had more conflicts with church philosophy on the question of equality between men and women than about sexuality, though of course the two are con-

Linda May Peterson lived in Oregon as a child, in Texas as a teenager, and in Utah as a B.A. and M.A. student in English at Brigham Young University. She has been living in Japan since 1979, where she is a teacher and writer.

nected. I felt that I could not be a "Mormon woman."

After being away for a while, I acknowledged to myself that I really was lesbian. Lesbians call this coming out to yourself. Having come out to myself, my choice was to leave the Mormon church. I am happy that I made that decision and did not choose to live with what I think are irreconcilable differences.

The next step was deciding that I still wanted to be a member of my family, that I wanted to maintain relationships with my mother, aunts, sisters, and others. I began the work of reshaping my relationships with Mormon relatives, work which I take very seriously. I think that all relationships are work and require constant negotiation and maintenance. Although I have been working on it for more than ten years, I'm not satisfied, but I'm not going to give up. I love my family. I *choose* to work on my relationships with them. It takes work to get along with people anyway, but when there are major differences in philosophy, as there are between me and my Mormon relatives, it can seem impossible.

I think there are good reasons that it seems impossible. I think that Mormonism and lesbianism are incompatible, and that's one of the reasons I left the church. However, I do not think that Mormons and lesbians are necessarily incompatible. I think it is a choice. Some lesbians and some families or family members decide that they are incompatible. I think it's sad, but one of the choices is to cut off contact. I know lesbians who have decided to separate from the family, and I also know of families who have disowned or rejected lesbian members. So far the choice made by me and most of my family most of the time has been to maintain contact.

Difficulties may start before the lesbian Mormon comes out. I felt completely unable to talk about my feelings about sexuality with members of my family. I started to separate from them in ways that felt significant to me long before I ran away to Japan when I was twenty-seven. My mother knew that something was wrong and knew that I was running away, and I found this both comforting and painful. I appreciated her attention to me, and I was sorry that I couldn't talk to her about what was going on.

Why Lesbians Don't Come Out

For most lesbians coming out to their families is a difficult thing. We start by concealing our thoughts, feelings, behavior, the changes that are taking place. For Mormon lesbians a major problem is that something that feels inevitable to us as lesbians is defined in Mormonism as a sinful choice, something to repent of. I tried repenting several times and always ended up feeling worse. At one point when I was at Brigham Young University, I became seriously depressed, sat on the balcony of my apartment crying for days. I went back to my parents house for a semester without telling them what was wrong. I talked to the stake president, repented, and went back to school, where shortly afterwards I met the woman who became my first lover. Repentance felt like a lie and meeting my lover felt like the truth. I suppose that this conflict is emphasized in Mormonism, in which a still small voice is supposed to tell you the truth. My still small voice gave me the wrong message according to the church. Of course I didn't tell my parents or anyone else about any of that either. And I repented again after the relationship ended, out of misery and still in secret. Concealment was a kind of safety. I could continue going to school. The external patterns of my life did not have to change.

Fear of change is part of the reason lesbians don't come out. We are afraid of losing the love of our families. We are afraid of losing money, support, a place to go for holidays. We are afraid of never being able to see our nieces again. We are afraid that everyone will be terribly upset. We are afraid of losing whatever peace and pleasantness we have built with our families. We are afraid that it will just kill Grandma and Grandpa or that Mom will never get over it. We are afraid that we will be accused of destroying the family. We are afraid that the love we thought we shared with our families will turn out not to be unconditional.

I have been lucky in being able to choose my times for coming out. For example I didn't get kicked out of BYU. No one in the family felt compelled to tell everyone. I haven't been excommunicated. I have had time and the luxury of changing my ideas and my relationships with my family members at my own speed. I don't believe lesbians and family members do ourselves or each other any good by protecting each other, by pretending that we don't know things, by pretending to be other than who or what we are, or by acting on the idea that anyone else's happiness depends on what we do.

Why Lesbians Do Come Out

I haven't come out to everyone. Usually there's a particular reason for coming out. One of my sisters started writing me letters asking lots of questions and saying that she wanted to continue our relationship on a deeper level. An aunt was coming to visit me and I was not willing to pretend in my own house. When I am going to visit someone and want to have more meaningful contact, I come out. I come out to people I trust or people who I think will try to listen to me and give us both a chance. One of the values I share with Mormons is that everyone gets a choice, and having decided to live as an open lesbian as much as possible, I want to give my relatives a share in the decision about whether to continue a relationship.

Another value I share with Mormons is honesty. I never was a good liar. I don't like lying for social reasons. I don't like avoiding issues. When I read my journals from when I was in the church I am amazed to see what I put in and what I left out. I was writing for my great-grandchildren and trying to make it faith-promoting, and faith-promoting was more important to me at that time than truth-promoting. I did not write about my doubts and fears. I did not write about my feelings and how confused I was about them until I had run away to Japan and given myself permission to really be honest. One of the reasons I love my mother is that as much as she likes to avoid unpleasantness, she doesn't like dishonesty. When she began to ask me about my life in Japan, I wanted to tell her the truth.

I did not take this lightly. Of course for a lesbian, it would be foolish not to expect some distress on the part of a Mormon relative to whom lesbianism is a sin. For the lesbian, coming out is an act of self empowerment, a claiming of an identity which has become or is becoming positive. For the Mormon it is an admission of guilt or sin or possibly illness or madness.

When I decided to come out to my mother, I planned it very carefully. I chose a time when we would be alone together with time to talk and work things through. I prepared by actually role-playing the conversation with friends and with a counselor. I tried to anticipate Mom's reactions, so that I would not find myself saying things I didn't want to say. I needed to be strong and clear. It was important to me to say what I wanted to say and get through to her. My message was "I am a lesbian, and I am happy about it."

I expected her to question whether I really knew what I was saying, to try to talk me out of it, to cry, to feel guilty. She did all of those things. I did not expect her to give me her blessing or to be happy about it. She did not. I was pleased that she talked, asked questions, expressed her feelings. I think what made the conversation a success was that we both loved each other, and neither of us wanted to hurt the other or shut the other out.

I have since come out to all of my sisters and some of my aunts and cousins. I don't want to be the sister, niece, cousin who just disappeared. That is what often happens to lesbians in Mormon families who don't come out. They just fade away or carry on superficial contact, going along with the idea that silence is best for everyone.

After Coming Out: Denial

Coming out may not change anything. One of the most surprising results of coming out is that sometimes absolutely nothing happens, and no one ever mentions it again. The lesbian may feel that at least she doesn't have a secret any more, and the others may be relieved that at least the lesbian isn't going to insist on talking about it. Any lovers remain "friends" or "roommates."

The problem with this kind of silence is that it begins to feel like a lie after a while. I know families in which everyone plays along with the idea that the lesbian is just an old maid, even though everyone guesses or suspects or even knows she's lesbian. I have come to believe that this kind of denial really is dangerous. From the Mormon side the message is that silence is the price of acceptance, even of love. Another message is that perhaps the reality will go away. From the lesbian side the message is "I know that the real me is not good enough." Or perhaps the message from both sides is the same: "I don't respect you enough to tell you the truth; we don't trust each other enough."

The other thing about silence is that superficial contact is boring. It is not surprising that lesbians sometimes look on family visits as uncomfortable, unpleasant duties. I think that it's possible for Mormons and lesbians to love and enjoy each other, but I don't think silence and denial will make it possible.

At the same time, silence really can buy privileges. One of my relatives changed her policy towards me drastically after we spoke about my being a lesbian, even though she admitted that she had been speculating about me long before we spoke. Some kind of moral imperative caused her to change her behavior after she *knew.* Perhaps she thought that after we had acknowledged the truth, I would behave less cautiously, be less "tactful." As a result of her changed behavior, I decided not to contact her. I want her to have time to think things through and decide whether she wants contact with me at all. I don't think of this as a permanent decision on my part. I think of it as a breathing spell until one of us decides to try again.

Unspoken Agreements, Unilateral Decisions

Coming out may mean that both sides try to outguess each other so as not to offend or to offend as little as possible. For myself, I have made some changes in my way of interacting with my family, mostly without discussing the changes with them. For example, instead of staying at my parents' or sisters' houses, which is considered normal in our family, I stay nearby in a motel, especially if my lover is with me. This was a decision I made for my own peace of mind, but I think it was helpful for my relatives as well, though they would never have suggested it or even agreed if I had discussed it with them. I just decided and did it.

I have found that this is a good way for me to handle interaction. I do a lot of thinking before an upcoming visit or gathering, even telephone calls sometimes. I make specific dates with the people I want to see. I invite my sister out to lunch if I want to talk to her. I don't expect it just to happen. I try to remember that I always have a choice, and I try to remind everyone else that they have choices too.

I tell people why I am doing things. For example, I explain that I want to have a chance to talk, and it's difficult to really talk with the kids around. A painful decision I made recently was not to go to a family reunion. I would like to see my nieces and nephews, and I like the idea of everyone getting together. But I thought I would be uncomfortable in the group, so I called the host sister and explained why I wasn't coming.

Ongoing Relationships

I'd like to be able to discuss things with my family much more openly than we can now. I'd like to be able to negotiate. For things to be negotiated, both sides have to be willing to talk about them. I am hopeful. One of my sisters surprised me by asking about terminology, whether she should say lesbian or gay or homosexual in referring to my sexuality. I was delighted to be able to explain that I prefer the word lesbian and that I feel that the terms gay and homosexual refer mostly to men and not to me. She and I have reached a level of communication in which we can discuss and negotiate. I send her my writing and she discusses it with me. She encouraged me to do this essay, and when I mentioned my hesitation about using my real name on it, she said of course you'll put your name on it.

I think of her as my ally. She does not approve of my lifestyle and makes that clear, but she supports me in my desire to continue being a member of the family and to work out better ways of getting along with everyone. I appreciate the risk she takes by being open with me, and I realize that part of the risk she takes is the possibility that other members of the family will not approve of her relationship with me.

It will be interesting to see what effect this essay will have on my family relationships. My previous writing about lesbianism has been directed at lesbians, so there was little chance of my relatives reading it. It's possible that some family members will be upset, but I have already decided that I have to live my life the best I know how and that I can't be responsible for someone else's feelings. I hope that the result will be positive, that my relatives and I can talk, that we can understand each other better, that we can respect each other's choices. I hope that we can love and enjoy each other in spite of our differences.

Partner's
Voices

EIGHT

Goodbye, I Love You

(an excerpt)

▼

Carol Lynn Pearson

"Trudy? This is Carol Lynn. Is Gerald there?"

"He is. We're having a wonderful visit. How are you, darling?"

"Fine. And you?"

"Wonderful! Here's Jerry."

"Hi sweetheart. I was going to call you." A long pause. "Blossom? Are you there?"

"Gerald?" I could hardly hear my own voice. I'd have to speak louder. "Gerald?"

"Yes?"

"I have to ask you a question. Gerald, since you and I have been married, have there been any . . . men?"

"Yes. Yes, there have been."

A long pause. "Gerald? What do you want to do?"

"What?"

Carol Lynn Pearson, *Goodbye, I Love You* (New York: Random House, 1986.) Ms. Pearson currently resides in Walnut Creek, California. She is a poet, playwright, and personal essayist. She lectures widely, and most recently has performed her one-woman play, *Mother Wove the Morning*, throughout the United States.

"Do you want to stay with us?"

"Blossom!" A world of pain was in Gerald's voice. "Oh, Blossom! Some questions don't even need to be asked."

"I'm asking."

"Of course I want to stay with you and the kids. Of *course* I do!"

"How?"

"Blossom, we can work it out." Gerald spoke firmly. "I've been trying to tell you. I've been preparing things so I could tell you. I feel awful that it happened like this. Please . . . just hang on until I get home. Please believe in me, believe in yourself, believe in us. We can find a way to work it out. Don't do anything, *anything* until I get home. Promise me that. Blossom?"

"Okay."

"What?"

"Okay."

"Blossom? I love you."

"I . . . love you too."

Both hands put the receiver back on the telephone. Slowly I crossed the room, turned out the light, closed the door, walked up the stairs, down the hall, and into the bathroom. I was shaking, shaking from the cold. I knelt down and turned on the water in the tub, only the hot water. I watched while the water filled the bathtub, while the steam rose and covered the walls and the mirror. Then I undressed and stepped into the tub. I shivered violently as the hot water met the chill of my feet and legs. Then I lowered myself into the water, feeling the heat travel upward to my neck and my chin. Still I shook.

The carillon bells on campus sounded the hour. Eight—nine—ten. And then I gave myself up to the moaning that rose in my throat in a primitive rhythm that made me hold myself and rock back and forth, back and forth to the strange, wounded sound of my own voice. . . .

Next morning Lynn Ann looked at me as if I had blood on my face.

"Carol Lynn! What's *wrong*?"

"I'm just tired. I didn't sleep much." That was not a lie. I hadn't slept at all. I had walked and rocked and lain down and gotten up and gone in to look at the children and picked Aaron up to hold because he was the smallest. Then, before they were to wake, I put a wet washcloth on my eyes. The world was still here and there were things to be done.

I had to move. I had to get ready to give a talk. Two hundred women would be waiting to hear me. One fulfills one's responsibilities. I could only move slowly. I got dressed and put on my makeup. I looked tired. Worse. Old. Worse. I looked ugly. I was overwhelmed at how ugly I looked. How could I ever have thought I had nice eyes?

At the luncheon, I stared at the elegantly arranged flowers in the centerpiece as my introduction was given. It was a lie. It was all a lie. I was not the person they had invited to speak. I didn't even know who she was. I was a fraud. *They* thought I was an example of good Mormon womanhood. They were proud of me. I had a wonderful husband and three children and I wrote lovely poems. They didn't know anything. They didn't know that my eternal marriage was in ruins. They didn't know that my children's father was a homosexual. What if they knew that? They wouldn't want me then. They wouldn't ask me to speak then. Still, I would give my talk. I would speak on the wonderful world of women. In spite of the fact that my husband preferred men, I would tell them what a thrilling thing it is to be a woman. I didn't have a master's degree in drama for nothing. I could pull it off. I could lie once. And then I would never speak again. I would go home and cancel all the speaking engagements I had accepted. I would resign my seat on the governor's commission to plan the bicentennial. I would cancel everything.

No one seemed to notice that I lied. Two hundred women applauded and many told me how much they'd enjoyed the speech and what an inspiration my writings were to them. I smiled and thanked them. If I could just get out the door and down the stairs, I would never, never have to do this again. How could they not know, I thought, as I finally opened the car door and sank into the driver's seat. I was saying the right words, and the right words were fine with them. Was that all they wanted? Is that all anybody wants. Just to hear the right words?

On the way home I stopped in to visit my father whom I hadn't seen for a couple of days. Would he be able to tell?

"How is he?" I asked Gladys as she opened the door for me.

"He's not eating again, that's how he is," my stepmother replied as if it were a personal affront. "That man is *so* stubborn! "

"Daddy?" I sat down beside his bed and touched his hand.

His eyes opened and he looked at me. "Hello, Sister."

"How are you feeling?"

"Not too good."

"Gladys says you won't eat."

He closed his eyes again and shook his head.

"I wish you would."

He made as firm a gesture as he could with his hands.

"Sister, I'm on my way out. If I could get better, I would. But I can't. Just leave me alone."

I took one of his hands and felt the tears come to my eyes. I didn't want him to be so frail, so helpless. But there was something else too. I felt relief. My father was going to die soon. He would never have to know what was happening to me. He would never have to know about Gerald. It would kill him. He had charged Gerald on our wedding day to take good care of me. Oh, Daddy, die soon, I thought. And then you'll never have to know.

And there was another thing I felt—I was envious of my father. *Envious!* He was going to die soon. He would be through with all of this. Wherever else there was, he would soon be there. Oh, Daddy, if I did not have three children, I would lie down too. I would lie down and not eat or drink, and soon I would not be here.

I let the children watch television all afternoon, something that never before had happened. I went upstairs to my room over the garage to try to think what to do. I had a dozen good friends I could call on for *anything*—anything except visiting upon them my enormous shame. I could tell no one.

If my house had been destroyed by fire, if my child had been run over, I could call on the church. The church would be wonderful. But not this. I could not bear it. Gerald might be excommunicated and I would be humiliated and pitied. Women with problems were encouraged to take them to the bishop or to the Relief Society president. I couldn't go to the bishop, not now. I had promised Gerald I'd do nothing until he got back.

And I *was* the Relief Society president. Women in the ward brought their problems to *me*. I had been amazed when the bishop called me to the job. "I'm not a Relief Society president," I had protested. "I'm a maverick—I'm strange—I'm nothing *like* a Relief Society president!" But he had insisted I was the one for the job. He wanted to strengthen the compassionate service aspects of the Relief Society and he thought I was the one who could do it. Compassion, love, helpfulness. That's what it was all about. CHARITY NEVER FAILETH. That was our motto. What did it mean? Compassion. But not for wickedness. Not for the very lowest of the low. Not for . . . homosexuals.

I groaned aloud. How could this be happening to me? I had been doing everything right. I was keeping all my covenants. I had promised in the temple to be honest and chaste and to obey all the commandments. I was doing that. I prayed. We had family prayer. I paid my tithing. I went to all my meetings. We had family home evening once a week to teach the children to be faithful. Nothing like this was supposed to happen. Illness and accidents, maybe, and maybe financial problems. There was no shame in those. But not this, not something so shameful, so sinful you could not even speak it. I had thought it was over, done with, washed clean. I had been promised!

, I went to my bookcase and pulled out the one book published by the church that I knew had some mention of it, *The Miracle of Forgiveness* by Spencer W. Kimball. There it was in black-and-white. Homosexuality was "an ugly sin . . . repugnant . . . embarrassing . . . perversion . . . sin of the ages . . . degenerate . . . revolting . . . abominable and detestable crime against nature . . . carnal . . . unnatural . . . wrong in the sight of God . . . deep, dark sin." Under Mosaic law it carried the death penalty. Those words—those awful words—I had only pictured them as applying to someone so low, so evil and beastly that he hardly deserved breath. But they were talking about Gerald. Gerald!

I read on. "Satan incites the carnal man to ever-deepening degeneracy in his search for excitement until in many instances he is lost to any former considerations of decency. Thus it is that through the ages, perhaps as an extension of homosexual practices, men and women have sunk even to seeking sexual satisfactions with animals."

The tears and the sobs came again. How could this be? Gerald was an unrepentant homosexual! Should I pack up the children and leave? Take them somewhere so he could never see them again? Where could I go?

I picked up the book and went on:

> After consideration of the evil aspects, the ugliness and prevalence of the evil of homosexuality, the glorious thing to remember is that it is curable and forgivable . . . if totally abandoned and the repentance is sincere and absolute. Certainly it can be overcome, for there are numerous happy people who were once involved in its clutches and who have since completely transformed their lives. Therefore to those who say that this practice or any other evil is incurable, I respond: "How can you say the door cannot be opened until your knuckles are bloody, till your head is bruised, till your muscles are sore? It can be done. . . ."
>
> Many yielding to this ugly practice are basically good people who have become trapped in sin. They yield to a kind, helpful approach. Those who do not must be disciplined when all other treatments fail. . . .
>
> Remember, the Lord loves the homosexual as he does all of his other children. When that person repents and corrects his life, the Lord will smile and receive him.

Slowly I closed the book and put it down. It had not occurred to me, not once in all our married life, that Gerald had not completely and fully repented. What was it? Was it *me*? Was I not sufficiently attractive? Had I not been enough of a woman to make it work?

I stared at my hands and turned them over. They were small, a woman's hands. Was there something wrong with having a woman's hands? Were big hands better? Was there something wrong with having a woman's face? Woman's skin? Woman's breasts?

I sank to my knees and buried my face in the gray couch. *What's wrong with being a woman?* The cry came from the depths of me. Where could I go to find healing for the wound to the woman in me? Only to God. But . . .

Didn't God prefer men too, in a spiritual sense? God *was* male. God associated with males, did business with males, spoke to males, called males to his work. God did not transact important business with people with small woman's hands and a woman's face. He loved all of us, of course, but he preferred men. My mind moaned under the weight of it.

And God's church preferred men. That was evident. Women were welcomed and respected and used, but not preferred. The hundred horror stories I had written out in my diary marched through my mind in sorry evidence. Only last month a rough cut of a film on Joseph Smith's early life had been shown to the Brethren. A scene at the kitchen table had panned the family group and ended on Lucy Mack Smith gazing devotedly at her son. One of the Brethren responded, "Why did that scene feature the mother? It should have featured the father. We're a priesthood-oriented church. We've got to feature the men. I'd like that scene shot over." No matter how many I heard, those stories hurt anew.

What's wrong with being a woman?

I had known all my life that somehow femaleness was second prize. But they had promised me, *promised* me that in this one thing I was safe. The man would want me, need me *because* I was a woman. My softer skin and woman's breasts would be indispensable. I had been cheated. I had been violated.

There must be some mistake. It could not be true that *everywhere I turned* they would rather I be male—not God and the church and my husband too. I did not want to be a man. I liked being a woman. There must be some mistake, something I couldn't see, something no one had told me. *I will not accept this answer,* I cried inside. *I will beat my small woman's hands against heaven until I get a better answer!*

On the next day the anger came. I had slept just enough to find a little strength, and I woke up furious. The enormous, staggering betrayal washed over me in waves. This must be what many of the early Mormon women had felt when they learned their husbands were being intimate with other women, or were planning to be, I thought. To know that the person you love is sharing that most private act with other people! How could they bear it? How could I bear it? How dare Gerald do that to me? How dare he do it to us? How dare he let his filthy habits destroy all we had been working for in this life and in the world to come? How dare he do this to Emily? To John? To Aaron? . . .

Another day to endure. Get dressed. Make breakfast. See Emily off to school. Find another answer if John asks again if I fell down and hurt myself. Go on.

When the visiting teachers rang my doorbell I was startled. I had forgotten that they had made an appointment for this morning. Once a month the visiting teachers went in pairs to call on all the women in the ward to give a short lesson and check on the welfare of the family. Good thing I had at least gotten dressed and combed my hair. . . .

[Later] as I watched the two women walk down the sidewalk, I remembered Sister Loper. She was bedridden again and was scheduled to be taken to a rest home near her daughter in Oregon, but until next Friday she was the responsibility of the Relief Society. For the past few weeks I had made sure her visiting teachers were having food brought in and were tending to her basic needs. I had been to see her several times and decided to go again today.

As I walked up the cracked sidewalk of the little green frame house, I noticed the dried grass and weeds in the yard and made a mental note to see if we could get one of the youth groups in the ward to come over and do some watering and a little weeding. I knocked lightly on the screen door, then opened it and went in.

"Sister Loper?"

"In here, Sister Pearson." . . .

I stayed and talked for a while and gave Sister Loper a backrub, going gently over the little bones. Then I rubbed her feet. She smiled and closed her eyes. What a pitiful, helpless little thing.

Suddenly I remembered a statement Gerald had read to me a few weeks before. I was nearly asleep and he had shaken me and said, "Now listen to this, Blossom. Are you listening?"

"Mmm hmm." I had turned toward him and tried to open my eyes.

"This is from Alan Watts. 'The thing is to see in *all* faces the masks of God.' That's *it*, Blossom. That's what it's all about. If we can look at each other and see *everyone*, no matter who they are, as a manifestation of God, we've solved the puzzle!"

I looked at Sister Loper's tight little wrinkled face. A mask of God. Gerald was not talking about Sister Loper. He was talking about himself! That's why he spoke it so urgently. That's why he shook me and insisted that I hear it two or three times. If only he could make me see *all* faces, even *his* face, as a mask of God. . . .

Waiting for the sound of the car in the driveway was excruciating.

"When will Daddy be here?" John asked, tearing through the kitchen with his truck. The children had asked that a dozen times already.

"Any time now. This afternoon. That's all I know."

Gerald had decided, instead of rushing right home to meet the crisis, to stay and go to the workshop. It might be part of the solution, he reasoned. If he could make some of these psychic-spiritual breakthroughs he'd been working on, perhaps he could see better his own situation, our situation, and what it all meant. Besides, staying away for a few days would give me a little time to recover before we saw each other.

One week. Had it only been one week? Years had gone faster. I had confided in no one, only gone over it and over it with myself.

Can you become
Acclimated to pain?
Can the shiver cease,
And some condition
Almost comfortable set in?

The polar bear has been
So long a resident of frost
That the ice he walks barefoot
Is not reported to the brain.

Can you become
Acclimated to pain?

I washed the kitchen cupboards as I listened for the car. Physical work was the only kind I'd been able to do for a week. Hands can move no matter what.

"I'm so glad when Daddy comes home," Emily sang from the front room. "Glad as I can be—"

Please, Emily. Please don't sing that song again, I begged silently, as I leaned over the counter and closed my eyes. The children had sung it in Sunday school on Father's Day a few months ago. Gerald had beamed as he'd watched his three little angels singing to him.

"I'll pat his cheek and give him what?" Emily sang on. "A great, big kiss!"

"Emily!" I called sharply. "John! Aaron!"

The three came running.

"Listen. Will you please go out on the front lawn and wait for Daddy out there? Here's a Popsicle."

The Popsicles did it. Happily the three children trudged out front to watch for Daddy. Why did I need so badly to be alone? Would I ever again have enough energy to have three children in the same room with me?

When I heard the sound of the car I had to take hold of the sink for a moment. I always knew when Gerald was home because he revved the motor a little before turning off the ignition. He said it made the car easier to start the next time you used it. There it was. The motor, the rev, the slam of the door, the shrieks of the children.

I lifted a corner of the curtain and looked out the window. I had opened none of the drapes for a week. Emily was in Gerald's arms. Then John and Aaron. They helped him lug his suitcase and his briefcase up the porch stairs. I straightened up beside the sink. If I could just keep the blood moving through my veins I would not keel over. I breathed deeply a few times, the way Sister Pardoe had taught me to do against stage fright. Fill the abdomen.

"Where's Mom?"

"In the kitchen. I finished my sculpture, Daddy. Do you want to see it?"

"In a minute."

Gerald walked into the kitchen. It was just . . . Gerald. He had done it hundreds of times before. It was just Gerald walking into the kitchen. I looked at him and listened to my voice say, "Hi, Gerald."

"Hi, Blossom."

We looked at one another, tentative, questioning.

"Emily's sculpture's real good, Daddy. And so's my kitty," said John. "You want to see them?"

"Daddy, did Mommy tell you what the *boys* did on the wall?"

"Emily," I said, "go turn on *Sesame*, would you please? We'll be out in a few minutes."

"Oh, all right," she said, and stomped off to the front room, followed by her brothers.

Gerald picked up his suitcase and walked down the hall. I followed him. I shut the door to our bedroom and watched Gerald put his suitcase down beside the closet. Then he turned around and looked at me.

The thing is to see in all faces the masks of God.

And then we were in each others arms, sobbing, pressing against each other and against the monumental mystery that lay between us and around us, that I knew would be there for the rest of our lives.

Had I been able to hate Gerald, it would have been simpler. I tried to let it happen and it would not. I watched him as I went through the rest of the day waiting for evening when we could be alone and talk. He appeared to be *the same person* that I had been living with for eight years. Was it possible?

At supper he told the children silly stories of things he had seen on his trip and made them laugh. "And there's this grimy little bag lady there on the same corner every night in San Francisco. She wears old slippers and doesn't have many teeth and she goes around singing as loud as she can, 'Gonna wash my back tonight— hallelujah—gonna wash my back tonight— hallelujah!'"

Was it possible that an unrepentant homosexual could still love his children? Or was I going a little mad? Was Satan making his first inroads against my sense of right and wrong? Should I even have let Gerald in the house? But there he was, *the same person* I had loved all these years. He was a little anxious. I could see that. But his light still shone. It had not gone out. Gerald had sold out to Satan. *Why didn't it show?*

When finally Emily's sculpture and Johnny's kitty and Aaron's rendition of "If You Chance to Meet a Frown" had been properly admired and the children had been put to bed (the children were to see nothing wrong; at all costs the children were to see nothing wrong), Gerald and I sat down on the couch and looked at each other.

"How was the workshop?" I asked quietly.

Gerald gave a short laugh. "I had diarrhea the whole time, from the moment of your phone call. Have you ever tried to have an out-of-the-body experience while you've got diarrhea?"

"No, I haven't. Sorry I spoiled your fun."

"Blossom." Gerald reached over and took my hand. I let him. "Please don't be caustic with me. You have such a way of being caustic when you want to. Please don't."

I stared at the floor and said nothing.

"I want to tell you everything," Gerald went on. "Everything. And I will answer every question you have. Please try not to judge. Please try just to listen."

Gerald thought a moment, then went on. "I was not being dishonest with you when we married. I loved you. You were wonderful and I really did love you. I thought that the *problem* would be taken care of. They told me it would be. I did everything they said to do. And I thought for a few months that everything was changed."

"But, Gerald," I interrupted, "we were—I was—happy!"

"And I was too, in many, many ways. Blossom, this is not your fault. Maybe you think it is, but it has nothing to do with you, only with me. Yes, we were happy. I liked being with you. I even liked being with you physically. But to me it was like . . . like we were such good friends that we shared everything with each other, even sex. It was never quite like . . . like lovers. There is this other thing in me, Blossom, and it has never gone away and I know now that it never will. There is this thing in me that needs, that *insists* that my strongest feelings be for a man. It is a need that seems to be as deep in me as my need for food and breath. I tried to beat it to death, to strangle it, to smother it. And it has not died. Blossom, I know the anguish you've been through this last week. Can you understand that I have been in anguish too? And for more than a week."

"Gerald," I said, "it's *wrong!*"

"Wrong!" Gerald put his face into his hands and then looked up. "I have taken that word and used it like a whip on myself. I have flagellated myself with that word until I'm bloody. But it does not change things. I have fasted, I have prayed. How many thousands of prayers I have prayed! And it does not change things. If my homosexuality is wrong, then *I* am wrong, the fact of my *being* is wrong. Because that's what *I am!*"

"When did you finally know?"

"About a year after we married."

"Did you . . . meet someone?"

"No. I just knew. Inside me. And I can tell you the exact moment. You won't remember this. It was Sunday morning and I turned on the program of poetry reading on KSL. 'The Buried Life' by Matthew Arnold. My own life, my buried life, came washing over me, drowning me. I just lay there and sobbed. 'Tricked in disguises, alien to the rest of men, and alien to themselves.' That was me. An alien. Disguised. Trying to give my all to being something that I really was not. An alien, trying to find home"

I heard all the words. The language was not foreign, but the sense was foreign. I felt we could continue to talk forever and I would still miss the sense of it. I had to take a deep breath before I could ask the next question.

"Gerald, when did you first . . . ?"

"Act on those feelings?"

I nodded.

"On the tour to Europe."

"While I was home, pregnant with your child?" I cried, remembering that "friendship ring," finally understanding it. "While I was pregnant, you and your roommate . . . all over Europe—"

"He wasn't my roommate."

"You and whoever were—" Angrily I stood up and walked away from the couch. "Why didn't you tell me before you went?" I whirled around to look at Gerald. "Why didn't you say, 'Look, we've made a terrible mistake. I can't keep my promises. Let me go!' Why didn't you say that to me?"

The hurt in Gerald's eyes was huge. "Because I never really thought it *was* a terrible mistake. In spite of this, we've had one of the best marriages I've known. I didn't want to leave you. And then Emily, and the boys. How could I leave them? Maybe I should have come to you and said let's end it, but I couldn't bear that. I decided maybe the best answer was just to let my buried life breathe from time to time. I thought maybe you would never have to know, never have to be hurt." Gerald heaved a long sigh and leaned back. "I found out it doesn't work that way. I hate not being honest. I hate it. I knew I'd have to tell you. I've been trying to. Oh, Blossom, you can't imagine how many of the things I have said over the last several years have had one goal in mind—to prepare you to accept me as I really am."

"Accept you?"

"Accept me. Look past the horror you've been conditioned to and really *see* me. Love me. And, if you can, stay with me."

"*How?* Gerald, what you're asking is crazy! I don't know any woman who could be in a marriage like that. You want *everything*!" Then it hit me, the memory of Gerald and Paul and me, in the car, close together, Gerald holding my hand. How cruel! To both Paul and me. That was the kind of life Gerald wanted?

"You could do it if you wanted to," Gerald said.

"I *don't* want to," I cried. "I don't want to and I couldn't if I did. It is not *in* me, and I'm glad it isn't because the whole thing is *wrong*!"

Gerald shook his head and spoke as if to himself. "Wrong."

"Listen, Gerald. You *can* change. I know you can. If you want to stay with us badly enough, if you want to make things work. Now that it's out in the open we'll work on it together. We'll get help, through the church, through counseling.

Tears of frustration filled Gerald's eyes and he clenched his fists. "Counseling! Oh, Blossom, I have had all I want of the church's counseling. Before I went on my mission, I went again and again to the church's top expert on this subject. He's a good man, a kind and loving man, but he does not even begin to understand the depth of the homosexual condition. He told me I would be all right if I would just continue in fasting and prayer and *not touch myself when I went to the bathroom*."

"But there must be other treatments, professional treatments." Gerald nodded his head and he looked tired and old. "And nobody I have ever known has gotten anything from the treatments but more guilt and more hopes smashed. Like Sam. Let me tell you about Sam. No. I want you to meet him. I want you to hear his story from himself. Will you?"

I didn't want to meet Sam or hear about treatments that didn't work. But I said I would meet him. If I was going to fight this thing, I had to know what I could about the enemy.

We got ready for bed as we had how many hundreds of times.

"Do you . . . . do you still want to pray?' I asked.

"Blossom, do you really think that homosexual people don't pray? Of course I still want to pray."

We knelt and Gerald offered the prayer as he had now many hundreds of times.

"And we're grateful for the love we share. Please bless us that during these difficult times we don't lose sight of that. I'm so grateful for Carol Lynn and for her goodness. Please bless her that her pain will be lightened. Help us to find answers to our problems. And bless the children that they will not be hurt . . ."

I managed to find enough voice to say "Amen."

NINE

The Long-Term
Lesbian Relationship

▼

Anonymous

Periodically my sister Laurie crashes on my couch for a couple of hours and bemoans a particular crisis she's weathering with husband Paul. Or Gail, a friend from college days, comes through town for a weekend and spends half the time recounting her marital ups and downs. On these occasions I'm expected to nod sympathetically and ask questions in the right places, but offering anything like advice or swapping similar tales is not an option. Despite my nineteen years with Barrie, despite interpersonal problems that are strikingly similar to Laurie's, I'm never asked for first-hand views on marriage. This is because my partner is another woman.

I really don't want to get into marriage counseling anyway. My job as owner-manager of a small business provides plenty of challenge. My point is that long-term lesbian relationships have much more in common with long-term straight relationships than people usually recognize. Most of the agonies and the ecstasies of an intimate relationship arise from similar sources, whether the people are gay or straight.

If you don't agree with that claim, just reflect a little. What makes an intimate relationship work? Closeness, sharing, give-and-take, a sense of each being central to the other's well-being, good communication, trust, commitment, a willingness to grow both as individuals and as a couple. If the relationship is sexual, add that spice along with an openness about what each wants and hopes for from physical encounters. The list is pretty much the same in a heterosexual liaison or a gay union.

And the obstacles are not very different, for the most part. What do married couples argue about? In-laws, money, chores, not enough time together, inconsiderateness, jealousy, even infidelity. You name it, everybody's got it.

On the other hand, some agonies and some ecstasies may be more prevalent in same-sex relationships. One of the major problems, of course, is that same-sex unions aren't sanctioned by society. This means that in addition to the anxiety about disclosure, fears and worries about jobs, family response, gay-bashing, and all the other unpleasantries, a lesbian couple doesn't get much support from the outside world to succeed as a couple. In fact, one of the major complaints of most lesbians I know is that well-intentioned family and friends so often ask, "Are you and X still together?" It's very unlikely for someone to ask a married woman, "Are you and Jim still together?" unless a split is imminent. Society at large wants married couples to stay married. So all the pressures and all the encouragement is in that direction. By contrast, society wants gay couples at best to stay invisible. So when rough waters loom for a lesbian couple, they get little outside shoring up.

There are other problems which characterize the typical lesbian partnership. Bluntly put, one is the question: "Who's the mommy?" The psychological dynamics between two women are very different from those between a woman and a man. A man may want some mothering from time to time—and it's very clear in a straight relationship who the "mommy" is. More often in heterosexual unions, the male, who has been trying since early childhood to achieve separation from his mother and establish his male identity, insists on a certain amount of distance from his female partner. He is probably unaware of this need, but it's still there. A female child, on the other hand, seeks to identify with her mother, and one of her tasks is individuation, making real the boundaries between herself and her sex-role model. When two women are lovers, those boundaries tend to blur, and the result is a circumstance that has taken on mythic proportions in the lesbian community: the infamous "merging." It means you get too close, too wrapped up in each other. She fights with her mother, and you get a headache. You feel you must do everything together, enjoy all the same things, dislike all the same things, or else the relationship is doomed. You monitor each other's comings and goings excessively, listen for the slightest nuance in everything the other person says, take each other's emotional temperature too often. It gets claustrophobic, but the first time anyone mentions the need for a little space, there's apt to be a scene that starts out, "Are we growing apart?" and ends up with someone sleeping on the couch, in the basement, or in the doghouse.

There are of course other obstacles unique to the lesbian couple, but since the down side is treated in some detail, I'd like to focus on the pluses of the long-term lesbian relationship. I'm only going to speak for myself here, but I have conferred with a number of friends in long-term relationships and find that they pretty much agree with my list.

Here are some of the joys of my relationship with Barrie:

1. A shared understanding of what intimacy means and an agreement about its importance in life. Barrie is a surgical nurse in a large medical center. Her work is demanding, important, and rewarding. So is mine. But there is no question in my mind or hers that our relationship comes first. And it comes first day-by-day, not just in times of crisis. Because of the trust I have in Barrie, because we have progressed to a place of genuine acceptance of each other (an acceptance which is far beyond mere lip service to the ideal) and because I know my discoveries about myself are almost as important to her as they are to me, I feel safe even when vulnerable.

Perhaps many straight women have such relationships with their husbands. All I know is that many married women seem to long for this kind of intimacy and turn to other women in platonic but intense friendships in order to find it.

2. Compatible ideas of the importance of affectionate touch. "Dear Abby" asked her women readers if they would give up sex in exchange for more cuddling, holding, and caressing. By a huge majority, the answer was Yes! The good news is that I can have both. Barrie and I, like a great many women, seem to have "skin hunger." Touching is important to us. From dreamy half-touches

in the middle of the night, to morning hugs and off-to-work kisses, from head-in-the-lap viewing of TV to foot massages and back-rubs, from giving each other shampoos to sharing a long slow bath or a quick, soapy shower, from semi-dangerous games of Distract-the-Driver while we're barreling down Highway 1 to spontaneous love-making in a thick grove of trees in the middle of a backpacking trip—we touch often.

In a lesbian relationship there is usually a pretty clear distinction between what is affectionate touch and what is sex, though naturally one often leads to the other and one includes the other. But many straight women tell me that with their partner's affection is generally an all-too-brief prelude to sex and rarely is offered independently by itself with no intention of sex. To keep the ledger balanced, I need to point out that lesbians (like heterosexual women) have plenty of problems about sex per se. Interest, preferences, frequency, style—all these have to be worked out. Studies confirm that lesbians in a long-term relationship have sex somewhat less frequently than heterosexual couples. But ah, those long evenings in front of the fire!

3. The concept of active listening as a major skill. Maybe this should be included under intimacy, but I think it's important enough to rate a category by itself. Barrie and I are both pretty heavy-duty talkers. My roots are southern with a long line of storytellers predominant. Barrie is both Italian and Jewish. Talking comes naturally; listening is an acquired skill, but we do listen to each other with, I think, a great deal of sensitivity. We listen to what's said and what's not said. And we listen to body language. I can sit in the passenger seat while Barrie's driving and tell from the merest flicker on the right side of her profile whether she wants to say something but needs prodding or whether she needs silence. Barrie can tell from my voice on the phone whether a quick, just-seeing-how-your-day-is-going call is enough or whether I need her to give me something more substantial even though I can't say what that might be.

Yes, sometimes this gets a little claustrophobic, and then we have to arrange for some space, some distance, one way or the other. I talked earlier about merging and its dangers. Research studies indicate that lesbians do a better job than straight folk at creating the close relationship but a worse job of establishing space between partners. When Barrie and I were first together (like for the first five years), I got upset if she went into her bedroom and shut the door. She got upset if I had plans for the evening that didn't include her. I used her towel, hairbrush, pillow, clothes, and car as if they were mine. She felt wounded if she learned anything about me—how a sales promotion went, that I'd had lunch with my sister, and so on— from someone else before I told her. ("I'm always the last to know!") We both automatically asked, "Who was that?" after any phone conversation the other had without even waiting for the information to be offered. It was all pretty smothering.

We've worked at that over the years. We grew to understand that things went better if we didn't try to live our lives in lockstep, but each went out and lived her own life, and then returned in the evening to share her different experiences and different perceptions. Now we purposely plan lunches, evenings at the theater, tennis games, and even weekend jaunts with other friends. For the last several years, Barrie has spent a couple of weeks each summer back east with her old high school cronies, and I've gone on travel expeditions to places that don't interest her. This feels good to us. We feel less merged, more independent, and yet in some way closer than ever. I think we're more interesting to each other. We also have some spelled-out understandings. If a door is shut, respect the other's privacy and give her the time alone. Ask before using someone else's things. Don't assume: don't assume Barrie will automatically meet me for lunch if I find I have a spare hour—ask. Don't assume I'll run an errand—ask, and make sure that "No" is an acceptable answer. Barrie and I both have worked steadily at learning to ask for what we need (instead of relying on the old route-to-hell: "If you loved me, you'd know what I want"). And we keep reminding each other that it's okay to say no. That's a very important kind of space. As to time, we're both over-programmed. We no longer assume that any spare time will be spent together, nor do we assume that our relationship will thrive on whatever scraps of leftover time we can manage. We plan for nice three-day weekends in a pampering bed-and-breakfast by the ocean or a long Sunday at a friend's cabin or just a little ritual such as a walk around the neighborhood before bedtime.

4. Less deliberate game-playing. All of us unwittingly play games based on our earliest childhood dynamics. I speak here of

conscious games learned and perfected during adolescence, games concocted in the male-female matrix. Indeed, for some lesbians their first clue as to their sexual identities came when they discovered how much they hated those games and how reluctant they were to play them. That discovery led to more probing questions. Barrie and I vowed in the earliest days of our relationship that we would work hard at not playing games. To an amazing degree we have succeeded. And as we have learned about sub-conscious games, manipulations arising out of the kinks in our psyches, we have worked hard to keep those from creating havoc as well. (By definition they are harder to eradicate.)

I say that lesbians do less deliberate game-playing because the built-in roles are not there. In male-female relationships we're taught to play Hard to Get, I'm Cool, Make Him Jealous, I'm Helpless, Anything You Say, Dear—the whole list. There are fewer publicly acknowledged games between two women, I think.

On the other hand, sometimes lesbians play the kind of game that involves acting contrary to our inner feelings because we really don't know what those feelings are. Everybody, gay and straight, plays this kind of game, of course, but if you have invested a lot of your life in not showing and even not feeling emotions which society frowns on, you're apt to make a habit of the ploy.

5. A strong sense of being valued for oneself, to grow and develop with less reference to roles and stereotypes. There is no role I am expected to play in this relationship. I do what I'm good at, Barrie does what she's good at. If after a while I grow tired of yard work, I can ask her to take it over, or she will toss me the household checkbook to manage. But the matter goes much deeper than a division of chores. Because there is no mold into which lesbian relationships can pour themselves, each one has to be worked out day by day, year by year. There are very few givens.

There are also more levels to the relationship than is traditional. Barrie and I are in one sense single women, in another sense a couple. We earn our own livings, have separate checkbooks, separate income taxes, separate retirement plans, even at this point lots in separate cemeteries. But we also have a shared household checkbook, we own a home together, we have yours-mine-and-ours Christmas card lists, have to negotiate where we'll spend holidays (your family or mine?). As Barrie's irascible Italian father ages, the possibility grows that he may one day have to live with us. My nephew will probably live with us while attending college. If I end up nursing Barrie's father, it will not be because it is "expected" of me but because I choose to do so, offer to do so. If Barrie helps finance my nephew's education, that too is a choice. Our relationship is filled with decisions (sometimes it seems there are far too many!) but it is also filled with option, with choice, with freedom to say No. Here's another blessing for which I'm grateful: it has never occurred to me to wonder if my greying hair, wrinkling skin, expanding tummy and other signs of wear and tear will lessen my value in Barrie's eyes.

6. Mutual sentimentality about birthdays, anniversaries, Valentine's Day, full moons, "our" songs, and so on. Frequently, before we drop off to sleep, we'll lie abed and sing a few songs together. Affectionate messages in soap appear on the bathroom mirror from time to time. Bouquets of flowers come for no special reason. (Once when Barrie was just developing the habit of this kind of thing, she had a dozen roses delivered to my store. The card read: "Thanks for everything." I was sure it meant she was leaving—"Thanks for everything, and good-bye.")

7. Unequivocal status as a peer. If Barrie and I wander around a car dealership with intent to buy a car, no salesperson automatically talks to her while leaving me to feel the upholstery. The waiter doesn't look to me to do the ordering for both. If Barrie were to change jobs and move to a hospital in another city, she wouldn't assume that I would automatically sell the business and follow her: it would be a matter for negotiation. And beyond how we are treated by others, there's a deeper issue: how we individually feel in the relationship. Let's have some—you'll pardon the expression—straight talk here: Anyone who lives in a given culture picks up the cultural attitudes of that culture, even if those attitudes reflect negatively on the person herself. For example, people of color are subject to racial slurs in our culture, and despite their own sense of pride and the knowledge that the stereotypes are stupid, some of the attitude rubs off on them. Jewish people all carry around a little anti-Semitism. All gays suffer from some homophobia. And all women have to deal with some sexism within themselves. Sad but true. And our culture has taught women that they are the party of the second part. The old saying was, "Man and wife shall be as

one—and that one is the husband." Even in this day traces of those attitudes remain deeply embedded in all of us. For Barrie and me that is one mine field we don't have to maneuver.

I began by talking about my sister Laurie. Sometimes, I wish I could talk with Laurie or other close friends about my domestic life. Sometimes, I'd like to use her as a sounding board or a shoulder to cry on or a resource for advice. And as I said up front, I wish she realized that I could offer her meaningful insights about marriage. But as long as she and other straight men and women view gay and lesbian unions as more different from their own than alike, I won't get my wish.

Despite the silences between Laurie and me on that subject, despite the secrets we still keep in certain quarters, and despite the ongoing societal rejection of our way of life, which continues day by day in a hundred ways large and small, Barrie and I continue. We do more than cope or survive: we thrive. At times, I think that our situation has required us to read more, think more, reflect more, and talk more about primary relationships than is the case in conventional marriages. And sometimes I think we're just plain lucky.

TEN

And Then There Was Light

▼

Jean Burgess

I did not become consciously aware of my homosexuality until I was thirty years old, the mother of four children, and the wife of a bishop. Ironically, as my self-awareness concerning my sexuality increased so did my spiritual awareness. The spiritual struggle resulting from the confrontation with my sexuality was an intense one lasting eighteen months and one that is documented in a journal which I began keeping shortly after the struggle began.

Before this period I had been a dedicated church member doing all that I could to ensure my salvation. I strived diligently to live the teachings of the gospel and to develop a closer relationship with my Heavenly Father and my savior Jesus Christ. My whole life revolved around church activities and all that went with being a member of the Mormon church. I had held numerous callings within the church and at that time was the children's Primary

Jean Burgess resides in Laurel, Maryland, where she is a social worker at the Montgomery County Crisis Center and also has a private practice. She holds a bachelor's degree from Auburn University and a Master of Social Work degree from Norfolk State University.

inservice leader. In addition, I supported my husband and the busy schedule he kept as bishop of our ward.

One evening I carefully outlined some goals that I had hoped to accomplish. In a sense those goals were prayers put to paper, a plea to my Heavenly Father to assist me in achieving an understanding and testimony regarding several aspects of my life, two of which were: (1) my relationship with my husband, specifically our sexual relationship, and (2) the importance of prayer and daily scripture reading.

At the time I did not realize that the initial answers would come to me in the form of a person, a former Relief Society president. She was introduced to me as someone who was struggling with her testimony, and it was suggested that I could somehow shepherd her back to the church. At our first meeting I felt a concern for Betti and sensed for some reason that both Satan and God were struggling for her in a real way. Upon returning from this luncheon, I commented to my husband that I felt certain that this sister's struggle was with homosexuality. Within several weeks I embarked on a struggle of my own which was intense enough to cause me eight consecutive sleepless days and nights as I began confronting feelings hidden for many long years.

The following is from the journal I began keeping several months after meeting Betti in the fall of 1983:

(14 March 1984) That was the beginning of an extremely intense relationship for me. Within 3-4 days I felt a sexual attraction towards her that I had felt towards no one. We could hardly avoid touching one another. At the same time it was a very spiritual relationship. . . . it seemed to me with each meeting (which was practically every single day for three to four weeks) new spiritual insights were given to me to share with her. It all seemed to be helping. She was drawing closer and closer to the church, but we were also becoming more and more physically involved. . . . We could hardly bear to be apart. Life took on a new meaning for me. I had never felt this way towards another person. I had never felt such a Christ-like love for anyone, meaning that it mattered not to me what she said, did, or felt, I knew I would always love her.

As these feelings surfaced, so much of my life which I had failed to understand took on a new meaning, and prayers that I had barely uttered were beginning to be answered. I realized I was gaining an understanding about myself and my relationship with God that I had been seeking for quite some time. I was also beginning to achieve those goals that I had so carefully outlined in my journal.

During those months of struggling to come to terms with my sexuality, a depression surfaced which I now think I had carried my entire lifetime. I had always had difficulty understanding my relationship with my husband. During the first few months after we were married, I experienced a void in our marriage that I was unable to put into words. I remember one particularly frantic night as I tried to express these feelings to Rick. I wanted to feel close to him, but for some reason I couldn't. At that point I thought somehow he was pushing me away—that he didn't want closeness. I became so frustrated with wanting the closeness but being unable to achieve it that I gave up trying to communicate this to Rick. I pulled my pillow from the bed to sleep on the floor, sobbing until I fell asleep. I was never again as closely in touch with those painful feelings of wanting a sense of intimacy which we seemed so unable to achieve.

The following eight years were spent in going about life as Mormon families live it. Rick and I had four beautiful girls, and I became fully engrossed in mothering them. Only occasionally did I allow the painful unanswered questions about our marriage to surface. Sex in no way appealed to me and became increasingly unenjoyable—so much so that I came to dread it. I had a difficult time feeling emotionally or physically close to Rick. Therefore, I could not bear for him to hug or kiss me. I constantly tried to change in this area, to make a real effort to feel closer to him. I even went as far as to commit in my mind to sex twice a week. If I didn't set some sort of schedule for myself, I knew I would end up avoiding it altogether.

Nothing seemed to work, and my aversion to sex with Rick was intensifying. As the long repressed homosexual feelings began to surface after meeting Betti, they seemed to offer some answers to my questions about the difficulties Rick and I had.

Following my meeting Betti, and after a couple of months of

seeing a male Latter-day Saint therapist, I realized it was time to involve Rick in all that was going on in my life. Telling him of the awakened awareness of my sexuality proved to be a good experience for both of us. My respect for him increased because of the mature way he handled the information. He was actually relieved, since it explained so much of what had gone on in our relationship and answered questions he also had been asking himself. Even though we were approaching a closeness we had not experienced in the past, I knew it was not an intimacy which would allow me to be close to him as my husband. There was simply too much unresolved within me.

Also during this period, Betti and I began making decisions about the relationship which had been developing between us. We both valued the church and knew we were playing with fire. We made the decision to end our physical relationship, which had progressed to kissing. We began seeing less and less of one another as I focused my energies on reconciling my newly acquired sexual awareness with my religious beliefs.

Five months after I met Betti, Rick and I moved. He was in the Navy and had received orders to the Norfolk area. In Virginia Beach I began the complicated task of locating a new therapist, someone who could assist me in the task of unraveling the confused feelings I felt would prevent Rick and me from continuing along the path towards celestial exaltation. With the help of our bishop and a Navy chaplain, I located another therapist, a woman.

During that time Rick would fluctuate between being very supportive of me as I dealt with many disturbing and painful feelings and having difficulty dealing with his own anger and pain at realizing he was married to a homosexual. I was also dealing with ambivalent feelings of my own.

(16 May 1984) I'm feeling at quite a loss as to where to turn. Maybe it's just impatience and a lack of humility that keeps me from approaching him [the bishop]. It would be different if an actual transgression was involved, but so far we're just dealing in feelings here. Sometimes when I think through all of this I wish I had never told anyone, just moved away and stuffed it all back in. All I know is that I

only want to be what the Lord wants me to be, but I am not sure how to come to know what that is.

Through the years as I had grown spiritually in the church, I had come to rely more and more on prayer. I was familiar with the feelings of assurance and peace which come when prayers are answered. I had most often relied on prayer in connection with church callings and had never had occasion to "pour out my heart" to God and, in fact, had difficulty relating to what that actually meant.

Now as I progressed in my struggle regarding my sexuality I relied heavily on scripture reading and prayer. I frequently "poured out my heart" as I searched for solutions to problems I never anticipated. Previously I had sought fast and easy solutions, so this proved a laborious process for me. There simply wasn't a quick answer this time.

(20 June 1984) I feel so much confusion right now and a lot of sadness. I have seen my new therapist (Rita) three times now, and I feel she is going to be really helpful to me—she has been able to do more than the others because she is willing to talk about my homosexual feelings—the others would not—they invariably changed the subject. Most importantly, she is skilled enough to help me to deal with it all on a much more emotional level. . . .

I talked to the Bishop last Sunday and told him in ways I was afraid my testimony was weakening. I feel as if I am being asked to live a lie by denying these feelings. Living with Rick in this relationship all seems like a lie to me. . . . I keep telling the Lord that this is very hard for me—the temptation to know and understand myself fully by acting on these feelings almost seems too strong. I've asked Him to protect me from this if all that I have believed in the past is true. Sometimes I just don't know how long I can hold up under this conflict.

As I progressed in therapy, no one was more disturbed than I to discover the direction in which my thoughts and feelings were taking me.

(31 July 1984) . . . I am feeling better emotionally than I have in a long time. I seem to be arriving at some sort of decision about all of this, and that is more or less to decide not to decide (I think I've been here before but each time it seems more correct). That is, I know I can't just leave the marriage and go live "the gay life" though that's what these very strong feelings I am experiencing could easily lead me to do. I can't because of my children, and I am just beginning to learn how to really love them. I cannot abandon my obligations or feelings in this area.

Also, I am not ready to deny the truthfulness of the gospel, though I am certainly questioning it as I never have before. . . . this is scary. . . . I'm not sure where these feelings are going to take me. Will I come to the conclusion that the church is not true and that in order to remain true to myself I'll have to "come out" as a lesbian, or am I going to become more and more sure that the church is true and exist in this life lonely? Or still a third alternative . . . will I find that I am able to love men and develop the kind of relationship with Rick that I have been promised by the Lord is possible?

Trying as these times seemed to be for me, they were not without hope. It was the search for truth that kept me going.

(5 August 1984). . . there does seem to be hope, a distinct feeling of being able to wait for some answers. I have felt a strong desire for even more earnest prayer and to go spend some time in the temple. Hopefully, I can make a trip up in the next couple of weeks and spend a few hours there. I've been told I can expect the answers that I need, and I do know from past experiences that the Lord hears and answers prayers—perhaps I just need to pray more fervently on this one.

During the summer and fall Rick had been away on a four-month deployment with the Navy, and I had become accustomed to his absence, which gave me time to think:

(18 October 1984) I'm having a lot of feelings about Rick's return as it gets nearer and nearer the time. None of them are good. I'm angry that he's coming back to complicate things for me. I'm angry that he's even a part of my life, and I'm angry at myself for ever making him a part of my life. I feel bad for him, too. It must be hard for him to come home knowing that he's coming home to a wife who does not love him as a husband. As hard as it is for me, I truly wish I felt the excitement that the other wives are experiencing. I'm also angry that my insides are so confused that I can't even consider that kind of a fulfilling relationship with anyone.

(31 October 1984) I feel so sad, so tired of all this, and I wonder if there ever will be a solution and a possibility of future happiness. There just seems no way out. It's scary when you find yourself feeling that dying seems the only good alternative. It's hard to imagine putting my children through all the pain of divorce, yet it's also hard to imagine enduring the pain and sadness of this unfulfilling relationship. . . . I know I've got to sort all of this out before I can make any decisions, but I wonder if I'll ever have that much strength.

Once Rick was home I continued to seek answers through therapy, fasting, and prayer, but I was becoming increasingly concerned about the conclusions to which I was coming.

(3 March 1985) I saw Dr. Taylor (from LDS Social Services) on Thursday because I have been so concerned about losing my testimony of the church and thought that maybe I should stop seeing Rita awhile and see him instead. He seemed to think that everything was going fine with Rita and that I should continue on as I am.

After talking with Dr. Taylor and meeting with the president of my new stake for the first time, I felt strongly impressed to go off completely alone to read the Book of Mormon from cover to cover and to think and pray. Rick and I talked it over, and he completely supported my decision to spend a weekend alone at the

beach to accomplish this. Several weeks later I recorded the following about that weekend:

> (21 April 1985) I wasn't sure what would be the result
> but felt that it would prove helpful in facing some of the
> decisions that are mine. It did. I read the Book of Mormon
> from start to finish in just under two days. I left the room
> once to go running along the beach and once to eat. It was
> a difficult thing to do, but I learned a lot from it and had
> some very meaningful prayers, the most meaningful of
> which was the prayer I said before I ever got started
> reading. I poured my heart out to my Heavenly Father. I
> expressed a great sadness to him for all of the pain that I
> have caused others (most particularly Rick) by not being
> true to my own feelings, even though I was not aware of it
> at the time.
>
> I also told him my feelings about my sexuality and
> about the church; that right now I am feeling very homo-
> sexual and that it is hard for me to conceive of being any
> other way. I told him that I felt that in order to maintain
> my integrity of self that I would need to accept and be at
> peace with my homosexuality. . . . I went on to pray to him
> that if his will for me included me not expressing my
> homosexual feelings and changing my sexual orientation,
> I was willing to do that as well. I completely trusted him to
> give me the answers that I was seeking. . . .

The answers that seemed to come to me that weekend were
not the ones I was expecting. They came as strong impressions
throughout the weekend as I was reading the Book of Mormon. As
my spiritual retreat was concluded, I came away knowing the
answers to the questions I had been asking for eighteen long
months. I left the beach that weekend with a completely different
understanding of the scriptures and knew that the church would
never again meet my needs in the way it had in the past. I also knew
that my Heavenly Father loved me as I was and not only wanted
me to accept my sexuality as part of his creation but to rejoice in
it as well. Before leaving I went down to the beach and composed
a letter to Betti. Even though I had seen her just briefly on a few

occasions during the past year, I remained deeply in love with her.

Within a week I received a reply from her clearly indicating she was not yet ready to consider a relationship together. So I went about doing what I needed to do as a result of that weekend spent at the beach. Three months after receiving the answers to my prayers and after careful consideration, I requested that my name be removed from church records. There were no other grounds for excommunication; however, for integrity's sake I felt I had to formalize my separation from the church before acting on my sexuality. The following July Rick and I were separated and then several months later divorced.

Four years later I find myself adjusting to more changes than I could have imagined. Rick and I now share joint custody of the children, and they spend equal time with the two of us. Rick has since remarried and lives in Florida. This past year I relocated to the Washington, D.C., area and live with Betti, who has gone through changes of her own. There are times when I experience pain and sadness as a result of the decision I made to leave the church and my marriage. I am also painfully aware that many of my choices have caused sadness in the lives of others as well. But because I arrived at my decision through what I believe was a spiritual process, I have never had the need to question the "rightness" of the choices I have made concerning my sexuality.

ELEVEN

After Marriage–What?

(an excerpt)

▼

Gordon Miller

I was born into the Mormon church. I was well indoctrinated in its teachings by both my parents and the church and have always been a dutiful and obedient member. Very early in my church life, I was given a great deal of responsibility and was made to feel the pressure of fulfilling a mission and marrying and having a family, both of which I did. In spite of the fact that I loved children, always had good rapport with them, and always wanted to have children of my own, I put off marriage as long as I could because I knew I was homosexual, felt no sexual attraction toward women, and feared the prospect of a heterosexual relationship. Finally at a late age, I married, hoping that might be the step which would "cure" me of my homosexuality. From what I have observed, I was eminently successful in hiding my sexual feelings from everyone, including my wife.

During the course of twelve years of marriage, my wife and I

Gordon Miller contributed this essay to *After Marriage–What?*, a collection of essays published by Affirmation (n.p.), 1980. Mr. Miller lived in Los Angeles until his death from AIDS in August 1986.

parented four beautiful children. Our marriage went well except in our sexual relations. This was the only matter concerning which we ever argued and had hard feelings. From the outset my wife realized that there was something different about me, but she never suspected that it had anything to do with homosexuality. In spite of a relationship which was relatively smooth functioning, there were a great number of things that bothered me and continuously preyed upon my thinking, things that constantly reminded me that basically I was sexually out of context. Some of them raised guilt feelings in relation to my marriage and were never to be resolved. I was never moved to initiate sexual relations with my wife. She was always dominant in that area, and if she didn't make an issue of it, there were no relations. As time went on sexual relations became much more infrequent, and the last two years of our marriage were void of any sexual relations. This was because I had become very adept at avoiding relations, not because my wife did not desire or press for them. I found from the outset of marriage that I had difficulty spending time alone with my wife. The children provided a great escape in this area of our relations. I could be out of town and not miss my wife but always missed the children immensely.

I found myself in the situation of constantly having to feign the small but necessary verbal and physical demonstrations of affection which are really vital to a loving relationship. I would more often than not be remiss in that department, and only at the behest of my wife would I revive my feigning hypocrisy. I always wished that I could really demonstrate spontaneously all of the things my wife needed and often asked for, but I couldn't, and it was very painful. Every time we were with another couple or I saw another couple who were spontaneous in their verbal and physical public demonstrations of affection, I felt a great deal of pain. It constantly reminded me of those things I did not feel for a woman and that I was denying my wife—things she wanted, needed, and deserved. My wife's family and other "outsiders" were somewhat aware of this void in our relationship, and I frequently had to endure little verbal barbs from others in this regard. But the best of intentions failed to produce genuine spontaneity, and I always felt guilty and hurt because of it.

Lest I be misunderstood, I would like to make it quite explicit that I loved and still love my ex-wife. However, it was and is an incomplete love for a married heterosexual couple. I loved my wife as best I could, but that was not enough, and to impose such a mold upon a homosexual is unnatural and emotionally suffocating. In the midst of all of this I was also attempting to be a good father—which I was. That was one area in which I excelled and which I enjoyed. I am not ashamed to say that I doubt anyone could be a better father to my children than I. In addition, I was trying to maintain a heavy activity in the church, which had always been a large part of my life. But being active in church also raised many guilt complexes within me, and the maintenance of that activity level sometimes required me to represent myself to others as someone I really was not.

I often pondered my marital relationship. I always ended up at the same point: I could not believe that I would be able to maintain my marriage throughout my whole life. That hurt. Yet I couldn't talk to anyone about it, and I was petrified at the thought of divorce and the loss of the close day-to-day association with my children. As things eventually developed, I fell in love with another man and carried on a clandestine love affair for some time. It was both wonderful and terribly painful. It was wonderful because for the first time in my life, I experienced the full and spontaneous expression of love. But it also showed me more graphically than ever before just how much I was denying my wife by trying to maintain a heterosexual marriage.

The future haunted me in advance: I knew that if I was able to maintain my marriage until my children were grown and out on their own, I would be unable to sustain a one-to-one solitary relationship with my wife and make it a happy experience for either of us.

In the midst of all of this, I broke down one morning, and with intermittent verbal accounting predominated by almost hysterical sobs, I began to tell my wife everything. This explanation went on at various appropriate times for several weeks. My wife was hero-ically gentle, gallant, and understanding and showed a great deal of concern and compassion for my condition. And although in retrospect I realize that she did not really understand everything I told her at that time, she was nevertheless more than completely forthcoming in attempting to understand and make things as easy as possible. We met with two psychiatrists, and she conferred with her family and the stake president. A divorce was chosen as the most proper resolution. I really did not want a divorce, and had it not been for the strength of my wife, the process would have been much more protracted.

I was relieved. A whole new peace which I had never before experienced enveloped me. I felt good, because for the first time in my life I had confronted my true identity and was open and honest with people. As much as many things hurt and in spite of a great deal of pain still to come, I felt really good—completely whole.

My wife at first believed that I could be helped and changed, and she was willing to go through anything to effect that change. But following our professional consultations, she realized that it would be best to let go. That period in our marriage—the end—was probably the closest we had ever been, because it was at that point that both of us were literally fighting to sustain ourselves and each other. It was a wonderfully moving and loving experience. The whole process was a relief for both of us. For the first time in our marriage, my wife understood just exactly what was different about me: that certain something which set me apart but which she had not been able to identify. Suddenly the many things which earlier had been inexplicable to her began to fall into place, and she understood why certain things had happened the way they had. At last a great burden had been lifted from her. She knew that she was all right. She knew that she was normal and that there was nothing about her that made her unattractive to men. This fear had constantly haunted her throughout our marriage. Now that she has remarried, she will be able to experience the full range of sexual expression open to the heterosexual couple.

My wife and I separated, the process of divorce began, and the children were told what was taking place. During the separation and after the divorce, I spent my spare time every day with the children. Now that she has remarried and lives approximately one hundred miles away, I don't see them that often, about every two weeks, but I am in constant telephone contact with them. We remain very close to each other emotionally.

The pain of separation from the children was and continues to be immense for me. Part of that pain is associated with the fact that now another man, not their real father, has the privilege of that close relationship with my children which I so much desire. While the sharp edge of the pain has since subsided, I doubt that it will ever disappear. It recurs with unpredictable frequency. Yet I am convinced that what happened was best for me and my wife at this time. I have a great deal of work ahead of me in order to maintain the type of relationship I desire with my children. I think it can be done.

As a final apology I must say that I will be eternally grateful for my wife. I regret having caused her pain and am sure that I will be eternally repentant of that fact. However, I do not regret having been married and having had four children with my wife. I do regret that I did not have the courage to be honest earlier in my life. I have always loved the church and the gospel of Jesus Christ, and I continue to do so today. However, I am convinced, based upon my own experience, that the church is ignorant of homosexuality and wrong in its treatment of the homosexual. I fervently hope and pray that this state of affairs may rapidly change. I have the assurance that God loves and understands me and accepts me as I am. I also know that my being homosexual was not a conscious behavioral choice on my part, but that I was created that way. I do not understand why.

TWELVE

One View of a
Troubled Relationship

▼

Karen Brown

I first heard of Carol Lynn Pearson's book after a relief society lesson I had given. I had used a poem of hers, and after the meeting a sister rushed up to ask me if I had read Pearson's new love poems. She explained that they had been written after her husband had died—after he had left her for the homosexual lifestyle and then returned to be cared for until he died of AIDS. "Now that's love," she said. "Real love." I am sure my astonished but polite "Ohs" were very inadequate and unappreciative. But what else could I have said—I who had had such a different response to a similar problem.

I met Gordon in my last year of college. He not only enchanted me but my friends and family as well. He was the "catch" of our singles ward. Our marriage a year-and-a-half later delighted all who knew us. We seemed the ideal couple.

"One View of a Troubled Relationship," by Karen Brown, originally appeared in *Exponent II,* Winter 1987. Ms. Brown lives in Vista, California. A native of southern California, she earned a B.A. in elementary education from the University of California at Los Angeles and currently teaches fourth grade.

Gordon had had only a few obligatory dates and no girl friends before we met, while I had had many boy friends, enough to be aware that Gordon's undue shyness and reserve were rare among young men. But I felt this was due to the newness of the romantic experience for him. Loving him as I did, I felt that hugging and physical affection would come naturally with time.

In many ways we had an excellent marriage, and he was a good father to his four sons as they came along. Hindsight, though, provides me with a better perspective. Looking back I can sense an ever-present restlessness in him; perhaps even a subconscious searching that was there even from the beginning of our marriage. Gordon never fulfilled the great potential he had. His spiritual experiences while serving on a German mission and in his home stake's presidency promised future spiritual growth and devotion. Yet he gradually moved further and further away from the church. On a full graduate fellowship to UCLA, he let his studies slide and eventually failed to attain or even attempt to attain the goals he had previously set. He began taking classes first to fill the unexpired time left on his fellowship and later towards one elusive goal after another.

I found our social life following a similar pattern. He would aggressively pursue a friendship with another couple or single male friend on an intense level for a period of time and then drop the relationship and move on to another. I found it difficult and even impossible to maintain the friendships we had formed as a couple. Formerly close friends and eventually even family members were no longer of interest to him.

About the time I became pregnant with our fourth son, Gordon's restlessness seemed to increase. He began spending every night away from home, telling me that he was practicing the organ at church, working late, or studying late. I worried and fretted while he was gone but immediately accepted his excuses when he returned. He formed new friends exclusive to him, and he took more classes that led nowhere. On the rare evening when he was home, he would fall asleep on the couch in front of the TV. Even holidays and vacations were divided between family and his new friends or work.

Our relationship began to deteriorate. I had always been able to rationalize the lack of physical affection in our marriage and balance it with the many good things. Few marriages were perfect, and Gordon had far more to offer me than anyone else I had known. When we argued about his unresponsiveness, he closed up and refused to share his real feelings. I would come away from the discussions with no more understanding of what was wrong but with more determination to be sweeter, more cheerful and supportive, and less demanding. I felt that the burden of making the marriage work was all mine. I hoped and prayed constantly that Gordon would love me as much as I loved him.

Finally the strain and hurt became too great. I had reached a point where I had to have better answers. The week before our thirteenth anniversary Gordon shared his problems and feelings with me for the very first time. His story was similar to so many I have read about recently. From early teenage years he had been attracted only to men. Childhood sexual experiences with an older boy had only intensified that feeling. But devoted to the church, he was determined to live an honorable life. During his mission interview with a stake president, he attempted for the first and only time to reveal his torment but was met only with an embarrassed rebuff.

He told me he had spent hours, even days, praying and fasting for help. But no relief had come, and then he had met me. He too wanted children, a family of his own, and he felt that perhaps this at long last could be the answer. But it was not. Pretense and repression of his real self continued until it became too much for him. While still married he began to investigate the homosexual community. He read its literature, had many liaisons, and finally formed an attachment that he hoped to make permanent. He told me that he finally knew what real love was for the very first time, and he did not ever want to go back to a heterosexual lifestyle.

During the ensuing discussions we had, I felt the anguish Gordon had suffered, the humiliation, abandonment, misunderstanding, and rejection he had experienced. While listening to him, I became completely convinced of his sincerity and truthfulness. God indeed had placed a burden on him too great even for Gordon to bear. But away from him, I began to re-evaluate and question. I knew I needed help and wanted it from a Mormon who would understand us both. I knew that eventually I would be all right. But I had four sons, and I had a great concern for them and for Gordon.

Gordon agreed to go with me once to see a prominent Mormon psychologist. Because the doctor could not name a homosexual who had been cured of the problem, Gordon refused to make a second appointment or to try anymore to change. After that he would go only to his own therapist—one who would help him accept his new lifestyle. But the Mormon doctor helped me. Though I saw him only twice, he helped me understand and cope with my nightmare. He explained that many of his patients had acute handicaps not of their own choosing or doing and yet were successfully and happily managing their lives in spite of their drastically limited potential. That option was still open to Gordon. After our session the doctor also gave me a priesthood blessing assuring me that the children and I would be fine.

The next few months were a testimony to me of the love the gospel helps us to share. As people in my ward gradually found out that something was wrong with this "ideal family," they responded with totally non-judgmental love and concern for the boys and me. No one was ever assigned or asked to help, but the calls, letters, cookies, dinners, garden produce, and bouquets arrived—usually just as I needed them. I shall never forget those true offerings of the heart.

Our bishop had recently handled a couple of excommunications in a rather sensational manner. Wishing to protect my children as much as possible, I went instead to our stake president. Again the guidance I needed was right there, and the anger I felt against God for letting this terrible thing happen was somewhat abated. Our stake president had a Down's Syndrome child, and while he could not understand how God could have done this to an innocent child, he knew that God had helped him and his family deal with the situation and grow from the experience.

Gordon was convinced that he could not change or live as a heterosexual. He now surrounded himself with gay friends, who of course supported and encouraged his new lifestyle and had only horror stories of those who had tried to be straight again.

For a while I maintained the structure of the marriage to allow Gordon the time to adjust to his chosen lifestyle. He had given up everything—his family, friends, and church—and the adjustment was agonizing. To ease his panic he became involved in the gay

Mormon support group, Affirmation. This group did provide him with desperately needed friends and a validation of self-worth, but it also gradually immersed him in the gay lifestyle and philosophy. His personality, appearance, and values began to change as he became more and more involved. He manned booths during Gay Pride weeks, held support meetings in his home, counseled other Mormon homosexuals, and wrote and telephoned church officials concerning the rightful place of the homosexual in the church.

When his attachment to his new friend ended somewhat bitterly, he began a search for a new friend. Eventually he found a young architect, who moved in with him permanently. Our marriage, of course, was over. I could not, as he once suggested, take a lover and still maintain our home, nor could I continue to pretend we had a marriage. I talked to the children and notified family members of our problem. The divorce which followed was painful. While I tried hard to be fair and nonjudgmental, disagreements and misunderstanding arose. We disagreed about the distribution of our belongings, the handling and rearing of our children, and our responsibilities and commitments to them.

I later remarried and moved one hundred miles away. The developing friction between us intensified as my new husband and I struggled to form a new family. The children kept in close contact with their father on the telephone and through occasional visits.

Early in 1985, we began to notice the frequency of Gordon's illnesses. Minor colds and irritations refused to go away. He lost weight and energy. By the summer of 1985, the diagnosis of AIDS was confirmed. He continued to work as much as possible, but it became increasingly difficult for him. His friend stayed on to nurse him. My husband Verl and I saw to it that the three older boys were with him as much as possible. They spent holidays and every weekend from then on at his house. They willingly gave up activities and parties. The oldest even flew home from college some weekends to care for him, care for the household and business errands, and to cheer him. Indeed the children were his main delight.

We did not expect Gordon to live through first Thanksgiving, then Christmas, and the winter. I notified his family and close friends and asked them to visit. Almost all responded willingly. Gordon continued to hang on. We were encouraged and even began to hope. The two oldest boys looked for jobs in the Los

Angeles area to spend their summer with him. By now he needed someone with him continually, and his friend needed a respite. Our oldest son Jeff lived with him all summer. His hours outside of work were spent nursing Gordon, working on the business and the household. Twice Jeff drove him to the emergency hospital when he had a seizure. Finally in August Gordon had another seizure and died virtually in Jeff's arms.

We had been expecting Gordon's death for almost a year, and yet when Jeff called that Sunday morning, it was a shock. It hurt—far more than I had guessed it would. We had shared thirteen years together, many of them rich and good. No matter what breach had developed, no matter what hurt Gordon may have caused, he had suffered and paid dearly for his choice. No one deserves to die like that—so young.

Gordon's friends wanted a memorial service at the house. They asked my family, many of whom had not spoken to Gordon since the divorce, to come. My uncle was asked to speak. Before the divorce he had been very close to Gordon and had gone out to visit him one Christmas when Gordon came to pick up the boys. This small kindness had been remembered and appreciated. Gordon's friends conducted a very Mormon service. Hymns were sung, prayers offered, and happier times remembered. Bitter feelings began to dissipate, and wounds began to heal.

It would be very easy for me to say that I would never have done what Gordon did. But I suppose that I really cannot know exactly how I would react. I hope I would make different choices. I would hope that I would seek counseling and help and seek it at the first sign of a problem—not after I had gone too far to want to change.

It is equally easy for the homosexual community to say that someone else cannot know what it is really like, that there is nothing anyone can do to change their sexual orientation, and that fighting their orientation and attempting to live a heterosexual lifestyle is doomed to eventual failure. Truly believing this is self-serving in that it justifies their presence in the gay community.

Deceit is never right or justified, particularly when the victims are innocent family members. I have too strong a Mormon background to feel that it is ever right to break a commitment. When we freely commit ourselves to a marriage and to parenthood, regardless of our naivete at the time, we undertake an obligation to those involved with us.

This is where, I suppose, I differ with Carol Lynn Pearson. It cannot ever be right to go blithefully on our own, searching for some elusive other self, some other lifestyle or fulfillment, at the expense of a family to whom we had committed our love and very life. I do not feel we should support one's efforts to do so nor to condone it. And I think that we should never allow our children to think that we believe it to be all right to break that commitment regardless of our love and concern for the suffering and unhappiness of a spouse.

While my experience can never be termed a good thing, I have learned from it. Now that I have remarried, I have experienced the joy of having someone love and treasure me, someone who willingly gives of himself to my growth and happiness and who is willing to share his strengths, his weaknesses, his beliefs, and his whole life with me.

THIRTEEN

A Wife's Story

▼

"Lynn Conley"

I am twenty-eight years old and my real name is not Lynn Conley. I use a fictitious name because my ex-husband is gay. Jim (also fictitious) and I were married a little over three years, and we have a two-year-old son. We filed for divorce in 1988, and our divorce was finalized in January 1989. I don't blame Jim for what happened in my life. I went through a stage where I wanted to blame anyone and everyone, but not any more.

I was born into an active Mormon family and lived a typical Mormon life, including going to Brigham Young University, completing a degree in nursing, and then serving a full-time mission. I continued to follow this path by marrying in the temple a fine young man with many talents and spiritual qualities. We had a wonderful marriage. It wasn't perfect, but we are now fond of saying that we had a better marriage in three years than many couples have in a lifetime. Jim has always been a good person. He fulfilled a productive mission for the church and was an assistant to the mission president. He has served well in many responsible positions in the church, and at the time of our marriage Jim was a member of the bishopric. I realize these are only titles, but I knew the man behind them and he truly strived to be a man of God.

Jim first expressed his true feelings to me when our son was two weeks old. Even though he didn't completely understand his desires, he believed that the church held the solutions to help him. To this point he had been true to his marriage and had never been sexually involved with another man. He knew he had some homosexual feelings growing up, but he had comforted himself by concluding that others must have similar feelings and that an active sexual relationship with a woman would decrease his homosexual urges. With time, righteous living, and a temple marriage, he was led to believe that these feelings would pass. They did not. Instead they intensified, though he tried valiantly to conquer them.

Homosexuality. The word had hardly entered my sheltered life previously and now it consumed my life. I searched my mind desperately for information connected with this word. Something about evil people and strange men waiting in the dark to abduct children. It made no sense and it was all too much for me to face, so we put it aside, almost pretending these feelings didn't exist. But they did. Jim continued to be faithful, but he grew very restless and extremely depressed.

Life was a nightmare of confusion and pain. Finally we got to the point where we had to have some answers. Jim was always afraid to ask because his greatest fear was that there would be negative answers. Many months and thousands of dollars later, his greatest fear was confirmed. For us this was a time of urgent hope, severe disappointment, and bitter despair. Counselors both in and out of the church basically told us there was nothing that could be done to change Jim's sexual orientation. And yet we continued together, because we both desperately wanted to stay married and continue our family. As bitter as it all has been, at least we can look back without regret and with the assurance that we tried everything we could.

During this time of searching, we had decided not to tell anyone. It was a very long and painful year of silence. How I withstood it, I will never know. Jim knew I needed to talk to someone. After hearing Carol Lynn Pearson speak at a conference, he knew she could be trusted. She would be understanding and empathetic. I longed to talk to someone, especially someone who knew what I was going through. I had felt that I was the only one in the universe who had gone through this. And now maybe there was one other. It took me three months to get up the courage to write her. Thank God for Carol Lynn! In two days there was a letter in my mailbox from her. I drove to the hills. I remember sitting there looking at it and shaking. Finally I opened it and read. She didn't say anything earth-shattering. She didn't even have the answers to my questions, but I will never forget the feeling I had. It was like the weight of the world had been lifted off my shoulders. Someone else had gone through what I was going through and survived it. Maybe, just maybe, I could too.

I love the church, but in all honesty it was not there for Jim and me in this time of crisis. We finally spoke to our bishop, who couldn't have been more supportive. I have since learned that we were very fortunate to have a bishop so understanding and open-minded. God was also there for me as he always is for his children. I had many more questions than he felt should be answered. But he gave me what I needed to make it through. Early on God let me know this was something I was supposed to be going through, which brought some comfort. He also let me know that he loves homosexuals and that he expected me to love them also.

Love them? I didn't even know who they were. At first I hated them. They were the enemy. Whoever they were, it was their fault that my life was falling apart. And yet I felt a desire to know them and understand them. I started by joining an AIDS Task Force, which has become one of the most rewarding experiences of my life. I also meet with other gay people both in and out of the church. I was afraid at first. What would they do to me? Would they accept me? What would we say? It now seems silly asking these questions because I now have many gay friends. Although homosexuals are as varied as heterosexuals, I find that generally they are a very kind, loving, and caring group of human beings. I am grateful for the blessings that this trial has brought me, one of which is my new-found homosexual friends who enrich my life.

I have found another purpose for this unusual journey of mine. I felt guided to start a support group. When I had looked for some help, anything, there was none to be found. I felt strongly about providing support for other women, if they existed, who might also be making this same journey. This was a challenge for me, because I had never attended a support group of any kind. How could I then start one of my own. My biggest obstacle was finding the women. We are a very closeted group. When a husband comes out of the closet, often his wife goes in. I didn't know where to locate wives, but I knew where some of the husbands were. So I made flyers and posted them in the gay bars. I also gave information to gay groups and publications and provided community organizations with similar information.

I wasn't sure what to expect, but slowly I started getting calls. My life will never be the same. I wish that I could express to you the hurt and pain for these women. I am constantly amazed at the stories I hear and the number of women who call. I feel that I have only scratched the surface. Our group meets twice a month and we have phone lists that can be used by both those who attend and those who cannot. Some women drive over seventy miles and rarely miss a meeting. I've had calls from throughout the United States. I have spoken to husbands who are married to lesbian women.

I would like to mention one other thing, the issue of openness and honesty. For me this was one of the hardest things I had to deal with. I have the philosophy that no matter what comes along, if you face it honestly, it can be dealt with. Fictitious names and secret lives go against my way of thinking. Yet did I have a choice due to the misunderstanding and prejudice of the church and society? I have slowly been able to open up to family and friends as I have gotten over my own paranoia and become more confident in myself. Then and only then did the healing begin. I hope soon to stand open to the church and society as an ex-wife of a gay man. I am not alone in these feelings. Others from my group have expressed the desire for "no more lies" and "no more hiding." Much has been said and written about the homosexual, and this is good. But what about the spouses of homosexuals? Why haven't their issues been addressed? I hope we can all work together for a better understanding of each other no matter what our situation is, so we can live honestly and love unconditionally as Christ taught us.

FOURTEEN

A Letter to a Church Authority

▼

"Jim Conley"

This letter accompanies my wife's request for a cancellation of our temple sealing following our divorce over a year ago. I support her in this action and want you to understand my position in our divorce. I also want you to understand that our situation as a couple is far from unique and plead with you most earnestly to help people like me.

I am homosexual.

Lynn and I met at BYU. We were both returned missionaries, very active in the church, and completely committed to gospel ideals. Our strong testimonies and the value we placed on spiritual things were factors in attracting us to each other. The church was simply the most important thing in our lives. Both of us came from active families and had tried in every way to live in harmony with the church's teachings. Our life goals were to live pure lives, serve others, and remain close to our Father in Heaven. Both of us were morally clean. Part of what we offered each other in our love was a virtuous life and commitment to be faithful to each other. I want to stress that both Lynn and I had kept this commitment.

Before marrying I did not fully understand myself. I knew that since childhood I had a curiosity about men that I could never quite define. During adolescence this curiosity deepened. It made me uncomfortable, but I decided that I must be jealous—wishing I could be as handsome or personable or athletically successful as the men I admired. I worked very hard at suppressing these feelings and by the time I was called on my mission had succeeded in forcing them out of my consciousness.

I did not know any homosexuals. I had never been sexually molested in any way. In short, there were simply no external influences which could have "suggested" any sexual orientation other than the normal heterosexual relationships that I saw between my parents and between the other couples in my ward.

Lynn and I began our temple marriage with high hopes and deep commitment. There was a great deal of tenderness and affection in our relationship. Our adjustment from virginity to marital sex was, I believe, healthy and normal. When she became pregnant soon after marriage, we anticipated the birth of our child with a great deal of joy.

Greatly to my surprise, however, I found myself attracted even more strongly to men once I had become sexually active with my wife, and these urges continued to grow until I could no longer pretend that my feelings for men were "admiration" or "jealousy."

These feelings were both horrifying and terrifying to me. I felt that they were a temptation from the devil and diligently did everything in my power to root them up. I also had unwavering faith at that period that with the help of my Heavenly Father, I could do so. I continued to fast, pray, and attend the temple. We both had challenging church callings, and I threw myself into church service, filling my life with activities I believed to be righteous and good. I systematically ignored and repressed my feelings as much as possible. But I was experiencing uncontrollable obsessions about men that I would struggle against in vain. I simply could not distract myself or control my thoughts. However, in spite of involuntary reactions, I want to stress that I never voluntarily sought out physical closeness to another man, let alone a sexual partner. I did not "indulge" myself in fantasies but struggled against them. I did not yield to these temptations or foster this appetite. When a particular episode was over, I was racked with depression and guilt so extreme that I became suicidal.

This cycle repeated itself relentlessly for the next two years. Two weeks after our beautiful son was born, I told Lynn of my struggles. It was very painful for her, but she rose above her own confusion and agony to help me. I never stopped struggling, but I was so emotionally lacerated by this experience that I deeply wanted to die. I thought about it so often. I had felt that repressing my homosexual feelings was becoming increasingly impossible and that suicide would be less of a sin than acting out these feelings.

Finally, during our second year of marriage, we realized that prayer, service, and faith were not sufficient to resolve this problem. I knew that I had to have help or my suicide was only a matter of time. As I had done during my entire life, I turned first to the church. It took a great deal of courage to make an appointment with an LDS Social Services counselor, but it was a great relief to explain my situation and I felt a great deal of hope. I was under the impression that the church had effective means of "curing" homosexuality, and I was desperately anxious to change. I was willing to do literally anything to become heterosexual. Surely, I thought, with my motivation and some help, I can resolve this problem.

For the next few months, I went from counselor to counselor within the LDS system, always with Lynn's total support. My love for Lynn and my commitment to our marriage had never faltered. Her support for me in spite of the devastating blow never wavered. We were determined to overcome this problem together. We were willing to fly anywhere, see anyone, move anywhere, and give up everything we owned to overcome this problem. Ultimately we budgeted up to $100,000 for treatments and counseling fees. But to no avail. Despite the hopefulness with which I approached each counselor and despite my diligent efforts to do whatever he suggested, I suffered disappointment after disappointment. The Social Service system finally declared that it had no effective treatment for me and many other homosexuals. I felt that the unresolved feelings inside me were quite literally driving me insane.

Next I began to believe that it was my calling to discover the "cure" so I could help others with this challenge. I had my own business and arranged to begin a full-time study of homosexuality. At this point Lynn and I had been married two years and our son was one year old. I began working on a master's degree in psychology and began searching outside the church for any system which had had success in treating homosexuals. During this time I also attended a two-day conference of the Association of Mormon Counselors and Psychotherapists (AMCAP) dealing with the theme of homosexuality. Although this organization was not sponsored by the church, it included as members many counselors with LDS backgrounds, and I hoped that I could hear about therapies or treatments which would encourage me in my quest for change. The meeting was sobering, even shocking. Few were talking about change. They discussed instead ways of helping homosexuals adjust to their condition and deal responsibly with it. When they talked about change, it was the attitude of the church and society at large toward homosexuality that they hoped would change.

Again discouraged, I branched out into an extensive reading program, surveying material that had been published anywhere in the world about the causes and treatments of homosexuality. I learned a great deal, but nothing that gave me much hope for change. After researching theories of development, theories and practices of change, and interviewing gay men, particularly those who claimed that they had successfully adapted themselves to heterosexuality, I concluded that a few homosexuals can change, for example if they are bisexual and have sexual feelings about both men and women. Through therapy and continued internal monitoring, they can train themselves to enhance the feelings they have about women and downplay those they have about men, essentially tilting their orientation toward heterosexuality.

Estimates indicate that 10 percent of the human race is homosexual. I believe that most of these individuals did not choose or desire this sexual preference. Many among them, like me, fought bitterly against such feelings. Many continue to fight. Some have come to terms with their homosexuality and found ways to adapt to it.

I have a difficult time with those who argue that homosexuals "choose" their lifestyle. Who would actually choose a lifestyle in our culture that has a high risk of job discrimination, prejudice, verbal abuse, violent physical attacks, and serious disease? When homosexuals are committed Mormons, they must also deal with additional depression, lack of self-esteem, feelings of unworthiness, and temptations to commit suicide.

I feel that I have achieved some measure of resolution about my homosexuality. I could not have been more motivated to change. I could not have tried harder to change. I say this with no sense of boasting or self-justification but simply because it is true. My sense of peace has come about not because I am "cured" of my homosexuality but because I have finally been able to accept that there is no cure. I accept that my homosexuality was not something I chose or created because I was evil. All my life I had been treating the symptoms of homosexuality and consequently struggling with depression, guilt, and anxiety. Facing the real cause of these feelings directly and understanding myself finally brought more clarity and peace to my life.

Lynn and I had decided that we would divorce if I could not change my feelings. Even though we loved each other very much, were totally committed to providing a high-quality family life for our son, and wanted to stay together, we felt that we could not have a true marriage that would allow both of us to reach our full potential. She has my support in establishing a new relationship with someone who can bring her happiness in this life and for eternity.

I too have needs to be fulfilled. Homosexuality is not about sexual fulfillment but rather about emotional fulfillment. Homosexuality is an internal drive for intimate companionship and bonding with one of one's own sex. Many homosexuals, confused by a lack of self-esteem and by social labeling as "perverts," "queers," and "degenerates," have fallen into the trap of sexual promiscuity, trying desperately to meet an inner need by changing partners continuously. Such promiscuity is as much a symptom of personal inadequacy and immaturity as promiscuity among heterosexuals.

Although this sad and despairing situation receives most of the press coverage and has become society's general image of homosexuality, it is far from universally true. In many communities throughout the world homosexual couples have established satisfying and emotionally mature long-term relationships. These couples have chosen to avoid publicity and cherish the privacy of their homes.

Perhaps because I am a Latter-day Saint, I have encountered a high percentage of homosexuals with Mormon backgrounds. And a high percentage of these are among the most promiscuous and psychologically disabled. Long periods of repression and self-misunderstanding seem to lead to greater explosiveness in terms of long-range consequences. Often suicide seems like a good option to these individuals. Frequently these suicides are denied or concealed, even by family members of the victims. "He seemed to have everything going for him," they say. "Why did he do it?" I believe it is safe to say that homosexual guilt and frustration lie at the root of many of these suicides. Yet these individuals did not create their condition.

I could easily have been one of these fatalities. Each time I considered it, however, someone or something intervened at the right moment to save me. During the last three years in particular, the support of a loving wife and my love for my little son have been strong deterrents. Since I have accepted my homosexuality, I still feel depression, but the suicidal tendencies have receded.

The church and its goals were the most important things in my life. I have served as a youth leader, a missionary, instructor at the Missionary Training Center, scoutmaster, young men's president, counselor in the elders quorum presidency, counselor to the bishop, among other callings. Believe me, if I could have changed, I would have. As someone who loved the church but has literally chosen between life and death, I beg you to consider these points:

1. Most homosexuality is biologically determined. It cannot be "unchosen" once it occurs.

2. Please allow homosexuals the choice to remain in the church on the same basis as heterosexual members, through sexual restraint rather than denial and change. I do not ask you to approve of gay sexual relations, but it is clear that those who understand their homosexual orientation early on in an acccepting environment have fewer difficulties adjusting, are less promiscuous, and have a better chance of achieving a healthy self-image and a positive lifestyle.

3. If and until a proven method of change becomes available, the burden of guilt could be lifted from those whose thoughts and feelings are homosexual. If the church recognized that homosexuals did not cause their condition and are not responsible for its continued existence, their self-esteem could be built and they could focus their energies on sexual self-restraint and acceptance

of themselves as gay individuals.

4. If members of the church were educated about what we currently know and do not know about homosexuality, this would alleviate much of the suffering experienced by parents, wives, children, friends, and the homosexual individual him- or herself. Such education may help to reduce the frequency of suicide among despairing gays.

Perhaps I have not communicated accurately and completely the depth of my pain. Accepting my homosexuality has meant giving up or altering every goal, hope, expectation, and dream that have been dearest in my life. I feel rejected by the church because of its position that I am somehow to blame for a characteristic I have no more control over than I have for the color of my eyes.

Truth is one of the cornerstones of the church. The church should not avoid truth or make it difficult to find. I pray that you will be part of the effort to promote honesty and truth about homosexuality. I pray that you will help bring about a greater understanding of this difficult subject so that families can come back together, individuals may begin healing, and we may all share a brighter future of love and understanding.

Voices of
Family Members
and Friends

FIFTEEN

Homosexuality, Mormon Doctrine, and Christianity: A Father's Perspective

▼

Wayne Schow

Mine is a Latter-day Saint family whose church roots go back for generations. I served a mission to Denmark, Sandra and I were married in the Logan temple, and we have raised four sons in the church, participating in its programs and trying diligently to create a vision and an example of the Christian life. Our boys were obedient and faithful to church standards as they grew up; they were good students, good citizens. As young men three of them carried the gospel message into the mission field. As a family we have enjoyed the good opinion of our LDS brothers and sisters in the wards and stakes in which we have resided. I mention these facts because they will help the reader evaluate the perspective from which I write.

Ten years ago, when he was twenty, our eldest son Brad came to his mother and me and told us he was homosexual. We were caught by surprise, for neither his appearance nor behavior would

---

"Homosexuality, Mormon Doctrine, and Christianity: A Father's Perspective," by Wayne Schow, originally appeared in slightly condensed form in *Sunstone,* February 1990.

have suggested this sexual orientation: he was a muscular, sturdy youth, not effeminate, and his social life had seemed normal enough. His friends included boys and girls equally, he spent many hours in mixed company, and he dated girls after he reached sixteen, though not frequently. The only unusual trait we had noted was his being somewhat more intellectual and more interested in serious music, art, and literature than the majority of his high school friends. There was, however, one sign that something was wrong (easier to recognize after the fact): he had been subject to periods of depression, which concerned us somewhat at the time but which we attributed to the general difficulties of adolescence.

We responded to his declaration with incredulity and predictable dismay (I had always had visceral negative feelings about homosexual people). Surely he was mistaken: since he had had no actual homosexual encounters, he couldn't be sure. We counseled him not to act on his "supposed" feelings, to date young women seriously, to wait and see. Possibly, we conceded, he could be bisexual and might still opt for a wife, a family, and a life acceptable to church and society, a life less problematic and more fulfilling. Homosexuality, we contended, is sterile; it does not contribute to perpetuating life. "Choose otherwise," we urged him.

This was, you see, the most compelling reason to deny his assertion: in my mind and in the doctrinal view of my church, homosexuality is an acquired behavior, a perverse—or at best, mistaken—choice of lifestyle. Our decent, loving son had not been reared for such a course.

Nevertheless he was convinced that the orientation of his sexual feelings was not voluntary, and he produced a folder full of articles whose authors, some of them homosexual themselves, some of them Latter-day Saints, concurred with him. (Clearly he had been doing a lot of reading. We devoured the articles, the first of many books and articles we would sift through in the following years, trying to make sense of the chaos of theories about sexual orientation.) Theories aside, we had to confront the reality of Brad's unequivocal sexual feelings for males, feelings he said he had known since his early years in grade school and which had become clearer in adolescence.

In retrospect we realize that Brad's periods of depression reflected the identity crisis he was experiencing. He told us that he prayed fervently over a long period that God would help him to reorient his feelings, and in return he promised God extraordinary devotion. (His personal journals from this period reveal a religious youth who had concluded from all the implicit messages of home, church, and society that he was flawed and sinful—cursed as it seemed to him—in spite of his wish to be otherwise.) Our immediate sorrow was all the greater because we realized how deeply he had suffered alone, while we unaware had done nothing to help him.

Following Brad's declaration we understood why he had finally decided not to fill a church mission. Though he had not at nineteen engaged in homosexual relations and was presumably worthy to serve, he could not square his troubled self-image with his understanding of what a missionary should be. He knew he could only represent the church by denying the legitimacy of his inner self, which seemed to him to be unfair both to the church, because it was hypocritical, and to himself, because it violated his very identity. There had been much personal integrity evidenced in that decision.

Meanwhile Sandra and I wrestled with demons of our own. What had we done wrong? Had she been domineering or overly protective? No. Had I been a wimpy father? No. Had I overpowered him, had I been distant, absent, had he and I failed to relate well to each other? No, no, no. Had he been Oedipally attracted to his mother? No. None of the facile theories about parental influence on the development of homosexual behavior made much sense in our case. Did real love exist in our family? Yes. Had we shared much quality time together? Yes. Had his parents' marriage been a good one? Better than average. Ultimately we came to the conclusion that Brad's homosexuality was not a result of failed parenting or inadequate family relationships.

After finishing his sophomore year at college, he returned from Salt Lake City and discussed his situation with us. He had during that semester made contact with the gay "underground," and he was planning to move with a close friend to Los Angeles. Moreover he had virtually dropped out of the church. Since gay people could not easily live openly in Idaho and Utah, he had to go where there were enough others of his kind that he could feel his essential identity was acceptable.

These decisions were deeply upsetting to his mother and me.

We feared the dangers of that city. We knew that the ballast he needed for stability was now lessened considerably. But from my present vantage point I see it was a risk he had to take; for the sake of his own self-esteem he had to discover and test the truth of his unique identity. He had emerged from his teen years with his self-worth severely undermined. Our culture had encouraged him to hate himself, and the church's attitude toward homosexuality had contributed substantially to that despair.

When Brad left for California, we were extraordinarily concerned about what we could do to help him. Clearly he had to establish his independence, and we had to allow him to determine his own course. We tried not to be intrusive while keeping our lines of communication open. We did not want to jeopardize the good relationship we had always had with him.

In Los Angeles Brad was thrown on his own resources, earning a living, making his own decisions, acquiring street-smarts, learning to negotiate traffic in the fast lane. Inevitably the values of his Idaho upbringing clashed with the aesthetic hedonism of West Holly-wood. He wanted to have the best of both lives, but he could not reconcile them. To us he praised his brave new world, yet it seemed he protested too much. His relationship with a lover came to an end. After two years he began to sense the desperation that lay beneath the surface of the frenzied life he was participating in. After the third year he saw clearly how self-destructive many of his gay friends were. Theirs was the behavior of people who do not accept themselves because society does not, who have little joy and hope in contemplating the future.

It was not easy to leave an accepting community, but Brad knew he needed to orient himself in a more positive direction. He felt a need to escape the isolation of the gay ghetto and renew contact with the mainstream. And he realized he must pursue an education for a meaningful career. But where to go? A return to Idaho and Utah would renew his earlier experience of cultural alienation and revive the tension between himself and the Latter-day Saints. On the other hand, he felt that his deeply loved mountain environment and nearness to his family might steady him. His decision to enroll at a university in Utah was a calculated risk: would he be saved by the moral influence of his cultural roots, or would he suffocate in a closed environment?

Brad returned and for two years pursued this experiment in personal growth and professional education. On the positive side, he left behind the promiscuity that had become part of his life in Los Angeles, and he was advancing toward a career. On the other hand, he felt terribly isolated in that Utah community, angry at smugly religious people surrounding him, concerned lest his homosexual identity be discovered by his acquaintances, fearful of the toll that would be exacted from him if it was.

At this stage Brad contemplated the future with great ambivalence. There were so many things in life that he loved—the beauty of the natural world, the monuments of human achievement in art and culture. But the family and children he had always wanted were inaccessible, for he now felt he could never in good conscience ask a woman to marry him. With reduced possibilities before him, he sometimes wondered if clinging to life was really worth the effort. Nevertheless, he was coping.

What happened next seems a cruel irony. When he came home in the summer of 1985 to help build our new family home, he was clearly not well. Apparently incubating in his blood since his time in Los Angeles, the AIDS virus had now begun its deadly work. As it turned out, his homecoming would last for the remainder of his life. His condition grew steadily worse over the summer and fall; in November he nearly died from pneumocystis pneumonia. A brief period of remission, during which he gamely attempted to continue studying part-time at our local university, was followed by inexorable decline. He died on 5 December 1986.

AIDS is a devastating antagonist. It dismantles a person ounce by ounce, nerve by nerve. Brad fought this horrible disease courageously with the independent, self-reliant spirit he always had, and he never attempted to evade responsibility for what was happening to him. At the same time he tried so hard to find some deeper religious significance in his physical and spiritual suffering (and so did we). To the very end of his life he struggled to find a faith that could comfort him. Indeed, he had been engaged in a spiritual odyssey for years. After he concluded that he was unacceptable to the LDS church—and therefore rejected fellowship in it—he looked at oriental religions, born-again Christianity, and pantheism. But he could not accept easy explanations that were incompatible with reality as he perceived it. We will never forget our conversations with him during that last year, by day, by night, conversations in which we shared our convictions and our uncertainties.

The final year of Brad's life was the most difficult our family has known, a year of perplexity, a year of grieving. Paradoxically it was also the most profoundly meaningful year of our lives. Sharing his ordeal enlarged our awareness of the human condition. We learned so much from the way he faced the difficult circumstances of his illness and his life. We are grateful to him; we are proud of him. He was such a fine young man. At this point we can say that we feel blessed to have had a son who was homosexual.

I have lingered over these narrative details partly because they are engraved so indelibly in my mind but also to make a point: the meaning and morality of homosexuality cannot be assessed in the abstract. It involves more than theology. It requires that we confront real people, their uniqueness, their fundamental integrity, their hopes and dreams; it requires that in the process we accept, not distort, their personal reality. For those of us grown used to viewing life from a fixed philosophical perspective, encountering homosexuality jars us out of our complacence because we find to our consternation that the conventional explanations don't adequately account for what is really happening to people.

I suppose many of our LDS friends, in extending their sympathies, have grieved for us, thinking we have lost a son for eternity; they see Brad as having been disobedient to the law and thereby cut off from any celestial reward. But to us who knew Brad well, who knew the intensity of his quest and the honesty of his response, such a conclusion is unthinkable. We find his life to have been lived well; it was a life of great value for us and others. We conclude that, as it was, it must have value also in God's eyes and that the possibility for a renewal of progress now lies open before him.

The unavoidable challenge that we faced during the past ten years has been to try to understand our son (and others like him) and evaluate his life experience fairly—all in the context of our religious philosophy. This has been difficult indeed, for our acceptance of LDS moral authority on the one hand and our loyalty to our son and respect for his integrity on the other seemed irreconcilable.

As we understood it, the LDS church's position in regard to homosexuality was (and is) as follows: (1) The practice of homosexuality is unnatural because it is biologically unfruitful; (2) only within heterosexual marriage may sexual desires be expressed with full intimacy; (3) homosexual inclination must be suppressed, either through celibacy or through reorientation of sexual feelings within heterosexual marriage; (4) suppression or reorientation is possible because homosexual inclination and practice are learned behaviors and lie within the control of personal choice; (5) indulgence in homosexual acts is a grave sin, punishable by excommunication. Confronted with these teachings, how were we to account for what had happened to Brad—and to us—when it seemed he had pursued his life with such honesty and courage? We gradually realized we would have to be open to the lessons of experience and would have to sort out a great many intricacies in light of the central tenets of Christianity as we understood them.

The crux of any humane assessment of homosexuality is the question of whether homosexual orientation is learned behavior and therefore alterable or whether it is deeply, indelibly imprinted in the physiological inheritance of the individual. We began with the assumption that it lies within the realm of free choice, that to choose it is at best unwise, at worst sinful. But gradually our view changed. For eight years we studied the scholarly literature on the subject. We learned to know more homosexual people than previously we knew existed, and we listened carefully to their personal accounts, trying to evaluate the complexities of their experience as objectively as possible. Above all, we watched our son to learn what we could of the sources of his feelings. From these observations we are persuaded that for many, probably the majority of gay people, it is not a choice—a conclusion consistent with recent scientific work which suggests that homosexual inclination is a matter of biochemistry and therefore originates outside the arena of moral choice.

And there are further, pragmatic arguments that homosexuality is not freely determined. Because our culture and our church are so predominantly opposed to homosexuality, who would voluntarily choose such a painful situation? Moreover, for persons like our son and many others of LDS upbringing, the desire to be comfortably affiliated with the church, to be approved according to its teachings, is so strong that it would prevail over homosexual identity if choice of orientation were really possible. Having come to know numerous homosexuals who agonize in their desire to be other than what they are, we can no longer believe that for them it is simply a matter of misdirected agency.

Once we accept the likelihood that homosexuality is an involuntary, biochemically-imprinted dimension of personal identity, suddenly the ontological implications of the condition shift dramatically, and we must see it in a different moral perspective. Suddenly we must acknowledge that to be homosexual is not ipso facto to be unnatural but rather part of a natural minority—with some distinctly separate possibilities and challenges. Not to allow that difference may be to violate unrighteously the given framework within which members of this natural minority must, for the time being, work out their salvation and progression. If homosexuality is not learned behavior, we must give up attempting to "cure" the "illness" and instead concentrate on helping the gay person express his or her natural sexuality in positive ways.

There remains, of course, the point of view that whether chosen or not, this condition—most certainly its expression—is necessarily condemned by most religions. According to this view, the biblical denunciations of homosexuality are undeniable, and it must therefore be sinful. I see two issues to be dealt with here: (1) what kind of moral authority is represented by those scriptural passages and pronouncements based on them? and (2) what precisely in the essence of homosexuality would make it sinful?

The Christian scriptures record the spiritual history of important groups within the human family. They demonstrate clearly a gradual growth in spiritual stature among the "chosen peoples" as higher principles have been revealed and understood. In the Bible we encounter numerous examples of attitudes (and commandments associated with them) that have been altered as humankind has progressed on its quest for higher truth. The Mosaic law became outmoded in many respects; cruel punishments and retributions deemed appropriate in Old Testament times are no longer seen as compatible with Christian love. Gradually it became clear that Jehovah was more than a tribal god and that the gospel was essential for all humankind, not just the Hebrews. Paul's disparaging attitude toward marriage has been revised; women are moving to a position of equality unthought of even by Paul. Blacks enjoy equal status formerly denied them. Continuing revelation and spiritual evolution have accomplished these changes.

Might not homosexuality be an analogous case, an issue which because of its complexity is as yet inadequately understood? Isn't it possible that biblical passages related to homosexuality are rooted in cultural biases rather than eternal truth, that they derive from homophobia based on ignorance and fear of nonconformity, which in turn produce intolerance? I don't believe that biblical cultures were—nor are we today—exempt from this kind of injustice. Clearly, the continual perfection of God's revelation is accessible only as we develop the capacity to receive it perfectly. In the church we learn line upon line, precept upon precept. Even prophets, whom we regard as neither infallible nor omniscient, feel the influence of cultural contexts. The Mormon church does not lose credibility by acknowledging that we are even now in the process of seeking a more nearly perfect perception of the meanings and applications of divine love.

It follows that to condemn homosexuality as sinful simply on the basis of appeal to biblical authority is insufficient. We must undertake a more painstaking moral assessment based on its effects. The highest criteria against which Latter-day Saint Christians should measure behavior (including homosexual behavior) were given us by Jesus Christ. He taught us to evaluate attitudes and actions not by their conformity to the letter of a generalized law but rather according to their compatibility with the spirit of love and the degree to which they promote self-development. In this light, sin is behavior that weakens our capacity for love, impedes our growth toward divine characteristics, and undermines our worth and dignity as offspring of God.

Homosexual expression should be evaluated according to this Christian teaching. I believe Jesus would not condemn gay people abstractly for a condition that, through no fault of their own, places them outside the majority and its establishment standards. Rather I believe he would recognize that they too have been given God's gift of sexuality for their potential benefit. To that end he would judge the expression of homosexuality by standards similar to those we apply to heterosexuals: is it committed and loving in a larger context rather than promiscuous, selfish, and merely sensual? "By their fruits ye shall know them," he taught, and the fruits of the homosexual life vary considerably, even as do the fruits of heterosexuality. Perhaps the appropriate question is not whether but how one is homosexual.

Would Jesus find homosexuality sinful because it is biologically infertile? I think not. Conceiving, bearing, and rearing children in this life may be a blessing, but it is not a *sine qua non* for salvation and continuing growth. Many married people do not produce offspring, and we do not regard this as evidence of moral failure. If homosexuals are biochemically unsuited for the psychological demands of heterosexual cohabitation, that is sufficient reason not to marry.

Would Jesus find homosexual expression sinful on grounds that sexual intimacy outside marriage is forbidden? I doubt he would look at the matter that simplistically. The God-man who said that "the Sabbath is made for man, not man for the Sabbath" would probably say something similar about marriage. He would recognize that for most of us, whatever our sexual orientation, a fulfilled life is more likely if an individual is sustained by the love of another person within the bonds of caring, committed intimacy—including certainly physical intimacy. He would recognize that marriage, through sharing and commitment, provides stability and mutual support conducive to maximum growth of the partners. For what sanctifies marriage is not its legal formality but rather the holy enterprise of bonding and complementing which is intrinsic to it.

I believe that Jesus would recognize that homosexuals, deprived of socially approved cohabitation, have nevertheless the same righteous needs for loving commitment. Would he deny them opportunities for growth that are compatible with their nature and with righteous love? That means, of course, that gays should enter into monogamous, faithful relationships analogous to our ideal of heterosexual marriage. Ultimately Jesus would, I believe, judge each human relationship on its own merits.

It is a painful irony that Jesus' church, which ought to assist all individuals in realizing their maximum development, offers little positive support for gays. Instead of helping heal those troubled in spirit, the church is itself one powerful cause of the condition that requires a physician. It ought to foster an environment in which unique personal growth can occur. But for homosexual people, the church has become—through its repressive condemnation—a stumbling block on the path to self-acceptance. Without self-acceptance, there can be no self-love, and without a true love of self as God's creature, there can be no true love of God and thus no fruitful progression toward divine perfection.

Consider the psychological burden borne by Mormon homosexuals in particular. From their youth the seeds of low self-esteem are planted. From both adults and peers they hear the deprecating epithets, the scornful aspersions, the biased misinformation about gays which cause them to feel contemptible. They struggle to understand their difference in an environment which demands conformity. They hide their feelings from the world, even from loved ones, and hate themselves for this deception. They discover that there are laws against homosexual intimacy. They read books confirming their fear that they are flawed or mentally ill. And when they desperately need to turn to the church for comfort and assurance, it proclaims its condemnation by counseling them to deny their own nature. Ironically, the more orthodox the individual, the more he believes he is wicked and the more he suffers from this institutional repudiation of his identity. His "tainted" sexuality seems to him the central fact of his existence and colors all facets of his life. How compatible is such a mental state with the self-love essential for spiritual progress?

If my critical assessment is correct, the church not only fails to comfort many of its own members who need a radically different kind of assistance, it also fails to promote tolerant understanding in the greater society. Think how many are adversely affected in that greater society—perhaps as many as 10 percent of the human family, certainly no fewer than 5 percent by the most conservative estimates. Within the church alone, there could be as many as three-quarters of a million homosexual persons struggling to overcome self-hatred and accept themselves against the grain of the church's moral authority. This estimate does not even take into account the many family members of gays whose self-esteem and peace of mind are sorely troubled by prevailing attitudes.

As I contemplate Brad's short life, I am haunted by awareness of lost opportunities and by a vision of what might have been. How much happier his teen years could have been, how much more productive his young manhood, had he not been burdened with an enervating ambivalence about the value of his life. I think of how much more his parents and teachers could have supported and assisted him if only their vision of homosexual potential had been freer, more informed, less fearful. I wonder, had he experienced in Idaho and Utah a community that accepted and encouraged a Christian expression of homosexual love, would he have found a loving companion with a shared cultural background and thus avoided the extremes of life in the gay ghetto which finally destroyed his health and took his life? How might the church have helped all of us, his family and friends, to cope with the challenge of difference if it had emphasized more the positive, liberating side of its doctrines instead of the negative, constricting side?

Indeed, I believe Latter-day Saint theology can accommodate the phenomenon of homosexuality in a positive, harmonious way. For example, I see the possibilities of compatibility under the doctrine of eternal progression. We Latter-day Saints believe that our individual development is ongoing, that it will continue over a very long period, much longer certainly than can be contained within a brief mortal lifetime. Could it be that we are not all learning in a lockstep sequence, that God's children may vary in their personal approaches to eternal progression? Some may learn one discipline now, while others may choose to defer the same experiences or learn the same truths by a different set of mortal conditions. Or perhaps not all of us experience this mortal life at the same stage of eternal development. From this perspective isn't it possible that some may have chosen to encounter the challenges of homosexuality in this mortal life, perhaps because its demands are great and its potential rewards valuable or even at some point indispensable? From a premortal perspective homosexuality might actually be based on agency and not mistaken choice at all. There is so much possible under our general philosophy, and yet so much we don't understand that I think we must withhold judgment and remain open-minded.

Undoubtedly Brad grew from his suffering, and we that knew him have similarly benefited from the challenging circumstances of his life. I suppose we all can profit from adversity if determined to do so. But that fact should not be interpreted as a justification for our causing pain to others, failing to ease their burdens when we can, failing to lift up and encourage and speed them along the path of their learning. It is perverse to cause suffering needlessly.

When I multiply Brad's experience, and ours, many times over and think of all those who need consolation, love, a chance to

overcome alienation, a chance to talk openly without being condemned—needs that exist in so many among us—I sincerely hope
the future will not continue to find Latter-day Saints and their
church deficient in openness and charity toward this significant
minority. Having placed so much emphasis on the moral aspects
of the behavior of homosexuals, we must not forget to address the
equally important moral obligations incumbent on the rest of us
in responding to them. If we do not discriminate sensitively and
fairly, if we yield to the ease of blanket condemnation, we undermine their chance to respond morally in their circumstances.
Certainly, it seems to me, if we err as a church on this particular
issue, it would be better to err on the side of love, acceptance, and
positive encouragement to those of our brothers and sisters whose
identities and experiences fall outside the typical pattern.

I trust it is clear that I am neither scientifically expert on the
causes of homosexuality nor able to speak with confident certainty
about God's will. I only know that elements in my life that matter
greatly to me—my son, my responsibility as a parent, my commitment to my church, my faith in the moral vision of Christianity—
have been thrust into confrontation in a way that challenges my
deeply-held convictions about life and its meaning. Ultimately, it
seems to me, one's belief and the lessons of one's experience
cannot exist in separate compartments. One must find a means to
bring the two into a compatible, complementary relationship—or
face absurdity. What I have written here, unorthodox as it may
seem, is an unavoidable attempt at such a reconciliation.

SIXTEEN

Finding People Who Care:
A Mother's Experience

▼

Gerry Johnston

"I thought about you when I saw the mother in the television movie 'An Early Frost.' You are so much like her—you know how to take care of your kids, how to take care of yourself, how to give and receive love. And like her, you have a son who is gay."

With these words, on page three of an eleven-page letter, my oldest son acknowledged to me his homosexuality. The reading of those eleven pages brought into my life such emotional upheaval, painful struggle, and eventually such learning and growth, as I could never have imagined.

That Thursday night in December 1985, I wrote in my journal at 1:30 a.m.: "The truth is so painful that I'm hard pressed to even think of words to describe my feelings, never mind write them down. All I'm aware of is numbness . . ." And then I cried the night

---

Gerry Johnston lives in Salt Lake City where she is a personnel director. A native of Canada, she earned a B.A. degree in public relations from Brigham Young University. She is coordinator of People Who Care, a support group for family members and friends of gays and lesbians.

through. Early the next morning I phoned my sister, and within minutes the caring support I needed was there. She spent most of that long day—and many times since—just being there for me.

I had been through many difficult experiences in my life. I had dealt with years of poor health, the death of a baby, the sudden end of a happy marriage, going to university as an older student, with uncertainty and financial instability, and with loneliness. So I knew from experience that I was a survivor. But homosexuality in *my* family? I wasn't sure I could survive that.

My son came to spend Christmas week with me and his two brothers and one sister. It was a long, heavy week, so untypical of the usual laugh-filled times when my four children and I had been together in the past. I wanted to understand him, to make him glad that he had come home, but every time I turned around, there were those tears again.

Since the subject of homosexuality was apparently not going to leave my life, I began the slow search to become informed. The public library was not much help. I talked with professionals, and I read a book with the wonderful title, *Where Does a Mother Go to Resign?*, the personal account of a woman's journey through a similar experience. Through it all I prayed and cried and wished for some other mother, right here in my community, to talk to. Surely in this whole valley I was not the only one. There must be *someone* else going through what I was going through. But I just couldn't find anyone.

In the spring I became aware of a support group for LDS women dealing with depression. I couldn't get there fast enough. I needed desperately to deal with my own deepening sense of depression. I found there a roomful of women struggling with that heavy, heavy burden, and I discovered that I was *not* indeed depressed. I was just sad. I continued to attend and acquired some coping skills that are with me still. It was there that I first met a woman dealing with homosexuality in her family. Over the course of the next three months, I met two other mothers and I began to feel the suffocation lifting.

Always in my mind was the question of how to locate and draw together other people facing the issue of homosexuality in their families, but I could not come up with a workable way to make it happen.

Then Carol Lynn Pearson came to Salt Lake City to speak and to promote her newly-published book, *Goodbye, I Love You*. I thought about other mothers who might hear her, and I sensed that they might want to find me in the same way I wanted to find them. I was already acquainted with Carol Lynn, and we spent a comfortable time in her hotel room talking and looking for solutions.

That afternoon I arranged for a post office box, gave her the number, and Carol Lynn made the initial announcement—several times that day—which resulted in an immediate flow of mail. One of the first letters, which was typical of many to follow, said, "I can't believe there's someone I can talk to after all these years!" The formation of a support group for families of people who are homosexual was begun. We call ourselves "People Who Care."

With the establishment of our support group, my personal growth took off in quantum leaps. As its coordinator I felt a responsibility to locate, study, copy, and share helpful materials. We acquired tapes, articles, personal papers, and eventually a full-blown lending library of publications intended to inform and support people, particularly families, who care about a homosexual person. I read and re-read it all.

My own initial experience with professional counseling left me feeling ambivalent about its usefulness. Not long after I received my son's coming-out letter, I talked at length with the therapist with whom I had successfully worked on my own issues the previous year. Then when my son arrived that Christmas, we visited together with the therapist and one of his colleagues, who claimed to have had some experience in counseling gay people in the San Francisco area. I came with my mind open to learning, but the hour spent in front of the "expert's" chalkboard was uncomfortable and the concepts he presented found no home in me.

My son and I spent the following hour alone with my therapist. It was a painfully disillusioning time. The therapist adopted a pious tone, quoted from the scriptures, talked at length about the use he makes of his personal beliefs in therapy, and was thoughtless and inconsiderate of my son and of me. I was truly sad as I left there. I had been wounded by someone I trusted, and my son had been stabbed.

Some weeks later on the recommendation of my daughter, a

registered nurse, I spent an hour with a counselor affiliated with a local hospital's counseling service. In the three contacts I had with him, I found warm, caring support, an understanding of my confusion and of my son's pain, and a healthy and helpful recognition of homosexuality itself. I felt affirmed and came away with a sense of confidence in my ability to indeed survive, to learn, and to grow.

My bishop gave me quality support and showed that he cared. To quote from my journal, Sunday, 15 December 1985: "Before I left his office, he gave me a warm hug and had tears in his eyes as he told me how he cared that I was feeling sad and lonely and uncertain. It was a Christ-like demonstration of love, and I shall not soon forget it." And my children and their spouses, while coping with my son's homosexuality in their own ways, have continually shown concern and affection, which has helped get me through this. I feel the confidence of my Heavenly Father who knows the end from the beginning and who helped my son grow up to be a good, kind, caring person, a fine man who did everything right that he could think of—and for right reasons.

Our heavenly parents must sigh when they observe the pain we inflict on homosexual people who, through no fault of their own, must pay such a painful life-long price because of society's homophobia. Joseph Smith said, "While one portion of the human race is judging and condemning the other without mercy, the Great Parent of the universe looks upon the whole of the human family with a fatherly care and paternal regard. He is a wise Lawgiver, and will judge all men, not according to the narrow, contracted notions of men, but according to the deeds done in the body, whether they be good or evil."

Church leaders with whom we have talked have expressed much deeper personal concern over homosexuality than has been publicly evident. There have been expressions of confidence that the answer will indeed come, that we will someday know the "why," and God's solution, which in the words of one authority will probably be so simple we'll wonder why we struggled so hard.

I make no pretext at understanding homosexuality. I have come to accept that things don't have to be perfect. I am hopeful that by service in the church I can perhaps contribute to an increase in understanding in the level of caring. I have made the determination that I will stay close to my Heavenly Father, who I know cares deeply about us all and through whom understanding of our sexuality will someday come.

Meanwhile there are a few things I can do. I can keep the love and open communication flowing to my son and to all my family. I can pray for my son and for all of us who care about someone who is homosexual—and especially for those who don't care and ought to. And like the psalmist David, I can "trust in the Lord, and do good. [I can] rest in the Lord and wait patiently for him." That I can and will do.

SEVENTEEN

My Brother is Gay

▼

Eileene Zimmer

Several months after my father's death I was informed by a neighbor of my oldest brother's homosexuality. My brother had apparently confided in him, and he felt that someone in the family should know. He selected me because he felt that my mother would be unable to cope due to the recent death of my father, and he thought that my other brother, who had just returned from a mission, would not handle the information appropriately.

My neighbor and I fumbled at first, feeling that we should involve the church. We told the elders quorum president, who told the bishop, who called my brother in under the pretext of interviewing all former missionaries. My brother later told me that the bishop had mishandled the situation.

This neighbor then proceeded to educate me about the prevalence of homosexuality at Brigham Young University and among missionaries. My brother's partner was also a former missionary. Within a year I developed a friendship with a girl who was in love

---

"My Brother is Gay," by Eileene Zimmer, originally appeared in *Exponent II,* Winter 1987.

in love with a homosexual. She described her situation and that of others she knew of on campus who had fallen in love with homosexuals. Some had decided to risk marriage. I would never have guessed the extent of the practice among active Mormons.

I finally told my mother about seven years later. I don't remember what her reaction was at the time, but she periodically quotes scripture to him and calls him to repentance. She feels that it is her responsibility to do so, so that she will be found blameless and that he will be in the celestial kingdom with us. She says that if I really loved him I would try to get him to repent also.

And I do really love him. He is so easy to love. He is one of the most accepting and caring people that I have in my life. How do I now deal with his homosexuality? I accept it as being a part of him. I do not try to change him. I am appalled at my previous attempts to do so.

I've read a fair amount about homosexuality in magazines and journals, and in Spencer W. Kimball's book, *The Miracle of Forgiveness*. I tried to reconcile the church's stand with what I felt was reality. I came to the personal conclusion that some homosexuals can change with counseling, fasting, and prayer but that others cannot.

I do feel that my brother is missing out on a greater joy that can be achieved through a heterosexual relationship and especially through having children but wish him all the happiness that he can get. He is currently in a relationship with a much younger man. It seems to be a good relationship and has already lasted for several years.

My main problem has been in accepting his partners. I have not known how to relate to them and have felt awkward. I'm working on accepting his current partner as family. It may take a while.

EIGHTEEN

New Friends

▼

Anonymous

The unsigned letter stunned me. It pleaded for help, but how could I offer anything to an unknown writer. He was male; he said he would contact me. I did not trust that he would. He thrust his pain upon me—pulled me into his anguish, expected me to somehow provide relief, to prevent the suicide he threatened. Yet he would not identify himself.

He described an inner turmoil that prevented him from sleep, estranged him from family, denied him appetite. He had lost so much weight he lacked strength to work, but work was his only escape. He stayed late at his office, fought the arrival of solitary weekends. He hated himself. As punishment he refused to eat. He was not worthy to live, he said. He needed to die, wanted to die. He made plans to die—one plan after another.

I tried to set the letter aside, reasoning that most people who commit suicide do it confidentially and those who threaten are mainly calling for help. Since he refused to sign the letter, the

---

"New Friends" originally appeared in *Dialogue: A Journal of Mormon Thought* 19 (Spring 1986).

responsibility would have to remain with him. If he contacted me I would respond, but even then I did not relish the idea of counseling with a homosexual.

Still I was troubled. The fact that he had sought my help seemed a positive sign. Was he a member of my ward—someone I had been called as bishop to lead? Did it really matter whether he lived in the boundaries?

As much as I thought about him, I also feared an encounter. Once years before I had counseled with someone I knew to be gay, face to face. Though I had tried to listen sympathetically, my uneasiness had shown. He had read my feelings and did not return.

After that the issue of homosexuality simply did not present itself to me. Admittedly I do not go in search of the suffering that slumbers below the surface of appearances—my Christianity does not extend that far. But I had learned a good deal in the decade since my last chance to listen. I had read, sought counsel.

He was right to give me a week to think. This time, I resolved, I would try harder. But then what?

I had no formula for recovery except dramatic repentance. I had seen some real miracles: transformations, forgiveness, spiritual awakening. They dealt with other problems, however. My soul was electrified as I watched people discover the simplicity of the Redemption, finding that they could actually change. They uncovered what had seemed trite but was actually hidden from them: that Christ was available to help pay the debt they could not. Homosexuality seemed tougher, more elusive, but I did not doubt that the Redemption embraced it too. The theology of repentance and redemption was valid, but the homosexuals I knew found it difficult to use religion as a catalyst for change, and I did not know anyone whose behavioral modification formulas worked very long. So I began to read again, seek more advice, and pray.

The writer did not contact me again. Two months passed. Some days I shrugged it off. Some days I scanned the obituaries. Then I reread his letter carefully with the hunch that he was waiting for a response. Maybe he wanted a signal that I could listen. I found some clues embedded in the text. Putting them together, I had an idea. Immediately I dialed a number.

After two rings he answered.

His voice was all business as he gave the name of the firm.

"Hello, Clarke, I received your letter."

Silence.

"Clarke, the letter is beautiful. It is honest."

Silence.

"Clarke, I've been waiting for your call. I'm ready. Do you want to see me?"

Silence. Then a whispered, "Yes."

"I will be at my office at ten tonight. Do you know where it is?" (I purposely chose a time when he would be free, when no one would be in the foyer.)

"Yes."

"I'll be waiting. Thank you for writing."

With time to weigh his choices, I wondered if he would come. He did.

Our first meeting was painful. He shivered. My stomach knotted. He spoke with great difficulty, sometimes gasping, heart pounding. I thought he needed immediate admission to the mental ward.

When he mentioned that he had been in therapy for a year, I was both relieved and bothered. At least I could depend on the psychiatrist to watch for anorexia, borderline personality, schizophrenia, but his emotional pain was more intense than I had ever encountered. I told him I would always be available; but I secretly wondered if he needed more help than I was competent to give. I was most disturbed that he had sought a second counseling relationship. Was he going to bounce from ear to ear, seeking sympathy, instead of acting to eliminate the source of misery? I also wondered if the psychiatrist had ordered a thorough physical examination. Was a chemical deficiency triggering this acute depression? Was the psychiatrist exacerbating Clarke's problem?

I listened to his story. It seemed quite conventional: estrangement from his father (though Clarke was still in touch with the family), secrecy to protect parents and grandparents from what he was sure they could not face. A younger brother had fulfilled the athletic and muscular expectations in the family. Clarke had made excuses, manipulated his parents, and connived to avoid the physical work his father demanded of him. The distance between Clark and his father had widened. There had been ugly encounters and long weeks of silence. A male cousin had introduced some sexual fondling at age twelve and again at sixteen, this time more pornographic and overt. The encounters had become more frequent. He had felt terrible guilt but had not discouraged his cousin's continuing invitations. But he also had a healthy and fulfilling high school romance with a neighborhood girlfriend.

Clarke had initiated a talk with his bishop, mentioning the homosexual experiments briefly, embarrassing both of them. He then prepared for a mission and entered the field—to the great relief of all concerned. He hoped for a transformation. His parents, who had imagined all sorts of deviancies but who had felt so guilty they were unable to discuss Clarke's feelings, tried to convince themselves that their worst fears would be quieted. Everyone breathed more easily as weeks stretched into months.

Clarke found missionary work agreeable. Despite constant intimate contact with desirable males, he suppressed his homosexual thoughts. Midway in the mission, Clarke began working more closely with the mission president, whose family became very fond of him. At times Clarke was haunted with the thought, "If they only knew what I am really like." At other times he tilted in the other direction, "That is only part of me. All people have a weak side; but I have a genuine spiritual side, too—and it is winning."

Eventually Clarke built the courage to tell his mission president what his bishop had not really wanted to hear. The president did not act shocked. In fact, he confronted Clarke, extracting an admission that there was more than Clarke had told the bishop. Clarke had no more extended talks with the president, but each day was like a heart-to-heart encounter. Their eyes met. Clarke felt trust and encouragement as the president continued to give him responsibility.

The mission ended on a high note, but the flight home was full of panic. At the airport Clarke could not embrace his father. As time passed he felt increasingly alone. He had no idea what to do next. His mission euphoria lasted about seven months. His high school girlfriend was unhappily married. He could not force himself to date anyone else. He continued to fantasize about males.

Now he was in my office. Four years of increasing involvement in the gay network had brought him here. He knew its seamy side and its tender side. He had tried a committed partnership, endured its catastrophic collapse, and resorted to the desperation of pickup points—well-established spots where gays go to meet others anonymously for a quick, one-time sexual encounter.

I ventured a blunt question, knowing I could offend him, "What pleasure is there in such a risky and fleeting encounter?"

"It is enough," he said, "to hope, even if it is only for five minutes, that someone wants me."

Church meetings exacerbated Clarke's crisis. Just seeing the sacrament emphasized his hypocrisy. He tried to change his values to meet his behavior. That took him out of church activity, away from temple commitments, but gave him no relief. He realized he could not discard the church, did not really want to, but his feelings of unworthiness overpowered him. His psychiatrist told Clarke that he was not really a homosexual—that his gay life was a mere symptom of his self-rejection. He punished himself with homosexual acts because he hated himself, and those acts triggered guilt because he was so intensely religious. The argument impressed me; but it led to no relief, no therapeutic success.

When Clarke left that evening I put my arms on both his shoulders, extending a cautious touch, looking closely in his eyes. I expressed my admiration for the courage it took to come. He warmed also, cautiously. He said his father had never held him so. He was barely able to talk. I worried that he might not be able to negotiate the roads. He insisted he could.

As the days went by, I realized that I did not fear further talks with Clarke. I was not repelled. I was not interested in intimate details. I did not fantasize about homosexuality. I was liberated.

Andy's way of contacting me was the opposite of Clarke's. He saw to it that we interacted often on other matters first. Rather naively I missed the testing that he was putting me through. Then one day he blurted out that he was gay. I knew enough to roll with it. He told me that he had driven past my home night after night, vacillating between stopping or prowling for a contact. He said that one of our other chats had so scared him that he stayed out most of the night trying to calm down. I had been oblivious to it all.

But there it was. It was out.

Andy was so different from Clarke. He did not seem depressed. He was witty, socially skilled, full of humor, at ease everywhere. I suspected that underneath there must be tension that would yet come when he could suppress it no longer, but his easy laughing belied the insecurity that seemed to dominate him behind his well-constructed facade. He wanted to disassociate himself from the gay scene, but he was deep in the net—gay bars, gay gyms, gay porn. He knew dozens of pickup points and many partners. He had completed a successful mission but now lingered about the edge of the church. He kept his secret from his family, safely distant in another state, who saw him as an active Mormon.

Andy decided that excommunication was the route for him. He overcame the fear of censure which causes many people to hesitate when the idea of a church court first arises. He sought forgiveness and felt he could not even start without a court.

He was so different from Clarke. He had had no long sessions of anguish, no intense battle with parents, no expressions about suicide. He withheld his inner self from me, perhaps even from himself. He had many friendships, both heterosexual and homosexual. He dated extensively before his mission and after; but his numerous homosexual encounters before his mission were repeated after, even though he had abstained completely during his mission. When he came home, he immersed himself in the gay world.

I wondered how Andy coped. I did not want to destroy his defense mechanisms and push him into a depression like Clarke's, but I could not penetrate his defenses. Because he was popular in both homosexual and heterosexual settings, he was not sure he wanted to get beyond his present lifestyle.

The court was held with modest success. There were no hard feelings. He spoke openly with the high council and expressed closeness to the stake president. When the president asked Andy if he could predict a break with the gay world, he said he could only hope. He and I felt we were on a common wavelength, at least as friends. Then he failed to come back for the regular counseling sessions the stake president had prescribed. He settled into the reality of living without the priesthood.

I'm fond of Andy. We trust each other. He has brought me reading material on homosexuality. He has advised me in my counseling with others and wants to help people break out of homosexuality. He says he fully intends to marry and raise a family in the gospel.

I am puzzled.

After Andy I began to develop a cautious hypothesis about male homosexuality. It is such a taboo that most of us wish to avoid the subject. We are repulsed. We condemn. But underneath I think we mostly fear homosexuality. We fear that maybe, just maybe, there is some of it in us all. Do we all have some degrees of heterosexuality and some degrees of homosexuality? Perhaps our youthful experiences reinforce one sexual preference over the other. At least when Ned came I found myself able to identify with him past stereotypes or fear. He had had early encounters with homosexuality as childhood experimenting—particularly in Boy Scouts. He certainly was not a confirmed gay before his mission; but he knew the fear of that question, "Am I gay?" He cleared matters with his bishop, then waited for a probation period. Finally he left for the mission field. A few months later he became sexually involved with a companion. Both were sent home for professional help. After a few months Ned returned and completed his mission. His parents were aware of his "problem." They appeared to be accepting, at least they were not driven with fear as they talked about it openly with me. Ned's mother continued to urge him to date. Though he felt that pressure from family and relatives, he could not get interested in a woman.

Ned was completely convinced that homosexuality was wrong. But he did not feel that he could ever be heterosexual. He avoided the gay world, knew nothing of its systems, and did not want to. Yet about once a year he fell into an encounter he did not seek. He immediately came to me. I supported him and kept in contact with our stake president. In the interim Ned carried out church assignments and was the backbone of many activities. He brought order to his vocation. He participated in community activities. He had dozens of friends, and he kept dating casually.

Ned's condition was in some ways similar to Tad's. Tad came to me with his homosexual experience behind him. It was expiated; he had completed the probation of disfellowshipment and was in total control. But now he could not take the next step. He simply could not feel physical affection for a woman. Was he doomed to celibacy? he asked. He desperately wanted a family but felt he could not use a wife to bear children and then have no further sexual interest in her. He recoiled from the suggestion of sharing his concern midway through courtship. He doubted that any woman could want him enough to gamble on such a threatening point. Because he is a wonderfully talented, handsome, and winning person, I hope otherwise. Tad has moved away. I miss his wholesome spirit.

My interaction with Antonio was as frustrating as my contact with Tad was uplifting. He made an appointment to see me on the advice of an anonymous friend. (I wondered just how well known I was among gays.) Antonio came to me angrily. He wanted me to explain why he could not be a Mormon and a gay at the same time.

He had joined the church a year before, after having the missionary lessons. The elders never mentioned homosexuality, so neither did he. His sexual choice became evident shortly after his baptism. I confronted him with the evidence. Antonio did not deny being homosexual. I asked him whether he was prepared to break with his sexual activity. Antonio said he was not, that he did not feel he could or should. He argued that all gay suffering was the fault of a bigoted, rejecting society, that homosexuality was a legitimate choice, that it hurt no one, was for consenting adults, had always been around. It was time the taboo ended. Other churches were coming around. Why not the Mormons? There were thousands of gay Mormons, he argued. Why persecute them? They cannot help being gay; they are made that way.

He and I ended up polarized both in words and feelings. Nothing happened for a few weeks. Then I asked Antonio to come to the office again. I explained to him that homosexual activity was just as serious as fornication and could not be countenanced, that the practice did indeed harm others, was forbidden by God, and was therefore a violation of baptism and sacrament covenants. Antonio would have to make a choice between homosexuality and his membership. I assured him that I would support him if he chose to change his sexual lifestyle and understood that changing could take time. I asked Antonio to think about it and especially to pray about it.

Antonio refused to see me again. I sent him notice to appear before a church court. He burned the letter. When I sent the second letter, that he had been excommunicated by a bishop's court, he brought it to me, asking how we could be Christians when Christ said, "Judge not, that ye be not judged."

Our chat was not helpful. He wanted to argue. He wanted to dump on me. I could not get through to him. He just kept reading a sentence in the letter about the court's obligation to protect the church. Then he would fume that no one cared, especially not the people who were supposed to—the priesthood.

That was my last visit with Antonio, but, ironically, he sent me Kirt. Like Clarke, Kirt came in a terrible physical condition. He was using medication to calm his nerves, but the medicine kept him from sleeping. Without the medication he was so nervous that he could not sit down.

Kirt was a farm boy and had grown up with easy experimentation with himself, with other boys, even with animals. A stunning physical specimen, he was sought by older gays. He kept the secret from his father with whom he worked. He went into the mission field without discussing the matter with his bishop and never talked with his mission president about it. He completed his mission without problems and returned home. His straight friends had either married or gone to college. He did not intend to associate with the old gang; but after a year he had added drugs to homosexuality. They were his only friends, and he had spent every weekend with them until he and his gay roommate had broken up. Now Kirt determined to break out.

Kirt had an interesting logic. He had asked for excommunication to get the pressure off. Now he was trying to decide whether to use excommunication as a license to stay gay or as a stimulus to make some changes. He was dating a number of women, about which he felt a tenuous hope, but he was still unemployed and unclear about a career. His dependence on medication was diminishing, but the only close friends he had were gay. His was a circle of captives.

Antonio also sent me Curtis, divorced and a life-long, active Mormon. He and Antonio had nothing in common except their message: they were both gay, and they both wanted to be in the church. Curtis, however, had leveled with bishops all along the way. Like many who try to use missions as a cure, Curtis entered marriage hoping for a change. His wife was aware of the experimental nature of their relationship. They were married long enough to have three children, and then they parted. Curtis's pain had been multiplied by that marriage. He is counseling regularly with me and the stake president and is moderately active in the church. He is resigned to permanent bachelorhood and has informed his parents why.

Counseling with lesbians was more difficult for me. Women hesitated to approach me; our discussions did not come as naturally as those with men. We were both uneasy. I realized that it took real conviction on their part to overcome the gender gap. Nonetheless they came.

Krista and Carla, both returned missionaries, came with both humility and humiliation. Their physical affection had begun as platonic respect for each other. They decided to become room-mates out of a longing for friendship, for spiritual support, for a Latter-day Saint lifestyle. Their normal touching had grown gradually into an involvement that did not seem indiscreet initially. They talked themselves into denying that they had passed the border of propriety. Three months later they had resolved to break what had become a habit. They had abstained for six weeks and then broken their resolve, abstained again, and now were ready to admit that they were fooling themselves. They wanted help, con-fidential help.

It was hard for them to come to me. They knew I would ask why they did not stop living together, but their friendship was almost all they had. Both came from unsatisfying families. Both were lonely. Both were highly competent professionally. Neither had any previous homosexual experience.

We met regularly but at widening intervals. Then Krista rather suddenly became engaged. A year later Carla too married. I con-tinue to observe them both from a distance. They each appear to have acceptable marital relationships. They have moved to dif-ferent communities and have established new circles of friends.

Dotty is a complete contrast; she has checkmated me. She knows that I know about her homosexuality, and she has enter-tained the idea of coming to see me—I think. I am not sure whether she resents me personally or whether she is convinced that no one has a right to interfere. I am pretty sure that she hates the homosexuality that encircles her; she is deeply depressed and turns increasingly to alcohol. It is unclear to me which of her defeating behaviors is causal and which is symptomatic. She is explosive, perhaps dangerous.

Dotty moves often, but the moves do not help her find a new beginning. She alternately breaks with her lover and then returns. Similarly she sees the church as a point of refuge at times and as her tormentor at other times. She seeks out people who have been excommunicated and convinces herself that a court would be her nemesis. We have never talked about her homosexuality. She will not let me. I'm torn between a destructive intervention and patience that may never produce results.

I believe that other women must also need to discuss their homosexuality but feel unable to. I feel inadequate; I suspect that some women are still bearing guilt about events long abandoned. But they hesitate to confide in me merely because I am a man. I am grateful for the few women therapists to whom I can refer people, but I wish homosexual women would at least give me a try.

Where does all this lead? Certainly these few cases are too limited to generate universal solutions. They have brought me, average church member that I am, to know that homosexuality exists and has likely always existed—facts I wanted to ignore. Knowing and loving these people has not diminished my conviction that homosexuality is unnatural and unholy. I have seen no positive long-run benefits from its practice. I have read of some moderately successful companionships but have never spoken to someone who has experienced one. Even without considering the spiritual implications, the results of living a homosexual lifestyle seem overwhelmingly negative. I do understand that homosexuality sometimes provides the tenderness and touching that everyone needs but some have been denied. The childlessness of homosexual relationships is only one shortcoming. There are many others: severe guilt, social estrangement, manipulative relationships.

These ideas are not new nor are demands for social justice for gays. However, I also understand that those demands, even if implemented, will not eliminate most of the pain that I see in each person who confides in me.

I have found that we really do not know enough about homosexuality to be dogmatic. The question of whether gay behavior is biologically determined or socially formed has not been answered. Another fifty years might bring us to a realization that both options are inadequate explanations.

If this is actually the case—that we know far too little—then we are in a delicate position when making judgments about homosexuality. Is it an illness? The American Psychological Association and the American Psychiatric Association have officially said no. Yet I know members of each organization who dissent from that stand. I have not seen evidence that contradicts our traditional views based on scriptural sanctions.

Is there a physiological cure awaiting discovery? Will our interventions or judgments hasten suicide? Is homosexuality a learned behavior that can be unlearned or sublimated? Can determined repentance effectively eliminate homosexuality? These are the sacred and secular questions I ponder.

The church leaders I have worked with are generally cautious on the matter. I sense that they are also searching for answers. The policy of deciding each case separately is wise, especially since clear information is lacking.

For example, Victor Brown, Jr.'s analysis of homosexuality is insightful in some cases but inadequate in others. He argues three points. First, male homosexuals feel they do not fulfill the gender expectations of their fathers. Furthermore, they lack relationship skills. Finally, they have frequent fantasies of their own sensual activities (Victor Brown, Jr., *Fred's Story*. Sacramento: H. R. Associates, 1985).

Some of the people I have met with fit Brown's description. Some completely defy his analysis. Nonetheless Brown's three ideas are helpful because each suggests preventative actions. Certainly fathers would be well advised to realize their key impact in their sons' lives. A boy needs to feel the warmth of his father's physical touch. He desperately needs his father's vocal acceptance too, even of choices that may not fill a father's hopes. Not all boys can be football players or should be. The need for much cross-generational talk between parents and offspring is well known and is especially important when viewed from the vantage point of homosexuality. The need for deep, lasting friendships within wholesome peer groups is central. A youth busy with many activities and aware of parental support will usually not drift to deviancy.

Brown's prescriptions are helpful as preventions but inadequate as cures. Most adult homosexuals have long histories of pain and addiction that cannot be undone. Some adolescent homo-sexuality is mere experimentation, but adult homosexuality is most often deeply rooted. My knowledge is too limited. What experts have written or told me is still too limited.

What I do know is that homosexuals are people I can associate with quite normally and with whom other church members can associate. I did not previously know that. I subconsciously feared they might entice me. They did not. I found no allurement in their histories. I know homosexuals who love the gospel and the church dearly. I know homosexuals for whom the gospel and the church are terrible obstacles. Thus far the most powerful tool I have found to help them is still the idea that change is possible, gradual as it may be.

NINETEEN

What to Do When Your Child
Comes Out of the Closet

▼

Jan Cameron

I have no experience as a homosexual nor as a professional studying homosexuality. My expertise comes solely from being a Latter-day Saint mother of a gay son. I did not choose to be a mother of a homosexual, and I don't have all the answers even after years of dealing with this issue. However, I now find that it has been an enlightening experience, and I consider myself a pioneer in sometimes uncharted waters from trying to assist other LDS parents who are out there floundering in the murky waves of dealing with homosexuality.

As the founder of HELP (Homosexual Education for Latter-day Saint Parents), I have found myself on a roller coaster of emotions, especially when I asked for church recognition, received

"What to Do When Your Child Comes Out of the Closet," by Jan Cameron, originally appeared in *Exponent II,* Spring 1989. Ms. Cameron lives in San Ramon, California, where she is administrative assistant to the senior vice-president of the Commonwealth Premium Finance Division of Pacific Bank. She holds a B.A. degree in management from St. Mary's College. She is founder of HELP, a support group for parents of gays and lesbians.

it, and then saw it dropped. However, after much soul searching, I've decided to forge on in an effort to help keep Mormon families together—and sane. The phone rings at least once a month with a troubled LDS family, so I am needed.

I would like to share some helpful hints if you discover a homosexual in your home closet.

1. Be careful not to say hurtful things to your child after he or she admits to his or her homosexuality.

Barbara Johnson, a Baptist mother of a gay son and founder of Spatula Ministries in La Habra, California, suggests that all parents gag themselves for the first three months after discovering their child's homosexuality because everything they say is the wrong thing. We hurt as parents because we see our hopes and dreams diminish for that child—no mission, no temple marriage, no grandchildren, and worse yet maybe no eternal family. We unload our anger on them because we cannot find anyone else to be the scapegoat.

There are many children (1,500 to 2,000 between the ages of eleven and seventeen years) from all walks of life who end up living on the streets of San Francisco. They survive by prostitution. Do not allow your anger at your child to force him or her into this vulnerable situation. Our children are not prepared for this; many are murdered or commit suicide. Bite your tongue.

2. Find someone to talk to about your feelings who will do nothing but listen.

Finding someone who will understand is not as difficult as it would first appear. It is a known statistic that one in ten people is homosexual, and one of every four families has a homosexual in their family. Because we are in a more relaxed society, more gay people are "coming out of the closet" and more parents are "coming out" with them. A child's homosexuality doesn't need to be hidden, and parents will meet many wonderful people—parents and gays—once they have developed positive rather than negative attitudes about homosexuality. Parents will find that they are able to reach out to others who are in the same situation once they have overcome their own feelings about having a gay child.

Unfortunately the church is sadly lacking in training their priesthood leaders about how to deal with homosexuality. There are too few LDS counselors prepared to help families in this situation. I even met one counselor from Church Social Services who had never read a book on homosexuality. Hopefully this situation will change as more and more homosexuals and their parents make their needs known.

3. Do not judge the homosexual.

A Methodist minister to the Indians often quoted a saying I have never forgotten: "Do not judge an Indian until you have walked one mile in his moccasins." You can read about the church's position on homosexuality and how your child fits in with it. You can even discuss with your child how he or she feels. But don't judge your child. Encourage your child to continue to be a part of your family; don't try to change him or her. Love is a mighty tool, and love within a family helps the homosexual not to be on the defensive.

4. Accept the fact that there is no "cure" for homosexuality.

Can you remember how or when you chose your sexuality? They can't remember either. The gay men and women whom I have met have always had homosexual feelings; their lifestyle might change as they try to live gospel principles, but they will always remain homosexual just as you will remain heterosexual. Some are bisexual—are able to marry and even have children. But more often than not, gays cannot marry a person of the opposite sex any more than the heterosexual could marry someone of his or her same sex. There are many former wives of gay men who will tell you about their attempts to do otherwise.

Some homosexuals find lifelong same-sex companions. I have met couples who have been together for over twenty years. Parents who do not welcome their child's companion into their home often drive their child further and further away. (You might be interested to know that one European country has passed a law allowing gay marriages; California is considering changing a current law to allow gay marriages.)

5. Read about homosexuality when you feel up to it.

If you think people choose to be gay, just read about the homosexuals who were persecuted during Hitler's regime, who had pink triangles placed on them for identification, and who were placed in extermination camps along with the Jews. Or you might want to learn how and why San Francisco and other port cities became homes for gay people. It happened because we heterosexuals didn't think it unchristian to dishonorably discharge gay men from the Navy for homosexuality, labeling their discharge certificates with a big "H." If you remember what people thought of homosexuals twenty or thirty years ago, you will understand why these people would not return home to their families. How could you show your parents a certificate labeling you as a disgrace? The heterosexuals caused the gays to reside in these cities.

Read about the research that has been done on homosexuality. One such article appeared in the October 1988 issue of *Parents Magazine* and described some new thinking and research on how children become gay. Don't be afraid to read about the subject of homosexuality.

6. Learn to deal with the guilt that is a natural by-product of having a gay child.

Parents often blame themselves for their child's homosexuality. If they are not careful, they will wallow in this stage forever. Excessive guilt sometimes causes parents of homosexuals to choose between the church and their child. Parents need to forgive themselves for whatever mistakes they feel they have made while parenting. You and I are not perfect. Give yourself a break. Seek out support groups for parents who have gay children. Our peers can help us work through our homophobia.

7. Join a support group.

One nationwide parent support group is PFLAG (Parents and Friends of Lesbians and Gays), which was founded by a mother. Originally based in Los Angeles, it is now located in Denver, Colorado. PFLAG has groups meeting monthly right in your own neighborhood. You will meet parents who have more than one gay child in the family; mothers who have twins, one gay, one straight; lesbian grandmothers; parents who have dealt with their children's homosexuality for many years; and parents who have dealt with their children's being gay for only one day. There will be gay children who are searching for advice because they are afraid to tell their parents. And, yes, you will run into Mormon mothers and Mormon children.

At my very first parent meeting at PFLAG, two chairs down from me sat a former Mormon. His mother and brother had rejected him, and he had suffered a mental breakdown. I felt sorry for him; his mom couldn't live the Word of Wisdom, but she felt she could judge him and how he should handle his life. HELP and People Who Care are organizations you can join for just a small donation. They will have information that can be mailed out to you immediately; care is used to be discreet and confidential.

8. Don't be terrified to reach out.

I was so scared at the first PFLAG meeting and the first Affirmation meeting (a support group for gay and lesbian Mormons) that I left an itinerary on my table in case something happened to me. Nothing will happen except you will return home feeling a lot better about the whole matter than when you left.

9. Remember that all homosexuals are not promiscuous.

I attended a Gay Pride Day parade in San Francisco several years ago. A group of gay Mormons stayed by my side and made me feel protected as I peered into their world. Homosexuals have immorality in their ranks, just as heterosexuals do, but they also have wonderful people and good causes and upstanding citizens. Sometimes I find gays to be more sensitive, caring, and loving people—perhaps because they have always felt unwanted and unloved and that something was terribly wrong with them. . . .

10. The church is not unfeeling toward you or your child.

Some of the church's general authorities have reached out to me, and I will never forget them. A homosexual office has been created at church headquarters to work with this particular issue. What strides will be made by this department remain to be seen. But until more LDS members can get over their homophobic feelings, acceptance will come slowly for gay Mormons. I feel that parents of gays can be instrumental in bridging this gap, and I consider every parent a pioneer in this area.

Learning about your gay child can be a marvelous blessing. What was at first a major tragedy in my life has given me great new friends, tolerance, and empathy I did not have before. Homosexuals have a part in the next world, and I know our Heavenly Father loves them as he loves us.

The most recent experience of great meaning to me was my decision to march this summer in the San Francisco Gay Pride Parade. There were about seventy-five to one hundred of us parents marching with PFLAG. As we began the parade route, the revelry stopped, the crowd began to clap, cry, and shout. The roar became louder and louder with the enthusiasm, and lots of love was showered upon us. As tears welled in my eyes, I turned to a woman marching beside me and asked her what was happening. She explained that the crowd had experienced such rejection in their lives from parents and relatives that they were showering their affections on us. We became their moms and dads, their grandmas and grandpas. Flowers were given to us, and many people ran out and hugged us with tears streaming down their faces. What an experience. I am so grateful that I was there to reach out and share a few moments with these lonely people.

I realize that some readers of this essay will be shocked. I understand where you are. I walked that road myself not too long ago. I'm glad I finally reached the top of the hill. The other side looks so promising.

II.

PROFESSIONAL

AND

CHRISTIAN

PERSPECTIVES

TWENTY

Kinsey and Beyond

▼

Ron Schow

Perhaps the most important, and certainly the most influential, sociological research on homosexuality was done by Alfred Kinsey and his associates and reported in two landmark publications, *Sexual Behavior in the Human Male* and *Sexual Behavior in the Human Female* (Kinsey et al. 1948; 1953). In the first of these, normative data were gathered for same-sex feelings and behavior from thorough interviews with 5,300 white males. In the second work, similar data were reported for females. To this day these studies remain among the more thorough and revealing statistical assessments of the incidence and nature of homosexuality in our society.

The data gathered by this family man and a one-time Sunday school teacher were revolutionary. They challenged several well-established assumptions. Notably the data suggested that not all individuals are exclusively homosexual or heterosexual but that those sexual postures are two poles on a sexual continuum, along which sexual behavior and feelings are distributed in a mixed fashion. Moreover, the data claimed to demonstrate that homosexuality, exclusively or in some varying degrees, is more widely manifest in the U.S. population than had been thought—for both men and women.

It was in the first of these studies that Kinsey began the use of homosexual-heterosexual scaling (or what is sometimes called the H-H Scale or the Kinsey Scale). This enabled interviewers to assess more precisely the variations in feeling and behavior which comprised the sexual histories of the interview subjects. Since that time the Kinsey Scale and the view of sexuality underlying it have been widely accepted by sex researchers.

The scale is described by the Kinsey authors as follows:

RATINGS:　　0　　1　　2　　3　　4　　5　　6

0. Exclusively heterosexual with no homosexual.
1. Predominantly heterosexual, only incidentally homosexual.
2. Predominantly heterosexual, but more than incidentally homosexual.
3. Equally heterosexual and homosexual.
4. Predominantly homosexual, but more than incidentally heterosexual.
5. Predominantly homosexual, but incidentally heterosexual.
6. Exclusively homosexual.

(Readers interested in a full explanation of the scale and its implications may consult Appendix I.)

Basing their collection and interpretation of data on this scale, the Kinsey researchers concluded that about 30 percent of males and nearly 20 percent of females in the general population have had some degree of homosexual feelings or experience. By using those with the highest degrees of homosexual orientation (5 and 6 on the scale), the Kinsey researchers arrived at the most quoted fact about homosexuality: 10 percent of males and about half that many females are more or less exclusively homosexual for at least three years from ages sixteen to fifty-five. In a slightly different casting of the data to look only at activity, they found about one-third of all adult males report overt homosexual experience to orgasm some time after the beginning of adolescence. The female percentage of such experience was more limited, some 13 percent, although 20 percent of females report same-sex physical contacts of a sexual nature (Kinsey et al. 1953, 487).

How valid are the Kinsey data? Some researchers have voiced concerns about the methodology employed in the Kinsey surveys and accordingly about conclusions based on it. Numerous studies, all more limited in scope than Kinsey's original efforts, have examined this or that dimension of the homosexual incidence data. Despite limitations in some portions of the sample, the original Kinsey studies have been generally confirmed and continue to be the standard against which the newer research efforts are measured (see, for example, Gebhard 1972; Bell 1976). In the last few years additional data have emerged to support Kinsey's idea of a continuum (McConaghy 1987; Ellis et al. 1987). In light of some challenges to Kinsey's data (for example, that by Reisman and Eichel 1990), a recently published report of a major Kinsey Institute survey using a population probability sample affords an opportunity for comparison on both males and females (Klassen et al. 1989). These data were derived in a 1970 survey and have recently been used as important estimates in connection with the AIDS crisis (Turner et al. 1989). Based on data derived from responses to a written questionnaire, in contrast to the direct interview method of the original Kinsey researchers, the outcomes of this latter study likely underestimate the prevalence of homosexual feelings and behavior. Nevertheless this more recent survey gives general support to Kinsey's original work. (A fuller description and comment on the 1970 Kinsey study, together with some representative data from it, are included in Appendix II.)

Perhaps the best indication of Kinsey's continued importance in this field is a recently published volume, *Homosexuality/ Heterosexuality: Concepts of Sexual Orientation* (McWhirter, Sanders, and Reinisch 1990). A collection of twenty-two essays by some of the most eminent researchers on homosexuality and scholars from a variety of disciplines, this anthology grew out of a 1986 conference at the Kinsey Institute devoted to examination of the current state of knowledge on homosexuality. In particular the essays consider Kinsey and the Kinsey Scale and their continuing scientific, historical, and cultural relevance for homosexual studies. The volume is characterized by diverse opinion; collectively the writers demonstrate that homosexuality is a complex phenomenon with manifold interrelated biological, social, psychological, political, historical dimensions. Yet all the contributors acknowledge that Kinsey played—and continues to play—a crucial role in advancing the understanding of homosexuals as individuals and as members of society.

References

Bell, Alan. "The Homosexual as Patient." In *Human Sexuality: A Health Practictioner's Text,* edited by Richard Green. Baltimore: Williams and Wilkins, 1976.

Ellis, Lee, Donald Burke, and Ashley Ames. "Sexual Orientation as a Continuous Variable: A Comparison Between the Sexes." *Archives of Sexual Behavior* 16 (1987): 523-29.

Gebhard, Paul. *Prevalence of Homosexuality.* Rockville, MD: National Institute of Mental Health, 1972.

Kinsey, A., W. Pomeroy, and C. Martin. "Homosexual Outlet." In *Sexual Behavior in the Human Male.* Philadelphia: W. B. Saunders, 1948.

————, and P. Gebhard. "Homosexual Responses and Contacts." In *Sexual Behavior in the Human Female.* Philadelphia: W. B. Saunders, 1953.

Klassen, Albert, Colin Williams, and Eugene Levitt. *Sex and Morality in the U.S.: An Empirical Inquiry Under the Auspices of the Kinsey Institute.* Middleton, CT: Wesleyan University Press, 1989.

McConaghy, Nathaniel. "Heterosexuality/Homosexuality: Dichotomy or Continuum." *Archives of Sexual Behavior* 16 (1987): 411-24.

McWhirter, David, Stephanie Sanders, and June Reinisch. *Homosexuality/ Heterosexuality: Concepts of Sexual Orientation.* New York: Oxford University Press, 1990.

Reisman, Judith and Edward Eichel. *Kinsey, Sex and Fraud: The Indoctrination of a People.* New York: Huntington House, 1990.

Turner, C., H. Miller, and L. Moses, eds. *AIDS: Sexual Behavior and Intravenous Drug Use.* Washington, D.C.: National Academy Press, 1989.

TWENTY-ONE

I Am Not a Good Egg

▼

Marvin Rytting

I do not remember the first time I was called an egg. I probably was not even aware of it because my awareness of eggness developed gradually. I was in Brazil, and it took time for my Portuguese ears to develop the ability to distinguish specific words and even more time to pick up on the word *ovo* and longer still to realize that the word was being directed at me. Finally I learned that *ovo* was a Brazilian slang for homosexual—their equivalent for queer or fag.

It really is not that strange that they would call us fags. We did look queer. We dressed funny. Not only did we live together, but we were *always* together. And we were never seen with women. Come now—twenty-year-old men who never look at women? From all outward appearances we seemed to be homosexual. (Some missionaries never realize that the nice man who keeps inviting them to visit but never comes to church does so because they are

"I Am Not a Good Egg," by Marvin Rytting, originally appeared in *Sunstone*, Fall 1985. Dr. Rytting is currently associate professor of psychology at Indiana University-Purdue University at Indianapolis, specializing in personality theory and human sexuality.

cute and he likes having gentlemen callers—the same reason that some women invite them to visit.) Of course, the members knew better. They could tell how much trouble we were having keeping our eyes off of the young women in the branch. They would joke that the shots we took at zone conference to protect us against hepatitis were actually some variation of saltpeter. My reaction to being called queer was not to blame the Brazilians or worry about my sexual orientation but to recognize the absurdity of dressing so that we stood out as being different. I concluded that missionaries should look like respectable businessmen in the community. So I grew a mustache.

I was not at all traumatized by being labeled as gay on my mission. Ever since I disbanded the girl-haters club when I was ten, I have been incorrigibly heterosexual. My experience in Brazil actually reduced any homoerotophobia which I picked up from the American culture because there I learned how to hug men. Brazilian men hug. Therefore, Brazilian missionaries hug. The practice in our mission was to hug our companions after prayers every morning and evening. And zone conferences were veritable orgies of *abracos*. I learned that men can hug without it being sexual and that it feels good. (The corollary that men can hug women without it being sexual and that this feels good too has not been lost on me either.)

As a confirmed heterosexual, I have found it paradoxically easy to form friendships with gays—both men and women. I am not threatened by closeness with them. I have no fear of latent homosexual tendencies arising nor do I fear being converted. Still, I must admit that traces of mild discomfort have come out in subtle ways. One gay friend once pointed out that whenever we met, instead of hugging him, I would give him a friendly slug on the shoulder. His comment made me realize that that was my way of being close and still maintaining distance. Thereafter I was able to change and start greeting him with a hug. However, when he offered to introduce me to a friend of his who he said would really like me because he was attracted to handsome men with beards, I declined. It was interesting to think that I could be a sex object for a man, and occasionally that thought occurs to me in locker rooms.

Because the study of sexuality has become my academic special-ty, I have ample opportunity to explore questions about homosexuality, including my personal reaction to it. I have become aware of the paradox that my firm commitment to heterosexuality makes it easy for me to empathize with gays and to have gay friends. In addition to not being threatened by the topic or the people, I am acutely aware of how strong sexual preference is. One of the big issues—particularly in the Mormon church—is whether sexual orientation can be changed through therapy or repentance. Although I do not know *the* answer, I am convinced that *my* sexual preference cannot be changed, so why should I assume that theirs can be? I discovered this through a fantasy, and I invite you to try the same one.

If I imagine that I have been transported to a culture where homosexuality is the norm, then I get a sense of what it is like to be a sexual minority. I imagine being told that I must be erotically aroused by men and that it is a sin, a crime, and an illness for me to be attracted to women. But I cannot picture me deciding to love men rather than women just because the society now says I should. I can decide not to be sexually active with women because I do not want to be arrested or lose my job, but I cannot imagine no longer desiring them. I fantasize about going into therapy with a good behaviorist and seeing pictures of naked women while being shocked, and I wonder how many shocks it will take before I no longer get a charge from women—500? 5,000? 50,000? 500,000? I can picture myself claiming to be cured to avoid the shocks, but I cannot imagine really being cured. I think of seeing pictures of naked men in pleasant surroundings and wonder how many years it will take before they succeed in arousing me—5? 50? 500?

I fantasize about attempting to have sex with a man. It is strange, but this is the easiest part of the fantasy if I can take a passive role. If I could close my eyes and not know if it is a man or a woman who is sexually stimulating me, it would not make any difference. My body would not care—only my mind does. So if I could close my eyes and pretend that it is a woman, I would be OK. It would be much more difficult if I had to be the active partner, but I could probably force myself to do it although I would have a hard time enjoying it. Still it is ironic that the sex part would be the easiest. The part of the homosexual relationship that I cannot imagine pulling off is the romantic part. I cannot picture myself kissing a man passionately or cuddling for hours looking lovingly into his eyes and saying sweet nothings or flirting playfully with him or pining for him when we are apart—listening to sad music and feeling the sweet longing of loving from a distance.

I think about what it would be like to be a Mormon in this alien culture: I not only have to deal with the guilt of wanting to have sex with a woman but also the shame of not being married to a man. I imagine trying to repent and praying that God will make me gay, but I do not believe that all the prayers in the world would make me love men rather than women. I can imagine deciding to be celibate, but I realize that even so, I shall never have any standing in the church and shall be under constant pressure to grow up and stop being selfish and get married. I imagine getting married and living a lie, fantasizing about women whenever I have sex with my man and feeling guilty about my heterosexual dreams. I think of what it would be like to become asexual and withdraw from life into a lonely shell. I picture leaving the church to escape. The vision which seems least likely is being happy within the church.

My fantasy may be similar to the experience of some gays, but it is surely not true of all. Every gay person I know has a different story. We should not try to fit them—or anyone—into a mold; not even my mold. We vary in so many ways and our sexual preference is only one of our many characteristics. It should not overshadow the rest.

I do have a fantasy in which I can imagine being homosexual. If I were a woman, I would be lesbian. It is easier for me to imagine being a woman loving another woman than being a woman romantically loving a man. Suddenly I understand. Not only does the homosexual question have little to do with sex, it has nothing to do with homo vs. hetero, same vs. different. I am not attracted to an opposite sex; I am attracted to women.

Men do not turn me on simply because they are men, not because they are the same gender. I am not sure why, but for some reason some people are romantically attracted to men and others to women (and some to both). Personally I love women, and I cannot imagine feeling erotic love for a man. But I accept the fact that most women feel what I cannot imagine feeling—and I accept the fact that some men do too. It is easy to accept lesbians because I agree with their preference. Perhaps we should divide people into the categories of *gynophile* and *androphile*—those who love women and those who love men—rather than worry so much about whether this attraction is homo or hetero. Or perhaps we should not divide people into categories at all.

My fantasies do not prove anything. They provide no answers. What they do for me is to make all of the answers I have heard thus far inadequate. For a while I was comfortable with the position that it was OK to have homoerotic feelings but not to act upon them. After all, the rest of us have to live without sex outside of marriage. But even that answer does not fit any more.

For me to have sex only with my wife is simply not the same as being eternally celibate. And it is not really the sex anyway. I can imagine giving up sex for the rest of my life (reluctantly, to be sure), but I would go crazy if I had to give up the love and affection in romance—the touching, the hugging, the cuddling. Is it really moral to ask people not to love? I do not know *the* answer. But I do know that I cannot condemn my gay friends. Nor can I insist that they change nor that they should forgo love. All I can do is care about them—and accept them. I am convinced that the gospel of Christ has room for them. I hope that some day the church can make room too.

TWENTY-TWO

Sin and Sexuality:
Psychobiology and the Development
of Homosexuality

▼

R. Jan Stout

In the fall of 1970, I was a young psychiatrist with five years of clinical experience in private practice. I had been certified by the American Board of Psychiatry and Neurology, and I felt that I grasped the basic and latest theories concerning the cause and cure of homosexuality and other so-called sexual deviations. I had been asked to participate in examining this provocative subject in a televised panel discussion on a local public television station. In preparation I reviewed various texts on the subject, which almost universally presented the prevailing thesis: Homosexuality is a learned behavior, an illness to be treated and corrected, and can with proper therapy be cured in over 25 percent of cases. Homosexuals have failed, psychoanalytically speaking, to successfully traverse the pitfalls of psychosexual development as outlined by

"Sin and Sexuality: Psychobiology and the Development of Homo-sexuality," by R. Jan Stout, originally appeared in *Dialogue: A Journal of Mormon Thought* 20 (Summer 1987). Dr. Stout is assistant professor of psychiatry at the University of Utah School of Medicine and has a private practice in psychiatry in Salt Lake City. He is past president of the Utah Psychiatric Association.

by Sigmund Freud. To be sure, scattered reports in the literature suggested a genetic or hormonal basis for the disorder but did not convince the majority of clinicians, including myself. That panel of 1970 certainly understood, even if they did not openly discuss, that homosexuality was, and still is, considered a major sexual sin by my church, culture, and the entire Judeo-Christian tradition stretching back more than two thousand years.

After presenting my views and reviewing current literature on the subject, I felt satisfied, confident, and correct. There was no serious debate on the issue, and I returned home to the congratulations of my wife, friends, and colleagues. Sixteen years later I can state that what I presented was wrong and simplistic. The evolving change in my views came by examining new research, gaining more clinical experience, and looking for alternate explanations to clarify some of the mystery surrounding the development of human sexuality and specifically homosexuality. Understanding these issues has enormous implications for our perception of sin and moral responsibility. No one should ignore the dilemma, for perhaps one in ten of all men and a smaller percentage of women are not heterosexual.

No consensus exists regarding the causes of homosexuality. As with virtually all other aspects of human behavior, we see a spectrum of opinions, theories, and conjecture. Different scientific disciplines advocate different points of view and bias and ignore important contributions from other disciplines. Behaviorists, biologists, sociologists, anthropologists, geneticists, historians, lawyers, and political scientists have all offered explanations. Judd Marmor, a highly respected psychiatrist, psychoanalyst, and authority on homosexuality, has observed:

> The most influential theory in modern psychiatry has been that of Sigmund Freud, who believed that homosexuality was the expression of a universal trend in all human beings, stemming from a biologically rooted bisexual predisposition. Freud, in line with the strong Darwinian influence on his thinking, believed that all humans went through an inevitable "homoerotic" phase in the process of achieving heterosexuality. Certain kinds of life experience could arrest the evolutionary process, and

the individual would then remain "fixated" at a homosexual level. Furthermore, even if the development were to proceed normally, certain vestiges of homosexuality would remain as permanent aspects of the personality, and these universal "latent homosexual" tendencies would be reflected in "sublimated" expressions of friendship for members of one's own sex and in patterns in behavior or interest more appropriate to the opposite sex—for example, artistic or culinary interests or "passive" attitudes in males and athletic or professional interests or "aggressive" attitudes in females (1965, 2).

Now, almost fifty years after his death, many continue to advocate Freud's controversial theories; but I suspect that he would be the first to revise those theories, given new information on human sexuality.

My own thinking on this subject has been influenced by a major shift in psychiatry's "nature-versus-nurture" debate of the past two decades. Behaviors once thought to be entirely psychological in origin have been demonstrated to be profoundly influenced by genes and neurochemistry. Disorders such as schizophrenia, manic-depression, panic attacks, and debilitating anxiety have now been shown to have strong biological causes and can no longer be adequately explained by the theoretical models of intrapsychic conflict, poor parenting, and social learning defects. A prominent psychoanalyst discussing the relationship between neurobiology and psychoanalysis, including research in sexuality, recently warned, "We should be extremely uncomfortable with any theory that is incongruent with neurobiologic discovery" (Cooper 1985, 1402).

The Complexities of Human Sexuality

Few subjects arouse, confuse, intrigue, and provoke like the study of human sexuality. The search for understanding extends from the book of Genesis to Freud, Masters and Johnson, and Desmond Morris's *The Naked Ape*. The music of sexuality plays from infancy to senescence, waxing and waning, reaching moments of intensity and long periods of plateau. Sexuality binds and splits relationships, confuses and enlightens, produces profound ecstasy and unbearable guilt.

Only in the twentieth century, using the scientific method, have we been able to study sexuality with sophisticated neurological, anatomical, and hormonal research. Much folklore surrounds this subject, and we are in the process of trying to separate fact from fiction. The brain is the ultimate sexual organ, and everything else flows from it. A complex interplay among the neocortex (cerebrum), the limbic system and hypothalamus, and the brain stem contributes to the sexual experience. Hormones, especially testosterone, fuel this interaction in both males and females (Hales 1984).

Embryology (Effects of Nature)

Sexual differentiation begins when by chance a sperm meets an egg and initiates a chain of events that ultimately produces a sexually-oriented male or female. To understand human sexuality, one must understand embryology, the science of intrauterine development of the fetus. John Money, founder of the Johns Hopkins Psychohormonal Research Unit, says that the basic embryonic plan, at least for mammals, is inherently female—the "Eve principle," as he calls it (1984). In embryo we all start out female. Then a little more than one-half of us respond to the Adam principle as the result of the Y chromosome, which acts on undifferentiated fetal gonads to create testes. Thereafter, the change to male is controlled by male hormones, the androgens. Nature seems to have more difficulty creating male sexual identity and anatomy, which helps explain why many more males than females experience sexual variations (Morano 1979). Testosterone makes the brain less feminine and more masculine. Animal studies have demonstrated that "depending on the amount of testosterone present in the environment, we can produce effeminate males, fully capable of male sexual function but with female behavioral traits, or we can produce demasculinized males, incapable of male sexual behavior later even in the presence of testosterone; the converse can be done to females. The fetal mouse brain is exquisitely sensitive to the organizing effect of hormones" (Cooper 1985, 1400).

A recent hypothesis suggests that neural pathways imprinted

at crucial stages of brain development later profoundly affect sexual behavior and choice of a sexual object. Certainly, without the secretions from the embryonic testis no male organs can develop. It now seems possible that subsequent sexual feelings and behavior will also be influenced by testosterone produced in utero. Variations in the amount secreted or blocking of the hormone's actions by maternal stress or drugs have been shown to make major differences in the eventual sexual life of the developing embryo (Dorner 1983). Animal studies, although difficult to generalize to humans, have confirmed the crucial role that prenatal androgens have in sex-role behavior when puberty arrives (MacCulloch and Waddington 1981).

A recent, unconfirmed study by Zuger suggested that early effeminate behavior in male children is congenital and is the best single indicator of later homosexuality (1984). A new book has suggested the same conclusion. Richard Green, a UCLA psychiatrist, in *The Sissy Boy Syndrome and the Development of Homosexuality* chronicles the development of forty-four boys who preferred traditionally feminine activities at an early age. Three-fourths of them grew up to be gay or bisexual, Green found. He felt that these boys' early preference for feminine activities may reflect an innate tendency toward homosexuality. A reviewer summarized:

> They were chosen for the study because from very early childhood, their behavior was considered out of the mainstream of normal sexual development. Many dressed up in girl's or women's clothing and reported that they wanted to be girls, not boys. When asked to draw pictures of people, they would often draw females rather than males. . . . Many scientists agree that the causes are complex and involve a combination of biological and environmental factors—some beyond parents' control. Green's research and similar studies contradict the belief that homosexuality is simply the result of a domineering mother and a weak father ("Sissy" 1986).

The effect of hormones on the brain is not inevitably all-or-nothing. It is possible to be masculine without being also completely unfeminine or conversely to be feminine without also remaining completely unmasculine (Money 1984). This may help explain why we see such a wide spectrum of human sexual behavior and appearance.

Duane Jeffery, a professor of zoology at Brigham Young University, has examined the problem of intersex developmental defects in humans. He states that primitive gonads, the "ovotestes," are each part female tissue (ovarian) and part male (testicular). Genetic and developmental conditions can produce syndromes of intersex confusion that lead to both medical and theological difficulties. He does not explore the question of homosexuality and limits his discussion to the anatomical and gender identity disorders, concluding, "The very existence of human intersexes poses some interesting unanswered questions in LDS traditions and beliefs" (1979, 108).

Jeffrey Keller recently (1986) addressed the question "Is sexual gender eternal?" Despite reassurances from various Mormon church authorities that "there is no mismatching of bodies and spirits," modern biology has demonstrated numerous examples of physical and hormonal miscues that challenge our theological concepts.

In a few females, the excessive production of testosterone by the adrenal glands during gestation causes a relatively rare condition called the andrenogenital syndrome (AGS). These girls are born with masculine genitalia that can be mistaken at birth for that of a boy. The condition can be surgically repaired and treated with hormones, and the girls develop a normal feminine physique and undergo normal puberty. Yet a large percentage of these girls grow up as tomboys who show little interest as teenagers in dating. As adults "a startling 37 percent are homosexual or bisexual or have sexual fantasies about women" (Hales 1984, 23). Again, testosterone is the powerful hormonal catalyst that affects the developing male and female prior to birth. Significantly, it is well known that testosterone given after puberty does not alter the direction of sexual choice but may intensify the general libido.

The regulation of testosterone in utero is a biological, congenital, developmental event and does not represent a true genetic disorder (that is, coded, specific, preembryonic information carried by DNA in the genes of chromosomes). The genetic (inherited) transmission of homosexuality has been suggested by some investigators, but current research, with the exception of a single study, does not seem to favor this thesis. Kallman (1952) studied 85 homosexuals who were twins; and although the concordance rates for overt homosexual behavior were only slightly higher than normal for the forty-five dizygotic pairs, the rate was 100 percent for the forty monozygotic pairs. This finding suggests the presence of a definite and decisive genetic factor in homosexuality, but Kallman's findings have not been confirmed by other researchers. On the contrary, quite the opposite was found by Kolb (1963), showing no concordance in his identical twin study (Marmor 1976). The development of sexual identity comes after conception and is unlikely to be the result of specific information carried in the chromosomes. I believe that the crucial factor is the timing and amount of testosterone released in utero by the developing embryo. We will all have to wait for further studies to illuminate these various biological hypotheses.

The Environment (Effects of Nurture)

It has long been argued that behavioral sex in human beings is learned. It has long been assumed that infants have a neutral gender role. Toys, dress, and play patterns all begin working to determine ultimate sexual orientation. Little girls are supposed to like pink, and boys are inclined to blue. Girls are given dolls, and boys receive toy trains and trucks. Sex roles are supposed to work out just fine if the child is given clear and unambiguous messages about his or her sexual destiny.

As early as 1905, Sigmund Freud began probing the family backgrounds that could produce homosexuality and other sexual deviations (Marmor 1976). Every clinician, including myself, learned that passive, weak, or absent fathers coupled with strong, dominant, and castrating mothers set up the perfect climate for induction of homosexuality. Inability to form a satisfactory identification with an adequate father figure and development of a strong, unconscious fear or hatred of women was the prerequisite for this psychosexual disorder. Indeed, many cases seemed to bear out Freud's observations, but all of these clinical studies are by their nature retrospective and in selected populations. Recent research on large, randomly selected populations of homosexuals shows no valid statistical correlation with this family pattern. Many men with backgrounds similar to those supposed to produce homosexuality do not grow up to become gay.

A similar type of reasoning regarding the cause of schizophrenia was suggested in the 1960s and was widely accepted. "Schizophrenogenic" mothers were accused of giving repeated double-bind messages to their offspring, creating bizarre thinking, delusions, and hallucinations. Few psychiatrists familiar with current research in genetics and brain chemistry would advocate the 1960s kind of explanation for a disorder that is now clearly seen as a brain disease.

Other learning theories and behavioral hypotheses have been suggested but generally are subject to flaws similar to those that we see in Freud's original postulates. A study from the Eastern Highlands of New Guinea involving Sambia men and boys revealed that strong homosexual conditioning did not result in adult homoerotic behavior. Despite heavy reinforcing of unlimited fellatio in prepubertal boys and youths and powerful teachings that female bodies are poisonously dangerous, Sambia men are almost always heterosexual. As youngsters the boys are very close to their mothers and are told the secret of masculinity—a man is only the shell of a man unless he drinks plenty of semen. The boys engage in homosexual activities which they regard as pleasant, and sexual relations with women are strictly taboo. As marriage time approaches, the young men develop the "desire for women as gripping for these tribesmen as it is anywhere else." Upon marriage, in the late teens or early twenties, the taboo is reversed—homosexuality is forbidden (Stoller 1985). This is a rather troublesome outcome for behaviorists who insist that positive and negative reinforcement shapes sexual preference. The results also imply that teaching or recruiting young males to become homosexual is unlikely to produce homosexuality except in those who are biologically predisposed. In addition, these learning theories blame parents and families, implying that in some mysterious way they cause or can prevent the emergence of homoerotic behavior. Although fascinating, these speculations ignore much of the biological basis for human sexuality.

However, environmental factors are not unimportant. On the contrary, we can say that homosexuality, transsexuality, and transvestitism are probably determined by many psychodynamic, biological, sociocultural, and situational factors. Environmental factors can profoundly shape the style, expression, and quality of sexual behavior in all of us, whether straight or gay. Yet as we have seen, considerable evidence exists for the fundamental biological determination of sexual identity and object choice, and evidence for core, environmental causes is questionable. Apparently environment fine tunes the instrument of sexuality but neither creates nor organizes its direction. More difficult research is needed, but the evidence accumulated over the past two decades for the biological causality of sexual and gender identity, although inconclusive, is persuasive.

Sin, Sexuality, and Religion

Religions have a vested interest in advocating a sexual code of conduct. The Judeo-Christian tradition has long regarded the monogamous human family as the finest and best way to provide offspring loving security and moral integrity. Anything that threatens this goal threatens achievement of a moral universe; it is not surprising that homosexuality and other sexual variations are met with such antipathy in our culture. Religious leaders from the apostle Paul to modern-day LDS prophets have strongly condemned sexual deviancy. For many years in the Mormon church, homosexuality was referred to as "the sin that has no name" (Anonymous 1978). Homosexuals have found no home in Christian or Jewish faiths.

In other cultures, attitudes toward homosexual activities vary widely. A 1952 study of seventy-six societies observed that in 64 percent of the societies homosexuality was considered normal and acceptable, at least for some members of the community. In the remaining 36 percent homosexuality, though condemned, continued to occur secretly (Marmor 1976).

The accepted assumption has been that homosexuals have chosen their lifestyle and have knowingly entered into sin. LDS apostle Spencer W. Kimball wrote, "Homosexuality is an ugly sin, repugnant to those who find no temptation in it, as well as to many past offenders who are seeking a way out of its clutches" (1969, 78). Society at large has generally agreed with this conclusion.

Nationally-syndicated newspaper columnist Patrick J. Buchanan implied divine punishment in the AIDS plague. In 1983 he wrote, "The poor homosexuals—they have declared war on nature, and now nature is exacting an awful retribution" (Clark et al. 1985, 20). He apparently made no reference to the plight of innocent children, hemophiliacs, and others who contracted the disease.

Do homosexuals consciously choose their sexual identities? Are they more capable of doing this than those of us who are heterosexual? Is not sexual identity something to which we awaken rather than something that we decide by some rational, moral process? Do you remember choosing to be straight when you were thirteen? I have never met or treated a homosexual who felt that he or she had a choice in the matter. From their earliest recollections, they knew that in some way they "were different," and all felt confused, guilty, and frightened.

Mormon homosexuals experience a special, poignant pain. How can they fit into the celestial plan of things? Where do they go to resolve the conflicts surging within their realm of moral responsibility? How do they reconcile their feelings with divine revelation?

Sensitive and thoughtful articles in *Sunstone* and *Dialogue: A Journal of Mormon Thought* have examined this issue. Marvin Rytting acknowledges, "I do not know *the* answer. But I do know that I cannot condemn my gay friends. Nor can I insist that they change nor that they should forgo love. All I can do is care about them—and accept them. I am convinced that the gospel of Jesus Christ has room for them. I hope that some day the church can make room, too" (1983, 78). The problem is illustrated in John Bennion's fictional interview between a tormented young man and his stake president who expresses acceptance, love, and empathy but offers no resolution to the agonizing dilemma of the young man's homosexuality (1985).

The Clinical Spectrum

The personality spectrum among homosexuals is as diverse and complex as it is among heterosexuals—"from passive ones to aggressive ones; from shy introverts to loud raucous extroverts; from theatrically hysterical personalities to rigid, compulsive-obsessive ones; from sexually inhibited, timid types to sexually promiscuous, flamboyant ones; from radical activists to staunch conservatives; from defiant atheists to devout churchgoers; and from unconscionable sociopaths to highly responsible, law-abiding citizens" (Marmor 1976, 382). The homosexual stereotype of the limp-wristed, effeminate fag is as distorted as is the Rambo stereotype for heterosexual men.

Every occupation, social class, race, and creed is represented in the gay and lesbian world. Many are married, have children, and lead quiet, conservative lives. Sexual drive and the exclusivity of homosexual interest vary widely. A 1970 study of participants in the impersonal sex of public restrooms found that 54 percent were married and living with their wives and children in middle-class homes and were, for all intents and purposes, just "average guys next door" (Humphreys 1970).

The same variations occur among Mormons. In an anonymous monograph published in 1978, the homosexual author states, "We belong to your priesthood quorum, we teach your Sunday school class, we pass the sacrament to you each Sunday, we attend your primary classes, your faculty meetings, your family reunions, and your youth conferences. We sell you your groceries, we keep your books, we police your streets, and we teach your children in school. We preside over your wards and even your stakes. We are your sons, your brothers, your grandsons, and who knows but by some riddle of nature, we would be you" (Anonymous 1978, 56). From my own clinical experience of twenty-four years, I can attest to this diversity.

The families of homosexuals, whether parents, wives, husbands, siblings, or children, must often live with confusion, anger, shame, and sorrow. They feel helpless and guilty. Perhaps several million homosexuals and lesbians have chosen marriage as the "perfect closet" in which to hide their secret. *Married and Gay* chronicles the poignant struggles experienced by those who find themselves living in these unions (Maddox 1982). Single-parent mothers worry that lack of a strong male figure will foster the development of sexual inversion in their sons. Yet in his famous "Letter to an American Mother" Sigmund Freud wrote, "Homosexuality is assuredly no advantage, but it is nothing to be ashamed of, no vice, no degradation, it cannot be classified as an illness; we consider it to be a variation of the sexual functions produced by a certain arrest of sexual development" (Marmor 1976, 385).

Some men struggle for years to change their orientation or to experience an inkling of heterosexual interest. Beyond traditional psychotherapy, scripture reading, and church counseling, some have sat for hours viewing pictures of naked men while receiving painful electric shocks for negative behavioral conditioning. Some claim a cure, which many view with skepticism. Others resignedly accept their situation, while still others become bitter, disillusioned, and nihilistic. Some claim they have found love, comfort, and self-acceptance in their homosexuality. The spectre of excommunication looms over all who refuse to change their ways. The most tragic cases seek the ultimate out of suicide. A minority choose to lead abstinate, celibate, or morally neutral lives. The capacity to choose this solution varies widely, just as it does for heterosexuals.

In addition to many homosexuals, I have worked with a few transsexuals and transvestites. These situations represent a different level of core sexual identity and sex role behavior, respectively. A female transsexual may live with the absolute belief that she is male and be willing to undergo multiple, painful surgical procedures to achieve this end. A pseudohermaphrodite, known to be genetically female, received hormonal therapy and a hysterectomy and eventually proceeded, as a male, to priesthood ordination and a temple marriage.

How can we understand and ultimately reconcile the biological, social, religious, and moral questions posed by such situations? Clearly, there is no easy solution to these most intimate of human circumstances.

Moral Responsibility and Treatability

Confusion and misunderstanding surround homosexuality, and blatant hostility, rejection, and scorn are often directed toward those involved. Critics are often unable to find any redeeming qualities in the homosexual and often see the lifestyle as chosen and learned, refusing to acknowledge possible biological origins. A *Church News* editorial observed in 1978, "Then on what basis do the adherents to this practice demand special privilege? Who are they that they should parade their debauchery and call it clean? They even form their own churches and profess to worship the very God who denounces their behavior—and they do not repent. They form their own political groups and seek to compel the public to respect them. Do other violators of the law of God receive special consideration? Do the robbers, the thieves, the adulterers?" (16 Dec. 1978, 16). Many gays internalize and accept religion and society's abhorrence of their sexual preference and become their own persecutors.

What lies behind these reactions to the homosexual? The severe homophobic is perhaps easiest to understand. These people often harbor serious fears about their own sexual identity. They overcompensate by bullying and brutally teasing gays. Projecting and displacing hatred is a common and convenient way to run from one's own inner conflict.

Many people in and out of the church seem to want homosexuals held fully accountable for their sexual feelings and behavior. Yet if conscious choice is not involved, can we legitimately invoke the charge of sin? And if homosexuals do not act on these sexual feelings, have they morally transgressed? Does the revealed word of God in the scriptures supersede the experience and reality of millions of homoerotic individuals? Is it morally responsible to offer promises of cure? What of the larger question in some minds: Would God have anything to do with the creation of homosexuals or transsexuals? What kind of tricks has nature played on us humans? Does the new psychobiology challenge our treasured concepts of human responsibility and free will? Does human destiny reside in the intricate workings of the hormones and the spiral helix of DNA?

The question of treatment and curability of homosexuality is just as controversial as is its causes. "Treatment implies disease. Disease implies cure and the duty to seek or to strive for cure. Many ordinary people, as well as those judges who sentence homosexuals to some form of therapy in lieu of prison, believe that homosexuality is like dandruff, a condition that one can get rid of if one will only take the trouble" (Maddox 1982, 156). In 1973 the American Psychiatric Association (APA) voted to remove homosexuality from its diagnostic manual of mental disorders. Gay activists demonstrated in San Francisco in support of this decision.

Homosexuals were to be distinguished from heterosexuals only by their choice of an erotic object. This variation of human sexuality implied no impairment in judgment, stability, or reliability. An APA statement issued after the vote said of the resolution, "This is not to say that homosexuality is 'normal' or that it is as desirable as heterosexuality" (Roche Report 1974, 8). The debate over treatment issues was never settled by the landmark decision, and attempts to change orientation and behavior of homosexuals continues.

Masters and Johnson's 1979 book, *Homosexuality in Perspective*, has been applauded for its aims but ridiculed for the secrecy surrounding the research techniques and claims of a nearly 75 percent cure rate. Treatment was concentrated in a fourteen-day format with a strong emphasis on behavioral change with a heterosexual partner of the opposite sex. Thoughtful critics suggested that Masters and Johnson were actually treating bisexuals or maladjusted heterosexuals and ignored the psychological aspects of fantasies, emotional attachments and crushes, and arousal patterns of true homosexuals (Marano 1979). Aversion therapy treats subjects with electric shocks or drugs designed to induce vomiting when they are shown pornographic male photos. Many homosexuals find these methods especially onerous. As poet W. H. Auden said, "Of course, Behaviorism 'works.' So does torture" (in Maddox 1982, 167).

In one elaborately structured, four-part study, N. McConaghy of the University of New South Wales, Sydney, Australia, asserted that while homosexual arousal and behavior can be reduced by aversive therapy, a true homosexual orientation cannot be reversed. One hundred and fifty-seven homosexual patients were treated with various forms of behavior therapy. The majority desired to have conscious homosexual feelings reduced or eliminated. The homosexuals lost their strong arousal patterns and sensed a resultant weakening of homosexual feelings. Their basic orientation, however, remained unaltered. No evidence indicates that other treatments are more effective in reducing homosexual and increasing heterosexual behavior (Coogan 1977).

In recent years attempts to cure homosexuality have been replaced by therapeutic goals and strategies designed to improve the quality of life for homosexuals (Lowenstein 1984; Davison

1976). My clinical experience demonstrates that fewer people enter treatment seeking to change their sexual orientation; rather they come to deal with the anxiety, depression, and conflict attendant to their specific interpersonal struggles, losses, and fears. From my perspective changing a patient's homosexual nature presents the same challenge as would changing the orientation of a committed heterosexual. Yet since sexuality represents a spectrum of feelings and behaviors, some individuals can plausibly shift along that spectrum to some degree. (The cure reports in the literature come most likely from those people who are both highly motivated to change and have a relatively modest move to make along the continuum between homosexuality and heterosexuality.)

Where does this leave the majority of homosexuals, male and female, who have never experienced significant heterosexual feelings or fantasies even though they may have struggled in vain to arouse them? They have been told, "Homosexuality and like practices are deep sins; they can be cured; they can be forgiven. Sin is still sin and always will be. It will not change. Society might relax in its expectations; it may accept improprieties but that does not make such right and approved. Total transformation in ideas, standards, actions, thoughts, and programs can cleanse you" (*Church News*, 16 Dec. 1978, 16).

To remain active, loyal, guilt-free, and accepted in the Mormon church, homosexuals must do two things—remain celibate and abstain from engaging in eroticism with a member of one's own sex. This is *the* moral choice with which they are faced. They did not choose to be homosexual with any conscious, reasoned intent. Nor for that matter did any heterosexual choose to be straight. As I have argued, we all awaken to our sexual identity. The questions of moral responsibility come after this awakening. The moral agony for the committed Latter-day Saint who happens to be gay will often last for a lifetime. As Brenda Maddox has stated, "Those who want their gayness and God too are going to have a long struggle. They are asking that the churches, by nature conservative, give up their interest in the personal life of their clergymen and change their philosophy of the purpose of marriage. For full equality under the sacrament, gay Christians may have to wait until easier questions are settled, questions like the ordination of women and the gender of God" (1982, 194).

My clinical experience has indicated that the majority of Mormon homosexuals eventually drift away from their faith, live tenuously in the closet, or react with angry disillusionment. They ask, "Why did God make me this way?" That question should trouble all of us. Granted we do live in a natural universe where biological uncertainties and ambiguities are obvious. Biological equality at birth is a myth. Intelligence, athletic skill, handedness, musical and artistic talent, and a host of other characteristics vary widely among Homo sapiens. Yet the Mormon homosexual faces a peculiar distress. He or she is commanded to reject the behavior as well as the feelings and fantasies that invade the consciousness of sexual awareness.

Marvin Rytting challenges us to imagine being a confirmed heterosexual suddenly transported to a culture where homosexuality is the norm. Consider the dilemma of facing a hostile majority who insists that, "I must be erotically aroused by men and that it is a sin, a crime, and an illness for me to be attracted to women." He describes the fantasy of going into therapy with a good behaviorist and submitting to multiple shocks to suppress his attraction to naked women. "I can picture myself claiming to be cured to avoid the shocks, but I cannot imagine really being cured," he admits (1983, 78). . . .

In many minds homosexuals do not love but only indulge their sexual appetites in an endless orgy of promiscuous encounters. During the pre-AIDS era, a substantial number of homosexuals did exhibit this behavior. A Kinsey Institute study completed on a large sample of San Francisco gays revealed that "the average male subject had had more than five hundred sexual partners in his lifetime. Among the white males in the study, 28 percent reported more than a thousand" (Maddox 1982, 195). I know of no post-AIDS figures, but I would suspect a significant drop in such behavior.

Such findings are repugnant to most people and reinforce the hostility to the homosexual population as a whole. Yet San Francisco, California, is not Provo, Utah, and sensitive, quiet, industrious gay people live in both communities. Love, commitment, sharing, and caring are not virtues restricted to heterosexuals.

Homosexuality is a part of the human condition. Concerns about responsibility swirl around this issue and range from the conviction that "everything is your fault" to "nothing is your fault." The same can be said for a myriad of other human conditions as diverse as poverty, mental illness, drug abuse, and obesity. Clearly pursuing an extreme position is pointless. We sometimes labor under the illusion that we have more free choice than we can sensibly expect. We are slowly learning the limitations that our biological nature imposes on us. Yet we are also intentional, rational, spiritual, and moral beings who cannot escape the freedom that consciousness and agency grant to us. How we balance this uneasy alliance between our nature and our nurture is what makes us human.

I do not know the answers, and I suspect that no one among us does. Perhaps the best we can hope for is the willingness to reject prejudice, ignorance, and self-righteousness and to embrace tolerance and understanding. Finally, only fools will fail to recognize that the world brims with such existential and spiritual dilemmas, and the vast majority of these riddles have no simple, tidy solutions. My final question is, "Which of you wishes to shoulder the ultimate moral responsibility when dealing with such profound mysteries?"

References

Anonymous. *Prologue.* Provo, UT: Prometheus Enterprises, 1978.

Bennion, John. "The Interview." *Dialogue: A Journal of Mormon Thought* 18 (Summer 1985): 167-76.

Clark, Matt, et al. "AIDS." *Newsweek,* 12 Aug. 1985, 20-27.

Coogan, J. P., ed. "Is Homosexuality Reversible?" *Today in Psychiatry,* 1977, 6.

Cooper, Arnold M. "Will Neurobiology Influence Psychoanalysis?" *The American Journal of Psychiatry* 142 (Dec. 1985): 1395-1402.

Davison, G. "Homosexuality: The Ethical Challenge." *Journal of Consulting and Clinical Psychiatry* 44 (1976): 157-62.

Dorner, G., et al. "Stressful Events in Prenatal Life of Bi- and Homosexual Men." *Experimental Clinical Endocrinology* 81 (1983): 83-87.

Hales, Dianne. "Testosterone, the Hormone of Desire." *XL,* Sept. 1984, 23.

Humphreys, Laud. *Tearoom Trade: Impersonal Sex in Public Places.* Chicago, IL: Aldine-Atherton, 1970.

Jeffery, Duane E. "Intersexes in Humans: An Introductory Exploration." *Dialogue: A Journal of Mormon Thought* 12 (Autumn 1979):
107-13.

Kallman, F. J. "A Comparative Twin Study on the Genetic Aspects of
Male Homosexuality." *Journal of Nervous and Mental Disorders* 115
(1952): 283.

Keller, Jeffrey E. "Question: Is Sexual Gender Eternal?" *Sunstone* 10
(1986): 38-39.

Kimball, Spencer W. *The Miracle of Forgiveness.* Salt Lake City:
Bookcraft, 1969.

Kolb, L. S. "Therapy of Homosexuality." In *Current Psychiatric Therapies,*
ed. J. Masserman. New York: Grune and Stratton, 1963. Vol. 3,
p. 3.

Lowenstein, L. F., and K. B. Lowenstein. "Homosexuality: A Review of
the Research Between 1978-1983." *British Journal of Project Psychology and Personality Study* 29 (Dec. 1984): 21-24.

McConaghy, N. In *British Journal of Psychiatry,* Dec. 1976. Summarized
as "Is Homosexuality Reversible?" in *Today in Psychiatry,* a leaflet
published monthly by Borland-Coogan Associated, Inc., for Abbott
Laboratories, North Chicago, IL.

MacCulloch, Malcolm J., and John L. Waddington. "Neuroendocrine
Mechanisms and Aetiology of Male and Female Homosexuality."
British Journal of Psychiatry 139 (Oct. 1981): 341-45.

Maddox, Brenda. *Married and Gay: An Intimate Look at a Different
Relationship.* New York: Harcourt Brace Jovanovich, 1982.

Marano, Hara. "New Light on Homosexuality." *Medical World News* 20
(30 Apr. 1979): 8-19.

Marmor, Judd. "Homosexuality and Sexual Orientation Disturbances."
In *The Sexual Experience.* Baltimore, MD: Williams & Williams,
1976, 374-90.

———, ed. *Sexual Inversion: The Multiple Roots of Homosexuality.* New
York: Basic Books, 1965.

Masters, William H., and Virginia E. Johnson. *Homosexuality in Perspective.* Boston: Little, Brown and Co., 1979.

Money, John W. "Gender-Transposition Theory and Homosexual
Genesis." *Journal of Sex & Marital Therapy* 10 (Summer 1984): 75-
82.

Roche Report. "Deleting Homosexuality as Illness: A Psychiatric Challenge to Values." *Frontiers of Psychiatry* 4 (1 Feb. 1974): 8.

Rytting, Marvin. "Paradoxes and Perplexities." *Sunstone* 8 (Jan.-Apr.
1983): 74-79.

Stoller, Robert J., and Gilbert H. Herdt. "Theories of Origins of Male
Homosexuality." *Archives of General Psychiatry* 42 (April 1985): 399-
404.

Zuger, B. "Early Effeminate Behavior in Boys: Outcome and Significance for Homosexuality." *Journal of Nervous and Mental Disorders* 172 (1984): 90-97.

TWENTY-THREE

A Therapist's Counsel
for Married Homosexuals

▼

Carlfred Broderick

I think we are seeing more husbands who, after several years of marriage, confess to their wives that they are gay. I suppose it happens the other way around too. What can a couple who loves each other do in such a case?

I do see couples who are faced with this issue. In my own experience it has mostly been the husband who is revealed to have been gay all those years. It makes a difference though how the revelation comes about. Often the wife simply discovers his homosexual activities as another woman might find out about her husband's heterosexual affair. She may get a tip from a friend. She may find incriminating notes or overhear a telephone conversation. She may discover she has contracted a venereal disease and confront him with the fact. In such cases there is not only the problem of the homosexuality itself but also resentment and the

---

"A Therapist's Counsel for Married Homosexuals" is excerpted from Carlfred Broderick, *Couples: How to Confront Problems and Maintain Loving Relationships* (New York: Simon and Schuster, 1979). Dr. Broderick is professor of sociology and Director of the Marriage and Family Therapy Program at the University of California at Los Angeles. He resides in Cerritos, California.

feeling of betrayal that is part of any infidelity.

It is substantially different when the gay partner comes to his wife and tells her that he loves her and has been struggling with a problem that has finally become too much for him to handle alone. He doesn't want to hurt her, but he feels she needs to know that he is gay. Often such scenes are tender. Tears are shed on both sides, and the couple works together on handling the problem without destroying their relationship.

. . . If a couple should agree that for them the solution is a renewed commitment to their relationship, with a forswearing on his part of all extramarital sexual activities, he may find it more difficult than would a man with a heterosexual involvement. In addition to detaching himself from a loving relationship with another person, he is likely to have to withdraw from a whole network of friends, from a covert life-style that may have been deeply valued, and from a definition of himself as intrinsically and irreversibly gay.

We don't know much about what makes one person gay, another straight, and a third capable of both kinds of attraction. It is my philosophy, however, that if the couple hopes to survive, the gay partner has to accept not only the fact that he is homosexual but also that he is a free agent, capable at least of choosing what he will *do* if not how he feels. There is a great deal of rhetoric in the gay movement to the effect that a person cannot and must not fight his own homosexual nature. I guess I believe that the fundamental human qualities of love, commitment, patience, and loyalty have almost nothing to do with whether a person is homosexual or heterosexual. When a person is in touch with these basic qualities in himself, he can handle the other issues with more confidence.

I would not pretend that this is an easy issue to deal with, but I have seen a number of couples who have dealt compassionately and constructively with the challenge and have achieved a deeper and more satisfying marriage as a result.

TWENTY-FOUR

Difficult Choices for Adolescents and Adults

▼

Ron Schow and Marybeth Raynes

In the past few years we have become acquainted with many Mormons who are struggling with their sexual orientation. Some are teenagers or young adults wondering how to build a life in a world of homophobia. Others are adult women and men who have struggled for years with their attraction and are in various stages of acceptance or ambivalence about their identity. Still others are partners in heterosexual marriages. Some hoped or expected that their homosexuality would disappear with marriage; some want children and an acceptable life regardless of the cost; some are living a double life.

As these people struggle with questions of sexual orientation, they seek advice from LDS church counselors, traditional psychotherapists, or counselors within the gay/lesbian community. We would like to describe here the approaches of these three groups. Then we will discuss a number of alternatives and choices we have seen Mormon homosexuals and bisexuals pursue.

Therapy services available within the church, such as LDS Social Services, are generally concerned with changing orientation and behavior. While this may be appropriate for some it is inappropriate for others. Some bishops and church counselors allow a

189

person to discover and/or acknowledge her or his sexual orientation, but the majority of church authorities or counselors view
homosexuality as deviant. Unfortunately the distinction between
feelings and behavior may not always be emphasized as being two
different things, and people may be made to feel sinful simply for
having homoerotic feelings.

Outside of church circles most academic and therapeutic experts argue that no attempt should be made to change homosexual
orientation or behavior. The best course is to discover for oneself
where one's deepest attractions lie and build a life around these.

The gay community often communicates to outsiders an
"either/or" mentality. People are either gay or straight. If someone
has gay tendencies he or she is most likely gay, and therefore there
is little that can be done about it. If men and women are to find
any measure of happiness, they must acknowledge their gayness or
straightness and live a life consistent with it.

Because of the current chasm between the religious and
therapeutic worlds, many Mormons who experience dissonance
remain confused and torn. In our view there are elements in these
different positions that are defensible and appropriate. We are
inclined to consider the possibility that homosexual orientation in
some circumstances is subject to accommodation, particularly
when it is not strongly preferred. To suggest that someone has
homosexual feelings and therefore has only one choice about how
he or she lives does not seem consistent to us. But we are also
impressed with the position that homosexuality simply is and that
the path toward mental health and integration is to acknowledge
this. Change will not occur easily and one may struggle all during
his or her life to do so without success. Nevertheless, many people
are left facing two diametrically opposed choices rather than a
number of possibilities. This either/or perception is particularly
difficult for adolescents who may not have more developed thinking skills or experience to inform their choices.

We believe these two narrow, opposite positions develop from
a limited view of love and sexuality. These views are often supported by the notion that sexual feeling has only one direction: it
is either homosexual or heterosexual. Kinsey and his associates
(1948) used a seven-point scale from zero (exclusively heterosexual)
to six (exclusively homosexual). The content of dreams and fan-

tasies, as well as thoughts, feelings, and activities of a sexual nature, were all used to place persons at an appropriate position on the scale. They found that about 70 percent of twenty-year-old men rated zero, nearly one-fourth rated from 1 to 5, and 5 percent rated 6 (Table 147). Thus it appears that of those with some homosexual orientation, there are many more bisexuals than exclusive homosexuals. The percentages for female homosexual orientations were approximately half what they were for males (Kinsey et al. 1953). Furthermore, the findings suggested that beginning in young adulthood 30 percent of all males between the ages of sixteen and fifty-five years experience some homosexual feeling or behavior for at least a three-year period. A much smaller percentage of the females continued their homosexual activities for as long as the males.

There is an additional component to homosexuality that is not often discussed: affectional orientation. In certain heterosexual relationships sexual feelings and behavior are an important but minor part. A larger concern is with whom one's affections, dreams, and closest emotional intimacy contacts are linked. Apart from sexual feeling, many people say that they identify more closely with, understand, and want to be around people of the same sex. Probably the majority of these people will identify themselves as heterosexual and will have a comfortable split between those to whom they are affectionately tied and those to whom they are sexually attracted. For others, the affectional and sexual are integrated.

How then should people go about deciding the sexual direction for their lives? This is a real dilemma, especially for the young person who is experiencing an emerging ambivalent sexuality. It is equally difficult for older men and women who may be single and have not solved this dilemma. And it is excruciating for people in heterosexual marriages who find themselves attracted (affectionally and sexually) to members of their own gender.

A productive approach, considering the high frequency of homosexual feeling, might be to move the emphasis from whether or not such feelings are sinful and a matter of choice to the more profitable discussion of how we express or direct same-sex feelings when they are present. People may not have a choice about where they are on the Kinsey Scale, but most men and women can decide how to proceed with living, especially if they are in the bisexual range (2-4 on the scale). Furthermore, it is fairly clear from research that even though positioning on the Kinsey Scale provides some clarification, it does not totally dictate one's behavioral choices. For some, their position on the scale shifts throughout life (Kinsey et al. 1948; McWhirter, Sanders, and Reinisch 1990).

Many homosexual Mormons have made a range of choices over the years. In Mormon society, we find many single individuals despite strong pressures to marry. Some of these people are doubtless strong in their heterosexual feelings, but a number of these single men and women are single because of homosexual feelings (sexual or affectional). An isolated example of such a single person and of one choice (celibacy) is illustrated in the personal essay "Solus" published anonymously in *Dialogue: A Journal of Mormon Thought* (1976). The author describes his difficulties as a former missionary who is still committed to the church but frustrated by his gay feelings which he has not acted upon. Another option is illustrated in the lives of some twenty-five lesbian women who lived together mainly as couples in Salt Lake City in the 1920s and 1930s. They maintained their church membership and were basically treated as widows or as inactives needing special church support (Bullough 1978).

Despite these limited examples, the secrecy and societal shame of homosexuality have generally left us with little public or private awareness that Mormons have been and are faced with these choices and that they have made them in diverse ways. To increase general awareness, we offer the following accounts to describe the options some LDS people have taken. Many of them are derived from actual clients, others are composites. In every case, the identities have been changed.

John is in his late twenties, has finished graduate school, and is about to embark on his first professional job. He has had a wide range of relationships with both sexes and describes his social life as lively and complex. He is about equally attracted to both sexes. In his words: "It is not easy for me to say 'I'm bisexual.' The term itself disturbs me because it expands my realm of intimacy in a way which actually imposes severe limitations on my life choices. I honestly wish that I was only attracted to one gender or the other. I look at my gay friends and wish that I had not had sexually satisfying experiences with women. I look at my heterosexual friends and hate them for not having the capacity to understand the part of me that has had sexually satisfying experiences with men."

John easily discusses his childhood in a traditional Mormon home in rural Utah with an accompanying strong belief in the church. He went on a mission, and although he was aware of sexual impulses and urges, he was completely celibate and lived church standards. Throughout college he dated, loved women, and became engaged. But judging himself not ready for marriage, he went to graduate school single. He found his first homosexual experience "wonderful." Since that time he has had relationships with both sexes but describes his actual sexual contact as limited. In fact he reports that "during this period I was also experiencing two forms of religious guilt. I was either feeling guilty for being homosexual or feeling guilty for having intimate sexual contact with women."

Currently John is looking for a committed relationship, which he wants to be life long and sexually monogamous. He says, "I can actually imagine having that relationship with either a woman or a man. I honestly believe the important questions for me will be whether I love the person and whether we are compatible. I hope that the person will be a woman, primarily because I realize that life would be easier in a heterosexual marriage and because the possibility of children is stronger. However, I also know that I could have that relationship with a man."

Dan has been aware of his interest in other boys since childhood and sought friendships with many. One or two felt like "true friends," his term for his same-sex attraction. Now fifteen, he feels caught by two opposing forces. He feels a growing sexual attraction to some of his friends and describes one or two periods in which he says he was intensely obsessed with one of them. Naturally friendly with girls, he reports no interest other than feeling they would make good sisters. He is religiously devout but has a difficult time listening to church leaders and others say homosexuality is a sin. Feelings of panic emerge when he thinks of his parents finding out about him. He also reports that his episodes of obsession were accompanied by increased prayer and guilt. His guilt rose dramatically when he had a couple of sexual encounters with other males. Currently he reports losing hope that he will find answers for himself and is gradually becoming depressed. Lately he describes spontaneous thoughts of dying as a way out.

Judy is in her late forties and has been single and celibate her entire life. She teaches school and has a wide range of experience with many types of students. She owns her own home, is physically active, and has many friends. She describes a Mormon childhood identical to most other Mormon childhoods on the outside. On the inside, her family is split into different factions, and she feels unseen and unsupported by them.

She has had the usual interest in marriage and children and feels sad, sometimes for years, that she never has had an intimate relationship with a man. Ten years ago she became emotionally intimate with a good friend, who gradually disclosed her lesbian orientation. Judy loved Sue but never felt she could become sexually involved because she was not interested in her erotically, nor did she want to disobey church teachings. Over time the relationship became polarized because Sue felt Judy was not willing to be close enough. A long difficult period ensued, and Judy finally left the relationship. She now feels that the relationship was abusive to her and clearly sees herself as not lesbian. She feels still strongly interested in women's issues and women friends. Judging from the range of activities and friends she has, she is at home with women.

Dirk grew up in a small community ward, filled a mission and then returned to work in his father's business. He lived at home with his parents, almost never dated, and in his late twenties and early thirties was assigned in the ward to work with the young men. He was the MIA secretary and assistant priesthood advisor over a period of several years. He clearly enjoyed working with these young men. He was attentive and interested in their activities and would systematically engage them in conversation. He never married but throughout his later life performed extensive church service.

Extreme shyness around women would have made it difficult for Dirk to marry under any circumstances. Yet his attraction for and fraternizing with young men made it appear that he was craving same-sex friendship. While many other shy men are drawn to women and marry, Dirk's life is an example of one choice which may be made by a young man with homosexual tendencies.

Bill, who also lived in an LDS ward, presents a contrast to Dirk. Bill was handsome, drove a flashy car, and lived with his parents. When he was in his late twenties or early thirties, he hired some young men from the ward to work for him, and word soon spread that Bill was gay and made sexual advances. He would take the young men who worked for him and treat them to bowling or to meals at a local fast-food outlet. He attended church intermittently and approached other young men at community events like ball games.

There is little doubt about Bill's homosexuality, but it is interesting to consider his similarity with Dirk. Both Bill and Dirk found ways to reach out for intimate friendship. What was different about Dirk was his outwardly circumspect behavior. We do not know the Kinsey Scale rating for either of these two men. Nor do we know the intensity of sex drive which may have been an even more important variable with which they had to deal in making life choices.

Diedre is a tall woman who loves many things: the outdoors, animals, art, music, and particularly women. She is very clear on this last point and says the journey to self-awareness has been long and hard.

She grew up in a small town in the west, a stepdaughter of a mother whom she felt never loved her after her own mother had died. Diedre was sexually abused by her father and uncle. The abuse was not discussed in the family and still has not been openly confronted.[1]

Diedre fell in love with a girlfriend when she was eight and says she has been having crushes and has been falling in love since then. She never has been interested in men and has never had a sexual encounter with a man since the abuse. She says she is not opposed to men or even sex with men but that she is not interested.

Several times while Diedre was a teenager, her stepmother accused her of being lesbian, before she even knew what the term meant. So she says she did not admit this even to herself. As an adolescent she was active in the church and later went on a foreign language mission. Afterwards, her interest in women grew, and gradually she became sexually active. Then began a series of cycles. She would be in a relationship, drop out of church activity, and feel that one part of her life was being nurtured. The relationship would subsequently break up, she would return to church activity, and another part of her life would find fulfillment. After several cycles she dropped out of the church completely. She says she is still spiritually committed but cannot decide what to do about her belief in the church. Currently she is becoming interested in other spiritual systems as a way to investigate the spiritual side of herself.

Annette and *Susan* have been friends for about twenty years. In fact they have lived together, owned the same house, and wound their lives around each other for almost as long as they have known each other. They even look alike and hold most things in common, including unconventional jobs. In the LDS ward which they attend, most people assume they belong together, and almost all ward members treat them as a couple. But hardly any one thinks of them as lesbian or not completely committed to the church. Neither do they—they are not sexually active and never have been. They simply describe themselves as never being interested in men, in getting married, or in having children. They say they have heard all of the church's teachings about marriage and family but that it has not interested them. They enjoy their life together and cannot imagine any other way of living.

Melanie is married, has four children, and works at home part time. She is delighted with her children and likes to talk about them with others. She and her husband are good friends, and although they have been close in the past, his job is now demanding and they lead separate lives.

Only one of her friends knows that Melanie would have at one time preferred to be with another woman. While in college Melanie fell in love with Jean. The two were committed for at least two years and talked of spending their lives together. But as time went on, Melanie knew she could not put aside her wish to have children. She was raised in a large, extended Mormon family and did not want to confront the problems being lesbian would create. So she consciously chose to leave Jean and find a husband.

Now, however, she reports that her longing for the closeness she shared with Jean is returning. She likes her women friends but wants more intimacy than those friendships offer. Her marriage has never provided the same understanding for her that her relationship with Jean did. Still she says her children, her family, and the church are important to her, and so she feels she will continue her life as currently structured.

Mark grew up in the Mormon church but by fifteen had experienced several homosexual episodes. Recognizing his persistent homosexual feelings, he talked with his bishop who advised fasting and prayer. By age nineteen he could report several years of total sexual abstinence which qualified him to go on a mission. However, he was still troubled and talked with his bishop and a general authority about his homosexuality. His feelings persisted in the mission field. Counseling with his mission president, he was advised to marry quickly after his release. Returning home, he married within six months, but he was able to have sex with his wife only by thinking of men. Discouraged, depressed, and devastated by guilt, he divorced and turned to substance abuse. Soon he was an alcoholic. Only after years of therapy, participation in Alcoholics Anonymous, and development of a stable committed relationship with another gay Mormon has he been able to put his life together. He says that through prayer he found that the Lord loves him. He no longer hates himself or considers his life sinful.

Gary also grew up in the Mormon tradition, dated girls in high school and college, and went on a mission. In high school he engaged in some homosexual activities. Of his ten missionary companions he claims that two were homosexual. With one of these he slept in the same double bed, and they were eventually involved in non-orgasmic genital caressing. When they confessed to the mission president, he was understanding and recognized their otherwise excellent missionary work. He asked them to get another apartment with single beds. They did and discontinued their sexual activity. After his mission Gary dropped out of the church, moved to a distant city, and adopted a life in the gay community. He has now been in a stable monogamous gay relationship for fourteen years.

Hank's story is similar. He grew up in the church, experimented with homosexuality, and filled a mission. Unlike Gary, however, he married, hoping he could become a typical heterosexual with a family. He discovered that he could "fall in love" with a woman, have erotic experiences with her, father children, and for several years maintain sufficient normality that his wife did not suspect him of homosexual tendencies. However, realizing that he still had homosexual feelings, he began to seek opportunities to give that side of himself some expression. Rating himself as a 5 on the Kinsey Scale, he says there was a part of himself that he had buried, and he eventually left his wife. We believe people should be allowed to adjust marriage decisions made when they were inexperienced. Intolerable mismatches should be corrected, but be aware that the issues in a decision to pursue a homosexual orientation may not be essentially different from those in a decision by a heterosexual to leave an intolerable relationship.

Jay's story is the opposite of Hank's. Jay converted to Mormonism in his early teens. He graduated from LDS seminary and institute, filled a mission, and married in his late twenties. Along the way he "fooled around" with both girls and boys. As a senior in high school, he "fell in love" with one of his male classmates and later with his roommate in college. Neither of these other men shared the same sexual feeling, though they seemed to feel the same intensity of friendship in a platonic way. He engaged in sexual activities—such as mutual masturbation—with several friends. As a missionary there were no sexual incidents with companions, although he fell in love with a new "greenie" he was asked to train. He did not reveal his orientation to any of his companions.

Jay dated women but was not aroused by them sexually. He liked females and eventually chose one to marry whom he felt he loved. The idea of pursuing a homosexual life never occurred to him. He thought he would simply get into heterosexual activities with his wife and homosexual feelings would never again surface. Like others he found this expectation was inaccurate, and he continued to feel strong sexual attractions toward men. Nevertheless he and his wife have built a happy marriage based on a strong friendship, and they have three children. Only after they had been married for several years did he fully come to accept his bisexuality. He now places himself at 4 on the Kinsey Scale. He wants to stay in his marriage where he continues to find a satisfying if somewhat less than total expression of his sexual feelings. He doubts that he could find a relationship to match his current one even if his homosexual feelings could be given expression.

Jay says that he feels heterosexual relationships are essentially the same as homosexual ones and that homosexual erotic experience is indistinguishable from heterosexual experience—only the inconsequential details of technique are different. Other bisexuals feel that heterosexual marriages are distinctly different from homosexual relationships, and they and others may be offended by Jay's insistence that there is no significant difference. One factor which is also involved but not sufficiently recognized is affectional bonding. If identification occurs more strongly with members of the same sex and accompanies sexual experiences with them, this may cause some bisexuals to feel that erotic experience with one sex is different from the other.

Linda recently made a startling discovery. She thinks she may be interested in women and is confused. She was staying overnight with some other young women at a high school function and noticed her feelings become more intense throughout the evening towards one of her friends. Both fell into a long discussion lasting the night and during which both were oblivious of the rest of the group. She felt happy the next day, and the details of the evening, including Janet's appearance, kept revolving in her head. A night dream of affectionate hugging startled her because the feelings were more intense than "just friends." Linda started dating in this last year and says she likes men but prefers going in groups of people to various activities. Nothing has happened like the evening talk with Janet. They see each other all the time, but Linda is confused about the exact nature of their friendship. She says she cannot talk to her mother as she once did, and her other friends say she is acting strangely.

Lyman has several children, twenty years of a good marriage, and works as a trade school instructor. He is another example of someone who seems to have made traditional marriage work. He has undergone excommunication from the LDS church to satisfy feelings of guilt for his homosexuality. Lyman reports that he finds quiet fulfillment for his sexual feelings with his students. Like heterosexual teachers who are attracted to their students, Lyman gives only non-sexual expression to these feelings.

Lyman's wife struggles with her husband's homosexuality. He has told her about his experiences before marriage and tries to keep the discussion open between them. Nevertheless she reports some fears and tries to monitor Lyman's activities, especially when they are going through times of stress. There have been a few blow-ups when she felt Lyman was hiding something. Additionally, she says that she misses being desired sexually. She also says that their sexual relationship is satisfying, but she does not feel cherished in the way that she dreamed of before marriage. Finally, she often feels alienated from other married women because she has kept the particulars of her own marriage secret.

Cheryl was converted to the Mormon church as a teenager and felt it was a help to her after years of depression and isolation. Within two years of joining, she attended Brigham Young University on a scholarship, graduating with honors four years later. While she was living in a dormitory, a roommate became emotionally close to her, then sexually intrusive, and finally abusive one night. Confused, Cheryl went to her bishop to sort things out. She felt blamed for what now to her was rape. The bishop asked her to return several times. After awhile she stopped going because she felt that although the bishop was well intentioned, he was not helpful. Within a few months she moved out.

Shortly afterward she met another woman with whom she felt attached. Then Cheryl says she understood that she had had small infatuations with other girls but that since she was so introverted and isolated, she had not had enough contact to know how much she enjoyed women. Despite this she wanted to get married and for several years wanted children. However, her relationships with men never had the same depth as with women.

Cheryl's commitment to the church continued, as did her interest in women. Her visits to various church leaders also continued episodically. Over time she says that the church was abusive and that in at least two cases bishops were so intrusive that it felt to her like "institutionalized voyeurism." As the conflict intensified over time, she felt no help was given and left the church.

She currently is in a long-term homosexual relationship which she describes as happy and fulfilling. Cheryl is not an idealist, not having had an idyllic life, and says that her relationship has the same issues and concerns that heterosexual relationships have and that the process of working through the issues is continuous. However, she says her relationship provides the depth and nourishment she wants.

Ellen is a professional woman in a lesbian relationship of four years. She has been married twice and has one adult child. She feels that she has been interested in men erotically and romantically for most of her life and indeed has had normal sexual interest during her two marriages despite conflict in both. However, she knows that she has always been more emotionally connected to women than to men. For years, since her mid-twenties, she has characterized herself as a feminist and has read widely in women's issues.

Some time after her second divorce, she fell in love for the first time with a woman, which happened quite unexpectedly. She then went through a two-year period of sifting out her inclinations and priorities regarding women and men, the LDS church, and herself. Although committed to the church until her early thirties, she had been only partly active at the time of her first experience with a woman because of a long-term crisis of faith surrounding many issues. That sifting process continued despite a break-up in her first relationship. She finally understood that it was not necessary to categorize herself as strictly straight or gay. She felt some core needs had been filled by a woman that she had never experienced with a man. She met her current partner within a year after her break-up and reports feeling more committed and connected with her partner than during either of her marriages.

These varied case studies illustrate a range of available choices. Clearly, it is difficult for a person who is Mormon and homosexual to make a choice or accommodation that fits both dimensions. The split between the Mormon world view and homosexual reality is so strong that many gay people, feeling caught between two forces that are of life-and-death importance to them, undergo years of intense turmoil.

Adolescents cannot easily choose any option. The possibility of a committed relationship, regardless of direction, will not come for years. Dating or feeling a bond of love may take a similar path of affectionate and sexual unfolding as for heterosexual teens—but this must occur secretly. Even if celibacy is chosen, what about the kissing and hugging that heterosexual teens find permissible and pleasurable? Any same-sex touching is defined by many as sinful, so celibacy can be more rigorous with more anxiety and guilt. Given the difficulties with keeping self-esteem intact during this period, it is probably important to establish an ongoing relationship with a therapist who understands both the homosexual and Mormon influence in an adolescent's life.

So what choices are available to someone who wishes to integrate both the Mormon and homosexual facets of their lives? The following are possible, but not all inclusive, alternatives.

Celibacy. One option is to remain celibate as Judy or Dirk have done. Within this choice, other alternatives emerge. For those who remain single, some may have relationships with no physical contact. Others may find affection and/or limited sexual interaction possible within their own ethical guidelines. Another choice is to enter a committed, but celibate, relationship in order to adhere to the church's moral code (as have Annette and Susan). This is most workable for those who normally have little interest in sex, but who are emotionally attached to or fall in love with someone of the same gender.

Single and Non-celibate. This choice is fraught with conflict for those who wish to remain Mormon. Some, however, choose the conflict and guilt rather than give up either side of their being. The toll of maintaining a delicate balance of secrecy and conflict is so great over time that either being actively Mormon or being sexually active will often predominate. For those who become inactive, the commitment to Mormon teachings may not wane, and so how one is Mormon and simultaneously homosexual continues as an important life issue. We strongly recommend that those choosing this alternative seek professional consultation while sorting through the intense conflict.

Homosexual Marriage. Another option is to choose a committed, monogamous relationship with a same sex partner as Gary did. Although not often legally sanctioned (some cities and insurance companies are increasingly recognizing long-term homosexual unions), the partners, as in Cheryl's case, view themselves as married and consider fidelity, commitment, and the need to work on the relationship as seriously as heterosexuals. They are also willing to face negative social responses in order to keep their commitment permanent. Committed homosexual relationships present challenges beyond the usual challenges in heterosexual marriages. Nevertheless, many gay or lesbian partnerships have been successful, as in Gary's and Cheryl's cases, and those individuals who have a life which includes many sexual partners or highly compulsive sexual activities do not characterize the values of many in the gay community at large. For gays and lesbians alike, committed relationships can be very satisfying. They are attracted to the person, his or her personality, his or her way of being—just as in heterosexual relationships. For lesbians particularly the ideal of monogamy is strong and interest in sexual activity varies greatly, just as with straight women. (For a discussion of lesbian and gay marriages, see Berzon 1988; Blumstein and Schwartz 1983.)

How a gay couple works out a committed relationship in the context of the Mormon culture is problematic. Regardless of how the gay/lesbian and Mormon influences are woven into the marriage, plenty of supporting resources and relationship skills are needed to confront additional dilemmas. Since it is impossible to be openly homosexually married and actively Mormon at the same time, finding role models is a rarity. The few examples cited above (Annette and Susan or Ellen) can be compared with other information on such couples outside Mormon culture.

Heterosexual Marriage. A heterosexual marriage may also be chosen. However, if one's preference for one's own sex is strong (a 5 or 6 on the Kinsey Scale, for example) the risks involved in marrying someone of the opposite gender are high. Increasingly within and without church circles, such marriages are discouraged. This choice should only be considered if a person has romantic, erotic feelings and inclinations toward the opposite sex that are nearly as strong if not stronger than toward one's own gender. The difficulties in keeping romance and sexual activity alive in heterosexual marriage are difficult enough without the impediment of little interest to start with.

There are those who choose marriage despite a strong history of same-sex activity or inclination. For those who decide to go ahead, one or two guidelines are important. The future spouse should know about one's sexual history, fantasies, and preferences. In heterosexual marriages in which the husband is gay and the wife is straight, the adjustment is more likely to be favorable if the wife knows ahead of time. The research regarding prior knowledge has found that wives who did not know prior to the marriage feel betrayed, with an accompanying loss of self-esteem. Most of these marriages never reach satisfactory adjustment. Partners who do know ahead of time make an informed choice, and their decision is based on friendship and willingness to work to achieve a life that includes social sanction, children, and church blessing. If indeed there is a strong friendship prior to marriage, the chances for adjustment are better.

After marriage couples should receive competent help if the marriage interaction is unsatisfactory or is deteriorating. It will probably not get better by itself. However, an effort to openly confront problems and see if a solid base underlies the difficulties is an important first step. Coleman (1985) provides additional insights into conflicts and resolutions in marriage for bisexual and gay men from a therapist's point of view.

As stated before, all alternatives are fraught with difficulty. There are no simple decisions that can bring one's faith and one's orientation into easy congruence. In addition to the options discussed, several other guidelines for making choices about one's life and loves are offered below.

1. *Carefully analyze feelings and experiences on the Kinsey Scale.* Bell (1976) recommends separate scale placement for feelings and for behavior as a beginning point in resolving sexual orientation difficulties. Those with homosexual feelings experience eroticism for those of the same sex. Eroticism implies erotic character or sentiment, sexual desire, or love in any of its physical or psychic manifestations. Many people, according to Kinsey, have some explicit homosexual experiences and even more have subtle feelings of attraction, dreams, fantasy, or near sexual responses at some time in connection with a member of the same sex. One should not assume, however, that same-sex feelings or activity necessarily reveal core identity. The Kinsey data show that half of all males and one fourth of all females have same-sex attractions or experiences after the beginning of adolescence, and that most who experiment with homosexuality eventually choose to accommodate their lives to heterosexual behavior. Apparently for them, sexual feelings and experiences with the opposite sex are dominant in their older teenage and mature years. They then move into a firm, heterosexual identity. Difficulties arise, however, when sexual and/or affectional desire for the same sex is more predominant and persists into adulthood.

2. *Be aware that homosexual feelings are not likely to disappear.* Those who have some homosexual orientation but are closer to the heterosexual end of the Kinsey Scale will likely have more chance for success in a heterosexual relationship, but they should not expect homosexual feelings to go away. They should base their judgment on the degree of heterosexuality they feel and consider

whether it is sufficient to sustain a long-term relationship. When homosexual orientation and eroticism are evident for a substantial time (perhaps as long as three years after reaching adulthood), such feelings probably will persist indefinitely, though change toward bisexuality may occur and allow some movement on the Kinsey Scale over time.

3. *Be aware that love and sexual feelings are often intense and decisions about their expression need to be made with care.* Young people with some degree of homosexual orientation may have special challenges in military and Mormon missionary service. For those who experience intense and frequent sexual impulses, the temptation to act without thinking is often overwhelming. If so, they should seek help to understand their feelings and possible actions and to understand their moral and ethical choices.

For those whose personal moral code is similar or identical to the church's, the struggle to abstain will be difficult and should be separated from the issue of sexual orientation. Should they violate their own value system, the road back to congruence is through change or, in church terms, repentance. In dealing with guilt, they should remember that change is a necessary part of coming back to congruence for anyone with an internalized conscience. However, going outside of one's values does not make one bad or evil. Internal worth is not tarnished; outside actions just need realignment.

Homosexual Mormons may eventually conclude that some form of sexual activity fits within their value code. Most people develop a complex and sensitive awareness of what is right and wrong as they pay attention to the effects of their actions on themselves and others. As that moral code develops, gay Mormons should pay attention to the effects on others and to their internal self worth and spiritual strength. Again, they should seek a trusted friend or therapist who values them above the individual choices they make on this difficult path.

4. *In the longer run, sexual satisfactions will probably be secondary to relationship satisfactions.* As choices are made people should try to place sexuality into appropriate perspective. Sexual activity is an important part of life. But it generally takes a secondary and complementary role to a greater goal—finding and developing fulfilling relationships with people who share similar values, goals,

and emotional ties. While the gender of these people may be male or female, one's happiness in life and quality of sexual activity will be tied to the strength of the overall relationship which one achieves.

5. *Be wary of seeking sexual fulfillment at any cost.* If people attach too many conditions to the kind of sexual activity they must have to achieve satisfaction, they are apt to be disappointed regardless of their sexual orientation. The most solid lives, celibate or sexually active, heterosexual or homosexual, are based on the quality of relationship, the depth of friendship between partners. The same principles apply for choosing and staying in committed relationships regardless of orientation.

6. *One must make his or her own inspired choices.* No one else can decide how important sexuality will be for a person in his or her life. People may seek the advice of friends, professional help, spiritual counsel, divine inspiration, but all of us are still ultimately responsible for our decisions. Sex is clearly more important for some than for others. There is ample evidence of the tragedies that occur when people are forced into normative behavior which is "unnatural" for them. Possibly more damage occurs when a coercive process is used to make a person be a certain way than when mistakes are evaluated and corrected. People should learn to find their own inner sources of inspiration so that they can put the advice of others into perspective, as important resources not as direct commands.

Everyone develops continually. In one's lifetime several choices may be made depending on what is right for the person at the time. Each major decision should be made using *all* available sources, so that haphazard choices do not create so much damage and confusion that a person or others around him or her may take years recovering.

This is particularly pertinent for adolescents, who for adequate emotional development need to make several choices of dating partners before making a permanent choice. Additionally, gay youth are vulnerable to violent reactions from peers, such as leers, threats, and physical violence. The prospect of dating in any normal fashion is limited, but they should take time to explore their feelings, choices, and implications without rushing to a decision.

7. *One must try to make his or her choices work.* Having committed

to a permanent relationship or to remain single or celibate, one should make every effort to succeed. The difficulties of fidelity and trust in marriage are no different in homosexual and heterosexual unions. If a person is already in a marriage and sexual orientation is one of the central issues, he or she should seek help from a therapist who is not biased about final answers but can assist with the central issues of the marriage as well as help the individual. Often other concerns besides orientation are just as important in the decision about the direction the marriage should take—or whether it should be terminated.

8. *If relationship adjustments become necessary, they should be made with integrity.* If the relationship ultimately requires adjustment or termination, every effort should be made to approach these changes with faithfulness and integrity. Each of us needs to make the best decisions we can and then if necessary make changes later. If we make a choice that turns out to be unproductive, we should carefully and prayerfully try to rectify the situation. These are not easy matters. No one should be condemned for doing the best he or she can. Rather, others should do their best to help and support thoughtful decisions made in these cases.

The problem with the position of many religious people is that they ask others to try to cure themselves of being attracted to the same sex, when in fact, they are and may always be so attracted regardless of attempts to change. The problem with the either/or mentality in the extreme gay position is that it insists that no accommodation is possible, that to have homosexual feeling means that all choices about heterosexual marriage are completely out of the question. Nor does it acknowledge differences of degree in homosexual orientation. We reject the inadequacies in both positions. Accepting honest feelings, prayerfully making choices, and living with those decisions in a spirit of integrity and readjustment provides a better alternative.

Note

1. Sexual abuse is an important issue among lesbians. Some observers speculate that lesbians were more often victims of sexual abuse than straight women. However, in a simple survey (Loulan 1987), 35 to 38

percent of gay and straight women reported that they had been sexually abused as children. Bell, Weinberg, and Hammersmith (1981) reported that more heterosexual men than homosexual men were seduced as children by men—21 percent compared to 10 percent.

References

Anonymous. "Solus." *Dialogue: A Journal of Mormon Thought* 10 (1976): 94–99.

Bell, Alan. "The Homosexual as Patient." *Human Sexuality: A Health Practictioner's Text,* ed. Richard Green. Baltimore: Williams and Wilkins, 1976.

————, and M. Weinberg. *Homosexualities: A Study of Diversity Among Men and Women.* New York: Simon and Schuster, 1978.

————, M. Weinberg, and Susan Hammersmith. *Sexual Preference: Its Development in Men and Women.* Bloomington: Indiana University Press,1981.

Berzon, Betty. *Permanent Partners: Building Gay and Lesbian Relationships That Last.* New York: E.P. Dutton, 1988.

Blumstein, P., and P. Schwartz. *American Couples: Money, Work, Sex.* New York: William Morrow & Company, Inc., 1983.

Bullough, Vern L. "Variant Life Styles: Homosexuality." *Exploring Intimate Life Styles,* ed. Bernard I. Murstein. New York: Springer Publishing Company, 1978.

Coleman, Eli. "Bisexual and Gay Men in Heterosexual Marriage: Conflicts and Resolutions in Therapy." *A Guide to Psychotherapy with Gay and Lesbian Clients,* ed. John C. Gonsiorek. New York: Harrington Park Press, 1985.

Hersch, Patricia. "Secret Lives: Lesbian and Gay Teens Live in Fear of Discovery." *Family Therapy Networker* 15 (Jan./Feb. 1991): 36-43.

Kinsey, A., W. Pomeroy, and C. Martin. "Homosexual Outlet." In *Sexual Behavior in the Human Male.* Philadelphia: W. B. Saunders, 1948.

————, W. Pomeroy, C. Martin, and P. Gebhard. "Homosexual Responses and Contacts." In *Sexual Behavior in the Human Female.* Philadelphia: W. B. Saunders, 1953.

Loulan, JoAnn. *Lesbian Passion: Loving Ourselves and Others.* San Francisco: spinsters/aunt lute, 1987.

Masters, William, and Virginia Johnson. *Homosexuality in Perspective.* Boston: Little Brown & Company, 1977.

McWhirter, David, Stephanie Sanders, and June Reinisch. *Homosexuality/ Heterosexuality: Concepts of Sexual Orientation.* New York: Oxford University Press, 1990.

TWENTY-FIVE

Developmental Tasks
of Gay Youth

▼

Robin Pfeiffer

Over the past six years I have come to know about 200 teenagers as a result of my work with the YWCA in Salt Lake City. Also, I am currently working with twenty gay and lesbian adolescents in my private practice. From these vantage points, I would like to share some common adolescent developmental tasks and explain the accompanying dilemmas a gay teenager faces.

Gay and lesbian adolescents encounter enormous problems in growing up. Their issues are more critical and their conflicts more serious than those heterosexual adolescents encounter because they cannot accomplish the tasks of adolescence in an open, socially-approved environment.

For some youth, acknowledging a gay or lesbian identity is a natural outcome of the developmental process, and growing up gay or lesbian is marked by its own set of dangers and obstacles. This is because the primary task of a gay adolescent is adjusting to a socially stigmatized role. Additionally, Mormon adolescents face

---

Robin Pfeiffer is a social worker residing in Salt Lake City.

conflicts not only within school and family but also at church. They must, in their own words, survive a hostile environment everywhere they turn. The resulting insecurities, secrets, low self-esteem, even self-contempt come not from being gay but from the messages they have received about what being gay means.

One of the first tasks of adolescence is individuation, which is creating a self that is more independent or distinct from the family of origin. For teens, this means trying to achieve independence by moving away from home to identify more closely with their peer group. For a homosexual adolescent, there is no peer group or role model with which to identify openly. They do not bring friends home, nor talk about new love interests, nor mention what they are excited about. These secrets start when they become attracted to others, at age twelve or thirteen or even younger.

Teens also establish an identity—or self-definition—both social and sexual at this time. Heterosexual adolescents often experience a wider variety of activities in social groups; gay adolescents experience social isolation. For Mormon gays, this isolation extends to church activities. Adolescent sexual identity has many facets: a sense of being male or female, gender role behavior, choice of dating partners, awareness of body changes, and sexual attraction. In all of these a gay youth has no way to establish healthy intimate relationships.

Adolescence is also a time when people establish a sense of integrity for themselves. They are examining the values they have been taught and are trying to determine what they believe and what is right for them. In my experience, teens report knowing the value system their parents and church holds by the time they are four or five years old. Now, at thirteen, fourteen, or fifteen they are trying to find out what *they* believe. This becomes critical for Mormon adolescents who identify themselves as gay or lesbian because they are in direct conflict not only with society and their peers but their family and church as well.

One of the final tasks of adolescence is establishing intimacy with people outside the family. In working with all types of teens, I have observed that the "Just Say No" approach to premarital sexual activity does not work. It creates, instead, considerable secrecy, guilt, and shame. Teenagers begin lying to themselves and to their parents about sexual experimentation. This is increased for gay adolescents who are not allowed to communicate to their families even short, intense love experiences, including infatuations. Nor are they able to attend dances and experience the same kind of excitement that someone does with the opposite sex. Consequently, chances for developing real intimacy are greatly diminished.

With the difficulty, even impossibility, of accomplishing these developmental tasks, gay youth are more vulnerable to psychosocial problems. Again, these do not stem from being gay but from what society says about being gay. In fact, many teens go through a painful process of saying to themselves, "Please don't let this be true about me," when they become aware of their own same-sex interest.

One of these psychosocial problems is a two-edged sword. Many gay teenagers not only face isolation but are afraid of exposure. They fear being disowned by their family, by their church, by their peers. Many LDS teens have told me about being betrayed by a bishop or family member. One example is a young man who was president of his senior class. His stepfather discovered a letter from this teen's lover and threatened to expose him to the principal of his school. For six weeks he was suicidal.

Another aspect of this isolation arises when teenagers do not have access to accurate information about homosexuality and automatically assume that people will dislike them because of their sexual preference. Another problem can be their family's reaction. Considerable shame, guilt, fear, anger, and alienation begin as the teen discovers that she or he is different from other family members. This may be more prevalent in Mormon adolescents because of the church's emphasis on the family.

Violence is yet another problem for gay youth. Many of these teens worry about emotional and physical abuse at the hands of family members. Fear turns into reality as many face threats of exposure, rape, and actual physical abuse.

So how do gay teens adapt to growing up? Some suppress their sexual desires, keeping their secret for a lifetime while raising a family. Some become homophobic, hoping their feelings will go away. Others date heterosexually, expecting to send a message that says, "I don't have a problem. I'm not gay."

Others openly acknowledge their homosexuality. Only a

minority of adolescents do so, however. In my experience, these come from open families who communicate about sexuality.

This coming out process is important to consider in the context of adolescent adaptive responses. Usually between the ages of six and nine, gay individuals become aware that they are different. Between eight and eleven, they begin to realize that they are attracted to the same sex. They may have their first same-sex experience between ten and thirteen. During the teen years a fuller understanding of what it means to be gay emerges, particularly the contempt some people have for gays and lesbians. This is when inner struggle, depression, and thoughts of suicide occur. Because they are struggling with such overwhelming tasks, homosexual teens need people whom they can love and trust. One of the funniest ways of coming out that I know of was from the teen who left a note on the refrigerator saying, "Hi, Mom. I'm a homosexual. I'll be home at 7. Love, John."

Another response of gay adolescents is to deny all other social roles. Part of the depression an adolescent experiences might be, "I can't be gay and Mormon . . . gay and a teacher . . . gay and a parent." As teens mature they begin to get more accurate information, but between ages twelve and fifteen these are some of the nightmares: "I'll never be happy. I'll never have a devoted partner or have children because I'm gay."

Truancy and failure in school are also prevalent. I have found that schools do not initiate conversations with adolescents about sexual orientation as a possible reason for truancy or failure. There is not one teen with whom I have talked who said, "Oh yes, my guidance counselor or social worker brought that up."

Chronic depression is common among gay teens trying to cope. With depression comes shame, guilt, doubt, thoughts of suicide, and often suicide itself. Studies in 1972 and 1987 found more than a third of gay, bisexual, and lesbian teens had attempted suicide. (Roesler and Deisher 1972; Remafedi 1987). Probably up to 30 percent of teen suicides annually are attributed to lesbian and gay youth (Gibson 1986).

Substance abuse and promiscuous sexual behavior are other responses gay and lesbian teens sometimes employ. Both behaviors put the teenager in danger. Because these youth are not openly allowed to show affection and have legitimate intimate relationships, they may choose situations that are not safe. They may be exposed to violence, rape, or disease simply to have contact with other people for short periods of time in secret. When gay or lesbian teens are denied social interaction, they are prevented from becoming healthy, whole, integrated persons.

Adolescents with whom I have worked generally do not want to leave the church. They do not want to leave their families. They want to be acknowledged, loved, and supported for who they are.

What are some interventions to help these teens? First, preaching, lecturing, and advocating a "Just Say No" strategy to sex does not work. Next, talking to teens directly about homosexuality, providing support, accurate information, and resources is essential. As adult friends or family members, we need to examine our own attitudes and beliefs, our own feelings about same-sex orientation.

When teens say they are gay or lesbian, parents should carefully consider this and not tell them they are confused. That admission is difficult to make openly. More likely, a teen will give no indication that homosexuality is a concern. Instead, truancy, poor grades, severe family conflict, depression, and/or isolation surface as clues of a deeper issue. As a therapist, when I notice these signs I try to build a trusting, open relationship with the teen. I must be comfortable talking about myself, including my own sexuality and relationships. When trust has emerged, I ask, "Are you dating? Are you attracted to men? To women?" I try to let them know that nothing they say will surprise or shock me as we explore their experience among the wide range of homosexual and heterosexual realities.

All teenagers deserve to accomplish the tasks of growing up successfully. They deserve our understanding, support, and love. Let us hope that more gay and lesbian adolescents will gain better understanding of themselves earlier in their lives as we begin to dispel the myths surrounding homosexuality.

References

Gibson, Paul. Commissioned paper, US Department of Health and Human Services, National Institute of Mental Health. Presented 11

June 1986.

Martin, A. Damien, and Emery S. Hetrick. "The Stigmatization of the Gay and Lesbian Adolescent." In *The Journal of Homosexuality* 15 (1988):163-84.

Roesler, T., and R. Deisher. "Youthful Male Homosexuality," *Journal of the American Medical Association* 219 (8): 1018-23.

Roesler, T. , R. Deisher, and G. J. Remafedi. *Project 10 Handbook, Addressing Gay and Lesbian Issues in Our Schools.* Los Angeles: Friends of Project 10, Inc., 1989.

TWENTY-SIX

Alternatives in Therapy
Approaches

▼

Marybeth Raynes

The alternatives for attempting to cure or help homosexuals have varied over time according to theories about cause. Those who feel homosexuality is a sin have chosen punitive measures, those who view same-sex attraction as a disease or pathological maladjustment try to find a cure, and those who view gay relationships as one of a variety of normal affectionate, romantic, or erotic relationships explore ways to help gay people adjust within themselves and the larger world.

All three approaches exist in the world today. The first approach, which seeks to cure the sin and the sinner, is largely the province of the religious world and is on the decline in most major religions of the west. This is particularly true of non-fundamentalist Christian faiths. For sharply conservative religions, punishing or rehabilitating the sinner is at the core of interaction with homosexuals. However, even in many fundamentalist faiths, there are signs that the second approach is gaining favor. And in non-fundamentalist religions many believers see the third approach as the only humane and defensible course of action.

Among psychotherapists the first approach is typically not addressed because therapy does not view people's behavior as sinful. Whatever the client's problem, most therapists view it as maladjusted, pathological, or normal suffering—never sinful. A minority of therapists may, because of religious beliefs or other convictions, view homosexuality as sinful. These beliefs enter into therapy even if never overtly expressed. And the convictions of both therapist and client certainly influence the process and outcome of therapy.

Although therapists as early as Freud (Wysor 1974, 186) said that there is no disease in homosexuality, the therapeutic world at large until approximately twenty years ago viewed same-sex attraction as dysfunctional and the result of a developmental arrest. In 1973 as the dynamics of homosexual behavior became better known through research and therapeutic experience, the American Psychiatric Association removed homosexuality from its list of psychiatric dysfunctions, except for ego-dystonic homosexuality (i.e., persistently disturbing to the core sense of self for the individual in which it occurs). Since that time the shift in the therapeutic community has largely been to accept homosexuality as a normal human experience for about 5 percent or more of the population (Moses and Hawkins 1982, 4; Kinsey 1948 and 1953). However, therapists are well aware of the societal, familial, and personal adjustments and crises that occur with any behavior that is seen by the society at large as wrong. So therapy journals, workshops, research, and associations increasingly address the problems homosexual people face. Yet despite the fact that most therapists in America now see homosexuality as normal, there are individuals and groups who maintain that same-sex attraction is pathological and is based on some dysfunction in the person's past.

Before looking at currently available approaches in more detail, I would like to discuss several issues that have generated much concern in the past twenty years. Two of these issues are: can people change sexual orientation, and how successful has therapy been in producing change? A more recent emphasis by those in the gay community is that causation is not always the central issue; one does not have to prove that he or she is not dysfunctional in order to make a healthy choice to be with a partner of the same sex. Therapy approaches have increasingly included family, friends, and the social community. Finally, the AIDS crisis has heated up questions on many sides and has increased discussions of caretaking efforts and the grieving process.

As approaches and beliefs have competed side by side in American and western culture, research about past approaches to homosexuality has been conducted. Briefly, no therapy approach has shown major statistical success in changing homosexual orientation over a long period of time particularly for those who are strongly homosexual.

In 1978 Elizabeth James, in a Ph.D. dissertation for Brigham Young University, analyzed the research results of numerous change-oriented therapies. She concluded that 35 percent of those studied, including bisexual persons, reported a major change in orientation, 22 percent said there was some change, and 37 percent stated no change occurred as a result of therapy. These results were not substantiated in long-term follow-up studies. In a recently published book, *Homosexuality: Research Implications for Public Policy,* Douglas Haldeman reports very low change rates as a result of therapy. He concludes that those who report exclusive heterosexual behavior several years after therapy "were bisexual to begin with; exclusively homosexual subjects reported little change."

The identification of oneself as homosexual is usually a long process with several stages, requiring several years if not decades. Given that most people experience this process as long, arduous, and secret, it is difficult for people to report accurately if they are gay and where they might fit on the Kinsey Scale. These stages of identification will be discussed later under the various therapy approaches.

Therapy Approaches Viewing Homosexuality as Normal

Most therapists today see homosexuality as one of many normal variations that occur in the field of sexuality and sex therapy. A core belief is that just as sexual interest varies from non-existent to highly intense and as interest in a particular type of sexual activity varies among people, so does interest in the same or opposite sex vary among all peoples. Briefly, most professionals agree that the exact causes of heterosexuality and homosexuality are unknown;

that homosexuality and heterosexuality are probably the result of an interaction of several different factors, including genetic, hormonal, and environmental factors; that psychological and social influences alone cannot cause homosexuality; that a biological (genetic, hormonal, neurological, or other) predisposition toward homosexuality, bisexuality, or heterosexuality is present at birth; and that none of the contributing factors alone can cause homosexuality (see Haase 1988, which summarizes the work of Bell et al. 1981; Ellis and Ames 1987; Green 1987; Herdt 1987; Kinsey et al. 1948; Marmor 1980; Money 1988; Pillard 1982; and Weinrich 1987).

For many therapists, the picture of evidence for any one cause is scanty, just as determinants for other personality factors are still inconclusive. Until we have clearer pictures, it may not be very important to know a cause. Homosexuality has always existed and has a sufficiently strong presence in many people's experience that it is normal and should be worked with on that basis. Yet others believe that even if the "cause" question can be answered, there is still the issue of choice: a person can choose his or her response.

Given these premises, most therapists advocate a general approach to working with homosexuals in roughly the following stages:

First is assessment, with the issue for which the client wants help being explored, clarified, and acknowledged as important. Then, a general assessment of the client is conducted. A general history of the individual's personal and family life, including sexual history, is taken. Special attention is paid to what the client finds troubling in his or her view, what strengths and resources she or he brings to the perceived problem. Also an assessment of the person's current state of stress and personality functioning is noted. The therapist finds out if the client is troubled with depression, anxiety, or any personality traits or problems of mental illness which provide roadblocks to solutions. Finally, most therapists want to know what the person has already done to try to solve the problem.

At this point assessing the stage of homosexual awareness and identity is crucial. Although different typologies are offered by different authors, the following by Lou Ann Lewis (1984, 464-69) concerning lesbian women is illustrative. Stage One is an awareness of being different, which is followed in Stage Two by an increase in dissonance within herself and with the forces of society outside herself, often accompanied by significant inner turmoil. Stage Three occurs when a relationship with another woman develops. During this stage the issue of telling family, friends, and others becomes crucial. "Coming out" is a lifelong process, which begins during this time. Stage Four develops when a stable lesbian identity emerges, and the woman is much more self-accepting than in the past. Stage Five is integration of all the elements and conflicts of her life into a cohesive sense of self. These stages normally take years. Knowing which particular stage a person is at and the concomitant issues gives the therapist a clue about where to start the therapy process.

Next, the therapist assesses or explores common problem areas most people with homosexual awareness experience. One is homophobia. This term, named in 1973 by George Weinberg (Margolies 1987; Weinberg 1973), is an "irrational fear, hatred, and intolerance of homosexual men and women." This exploration includes looking for areas of self-hatred or hatred of others that would prevent a person solving his or her problem. Another area of concern is how the client deals with his or her homosexual feelings or behavior in relationship to others. Is he "out" to some people but not to his family? Does she reveal herself appropriately when she talks to others, or is she creating some problems for herself by how she interacts?

Still in the assessment phase, the therapist probably wants to know the actual patterns of behavior the person is exhibiting concerning the problem. If it is a relationship problem, what is actually happening? If it is a concern with family or church, what is the person presently doing? Is she or he talking to some family members but not to others? Where are the congruities and incongruities between how the person describes him- or herself and how he or she lives?

Finally, the therapist tries to get a clear picture of what the person wants. What does the solution to this problem look like?

Before moving to particular treatments, I would like to note that the above steps are typical of almost any therapy process. By accepting homosexuality as normal, the general therapy approach used for homosexual issues follows roughly the same course as for other concerns. In other words, the therapist does not see the homosexuality as the problem; rather the person's stated conflict is the problem. That problem is then investigated with the person's stated homosexual concerns in mind.

The second stage is the treatment phase. At this point, the therapist starts to employ certain therapy techniques. If she is from the psychoanalytic school of thought (commonly called psychodynamic, object relations, or other terms), she employs techniques commensurate with those theories. She will use family history and a re-working of the past. If the person is at the initial stages of identifying him- or herself as gay, then this past history becomes crucial, and the person's increased awareness of his or her own history may comprise the major part of therapy.

If the therapist is a behavioral or problem-centered therapist, then the client's problems are examined as they come up, and practical solutions, which the client tries out, are recommended. A guided trial-and-error approach is used to solve the problem.

Most therapists today say that although they employ one central method or approach, they really are eclectic. That means that they employ techniques and skills from all therapy approaches. Essentially the therapist picks from as large a tool kit as his or her repertoire allows.

If the problem is large or difficult, the therapist probably enters into a long-term relationship with the client. Some clients, of course, see their whole life as the problem. Picking through each area of concern, including the many areas that the person's homosexual feelings and actions can encompass, is the therapy task. Such a person often wants to grow developmentally, to rework his or her whole life. Again the person's homosexuality is an integral part but not the whole work. Given the negative reaction of society at large and fears about family, church, friends, work, and so on, many people feel that they have never had a place to talk openly and freely about all of their concerns.

If this is the case, a person may not have as fully developed a sense of self as others. One commonly held belief in the therapeutic community is that the "self" must have a place to grow freely, to be seen, to be mirrored, and to be loved in order to develop. If a major part of a person's sense of self must be kept secret or is confused and conflicted, the self must develop underground or it develops in ways not usual to people who can freely show most of their self.

An analogy may help. As I was growing up in the LDS church, I repeatedly heard stories of how early Mormons were persecuted. Given that much of church doctrine was perceived as heretical to the bulk of the American public, a major part of the Mormon identity was built around hardships (and stories of hardships) that occurred as a result of being different. In fact, being a "peculiar people" was a point of pride when I was young. Much of what occurred in polygamous families had to remain secret in order for them to live. And the selves of those people developed around the secret, around the hardships.

Likewise much of a homosexual's sense of self derives from the difference he or she perceives between him- or herself and the rest of the world. If the sense of difference is profound and if it has never been aired and reviewed, the process of therapy will take a long time. Again, homosexuality is not the issue for the therapist, but how the self has had to develop and what steps a person must take to develop healthily.

The third stage of therapy is the termination phase. As the problem is being solved, the therapist and client decide together on closure. Many times a person drops out of therapy when she or he thinks things are better or when tough spots are approached. The disadvantage is that it leaves many threads hanging. It is important for both therapist and client to say how they think the process is going. If the client has experienced much of the world as being difficult to control, deciding when and how to terminate therapy is an important step towards control. It is also important to confront difficult areas in a client's relationship with the therapist and to review when a return for additional sessions might be helpful.

Since confronting or dealing with one's family is a crucial issue, discontinuing therapy before this is explored is often counter-productive. In many Mormon families there is a strong belief that how people live their lives will determine whether they will be together in the eternities. So for many gays it becomes additionally fearful to approach their families when they know their parents, siblings, and others will see them as lost forever. Gay people are afraid of both the critical judgment they will receive, as well as worry about the pain that their family will feel. Whether the gay person accepts her or his homosexuality, she or he has had internal experiences that she or he believes cannot possibly be understood by the family. In the words of one client: "How can I communicate such peace and joy I have about myself, when the first thing they will be hit with is overwhelming pain and disbelief?"

Therapy Approaches Viewing Homosexuality as Dysfunctional

Throughout the history of psychotherapy, there have been possibly four basic approaches to "curing" or "correcting" homosexual feelings and behavior: psychodynamic therapy, aversion therapy, behavioral modification, and re-education or re-orientation therapy.

Therapies for homosexuality using psychoanalytic theory derive from a premise that something negative happened or something positive did not happen during the early years of childhood. One did not sufficiently bond with one's mother; one's mother was overbearing and one's father was distant; or one did not sufficiently bond with one's father. In sum the family did not provide the right atmosphere or was so organized that it provided the wrong one. Since the homosexual orientation was learned, it could be unlearned. The therapy methods relied primarily on uncovering past childhood memories or patterns and trying to devise new experiences which would correct them. The relationship with the therapist was important, because it helped the person have a safe place to let the past come forth and an enriching environment for new growth to occur.

Most therapists agree that early experience is important; but how important, and if someone is to blame, and what is possible in terms of change are all current subjects of long, intense debate—not just about homosexuality but about almost every personality trait. The nature-nurture puzzle is still being pieced together slowly, with no overall consensus among therapists and scientists.

Behavioral and aversion therapies came into vogue during the 1960s. Awareness about homosexuality arose during those years just as awareness about many other aspects of sexuality was increasing. Behavioral theories and practices came first, and aversion therapy techniques came from behavioral theory and methods. Basically behavioral therapy methods rely on the idea that human behavior can be changed by "shaping" behavior through rewards and consequences. Little and sometimes no attention is paid to the inner experience of the person who is trying to change; focus is instead on rewards and sanctions that motivate a person to change his or her actions. The theory goes that after sufficient time with the reward or consequence in place, the new pattern of behavior takes root and becomes permanent—or at least easily maintained. The basis for most parenting books and diet plans today is behavioral techniques and methods.

Behavioral methods have been used to try to cure homosexuality as an illness, disease, or dysfunction. Even though behavior methods are successful with many problems, they have not proved helpful overall (James 1978; Haldeman 1990). Basically many therapists say that the issue is larger than behavior and action. The core of same-sex attraction comes long before behavior (Money 1988), so of course behavior methods are not sufficient. The issue of how to shape any personality trait or behavior that occurs among a predictable portion of the population and is deeply ingrained seems larger than any one therapy method.

This conclusion seems particularly true in light of aversion therapy. Essentially, aversion therapists working with homosexual clients use negative treatment approaches such as shock therapy to orient a person's sexual impulses away from the same sex. After the aversive techniques are applied, then positive or rewarding techniques are employed to reinforce positive attraction to the opposite sex.

Not only have aversive methods proved ineffective, there has been considerable debate over the ethics involved. Many see punishing methods as coercive, particularly since many clients come to therapy under pressure from friends, church, or therapy authorities. Additionally, since explicit heterosexual visual material has sometimes been used to reinforce heterosexual impulses, many say that the method reinforces the use of pornography. Many women writers say that it uses women as sex objects—that loving sexual interaction is not being taught, just sexual response. Also, some former clients have reported severe long-lasting negative effects.

Aversive methods are largely discredited today. One of the proponents of these methods has admitted that even though homosexual impulse may be curbed, there is little success in triggering positive heterosexual impulse (Card 1988). Also, his research about these clients has not been published, and to my knowledge the accounts are only available from reports at public presentations.

Re-education approaches recently emerged with increased emphasis. Elizabeth Moberly has formulated a theory outlined in her book *Homosexuality: The New Christian Ethic*. In this work she spells out her theory of males insufficiently attaching to emotionally-absent fathers as the cause of homosexuality. Her theory is essentially the same as psychoanalytic theory with a Christian basis.

Re-education approaches acknowledge that homosexuality therapies have been ineffective. The emphasis is on understanding and helping the individual in his or her own chosen process. Few claims are made for absolute cure. They hold open the door that basic homosexual orientation may remain but say that choices toward a more normal or healthy lifestyle can be made and maintained. There is no outcome research available on these approaches that I am aware of.

Comparison of Therapy Approaches

	Dysfunctional	**Normal**
PREMISE	Homosexuality is dysfunctional, abnormal, or an arrested development; a minority see as sinful.	Homosexuality is a normal variation of human sexual bonding and response.
ETIOLOGY	Learned: 1. Impaired bonding with opposite sex parent. 2. Impaired bonding with same sex parent.	Not learned: 1. Biological. 2. Biological plus early learning similar to imprinting. 3. Irrelevant.

BELIEF ABOUT CHANGE	Attraction to same sex can be changed or unlearned; interest in opposite sex can be learned. Difficulty of change acknowledged.	Basic attraction pattern cannot be modified. No need to change attraction. Homosexual pattern should be affirmed.
GOAL OF THERAPY	Change of orientation; instigate growth past developmental arrest or dysfunction.	Goals chosen by individual client's wishes; general goal is for clarification of identity issues or healthy growth within gender preference indicated by client.
THERAPY METHODS	Exploration of early childhood and family patterns to increase insight; behavioral assignments, individual or group activities to increase heterosexual bonding and activity; in such cases aversive techniques used (now out of vogue, commonly seen as abusive).	Exploration of issues client brings to therapy; use of many techniques (cognitive, behavioral, and emotional) devised by the therapist.

Seeking Therapy

It is important in seeking therapy to know not only what is available but to be aware of one's own needs, to make an informed choice of therapist, and to keep one's needs paramount in the therapy process. The following guidelines may be helpful for people embarking on a therapy process. These guidelines are valid regardless of one's particular needs.

1. Is therapy your choice? Do you feel free to make this choice?

If you are afraid of another person's opinion, therapy is probably not entirely your choice. This should be the first issue addressed if you decide to go.

2. Does the therapist have the ability to see your conflicts in such a way that you feel understood? Does he or she accept your view of the problem and the goals you want to achieve? Any therapist has her or his personal bias, theories, and methods about homosexuality. Is she or he willing to let you and your concerns be paramount in the therapy process? You are embarking on a process to know yourself; that self must be seen acceptingly from every angle.

3. If you want to explore your underlying sexual orientation, is the therapist open-minded about whatever outcome fits you?

4. Does the therapist see homosexual and heterosexual orientation along a continuum, or does he or she see it as an all or nothing issue? Is he or she willing to explore where you might rate yourself along the Kinsey Scale and on other variables in order to assess what choices might be available to you?

5. Is your therapist willing to discuss the theory and therapy methods he or she employs, why he or she chooses those particular ones, and what previous experience and training he or she has had in working with gay men and lesbians?

6. If you seek therapy for changing your current orientation, impulses, or lifestyle, does the therapist acknowledge how tentative any methods are for producing lasting change? Is she or he open to discussing the research on changing sexual orientation, and is she or he willing to explore how the low rate of change might affect your current efforts?

7. If part of your concern is spiritual or religious, is your therapist willing to consider those issues valid, and is she or he willing to approach them from your vantage point as well as her or his own? Does she or he understand the particular conflicts in Mormon culture? Is she or he willing to hear your view of your Mormon issues or to consult with someone else regarding spiritual issues?

8. If part of your concern involves your family, is the therapist trained in marriage and family therapy techniques? Is he or she willing to face the intensity that such issues can generate? Is he or she willing to meet with your family?

Beyond making sure that the therapist is competent and appropriate, there are several other questions you may want to ask as you seek help.

1. Do you really want to discover more about yourself? If you only want to stop the misery you feel, the outcome of therapy will probably be limited. Therapy that considers the issues of homosexuality fully includes more than just the behavior; it opens up all areas of self so that you can look deeper into your full self. Many of the questions and riddles that come up might initially make the whole issue more troubling, not less. Are you willing to entertain more troubling concerns and perplexing questions on the way to finding peace with yourself? Remember this is a complex issue and has many uncertain answers.

2. Are you willing to let the process take time? To be sure, if there are some crisis issues brewing, there should be some immediate help. But the growth of self—individually or in relation to others—is a long-term process. I am not suggesting that therapy is needed every week or that therapy is the only vehicle for solving the dilemmas you face. But whatever process or methods you use, allow a period of time for resolution and growth.

3. It is helpful to be aware that many aspects of your problem may be separate issues. For example, suppose that you have had periods of depression for years. Because the unresolved feelings about homosexuality have been also going on for years, you may assume that they are related. This may be the case, yet it is also possible that the depression comes from another source within yourself (perhaps it is biochemical) and can be dealt with as a separate therapeutic issue.

4. Are you willing to consider that you might revise your feelings and thinking about your family, friends, and others? This is especially important if you are angry or isolated from family members. However numerous the issues on both sides, therapy is a healing process and should help with reconciliation within the self and with others.

In listing these possible questions, I do not want to make the therapy process seem too formidable. It is taken one step at a time, but enormous changes can result from small steps. The first steps are making an informed choice about what therapy method to choose and finding a therapist you can trust.

References

Bell, Alan P., Martin S. Weinberg, and Sue Kiefer Hammersmith. *Sexual Preference: Its Development in Men and Women.* Bloomington: Indiana University Press, 1981.

Card, Robert. "Presentation on Homosexual Re-orientation." At AMCAP Conference. Salt Lake City, Oct. 1987.

—————. "Presentation on Homosexuality." At Sunstone Symposium. Salt Lake City, Aug. 1988.

Ellis, Lee, and M. Ashley Ames. *Neurohormonal Functioning and Sexual Orientation: A Theory of Homosexuality-Heterosexuality.* New Orleans: PFLAG, 1987.

Green, Richard. *The Sissy-Boy Syndrome and the Development of Homosexuality.* New Haven, CT: Yale University Press, 1987.

Haldeman, Douglas C. "Sexual Orientation Conversion Therapy for Gay Men and Lesbians: A Scientific Examination." In *Homosexuality: Research Implications for Public Policy.* London: Sage Publications, 1990.

Hasse, Tineke Bodde. "Why is My Child Gay?" Pamphlet, n.p. Parents and Friends of Lesbians and Gays, Inc., 1988.

Herdt, Gilbert. *The Sambia: Ritual and Gender in New Guinea.* New York: Holt, Rinehart and Winston, 1987.

James, Elizabeth C. "Treatment of Homosexuality: A Reanalysis and Synthesis of Outcome Studies." Ph.D. diss., Brigham Young University, 1978.

Kinsey, Alfred C., Wardell B. Pomeroy, and Clyde E. Martin. *Sexual Behavior in the Human Male.* Philadelphia: W. B. Saunders, 1948.

—————, W. Pomeroy, C. Martin, and P. Gebhard. *Sexual Behavior in the Human Female.* Philadelphia: W. B. Saunders, 1953.

Lewis, Lou Ann. "The Coming-out Process for Lesbians: Integrating a Stable Identity." *Journal of Social Work,* Sept.-Oct. 1984, 464-69.

Margolies, Liz, Martha Becker, and Karla Jackson-Brewer. "Internalized Homophobia: Identifying and Treating the Oppressor Within." In *Lesbian Psychologies: Explorations and Challenges,* ed. Boston Lesbian Psychologies Collective. Urbana: University of Illinois Press, 1987.

Money, John. *Gay, Straight, and In-Between: The Sexology of Erotic Orientation.* New York: Oxford University Press, 1988.

Moses, A. Elfin, and Robert O. Hawkins, Jr. *Counseling Lesbian Women and Gay Men: A Life-Issues Approach.* St. Louis: The C. V. Mosby Company, Inc., 1982.

Marmor, Judd. *Homosexual Behavior: A Modern Reappraisal.* New York: Basic Books, 1980.

Pillard, Richard C. "Psychotherapeutic Treatment for the Invisible Minority." In W. Paul, et al., eds. *Homosexuality: Social, Psychological,*

and Biological Issues. Beverly Hills, CA: Sage Publications, 1982.
Weinberg, George. *Society and the Healthy Homosexual.* New York: Anchor/Doubleday, 1973.
Weinrich, James D. *Sexual Landscapes: Why We Are What We Are, Why We Love Whom We Love.* New York: Scribners/Macmillan, 1987.
Wysor, B. *The Lesbian Myth.* New York: Random House, 1974.

TWENTY-SEVEN

A Survey of Scientific Views on Homosexual Orientation

▼

Tineke Bodde Haase

Current estimates, first advanced by Dr. Alfred Kinsey, indicate that about 10 percent of the population is gay. This statistic is believed to be roughly the same all over the world, in all times, cultures, and climates. Feelings of same-gender attraction usually appear to be affectional as well as physical.

The first scientist to examine the mental health of homosexuals in an objective, controlled study was Dr. Evelyn Hooker of the University of California at Los Angeles. Her research in the late 1950s demonstrated that there was no difference in emotional stability and mental health between gay men and nongay men. More recently, researchers have begun to examine lesbianism and its origins. Through the centuries, male homosexuality has been more visible and received more attention than lesbianism.

Until the early 1970s, the study of homosexuality remained mostly in the domain of psychiatry. Researchers obtained their data

"A Survey of Scientific Views on Homosexual Orientation," by Tineke Bodde Haase, is excerpted from "Why Is My Child Gay?" Pamphlet (N.p.: copyrighted by Parents and Friends of Lesbians and Gays, Inc, 1988). Ms. Haase is a free-lance medical writer and member of Parents and Friends of Lesbians and Gays of Metropolitan Washington, Inc.

from people in therapy who had mental or emotional problems, which skewed their appraisal of homosexuals in general. But in the late 1970s the National Institute of Mental Health embarked on a major study to examine whether homosexuality could be the result of family environment, poor role models, or other psychological or social factors. The research findings were published in 1981 as *Sexual Preference: Its Development in Men and Women.* It was clear that there was more involved in determining gender orientation than family dynamics.

To provide a range of opinions about more recent research into homosexuality, two of the contributors to *Sexual Preference* and twelve other scientists were approached by the author with a uniform list of questions. Eleven of the fourteen scientists contacted responded, and their answers—printed *verbatim*—follow. Two of the scientists did not answer because of time pressures; one biologist declined to return the survey because her study findings are based on research in rodents and are not necessarily applicable to human behavior.

The respondents:

1. Alan T. Bell, Ph.D., is a psychotherapist and director of the Counseling and Psychology Department at Indiana University in Bloomington, and co-author of *Sexual Preference: Its Development in Men and Women.*

2. Lee Ellis, Ph.D., is a sociologist and received his doctoral degree from Florida State University. He is chair of the Department of Sociology at Minot State University in North Dakota.

3. Richard Green, M.D., J.D., is a psychiatrist at the University of California, Los Angeles, Medical Center. He served from 1974-86 as professor of psychiatry at the State University of New York at Stoney Brook and is author of *The Sissy-Boy Syndrome and the Development of Homosexuality.*

4. Gilbert Herdt, Ph.D., an anthropologist, is associate professor in the Department of Behavioral Sciences at the University of Chicago. He has studied homosexuality and gender identity development in Melanesia (near Australia). His research in New Guinea is described in *Guardians of the Flutes: Idioms of Masculinity* and *The Sambia: Ritual and Gender in New Guinea.*

5. Evelyn Hooker, Ph.D., was among the first researchers to do an objective, controlled study of the psychological characteristics

of gay men and nongay men. Her study disproved the then-popular theory that homosexuality was a mental illness.

6. Judd Marmor, M.D., of the University of California at Los Angeles, is a psychiatrist and a past president of the American Psychiatric Association. In the late 1960s he served on the NIMH Task Force on Homosexuality and was a leader in the movement to remove homosexuality from the diagnostic manual of the American Psychiatric Association in the early 1970s. Dr. Marmor is also one of the editors and co-authors of *Homosexual Behavior: A Modern Reappraisal.*

7. John Money, Ph.D., graduated from the University of New Zealand in 1943 and received his Ph.D. from Harvard University in 1952. He is director of the Psychohormonal Research Unit, professor of medical psychology, and professor emeritus of pediatrics at Johns Hopkins University and Hospital School of Medicine in Baltimore.

8. Richard C. Pillard, M.D., is director of the Family Studies Laboratory and professor of psychiatry of the Boston University School of Medicine. Dr. Pillard and his research team found "22 percent of the brothers of gay men appear also to be homosexual" (compared to about 10 percent in the population at large). He did not find this to be so for sisters or female relatives of the gay males.

9. June Machover Reinisch, Ph.D., is director of The Kinsey Institute for Research in Sex, Gender, and Reproduction at Indiana University, Bloomington. She is also a professor in the departments of psychology and psychiatry at Indiana University. She is the author of numerous scientific papers and writes the *Kinsey Report,* an internationally syndicated newspaper column on sex, gender, and reproduction.

10. Martin S. Weinberg, Ph.D., is professor of sociology at Indiana University, Bloomington and co-author of several books, including *Male Homosexuals: Their Problems and Adaptations* and *Sexual Preference: Its Development in Men and Women.*

11. James D. Weinrich, Ph.D., a sociobiologist, received his doctoral degree from Harvard University. He served for many years as a researcher at the Boston University Medical Center and is currently project manager for an NIMH-funded AIDS grant at the University of California, San Diego. He is the author of several scholarly research papers and of the popular book *Sexual*

Landscapes: Why We Are What We Are, Why We Love Whom We Love.

Question #1: *Many observers believe that a person's sexual orientation (homosexual, heterosexual, bisexual) is determined by one or more of
the following factors: genetic, hormonal, psychological, or social. Based on
today's state-of-the-science, what is your opinion?*

Dr. Bell: I believe that one's sexual orientation is determined
by all of the above in concert and that the relative weight of each
factor depends upon the individual involved. Prenatal, biological
events strongly influence a child's potential for gender conformity,
and this in turn profoundly influences his perceptions of males vs.
females and their love object potential.

Dr. Ellis: Based upon the most current scientific evidence, the
most significant factors responsible for variation in sexual orientation appear to occur prior to birth. Among these prenatal factors
are the influence of various sex hormones on brain functioning in
and around a primary drive control center, called the hypothalamus. This area of the brain not only appears to largely control
sexual orientation but has been shown to be organized differently
for males and females (albeit to varying degrees, depending upon
the amount and timing of exposure to testosterone and other sex
hormones).

Several categories of factors appear capable of altering how
much the hypothalamus and surrounding brain centers are exposed to sex hormones, one category being various genetic factors
controlling the synthesis of sex hormones. Studies with laboratory
animals indicate that exposing mothers to various neurologically
active drugs, and even to severe stress during pregnancy are also
among the prenatal factors which can invert sexual orientation. A
recent study by myself and associates (*Journal of Sex Research*, Feb.
1988, 152-57) found evidence that severe maternal stress may be a
cause of male homosexuality among humans. Nevertheless, a great
deal of scientific research is needed in this area.

Dr. Green: If this were a true/false question, the answer would
be "true." There is a growing body of evidence pointing to all of
these variables as influencing sexual orientation. Probably, the
proportion of each ingredient varies from person to person, but
the ingredients are all there.

Dr. Herdt: The determination of sexual orientation is complex and probably multi-causal. One problem in theorizing the determinants of sexual orientation is that there are probably several different pathways to arrive at the "same" sexual orientation (e.g., heterosexual). Another problem is that there is great variation in the meanings and practice of a sexual orientation (e.g., homosexual) in our society. In my opinion, multiple factors (biological, social, psychological) interact across the developmental cycle to produce sexual orientation outcomes.

Dr. Hooker: I believe that sexual orientation is determined by a combination of all the factors named, and that the weight or importance of each factor will vary greatly from one individual to another. There is no single "cause." Just as homosexuality and heterosexuality are enormously complex, so must the factors be which determine their respective development. I believe that those who seek a cause in a single factor such as "close-intimate-binding mothers" and "hostile-detached or absent fathers" fail to see beyond their own blinders.

Dr. Marmor: All of these factors may be involved, and more than one usually is.

Dr. Money: The determinants of gay, straight, and bisexual (orientation) may be genetic, hormonal, or transmitted *in utero* (via the bloodstream through the placenta and umbilical cord to the fetus). There is presently no incontrovertible evidence of a genetic determinant. Evidence of *in utero* transmission needs to be more strongly confirmed. Prenatal hormonal evidence differs for four-legged animals as compared with primates, especially human primates. In the four-legged species, prenatal hormones can be experimentally manipulated so as to influence the sexual pathways of the brain and determine whether the animal will be exclusively homosexual or heterosexual in mating. In the human and other primate species, prenatal hormones have a less absolute influence. They create only a predisposition toward exclusive homosexuality or heterosexuality in adulthood, or toward bisexual adaptability.

Especially on the basis of anthropological evidence, and the evidence of child development, it would appear that most human beings are born with a bisexual potential. Whether this potential is retained, or whether it becomes predominantly heterosexual or homosexual is, by analogy with native language, determined by influences (usually referred to as psychological and social) that reach the brain through the senses, especially the skin senses, vision, and hearing. The period of juvenile sexual rehearsal play, especially between the ages of five and eight, is particularly important with respect to establishing whether erotic attraction will subsequently be toward a male or a female, and whether the first experience of falling in love will be homosexual or heterosexual. Homosexuality, as well as heterosexuality, is ultimately defined by the sex of the partner with whom one is capable of falling in love.

Dr. Pillard: Sexual orientation probably results from a combination of causes—genetic, congenital, developmental—and this combination is probably different for each individual. What impresses me is that sexual orientation appears to be *innate* by which I mean that it is a deeply embedded personality trait, arising in the earliest years of life, however that may come about.

I qualify the above by saying that it seems to be true for men. Women appear to be more flexible in their orientation and seem to be able to modify it depending on circumstances. The aphorism is: men *discover* their sexual orientation, women choose theirs.

Dr. Reinisch: No one knows what "causes" homosexuality. For that matter, the cause of heterosexuality has not been determined either. Various theories have been proposed, but so far, none has held up under careful scrutiny. In fact, scientists probably have a clearer idea what does *not* cause people to prefer a same-sex sexual partner. For example, children raised by gay or lesbian parents or couples are no more likely to be homosexual than are children raised by heterosexual parents.

There also is no evidence that male homosexuality is caused by a dominant mother or a weak father, or that female homosexuality is caused by girls choosing male role models. There is evidence, in fact, that parents have very little influence on the outcome of their children's sexual orientation under normal upbringing conditions.

It also is not true that people become homosexuals because they were seduced by an older, same-sex person in their youth. The childhood and adolescent sexual experiences of both homosexuals and heterosexuals are fairly similar, except that homosexuals find the opposite-sex encounters less satisfying than do heterosexuals.

Both homosexuals and heterosexuals range in behavior from very masculine to very feminine, which suggests that there is a combination of factors involved in the expression of sexual orientation, and gender identity/role.

Dr. Weinberg: My guess: Biological factors for homosexuality and heterosexuality; conditioning for various degrees of bi-sexuality.

Dr. Weinrich: To answer this question properly, you have to be precise about the definition of "homosexuality." In the defini-tion I use, a homosexual orientation is probably caused by genetic and hormonal factors, and perhaps also by some early childhood experiences of a psychological or social nature. How these factors are expressed in an adult sexual orientation depends upon the society and a family's environment.

Question #2: *Do you believe that any of the above factors alone could determine whether a person will become gay, straight or bisexual?*

Dr. Bell: Every human being is the occasion for the meeting of all four factors, an indissoluble union of body and mind and emotion. Thus, it would be impossible for me to account for any human matter, including sexual orientation, on the basis of one single factor.

Dr. Ellis: No.

Dr. Green: Probably not. Sexual identity is too complex at the human level to be influenced solely by any of these factors.

Dr. Herdt: We cannot know for sure if any of these factors taken alone result in the self-identification states of "gay," "straight," or "bisexual." But in my opinion this is doubtful.

Dr. Hooker: No, I do not believe that any of these factors alone could determine a person's sexual orientation. As indicated above, sexual orientation is enormously complex and the factors which determine it must be equally so. Even genetic predisposition by itself would not determine the ultimate outcome.

Dr. Marmor. Genetic or hormonal factors may create a power-ful *predisposition* to becoming gay, straight, or bisexual, but psych-ological and social (cultural) factors usually play a contributory role in ultimate sexual orientation.

Dr. Money: No.

Dr. Pillard: Since we know so little about causes, it is premature to speculate whether one factor alone could serve as a cause.

Dr. Reinisch: No.

Dr. Weinberg: Yes, but only for a gay and straight orientation, not for bisexuality.

Dr. Weinrich: No, none of the factors *alone* do so, because in theory, at least, none of the factors operate independently of any of the others.

Question #3: *Can lesbians and gays change their sexual orientation through therapy or other means?*

Dr. Bell: Lesbians and gays may be able to increase their potential for heterosexual experience, at least some of them can, and to behave sexually in a heterosexual manner, but their basic orientation would be virtually unchanged. The latter is too complex a thing, too profound, to be amenable to change to any substantial degree.

Dr. Ellis: If, as I have argued, neurohormonal factors are responsible for variations in sexual orientation, it should be just as difficult to make a homosexual prefer to sexually interact with a member of the opposite sex as to make a heterosexual prefer to sexually interact with a member of the same sex. However, regarding bisexuals, since their sexual orientation is ambivalent to begin with, therapy could be used to direct their sexual inclinations more or less exclusively toward heterosexual activities. Whether or not it would be desirable to do so, however, would have to be decided on a case-by-case basis.

Dr. Green: Research data on lesbians seeking to change sexual orientation are too sparse to offer a meaningful reply. The data on gay men shows that the majority who seek to change sexual orientation do not, either regarding fantasy or overt behavior. Some change behavior markedly, but fantasy minimally. A few case reports claim that via religious therapy or psychiatric or psychologic therapy, sexual reorientation of both fantasy and behavior has occurred.

Dr. Herdt: There is virtually no evidence to suggest that lesbians or gays can reverse their orientation through normal therapeutic procedures.

Dr. Hooker: I know of *no* evidence that lesbians or gays can change their sexual orientation through therapy or any other means. All of the evidence that I have seen shows that they cannot.

Dr. Marmor: I do not believe that the capacity to become erotically aroused by members of the same sex can ever be totally eradicated. A minority of gays and lesbians (usually with a bisexual capacity) can—if strongly enough motivated—learn (through therapy or other means) to suppress their homosexual *behavior*. But the *inclination* usually persists in dreams and/or fantasies.

Dr. Money: No. However, for those whose bisexual ratio is in the range of 60/40 to 50/50 to 40/60, it may be claimed that they can change—even without therapy.

Dr. Pillard: The answer to this question depends upon whether you consider sexual orientation as an innate trait as I suggested above or rather something like a habit which, having been "learned," can also be unlearned. I would say in either case, that many individuals can modify an exclusive homo- or heterosexuality if they wish to do so. Women, in particular, probably have a bisexual orientation more often than not. At the same time, no "therapy" can currently claim to be able to permanently and reliably alter sexual orientation. And one wonders why an individual would *want* to change his or her orientation if we are serious about regarding either as morally equivalent.

Dr. Reinisch: No. We know that homosexuality is not a learned phenomenon. This is evident from anthropological studies of natives in New Guinea whose boys regularly participate in homosexual acts from ages 6 through 19. (It is believed that without the daily ingestation of semen the boys will not become men and procreate). Despite this daily exposure to homosexual acts for 13 years, 99 percent of the boys never again practice homosexuality after age 19, when they are matched with a woman. We also know from studies of twin brothers reared apart that if one twin is gay, it is likely that the second twin will be gay as well (but that is not true for lesbians). As I said earlier, children brought up by homosexuals or lesbians are no more likely to grow up homosexual than are children raised by heterosexual parents.

These data indicate that homosexuality is not necessarily a learned behavior. Permanent change through therapy in the attraction and emotional components dictating with whom an individual falls in love is therefore not likely.

Dr. Weinberg: No.

Dr. Weinrich: Again, this depends upon the definitions used. A homosexual orientation, as I define it, is apparently rarely (possibly never) changed by therapy or other means.

Reading List

Bell, Alan P., Martin S. Weinberg, and Sue Kiefer Hammersmith. *Sexual Preference: Its Development in Men and Women.* Bloomington: Indiana University Press, 1981.

Ellis, Lee Ellis, and M. Ashley Ames. *Neurohormonal Functioning and Sexual Orientation: A Theory of Homosexuality-Heterosexuality.* New Orleans: PFLAG, 1987.

Green, Richard. *The Sissy-Boy Syndrome and the Development of Homosexuality.* New Haven, CT: Yale University Press, 1987.

Herdt, Gilbert. *The Sambia: Ritual and Gender in New Guinea.* New York: Holt, Rinehart and Winston, 1987.

Kinsey, Alfred C., Wardell B. Pomeroy, and Clyde E. Martin. *Sexual Behavior in the Human Male.* Philadelphia: W. B. Saunders, 1948.

Marmor, Judd. *Homosexual Behavior: A Modern Reappraisal.* New York: Basic Books, 1980.

Money, John. *Gay, Straight, and In-Between: The Sexology of Erotic Orientation.* New York: Oxford University Press, 1988.

Pillard, Richard C. "Psychotherapeutic Treatment for the Invisible Minority." In W. Paul et al., eds., *Homosexuality: Social, Psychological, and Biological Issues.* Beverly Hills, CA: Sage Publications, 1982.

Weinrich, James D. *Sexual Landscapes: Why We Are What We Are, Why We Love Whom We Love.* New York: Scribners/Macmillan, 1987.

TWENTY-EIGHT

Encountering Homosexuality:
A Physician Responds

▼

Anonymous

We are a close and loving family. As parents we have tried to teach righteous living, personal sacrifice, benefits of education and career preparation, respect for others, personal integrity, and faith in God and church. All of these precepts have been accepted and lived by our children. College degrees with honors, respect from peers, service to community and church, happy homes have been the fruits of our parenting.

Into this apparently happy setting came the disclosure from one of our unwed sons that he had since age fifteen struggled with homosexual feelings. In spite of this he had served his church for two years as a missionary, achieved a post-graduate degree, and was embarking on a professional career.

For fifteen years he had conducted his private battle against these feelings, and through it all he had remained chaste and celibate. He had pursued counseling from local medical authorities. He had sought religious direction in prayers, fasting, and study. He did not like this facet of his temperament and sought to control and eliminate these feelings. He did not turn to substance abuse or acting out rebellion or suicide as so many others do. He continued to be a church-attending, loyal, obedient member of the family. But he could not, he felt, talk with us about his homosexuality. Increasingly his circle of friends became others of his same orientation because they could advise and support each other without fear of rejection or exposure.

When he finally told us, we wanted to deny it all and hoped his problem would go away. Yet it did not for us, as it had not for our son over those fifteen years. We resolved to fight the problem through study and by getting help from the experts. We sought out local authorities in psychiatry, psychology, and sociology. All of them told us that this was a difficult, unmanageable problem in an intolerant, uninformed community. We were told that our local community was even less accepting of homosexuality than in other areas. We then sought advice from national and international authorities on homosexuality. Specifically, we communicated with Dr. Gene Abel, behavioral medicine, Emory University; Dr. Irving Bieber, New York Medical College; Dr. Charles W. Socaridies, psychoanalysis, Albert Einstein University; Dr. Brian Gladue, human sexuality, North Dakota University; Dr. James Weinrich, psychiatry, University of California-San Diego; Dr. Julia Heiman, psychiatry and behavioral medicine, University of Washington; Dr. Gunter Dorner, pathology, gynecology and endocrinology, Humbolt University, East Germany; Dr. G. L. Gessa, Institute of Pharmacology, University of Cagliari, Italy; and Dr. John Money, psychology, Johns Hopkins University.

We were informed by all of these experts that change/cure potential was dependent upon the Kinsey Scale placement of our son. Our son gave us to believe, as did local specialists, that he was in category 6, exclusively homosexual. The potential for true and permanent sexual reorientation in category 6 has been found by all experts to be extremely limited. Since none of these authorities held out hope of cure for our son, we elected to research the causes of homosexuality. Perhaps the answers for treatment would follow the explanation of cause.

Sigmund Freud proposed that an abnormal arrest in the psychological-social development of male sexuality contributes to homosexuality. Freud continues to be popular with many psychiatrists and psychologists but is rejected by sex researchers. His notions have wide currency with the general public despite scientific research which indicates they have little validity. As our research continued, we found a growing body of scientific information suggesting that homosexuality may be biologically determined.

Scientific research in human sexuality has made great strides in the past twenty years. Prior to the 1970s sexual orientation was thought to be entirely self-chosen, self-imposed. Social and psychological determinants are still thought to play a role in the multiple causes of sexual orientation. However, animal as well as human research now supports the hypothesis that there are hormonal and genetic influences on the developing prenatal brain that influence eventual sexual orientation. These prenatal effects are not detectable, preventable, or treatable during fetal brain embryogenesis. They do, however, feminize or masculinize the fetal brain, whatever the gender determination of the fetus. At puberty this predetermined sexual orientation becomes apparent regardless of gender. Homosexuality, bisexuality, or heterosexuality results. (See Scientific Notes.)

Most religions have taught that homosexuality is purely behavioral and self-determined. They declare it within the scope of human self-control. In the LDS church aversion therapy along with counseling has been the mode of treatment generally advocated, with conversion to heterosexuality as the goal and with excommunication as the cost for failure.

Yet the *British Journal of Psychiatry* reported that in a study of 157 homosexual patients who were treated with numerous behavioral approaches, the basic sexual orientation was not changed. The researchers found no evidence of reduced homosexual feeling and increased heterosexual behavior (McConaghy 1976). These facts notwithstanding, churches in general continue to press homosexuals to change their orientation.

We have come to several conclusions about our son and based on these a course of action:

1. We accept homosexuality as an attribute from birth in him. We know that it is common, that one of every four families will be touched somehow by it. It is not avoidable, identifiable, or treatable before birth. Neither he nor we had a choice in his orientation—which became apparent at puberty.

2. His sexual expression is self-determined. His conduct will be dictated by his social needs, his values, his religious training, and

his strengths. We recognize in him all the basic good traits we have known him for always. His sexual orientation is only part of his personality makeup.

3. Our homosexual son deserves the same opportunities—social and religious—as the heterosexual receives. His life is meant to be full of joy and satisfactions just as the heterosexual receives. There should be no room for discrimination, hatred, rejection, or persecution. Who would render these feelings against the blind, the deaf, or the handicapped because they were born different from the norm?

4. Homosexuality does not equate with promiscuity, exhibitionism, voyeurism, cross-dressing, pedophilia, or any other extreme sexual behaviors. These behaviors relate to the moral values and controls of the person rather than to his or her orientation.

5. We accept our loved one as he is, just as he has learned to do. There can be no feasible change despite psychological and religious claims. We know that his future is fraught with risks of persecution, prejudice, church rejections, physical intimidation, and even AIDS. He will never know the joys of a wife or family. He cannot control his destiny for change. He can determine his level of sexual activity, but this will be dictated by his own basic emotional, social-sexual drives. All of these drives are God-given.

6. We will not reject or cast him out of our family as evil or perverse. Nor do we feel that any compassionate charitable person or group should. That merely adds pain and suffering to an already strained life.

7. We see in him all of the Christlike traits that he has had from birth. His homosexuality does not detract from these admirable characteristics.

8. We intend to keep his homosexuality a secret. Church and society are not prepared or able to accept his condition at this time. Unfortunately, most families revealing this heartache to church authorities have not been helped, understood, or accepted. The exact opposite has often been the result, with the involved individuals and their families being threatened with disciplinary action.

9. We intend to continue studying, researching, and expanding our knowledge. One cannot imagine the pain and suffering without being there. It is far worse for the affected individual, but it is

difficult for the families as well.

10. We have seen the faith of our son waver and weaken in response to rejection and accusation by his church. We have felt this same threat to our own faith. We wish there could be tolerance and support for this minority. If they could have religious acceptance and church organizational support, they could at least find others of their orientation with high values, ideals, and hopes. We will press for such acceptance.

11. We as well as he have an abiding understanding of and hope in the love, justice, and mercy of God. We do not understand this assignment to our son. We hope that it will not be more than he or we can bear. We do not want it to destroy his or our faith. We can't see the purpose of it, but we are willing to view it in positive terms, as compatible with a fulfilled life. He has expressed the same hopeful intent.

Scientific Notes

Most scientists have now reached the following conclusions regarding the development of human sexuality:

1. Life in general (and sexual life in particular) is based on interactions between genetic material and the natural and psychosocial environment. Such interactions are controlled by the brain, mediated by systemic hormones and neurotransmitters (Dorner 1988a).

2. Altering levels of neurotransmitters such as brain serotonin or dopamine in laboratory animals has a direct effect upon their sexual orientation. Dopamine agonists stimulate only male-type sexual behavior, while serotonin agonists stimulate only female-type behavior (Gessa and Tagliamonte 1975).

3. The neuroendocrine component, the positive estrogen feedback effect thought to be related to sexual orientation and indirectly to sexual differentiation, has been evaluated in heterosexual and homosexual individuals. The response in homosexual men is not the same as in heterosexual men. It falls more toward the response of women rather than the male response (Dorner et al. 1975; Gladue 1983).

4. Altering levels of brain catecholamines has an effect upon sexual interest and behavior. This is seen as a side effect in the

Parkinson patient when treated with L Dopa (Sjoerdsma et al. 1970).

5. The development of a sexual orientation in heterosexuals or homosexuals does not seem to depend on pubertal hormones. The evidence for a role of fetal hormones is suggested (Meyer-Bahlburg 1982).

6. Sexual orientation is not a matter of choice but is an effect of prenatal hormones on the dimorphic fetal brain which has the potential to develop in a masculine, feminine, or bisexual direction (Money 1988).

7. There are a number of medical syndromes which represent nature's experiment with gender assignment and sexual preference. These relate to hormonal or chromosomal abnormalities in development. The end result of these errors in morphology are patients with abnormal gender (Money 1988).

8. Identical twins raised in different homes have been studied to look at nature versus nurture in their effects upon sexuality. There is a higher rate of homosexuality found among the monozygotic (identical) twins than the dizygotic (fraternal) twins. It is hard to deny a genetic factor playing a causative role (Eckert et al. 1986).

9. A reproductive dictum suggests that if heterosexuality is essential for reproduction and is biologically determined, variations in sexual orientation must also have biological origins (Gladue 1984).

10. A positive estrogen feedback sex-specific reaction of the hypothalamo-hypophyseal system has been found in rats as well as humans. It is dependent on the estrogen-convertible androgen level during sexual brain differentiation and also on estrogen priming in adulthood. The lower the estrogen (primary) level during brain differentiation, the higher the evocability of a positive estrogen action on the luteinizing hormone secretion in late life. In clinical studies a distinct difference was found in the positive estrogen feedback luteinizing hormone secretion in homosexual men compared to heterosexual or bisexual men (Dorner 1988b).

11. Female- as well as male-brain differentiation may be hormonally determined. This could be due to abnormalities in fetal exposure to hormones, leading first to physical mis-differentiation and later to homosexual behavior in genetically and phenotypically

normal men and women (MacCulloch and Waddington 1981).

12. Aversive therapies do not appear to alter sexual orientation. No evidence is yet available indicating that other treatments are more effective in reducing homosexual and increasing heterosexual behavior (McConaghy 1976).

13. The brain is prenatally influenced by hormones. Both estrogen and androgen occurring during brain fetal differentiation predetermine sexual orientation (Dorner 1988b).

References

Dorner, G. "Hormone Dependent Differentiation: Maturation and Function of the Brain and Sexual Behavior." *Endocrinology* 69:3 (1977), 306-20.

———. "Sexual Endocrinology and Terminology in Sexology." *Experimental and Clinological Endocrinology* 91:2 (May 1988a), 129-34.

———. "Neuroendocrine Response to Estrogen and Brain Differentiation in Heterosexuals, Homosexuals and Transexuals." *Archives of Sexual Behavior* 17:1 (Feb. 1988b), 57-75.

——— et al. "A Neuroendocrine Predisposition for Homosexuality in Men." *Archives of Sexual Behavior* 4 (1975):1.

———. "On the LH Response to Estrogen and LH-RH in Transexual Men." *Experimental and Clinological Endocrinology* 3 (Nov. 1983): 257-67.

Eckert, E., et al. "Homosexuality in Monozygotic Twins Reared Apart." *British Journal of Psychiatry* 148 (1986): 421-25.

Federation of Parents and Friends of Lesbians and Gays. Inc. *Why Is My Child Gay?* 1988.

Gessa, G., and A. Tagliamonte. "Role of Brain Serotonin and Dopamine in Male Sexual Behavior." In *Sexual Behavior, Pharmacology and Biochemistry,* eds. M. Sandler and G. Gessa. New York: Raven Press, 1974a.

———. "Possible Role of Brain Serotonin and Dopamine in Controlling Male Sexual Behavior." In *Advances in Biochemical Psychopharmacology*, Vol. 11. New York: Raven Press, 1974.

Gladue, Brian A. "Neuroendocrine Response to Estrogen and Sexual Orientation." *Science* 225 (28 Sept. 1984): 1496-99.

———. "Hormones in Relationship to Homosexual/Bisexual Gender Orientation." In *Handbook of Sexology, Vol. 6, The Pharmacology and Endocrinology of Sexual Function.* Elsevier, 1988.

McConaghy, N. "Is Homosexual Orientation Irreversible?" *British Journal of Psychiatry* 129 (1976): 556-63.

MacCulloch, M. J., and John Waddington. "Neuroendocrine Mechanisms and the Aetiology of Male and Female Homosexuality." *British Journal of Psychiatry* 139 (1981): 341-45.

Meyer-Bahlburg, H. F. "Hormones and Psychosexual Differentiation: Implications for the Management of Intersexuality, Homosexuality and Transexuality." *Clin Endocrinology and Metabolism* 11:3 (Nov. 1982), 681-701.

Money, John. *Gay, Straight, or In-between.* New York: Oxford University Press, 1988.

Sjoerdsma, A., et al. "Serotonin Now: Clinical Implications of Inhibiting Its Synthesis with Para-chlorophenylalanine." *Annals of Internal Medicine* 73 (1970): 607-29.

TWENTY-NINE

Homophobia–Do I Have It?

▼

George Weinberg

In the late 1970s a young psychiatrist telephoned his wife who was at home with their infant child. "I'll be late tonight. Better have dinner without me," he said. They had been having some trouble in their marriage, but she gave no heed to his call. She did not know that her husband was about to kill himself. He went to a hotel room alone and took a fatal dose of poison. The reason: he was homosexual, and could stand the pain no longer.

The doctor had received his M.D. degree four years before. At the same time he had begun a long psychoanalysis aimed at eradicating his powerful attraction to men. His psychiatrist concurred that homosexuality was a serious problem that would utterly disqualify him from becoming a psychiatrist himself. They tore at the problem, presumably looking at it from various angles but never doubting that it was of a heinous nature.

Dr. George Weinberg is a psychotherapist in private practice and author living in New York City. He received an award from the American Psychological Association for coining the term "homophobia" and for its analysis. His best-known works are *Society and the Healthy Homosexual* and *Self Creation*.

I believe that their work must have intensified the young man's self-hate. Any act based on repugnance toward a part of oneself can only increase that repugnance. In the end his love for men seemed wrong and unconquerable; he had engaged in homosexual sex with several partners and could not talk himself out of his desire. The doctor confided in his brother, who told me more details than I can recount here. When the brother called the psychiatrist after the suicide, the latter at first refused to talk to him and then consented, commenting succinctly that this is the course the disease often takes.

I was reminded of the often-repeated sentiment that one of the puzzling things about homosexuality is that some people hate themselves for it, while others seem to adapt, often with little difficulty. Society, not just ours but virtually all modern cultures, sees in homosexuality something opprobrious, immoral, and even pathological. Without understanding the causes or implications of homosexuality, societies have punished homosexual men and women in ways ranging from subtle ostracism to physical brutality and murder.

In recent years the penalties have become less and in many places are not so often enforced. But homosexuality still remains a "problem." The prevalent negative attitudes toward homosexuals still cause immense harm, not just to gays but to those close to them and to all the righteous.

About fifteen years ago I became interested in the hostility shown by most people to homosexuals. I was spurred to examine this dynamic when I recognized that fear, revulsion, and distrust of homosexuals are often converted into great rage toward them. Apart from the evil done to homosexuals, many people who do not act overtly against them want to erase them from the mind, to annihilate them mentally. Why, I wondered, should people who engage in sexual acts not intrinsically harmful to anyone elicit such anxiety and dread in other people?

I soon realized the considerable importance of the attitude I was investigating.

The majority of people whose collective voice has opposed the rights of homosexuals is diverse. It is composed of liberals and conservatives, the sophisticated and the naive, the trained and the untrained. Its members come from every walk of life and every profession. This majority regards homosexuals as loathsome, freakish things—criminals at worst or pathetic strangers at best— whose conduct must be curbed for society's protection. To this group it seems that no injustice is done. Homosexuals, they feel, do not deserve to be on a par with others—since they make a mockery of society and its public morality.

I concluded that I was dealing with a phobia. Because the majority shared this phobia, it had gone overlooked as such. In 1967 I gave it the name *homophobia*. Like any phobia it is an obsessive, irrational fear. At the root of any phobia, there always lies some personal problem for which the stimulus is a symbol. The person with the phobia feels dread at the sight of or at any reminders of the dreaded. The word "thing" is significant. In this case homosexuals are the stimulus for dread, and the reaction of the *homophobe* is to dehumanize homosexuals, to perceive them as things not as people, thus the startling absence of concern in otherwise conscionable people over the systematic legal and social persecution of homosexuals. Thus do millions of concerned parents suddenly shun their sons and daughters for being homosexual. Their very blindness to the human consequences is a measure of the phobia.

Homophobia ranges in intensity from mild to acute forms. In mild cases the person seeks only to avoid homosexuals and perhaps demands that they remain socially anonymous. Such a person sees no reason for legislation to protect homosexuals since, if homosexuals "behave properly," they will get by.

At the next level of homophobia is the morbid desire to have homosexuals disappear, somehow. "If I had the power to do so," wrote Joseph Epstein in *Harpers,* "I would wish homosexuality off the face of the earth."

The still more intensely homophobic person actively seeks to enflame others against homosexuals and perhaps accomplish Epstein's aspiration by direct means. For example, there have been those who accuse homosexuals of bringing Hitler to power. "One cannot regard it as coincidence," wrote conservative commentator Jeffrey St. John, "that the Houston murders began at the time the gay militants took to the streets in 1970."

The nonintellectual form of this severe homophobia manifests itself in actual physical attacks on homosexuals. A chief reason given by New York City's Uniformed Fire Officers Association for opposing gay rights was that many of their own men would "go berserk" and beat up homosexuals if forced to interact closely with them. But homophobia in all its manifestations is much more subtle than even homosexuals imagined. It took a decade for gay activists to realize what they were up against.

For years advocates of gay rights imagined their opponents ranging between two polar positions—conservative and liberal. The conservatives, adhering to a literal interpretation of the Bible that condemns homosexual acts as evil, conceive of homosexuals as sinners and demand that they be punished. To gays it seemed virtually hopeless to expect conservatives to acknowledge their civil and constitutional rights. All hope lay with the liberals, large numbers of whom the gays imagined were simply misinformed about homosexuality. Liberals generally prided themselves on their desire for equality and on their willingness to listen and consider the evidence. Accordingly, liberals became the natural target of gay educational activities. The widespread assumption in the gay world was that liberals would be eager to rectify their tragic misunderstanding of what homosexuals are like.

Up to a point the liberals have been living up to the homosexuals' expectations. In the 1960s the ACLU began taking up homosexuals' cases for the first time. Many liberals began listening with genuine interest to gays' appeals. Liberals typically held several misconceptions about homosexuals which, the gays thought, could be easily set right by pure factual information. So they poured forth data. It was widely believed, for instance, that homosexuals as a group are guilty of molesting children. The Kinsey Institute volume *Sex Offenders* dispelled this myth. Recent studies corroborate their finding: virtually all child molestation is done not by homosexuals but by adult, heterosexual men with little girls. It was also widely accepted that homosexuals are prone to violence; the facts refuted this. It is given that homosexuals are especially vulnerable to blackmail. There is no evidence to support this, and a professed homosexual obviously cannot be blackmailed on that score at all. The liberals listened to arguments, absorbed data. As momentum gathered behind the various gay rights bills in different states, they seemed only a decimal point away from granting homosexuals their rights.

But the necessary margin was to remain beyond reach in many places.

Gradually, gay activists have begun to see that the liberal reaction, though flexible, is often of no more help to them than the conservative reaction. Liberals listen but somehow they are seldom persuaded. As soon as one myth about homosexuals is punctured the listener offers another. And as specific arguments are rebutted one by one, they fall back on others harder to prove or disprove, such as the one that homosexuals are "sick." Even the decision by the American Psychiatric Association that homosexuality is not a mental illness has not changed the attitudes of many who had used the sickness argument. This practice of replacing one misgiving with another enables the liberals to listen continuously and thus go on appearing deeply concerned about all minorities while doing nothing about the rights of homosexuals.

The true homophobe often displays another mechanism—that of having to "learn" the same information over and over again. Many of these listeners are continuously astounded by information showing that the homosexual community is actually deprived of its rights, as if they have never heard it before. The hard facts seem to disappear from memory and must be learned anew, time and time again.

In some cases homophobes show a remarkable ability to retain the facts, grasp the arguments, concede the harm done to homosexuals, and yet stand staunchly against a legal remedy. For example, syndicated columnist Nicholas von Hoffman described the existing punitive legislation against homosexuals as "crazy," advocated its repeal, and declared that many homosexuals have been "cruelly used, terribly mistreated, hounded, disgraced, and deprived of a living." Having thus demonstrated his humanity and liberality, he went on to declaim against a gay rights bill as unnecessary. After all, wrote von Hoffman, homosexuals are doing very well as compared to blacks and women.

It becomes increasingly clear that people's attitudes toward homosexuality do not fit logically into the structure of their own beliefs. It becomes apparent, in fact, that the real problem is not a matter of logic. Gays themselves began to grasp that they were up against a phenomenon deeper than mere intellectual opposition, that they were confronting an alternate fear—homophobia. After the publication of my book, *Society and the Healthy Homosexual*, in which I presented homophobia as an idea and analyzed it, gays seized the concept as one which genuinely explained their experience.

Within the last few years many more people have become aware that the hatred of homosexuals is itself a psychological problem. "We are presenting a new kind of target as we become visible and stronger," said Nathalie Rockhill, former National Coordinator of the Gay Task Force. "We have become the focus of the inchoate fears that people have."

What are the imagined threats that homosexuals bring? What fears plague the person who finds it distressing to work or pray or eat alongside a homosexual?

More than any other single correlate is what might be called the irrational *dread of contagion.* Barbara Gittings, one of the most prolific and articulate speakers on gay rights in America, told me, "The question seems always to come up in one form or another. 'What if everybody became homosexual, how would the race continue?'" One city councilman said in vetoing gay rights, "I cannot accept a homosexual lifestyle for my three children." Apparently that was the question he thought he was being asked to vote on. There is widespread fear that great numbers of people would find homosexuality desirable and must be discouraged.

So irrational is the fear, that many people imagine the mere statement that one is homosexual could make homosexuality irresistibly attractive to others, especially to the young.

Some fraction of homophobes are afraid of homosexuality in themselves. One advocate of gay rights encountered the objection, "If we drop the stigmas against homosexuality, and all the laws, why then *everyone* will be homosexual!" So apparently this man was using the law to help him with his own self-restraint.

Freud speculated that great rage toward homosexuals is always a defense against the recognition of one's own homosexuality. Many people continue to think this. But various follow-up studies of homophobia done in colleges around the country corroborate my own findings that this motivation appears relatively rarely. Most self-denied homosexuals painstakingly avoid the topic. The motivations for homophobia are more complex.

Freud, by the way, identified repressed homosexuality as an

invariable concomitant of paranoia. He observed many repressed homosexuals who had, in his opinion, a morbid fear of persecution. The saying became popular in psychoanalytic circles: "Scratch a paranoid and you'll find a homosexual underneath." However, the homosexual has always had reason for fear in modern western society. Paradoxically, the homophobic person, who has nothing real to fear from homosexuals, is the true paranoid.

Another prevalent reason for the dislike or dread of homosexuals astonished me when I started noticing it in different people. Though homosexuals have been outcasts and people believe that they suffer because of their orientation in the long run, there is a strong motif of repressed envy of homosexuals. The housewife who wonders whether she has chosen a life unduly difficult and the husband burdened with family obligations and resentful of his marriage contract are both likely to yearn for the freedom which they imagine homosexuals enjoy. Such people may perceive the homosexual as mockingly reminding them of their own choice, as if to say, "Look at all you have given up. And for what?" These people do not themselves want to be homosexual, but they envy the life they attribute to homosexuals. It feels as if the present penalties against homosexuals are needed to compensate for the unfair advantages they believe homosexuals enjoy.

Homosexuals in this view are avoiding obligations imposed upon the rest of us and for this reason should be punished. A wretched homosexual is not nearly so troublesome to these people as one who seems to be delighting in life. I am reminded of H. L. Mencken's comment that puritanism is "the lurking fear that someone, somewhere may be happy." Some of the very people who preach that the lives of homosexuals invariably end in misery are secretly afraid that they are wrong. Otherwise they would willingly let homosexuals suffer the consequences of their behavior and would see no need for social or legal penalties.

Among the most virulent homophobes are people who regard the homosexual man as having abandoned manhood and the lesbian as having abandoned womanhood. For instance, men who emphasize power, conquest, and "masculinity" are apt to dislike homosexual men. Several studies, and my own observations, suggest that the more important conventional "masculinity" is to a man and the more he fears passivity and traits which he regards as feminine, the more he is apt to dislike homosexual men. Such men regard homosexuals as lowering the "male standard." This brings terror to them because so much of their own sense of worth rests on their being men and not women. To many such people, granting privileges to homosexuals is exactly like granting privileges to women.

To men whose macho psychology is behind their opposition to gays, lesbians are apart from the issue. In fact, the form of the prejudice against women is very different from that of the prejudice against gay men. Some years ago a New York City judge threw out a case against a woman accused of lesbianism, saying there was no such thing. To some degree that attitude persists. Few consider lesbians as child-molesting or being violent or paying blackmail money. Lesbians endure the various social consequences that gay men do without being thought of a tenth as often. Lesbian rights bills would probably pass without raising as great a commotion.

One reason for this is that masculinity connotes prestige and power in our society. For a man to "act like a woman" seems more shocking, less explicable, than for a woman to "act like a man." Our dress codes, for instance, are evidence of this—women wear pants, but men may not wear skirts. The man who acts like a woman is seen as violating the basic rule of upward mobility. The woman who acts like a man is seen as doing so to gain real advantages. This view completely refuses to consider that lesbians are women in every sense and differ from certain other women only in their sexual orientation.

A second reason why lesbianism arouses less opposition is simply that women, being regarded as less important than men, are taken less seriously when they become homosexual. As feminist leader Dr. Catherine R. Stimpson put it, "Many men regard the lesbian choice as that of a lesser for a lesser."

Whatever the reason for any single homophobe, many expect homosexuals to bring catastrophe to society. This fear is linked to the dread of Judgment Day. It has a biblical origin—opposition to most gay rights legislation comes notably from the Hasidim and the Roman Catholic Church. And many people who have given up formal religion retain a sense of dread about sexual privileges. Though they no longer literally believe in Judgment Day, they fear the collapse of society here and now if further sexual permissions are granted. They see our society as already at the brink. Sexual privileges in this view might be likened to a deck of cards. If you remove the top card from the deck, others come closer to the top. For instance, if nudity is allowed, homosexuality comes closer; if homosexuality, then incest. When a gay rights bill was first proposed in New York, liberal columnist Mike Royko sardonically raised the question of whether marriage between men and monkeys would next be condoned. To such people it is as if there is in the deck a wild card, a joker, which, when it comes to the top, will destroy society altogether. Looking back over the past, these people may regard the civil rights movement as good; but looking toward the future, they fear a cataclysm if yet more rights are granted.

To solve the problem of homophobia would in my opinion do much more than give homosexuals a fair chance. It would release the homophobe from the bonds of his own fears and in many cases his own obsessions.

THIRTY

Suicidal Behavior in
Gay and Lesbian Mormons

▼

Christopher J. Alexander

During the last few years I have been a member of Affirmation, an organization of gay and lesbian Mormons who seek to build bridges between homosexuality and Mormonism. In 1987 I served as general coordinator and in this capacity maintained regular contact with chapter leaders and other members. Often I was the first person to be contacted by someone who was just learning of Affirmation. I answered their questions, provided emotional support, and referred them to the nearest chapter.

From this vantage point I came in contact with many men and women from around the country. I talked with people who had never before disclosed to anyone their feelings of being gay, lesbian, or bisexual. I talked with those who were active in the LDS church in varying degrees, and I met with church authorities to discuss issues surrounding homosexuality. I shared in the excite-

"Suicidal Behavior in Gay and Lesbian Mormons," by Christopher J. Alexander, originally appeared in slightly different form in *Affinity*, November 1989. Dr. Alexander holds a Ph.D. in clinical counseling from the Professional School of Psychology, San Francisco. He is currently a psychotherapist at the Children's Hospital, Oakland, California, and is in private practice.

ment of some who learned they were not alone as homosexuals in the Mormon community. I also saw the pain, sorrow, and struggle that many of these men and women were experiencing. One of the most alarming insights that came to me before and and during my tenure in office was the frequency of suicidal fantasies, attempts, or deaths occurring among homosexual Mormons.

Rofes (1983) points out that assessing the rate of suicide in any population is difficult given the shame, inadequacy, and failure felt by survivors and their families. The stigma is great enough that many families succeed in having coroners list the death as something other than suicide, and some coroners only list the death as suicide if a suicide note is present. Less than 40 percent of people who kill themselves leave notes. These facts notwithstanding, there are 35,000 suicides reported each year in the U.S., and it is the tenth leading cause of death.

Several research studies have gleaned the following information about gays and suicide:

—40 percent of men and 39 percent of women among a sample of 5,000 had attempted or seriously contemplated suicide (Jay and Young 1977).

—53 percent of the suicidal men and 33 percent of the suicidal women in this same study said that their homosexuality was a factor in their suicidal impulses and actions.

—37 percent of white homosexual males had attempted or seriously considered suicide compared to 13 percent of white heterosexual males in a research study of 575 gay men and 284 heterosexual men (Bell and Weinberg 1978).

—41 percent of white lesbians versus 26 percent of white heterosexual women contemplated or attempted suicide in the Bell and Weinberg study of 229 lesbians and 101 heterosexual women.

—50 percent of the gay men and lesbian women in the Bell and Weinberg study reported that their attempts were related to their homosexuality.

—over 50 percent of the gays and lesbians in the Bell and Weinberg study who had attempted suicide did so before the age of twenty.

—12 percent of lesbians and 7 percent of gay men had attempted suicide in a study of 146 homosexual persons (Saghir and Robins 1973).

It is important to acknowledge that these are statistics of survivors. We have no reliable data on actual suicides among gay men or lesbian women.

My interest in the incidence of suicide among gay Mormons grew as I read the research and talked to others. In the spring of 1985 I began a research project to examine the frequency of suicidal fantasies, attempts, and completions among gay and lesbian Mormons. I solicited biographies and autobiographies from participants at local and national Affirmation gatherings. I hoped that I would be able to gather enough data to warrant a dissertation project for my doctorate in clinical psychology.

Unfortunately several requests yielded only a handful of written narratives. The content of these letters spoke to the magnitude of the problem and provided some chilling insights. All of the letters sent to me were from men who spoke about their own suicidal ideas or told me about the completed suicide of another man. My correspondents were from all regions of the country. All but one person gave me a return address, although some chose not to use their real names. Perhaps the most striking thing was the obvious apprehension most writers had about putting their stories into words—for many it was the first time. Yet there was an increasing tone of relief toward the end of each letter.

A few of the suicidal men described to me were married. In some cases the wife knew about her husband's sexuality struggles, but for the most part the topic was not discussed in the relationship. One wife became nervous whenever her husband was around gay people for fear he would leave her. Her husband overdosed on prescription medications and drowned himself. One man who wrote to me about his suicidal feelings is still married. He feels that he goes through life with the feeling of "holding my breath, leading a life of introversion and morbid self-analysis." He writes, "The act or completion of suicide is when you can't hold your breath any longer." Reflecting on his fear of divorce, excommunication, and rejection, he said, "With such losses there would be no choice for me but the ultimate choice—death."

For a few men who wrote, the biggest struggle occurred as they were expected to go on a mission. Some felt that they were not "worthy" enough, and others felt that it would be a lie to go on a mission. As family influence mounted, the thoughts of suicide increased. One writer reported, "The pressure started from my family every time I saw them, adding to my own guilty conviction that what I felt was totally wrong. I was terrified of the possibility of excommunication. I couldn't stay concentrated on anything. I couldn't hold a job. Nothing in my life worked. Depression was always just around the corner. At eighteen it looked like the end of the world to me. I went home one weekend and spent the time with my family. Before I left I borrowed my father's .22 automatic. I thought about it for one entire week. I put it off and finally ended up at a bar. . . . I met a girl who told me that God didn't hate homosexuals. I began to realize that there was more thinking to do."

One of the major factors contributing to the suicides of lesbians, gays, and bisexuals is estrangement from the traditional support systems within our culture that people turn to in times of crisis: family, church, and school. As is clear from the above examples, these men did not see family or church as a support. Some of the men who wrote me harbor considerable anger and blame the church. One lamented, "The biggest agony I went through was my attempt to understand the suffering, my own and that of my friends. During a one week period I was able to count thirty friends who had seriously contemplated suicide because of their feelings about being gay. The Mormon church was the biggest factor, so I thought, in the origins of these suicidal feelings and fantasies."

Nineteenth-century French sociologist Emile Durkheim wrote, "If religion protects one from the desire for self-destruction, it is not because it preaches to him, with elements of religious origin; it is because it forms a social group." Durkheim was talking not only of social integration within the church as a community but also of personal identification with the church. The church is part of the self. I believe we should not underestimate the power of being raised Mormon. It is as potent to identity as being raised Jewish, Catholic, Irish, or Chinese. For gays, lesbians or bisexuals, this upbringing increases the feelings of isolation when they think they cannot turn to anyone for help. Motto (1975) notes that the second most common reason why someone commits suicide is that the person, who normally displays strength and ability in many areas of life, experiences a gradual, relentless shrinkage in his or her sources of emotional support.

Some of the respondents who are still alive continue to struggle with fleeting thoughts of suicide. Others have overcome their impulses and are living well-adjusted lives. One person wrote: "I am honest, hardworking, loving, happy, and gay. My family loves me. I am living life for me. I have never thought of suicide since that time. I have also never been back to church."

Of particular concern to me is the incidence of suicidal urges, attempts, and completions among teenagers, gay and straight, Mormon and non-Mormon. Current statistics indicate that the incidence of suicide among our nation's adolescent population is soaring. In the past thirty-five years the suicide rate for those aged fifteen to twenty-four years has risen from 4.5 per 100,000 to 12.8 per 100,000. This is a 284 percent increase. These figures include gay teenagers, and as Bell and Weinberg discovered, more than half of gays who attempt suicide do so while under twenty years of age.

The struggles of adolescents in today's world are well known. In addition to normal challenges, drugs and world conditions make growing up more difficult. For many Mormon youths high expectations add to the developmental challenges. When in addition to all of this, a youth struggles with homosexual urges that occur to him or her without bidding but are anathema to the church, the pressure becomes extreme.

Ann Landers writes of letters received from teenage homosexuals: "Most of the boys who write are tortured with guilt and self-hatred. Most live on the razor's edge, terrified that someone might learn they aren't like everybody else. Many who write are so ashamed of their physical desires for members of their own sex that they speak of suicide. One seventeen-year old Chicago boy wrote, 'If I can't get cured I would rather kill myself than be a pansy all my life.'"

A 1978 article in *The Advocate* contained the following by a gay Mormon, "In almost every case, the church overwhelms the young man with guilt. In some cases the guilt produces panic, desperate unpredictability, and even suicide. I have been rather close to several such individuals and know of other young returned missionaries who were unable to accept their sexuality and took their lives."

We need to understand the magnitude of guilt, shame, difference, and isolation that many men and women still feel today about their sexuality. We are each responsible to learn the signs of suicidal feelings and behavior and to know how to respond when we see those signs. Leaders should learn some suicide prevention and intervention skills. I vividly remember as an officer in Affirmation receiving calls from members struggling with suicide. These people need a place to come, someone to turn to for support and guidance.

I expect the church to perceive a responsibility concerning the number of suicides among gay and lesbian Mormons. Church officials and church members who work for LDS Social Services need to become more sensitive to the impact of their recommendations and treatment. Recently Affirmation was contacted by a bishop in northern California shocked by the suicides of two gay men in his ward. He was seeking advice on how to deal with this issue. This kind of openness is needed churchwide to help curb the numbers of men and women who are killing themselves because of sexual identity struggles. AIDS is more a part of our lives now, and there are those who know of "AIDS suicides" committed while the person is ill. Based on my conversations with church authorities, I believe many see this as a minor issue. It is not.

My concern extends to how therapists treat Mormon gay persons. Lovinger (1984) advises about religious issues in therapy, "There are some churches or synagogues that will accept homosexual members, and some, in larger cities that will welcome them. Perhaps all that is needed is to point this out." I wish this simple advice were sufficient in Mormon culture. As it is not, Mormon therapists need to explore thoroughly the cultural, personal, and spiritual impact of being Mormon on the gay person who is struggling with whatever issues are brought into therapy, particularly if depression or suicidal ideation is present.

Finally, whether church member, family member, church authority, friend, or therapist, we should all work toward loving and accepting each other. We must provide an atmosphere where people can discuss their struggles openly and perhaps finally start to reverse the high number of suicides in our communities.

References

Bell, Alan, and Martin Weinberg. *Homosexualities.* New York: Simon and Schuster, 1978.

Jay, Karla and Allen Young. *The Gay Report: Lesbians and Gay Men Speak Out About Sexual Experiences and Lifestyles.* New York: Summit Books, 1979.

Lovinger, Robert. *Working with Religious Issues in Therapy.* New York: Jason Aronson, Inc., 1984.

Motto, J. A. Personal communication, 1975.

Rofes, Eric. *I Thought People Like That Killed Themselves: Lesbians, Gay Men and Suicide.* San Francisco: Grey Fox Press, 1983.

Saghir, Marcel and Ell Robins. *Male and Female Homosexuality: A Comprehensive Investigation.* Baltimore: Williams and Wilkins, 1973.

THIRTY-ONE

Homosexuality:
A Part of Life, Not a Curse

▼

John S. Spong

The verb "to be" is the key verb in every human language. We use it to describe that which is of our very essence. If I have a broken leg I do not say, "I am a broken leg." But if my leg has been amputated, I might well say, "I am an amputee." The amputation has redefined my being. I might say, "I have measles" to explain a rash, or "I have cancer" to explain a physical pain. The verb "to be" is used when we say, "I am tall," "I am blue-eyed," "I am male," or "I am female." It is employed to describe the essential characteristics of life over which we have no control or that which is so much a part of our identity we cannot think of ourselves apart from it. Language reveals far more than we imagine when we say, "I am heterosexual," or "I am gay," or "I am a lesbian." We now know that homosexuality is part of the essential nature of approximately ten percent of the population. Statistically this means that in the United States of America, homosexuality is the sexual orientation

"Homosexuality: A Part of Life, Not a Curse" is excerpted from John S. Spong, *Living in Sin: A Bishop Rethinks Human Sexuality* (San Francisco: Harper & Row, 1989). John Spong is Bishop of Newark, the Episcopal Church, and author of nine other books.

of some twenty-eight million citizens. It means that every time one hundred people gather in a church anywhere in this nation, the mathematical probability is that ten of them are gay or lesbian persons. It means that no one of us ever goes through a day encountering or transacting business with as few as ten people without the probability that one of those ten is a homosexual person. It means that in every core family or extended family, when the circle expands to ten persons, there is a mathematical probability that one member will be gay or lesbian. The gay and lesbian population is all around us, touching our lives at numerous points, receiving our love and friendship, serving us with professional competence in a myriad of ways, even listening to and laughing at our jokes and our not-so-subtle innuendoes about homosexuality.

In prior generations these homosexual individuals have lived in silence, hiding in the shadows or blending unnoticed into the majority society. Today gay and lesbian persons are emerging from their closets, identifying themselves publicly, and demanding justice, recognition, and acceptance. They represent one additional factor in the changing sexual landscape. No treatment of human sexuality can avoid confrontation with the prevailing cultural prejudices against gay and lesbian people, nor can the ever-present phenomenon of homosexuality itself be ignored.

Homosexuality has been diagnosed in the past as a mental sickness, a medical model that persists in the minds of many. Homosexuality as an illness, however, began to be questioned with the publication of the Kinsey reports in 1948 and 1953.[1] That questioning grew until the board of trustees of the American Psychiatric Association officially removed it in 1973 from the second edition of *The Diagnostic and Statistical Manual of Mental Disorders*. As the manual explains the decision:

> The crucial issue in determining whether or not homosexuality per se should be regarded as a mental disorder is . . . its consequences and the definition of mental disorder. A significant proportion of homosexuals are apparently satisfied with their sexual orientation, show no significant signs of manifest psychopathology . . . and are able to function socially and occupationally with no impairment. If one uses the criteria of *distress or disability*, homosexuality

per se is not a mental disorder. If one uses the criterion of disadvantage, it is not at all clear that homosexuality is a disadvantage in all cultures or subcultures.[2]

Anthropological studies affirm that latter conclusion. There have been some primitive societies in which male homosexuality, far from being treated as a perversion to be shunned, was looked upon as an honor, even as a special blessing from the deity. The homosexual man quite often was assigned the role of the shaman or holy man. He was sometimes thought of as a third sex and given tribal permission to wear female clothes and to perform, liturgically, acts that outside the liturgy would be thought of as belonging to the female domain.[3]

The lesbian received no such honors as far as anthropological studies indicate. As a subjected member of society, she was forced to undergo the regular sexual rituals of the tribe, to mate, and to reproduce, with or without her consent. It was and is more difficult to discern her as separate and distinct in the society. Even our prejudice has a patriarchal stamp.

The modern, prevailing notion that homosexuality is a mental disorder is rooted in Sigmund Freud's theory that it is an aberration that occurs when normal development is somehow distorted between the ages of four and nine.[4] Others, inspired by Freud, speculated on the psychic makeup and influence of the primary adults (usually the parents) in the maturation of the gay or lesbian person. This was a particularly cruel theory, for it placed on the parents blame for what was thought to be a neurotic development, and it fed the guilt and rejection that so often characterized the relationship of a homosexual son or daughter with his or her parents. Nonetheless, because these early medical theories promoted homosexuality as an illness of maladjustment, there was hope of cure. Psychoanalysis in the medical community, or prayer therapy and faith healing in the religious community, were the proffered treatment. A behavior pattern that is maladaptive or learned can presumably be changed into what the majority regards as wholeness.

Continued research in this area, however, has not produced such a cure. Instead it has increasingly falsified the idea that homosexuality is a mental illness. Many researchers believe that not one shred of reproducible evidence has come to light to substantiate clinically the illness theory. If, as is the case today, leading medical practitioners are no longer able to call homosexuality an illness, it then seems inappropriate for official church bodies to continue to pass resolutions based on this discredited medical premise. The church is either failing to realize its ignorance or is acting as if its leaders are privy to some special source of expertise.

There are others who judge homosexuality as a perversion deliberately chosen by those of a depraved or sinful nature. Many heterosexual people cannot imagine that homosexual lovemaking could be pleasurable; some even say they are revolted at the thought of it. Members of the dominant sexual orientation reason that what is normal for them is also natural; if something is not normal for them it must be deviant and, thus, depraved. A variation of this conclusion argues that since homosexual behavior is "unnatural," it is contrary to the order of creation. Behind this pronouncement are stereotypic definitions of masculinity and femininity that reflect the rigid gender categories that arise out of patriarchal society. "Natural" sex is based on the complementary aspects of male and female genitalia. But the urgent question is, How important are the genitalia to sexual desire?

Rosemary Ruether has argued that men and women possess equally the physical apparatus necessary for emotional intimacy.[5] But human thinking has been so influenced by patriarchal values that the male-female relationship can be imagined only in terms of a power equation involving domination and subjection. Female receptivity to male penetration in the sex act has become a paradigm and a synonym for the natural. In this scheme, heterosexual activity is defined as the only valid expression of love. A corollary of this assumption suggests that the man has a gender-specific capacity for decisive action and the woman has a gender-specific capacity for passive intuition—a sixth sense, if you will.

We are moving away from that mentality. Personhood emerges not out of an imposed sexual role but out of the human ability to hear, feel, think, and relate. None of these abilities requires sex organs of any shape or description. Men and women alike have the physiology necessary to speak and hear, to love and be loved. Personal unity comes, Dr. Ruether attests, when one connects "the many parts of the self through multiple relationships with other people."[6] There is nothing unnatural about any shared love, even between two of the same gender, if that experience calls both partners into a fuller state of being. Can a religious tradition that has long practiced circumcision and institutionalized celibacy ever dismiss any other practice on the basis of its unnaturalness?

Contemporary research is today uncovering new facts that are producing a rising conviction that homosexuality, far from being a sickness, sin, perversion, or unnatural act, is a healthy, natural, and affirming form of human sexuality for some people. This research is still in its infancy, relatively speaking, but it has demonstrated a capacity to confront and challenge sexual fear and prejudice that has become entrenched by centuries of repetition. Only in the last few decades have we begun to understand such things as the structure and various functions of the brain, to say nothing of the importance of chromosomes. Discoveries in these areas have had a dramatic effect on our knowledge of human behavior. Specifically, research consistently seems to support the assertion that sexual orientation is not a matter of choice; that it is not related to any environmental influence; that it is not the result of an overbearing mother or an effeminate or absent father or a seductive sexual encounter. Some researchers are finding that certain biochemical events during prenatal life may determine adult sexual orientation, and that once set it is not amenable to change. Though new data are being gathered almost daily, few people working in the area of brain research expect these conclusions to be overturned.

Despite centuries of belief to the contrary, it is slowly dawning on us that the seat of sexual arousal is the brain, not the genitalia. To put it bluntly, this means that the brain is the primary sex organ of the body. A person's sexual orientation and what he or she finds sexually exciting are functions of that person's brain. . . .

Since the evidence points to the conclusion that homosexual persons do not choose their sexual orientation, cannot change it, and constitute a quite normal but minority expression of human sexuality, it is clear that heterosexual prejudice against homosexuals must take its place alongside witchcraft, slavery, and other ignorant beliefs and oppressive institutions that we have abandoned.

Some people fear that accepting this stance will mean that

critical judgment must be suspended from all forms of homosexual behavior. That, too, is an irrational manifestation of prejudice. All forms of heterosexual behavior do not receive approval just because we affirm the goodness of heterosexuality. Any sexual behavior can be destructive, exploitative, predatory, or promiscuous, and therefore evil, regardless of the sexes of the parties involved. Whenever any of those conditions exist, a word of moral judgment needs to be spoken. The difficulty comes when a society evaluates heterosexuality *per se* as good and homosexuality *per se* as evil. Such moral absolutes eventuate in preferential ethical treatment for heterosexuals. Distinctions will be made for heterosexual people between life-giving and life-destroying behavior, while any and all patterns of sexual behavior arising from a homosexual orientation are condemned as sinful. Such a moral position leaves gay and lesbian persons with no options save denial or suppression. Indeed, many an ecclesiastical body has suggested that these are in fact the only moral choices open to homosexually oriented people. Perhaps we need to be reminded that large numbers of heterosexual people engage in promiscuity, prostitution, rape, child molestation, incest, and every conceivable form of sadomasochism. Further, by refusing to accept any homosexual behavior as normal, this homophobic society drives many gay and lesbian people into the very behavior patterns that the straight world most fears and condemns.

Prejudice always defines its victims negatively, blanketing them with stereotypes that hide from view their individual humanity. This principle was illustrated for me recently when I had to deal with a church that had called a woman to be its rector (or pastor). The lay leaders of this congregation were very proud of this courageous selection, unprecedented in the life of their parish and still unusual for the church at large. However, this particular pastor proved not to be a good choice on a number of levels. Within a short time of her coming a departure was negotiated, and the church began a search for a new pastor. When the name of a second woman candidate was proposed, the search committee chair announced rather firmly that the committee could not consider a female prospect this time. "We tried that and it failed," he asserted. Around the table there were nods of general agreement.

"If you had had an unsatisfactory male pastor," I inquired, "would you now be saying 'We had a male minister and he just didn't work out, so we will not consider another male?'" There was silence in the room. Prejudice always masquerades as rationality until it is exposed.

Prejudice is enforced and reinforced by the corporate wisdom of the community in which it is upheld, until it is thought to be God's self-evident truth. Prejudice withers only when two things occur: when new knowledge undercuts its intellectual basis and when people begin to observe and experience in those they reject a distinction between behavior that is destructive and behavior that is life giving. A strong signal that a prejudice is becoming moribund is communicated when the victimized group refuses to accept being defined by others as evil. All of us should welcome the cry of "gay pride." It is the emotional equivalent of "Black is beautiful." Self-acceptance, a defiance of the definition of the majority, is now a major force at work in the gay and lesbian world.

Even conservative expressions of Christianity show signs these days of being influenced by the movement toward acceptance of gay and lesbian persons—quite a change, considering the history of church attitudes toward them. So widely was homosexuality condemned in the early days of this century that it was rarely even mentioned in ecclesiastical gatherings. One does not debate such self-evident evils as murder, rape, arson, and child molesting. Homosexuality was once thought of as being in such a category.

As it has become more difficult to define evil quite so simply, perceptions have changed and judgment on this and a whole host of moral categories has begun to be tempered. Today almost every church body responding to this debate has passed some sort of justifying resolution designed to alleviate the sense of dis-ease that continued prejudice against gay and lesbian people is beginning to create. The earliest of these resolutions were couched in the sweet rhetoric of piety. Homosexual persons were declared to be the children of God and commended to the pastoral ministry of the church. That stance satisfied the church for a decade or so, because no one bothered to define "pastoral ministry." One patronizing form this attitude took was the suggestion that the church should "love the sinner while it hates the sin." Funny how it was that none of those defined as sinners experienced that love. Most gay and lesbian people learned not to trust the church's pastoral sensitivity to members of a group that the church corporately rejects. Despite the negativity in this type of resolution, however, it still represented a small step forward. At least the prejudice was having to be defended—a sure sign that it was beginning to waver. It also indicated that the issue was now important enough to demand consideration.

The second stage in the debate came when the civil rights and economic well-being of the homosexual population were threatened. Then the church, ever on the side of the victim, passed resolutions designed to urge justice before the law when dealing with *all* people, even homosexual people. A person should not be fired for being gay or lesbian, the church asserted. A person could not be physically abused just because of his or her sexual orientation. Gay and lesbian persons should be granted a bank loan with the same ease and at the same interest rate as anyone else with a similar financial history. Churches felt quite proud of these "liberal" resolutions. Once again, they did not press the implications of these actions. Consider the economic penalty a gay or lesbian person pays when not able to claim his or her mate as a dependent under the internal revenue code, or the lack of legal status of gay and lesbian people if their partners die intestate. Can such practices be just when ten percent of the population cannot marry according to the laws of the state? If a mortgage is sought by a gay or lesbian couple to buy a home in our particular neighborhood, are we still quite so open?

Politicians seeking election quite often have to address the various political ramifications of prejudice against homosexuality. Championing the cause of the gay and lesbian population is not the way to collect winning votes. The negative emotions that such campaigns release usually burn brightly until they expend themselves in their own excesses. Even the witch hunts in Salem, Massachusetts, in the seventeenth century finally ended in public revulsion. Until that happened, however, many women were charged, tried, convicted, imprisoned, and even executed for witchcraft—so it has been with sickening frequency whenever homosexuality has been raised as a political issue. Yet as costly as these episodes are, they are part of the process that alters public consciousness. Persecution of minority people always seems to mark the time of transition. When the restraints that the majority places on those who they believe are evil become evil themselves, then men and women of conscience revise their thinking and take action on behalf of the victims to guarantee, at a minimum, their civil rights. Most church groups today have moved at least to this second stage.

The next step follows on the heels of the decision to end persecution. It is a strange step, in that it is appealing despite an incredible level of naivete. It is articulated in those resolutions and statements from church leaders and official bodies specifying that a distinction is to be drawn between sexual orientation and sexual behavior. They suggest that since one might not be able to choose one's sexual orientation, that orientation cannot be considered sinful. But since one can choose how to act no matter what one's ontological orientation, and since the sexual acts of the homosexually oriented person are evil, they are therefore not allowable inside the sanctions of the church. So if you are born with a homosexual predisposition, you cannot act on the basis of this predisposition. Your sexual energy must be contained, suppressed, sublimated.

The positive thing about this sort of resolution is that it signals a dawning realization that homosexuality is not an orientation that is chosen but rather a reality that is given. Once that watershed truth is accepted, the attitudes and behaviors of heterosexuals do begin to adapt, just as they adapted when we stopped thinking that left-handedness was abnormal. It is certainly a step forward to recognize that a minority characteristic might not necessarily be abnormal but rather a reflection of the rich variety of human life. As the realization that one cannot choose one's sexual orientation any more than one can choose to be right-handed begins to win its way, certain prejudicial words and phrases begin to drop from our vocabulary. "Sexual preference" is one such phrase, implying that one can stand at a crossroads and decide whether to become heterosexual or homosexual.

However, before extolling too highly this kind of resolution, let me point out its incredible naivete. It suggests that those who have a homosexual orientation also have a capacity to refrain from all sexual activity. It assumes that ten percent of the population can or will be willing to affirm and accept the vocation of celibacy that someone other than themselves has approved for them.

Those who know anything about celibacy know that true celibacy is a rare and unique vocation to which few are called. This vocation or lifestyle cannot be imposed involuntarily. The experience of the Roman Catholic church, which requires celibacy of its priests, is that even with all the external structure of the priestly life—the unique clergy dress, the rigid prayer disciplines, the aloof paternal titles, the cultivated image of set-apartness—the life of true celibacy is difficult to sustain, and the vow of celibacy is still broken with dismaying regularity. Yet those who support resolutions of this genre act as if celibacy can be mandated for the gay and lesbian population. Acceptance of this imposed celibacy becomes the price gays and lesbians must pay to receive the church's blessing upon their lives. Imagine the response that would be forthcoming if some ecclesiastical body, in the name of God and morality, announced that henceforth an arbitrary ten percent of the heterosexual world would have to live in sexual abstinence if it wished to participate in or be blessed by that church. It is almost unbelievable that this level of logic informs the majority viewpoint of solemn assemblies of influential and well-meaning bishops, representative clergy and lay people, or even seminary faculties where higher learning is presumed to prevail.

Nevertheless, this point of view, with all its ambiguity and naivete, is still an expression of forward movement, but quite obviously it cannot be the concluding word in the debate. It finally sinks into its own internal contradictions and unrealistic expectations.

In time a new understanding of the origin of homosexuality will cause us to lose the irrational anxiety that our children might be seduced into a homosexual lifestyle by some chance encounter. Witch hunts aimed at removing "those people" from positions where they might be quite influential in the lives of our children will be revealed for what they are and will cease. No longer will our own anxiety overwhelm us when we have a fantasy or dream that we fear might be an expression of latent homosexuality. No longer will men have to hide their softer, yielding sides and women their athletic competence, in order to make sure no one suspects them of an evil orientation.

The next stage is being entered when we begin to regard both the homosexual orientation and the heterosexual orientation in and of themselves as neither good nor evil, but only as real and true. Both aspects of human sexuality will ultimately be seen as natural. The recognition is growing that there is a majority orientation and a minority orientation and that both have roles in the enrichment of human life. This change will take time, for ignorance and fear are both tenacious, and prejudice covers human irrationality, making it difficult and frightening to relinquish.

Once the naturalness of majority and minority orientations is established, and the expectation of celibacy for gay and lesbian people is removed, the question of the moment will then become, How does a gay or lesbian person lead a responsible sexual life? Surely the laws of church and state must give equal protection and affirmation to this group. Our pious conditional resolutions binding moral homosexuality to celibacy reveal nothing less than an irrational belief in a sadistic God, in the light of new knowledge. This God created gay and lesbian people only to punish them. God made them in creation complete with sexual drive and then said that morality demanded that this drive be repressed. Once again we are confronted with the dictum that bad biology and bad biochemistry result in bad theology.

The traditional position of the church, based on the false premise that loving sexual expressions between persons of the same gender are always evil, must come face to face with the evil this stance has itself created. How can the fullness of life be achieved when some of God's children are barraged by consistent messages proclaiming them to be immoral? How can any person, in the face of constant disparagement, ever develop a positive self-image? We cannot really give ourselves in a loving commitment to others unless we believe that we have some value. Two broken, fragile egos that are daily downgraded and humiliated will not be able to sustain each other easily in a mutually monogamous relationship. The lack of community support and the necessity to hide a relationship from public life puts enormous strain on a couple's psychological resources.

In turning away from its self-righteous condemnation and grudging allowances, the church might first confess its own hardness of heart: "Lord have mercy upon us and forgive us for that evil judgment that has twisted and distorted your sons and daughters in every generation of your church's life."

Second, the church must set about the task of rethinking the ethics of human sexuality. . . . Suffice it to be stated now that the

intimacy of love, the legitimacy of a publicly recognized relationship, the joy of companionship, and the peace of a life without
secrets are not to be denied to anyone in his or her pursuit of
happiness and the abundance of life about which the gospel speaks
(see John 10:10).

The issue of what is permissible behavior in public life con-
trasted with private life comes to a head in the church's rules for
ordination. Should the church ordain a gay person who is neither
duplicitous nor celibate? The question itself, when publicly debat-
ed, indicates a leap forward in ethical consciousness. The fact
remains, however, that there have always been gay people among
the ordained and in religious orders. For two thousand years the
church has had gay clergy in numbers far beyond what most people
have dared to imagine. They have occupied every position in every
ecclesiastical hierarchy. They have assisted in the fashioning of the
doctrine, discipline, worship, and ecclesiastical dress of the church.
When celibacy was mandated as the only proper lifestyle for the
ordained, in the twelfth century, the doors were opened for gay
males to find in the church's priesthood a legitimizing place where
their single status would be turned from a liability to a virtue and
where their lives could experience creativity and community. If gay
people were excised from the ordained ministry throughout the
church's history, enormous gaps would appear, perhaps as much
as 80 percent in certain periods of history. Indeed, there was a time
when all under the vows of celibacy were suspected of being gay.[7]

The argument now about whether or not gay people should be
ordained is, in one sense, almost ludicrous. The outcome of the
debate will not change the constituency; it will change the public
face of the church. Moralistic voices want to keep "the secret." The
Roman Catholic church, among others, goes so far as to suspend,
expel, or silence members of its clergy who publicly admit their
preference for the same gender.[8] Of course gay people should be
considered without prejudice for the ordination process. They
should be screened like all other candidates, with a view toward
examining the integrity of their calls, the gifts they have to bring
to the church, and their intelligence, sensitivity, devotion to God,
willingness to work, and competence to handle their sexual energy
with responsibility and commitment.

Would a particular congregation call or accept a gay or lesbian pastor who had formed a monogamous, loving relationship and who did not want either to abandon that partner or to live a lie? It is happening at this moment, but primarily in cities and urban areas where anonymity in the larger community is possible. I personally know such clergy, who have the loving support of their people, and I do see the gospel of Jesus Christ being lived out in those congregations. I applaud these clerics, their partners, and the people of their churches for having the ability to transcend the prejudice that still surrounds us on every side.

Regrettably, there are others who live at this moment in a fear that will not allow openness. They operate under various protective covers, always wondering whom they can trust. Some have shared their life stories with me. My support for them in their heroic struggle to live in both love and integrity is firm. They have taught me much. I am in their debt.

Some will read these words and suggest vigorously that this stance puts me as a bishop into opposition with the official stand of the church I represent, and to the historic position of the church catholic. They are correct. I am a minority voice in that ecclesiastical structure. That minority is growing, as new knowledge permeates the whole society. It will not be a minority forever. The church has changed its mind many times in history and will do so again. . . .

Notes

1. Alfred Kinsey et al., *Sexual Behavior in the Human Male* (Philadelphia: Saunders, 1948); *Sexual Behavior in the Human Female* (Philadelphia: Saunders, 1953).
2. John Fortunato, "Should the Church Bless and Affirm Committed Gay Relationships?" *The Episcopalian*, April 1987.
3. John S. Spong, *Into the Whirlwind* (San Francisco: Harper & Row, 1983), chap. 8.
4. Sigmund Freud, *Three Contributions to the Theory of Sex* (New York: Dutton, 1962); *Totem and Taboo* (New York: Vintage Press, 1946).
5. Rosemary Ruether, "From Machismo to Maturity," in Edward Batchelor, Jr., *Homosexuality and Ethics* (New York: Pilgrim Press, 1980), pp. 28ff.
6. Ibid.
7. Spong, *Into the Whirlwind*, chap. 8.

8. John J. McNeill, "Homosexuality—The Challenge to the Church," *The Christian Century* 104 (Mar. 1987): 242-46.

THIRTY-TWO

A Case for Celibacy

▼

Eugene England

Recent scientific articles on homosexuality assist us in understanding better the causes of sexual difference and should increase our openness and empathy. But I find a serious problem with some of the arguments in these articles, which, I fear, increase moral and spiritual confusion for homosexuals and for all of us.

These articles review the evidence that has been developed in the last ten years that homosexuality and other conditions once thought to be psychological in origin are influenced as well by genes and neurochemistry. The evidence, though as yet inconclusive, is quite strong, and it seems to me probably true that a large proportion, if not all, of those attracted to their own sex do not "choose" that attraction and therefore are not morally responsible for their *condition*. The problem with these arguments is that they move beyond this insight to a logical breakdown that is morally dangerous. For example, R. Jan Stout argues, "Many people, in and out of the church, seem to want homosexuals held fully account-

Eugene England is professor of English at Brigham Young University, past editor of *Dialogue: A Journal of Mormon Thought*, and a frequent essayist on Mormon subjects. An earlier version of "A Case for Celibacy" appeared in *Dialogue: A Journal of Mormon Thought* 20 (Fall 1987): 6–8.

able for their sexual feelings and behavior. Yet, if conscious choice is not involved, can we legitimately invoke the charge of sin?" ("Sin and Sexuality," *Dialogue: A Journal of Mormon Thought* 20 [Summer 1987]). Sexual feelings may not be consciously chosen, but sexual behavior can be, and when sexual behavior of any kind consciously violates understood commandments or ignores natural laws, then it surely is sin—and inevitably destructive.

Unfortunately, many in our society, including many Mormons, fail to distinguish between homosexual feelings and homosexual activity, condemning both as sinful—sometimes in ways that are ignorant, intolerant, certainly unChristian. But many homosexuals, and many therapists who obviously feel great empathy for the suffering of homosexuals, react in ways that merely compound the same confusion: They suggest that since the feelings are not sinful then neither is related sexual expression. I think both positions are wrong and that LDS scriptures and church leaders are right when they make no judgment of homosexual feeling but speak out on homosexual intercourse.

It seems to me that the proper model for Mormons is to hold firmly to the ideal of celestial marriage and the laws of married fidelity. Mormons should make no judgments about same-sex orientation, unless of course such feelings are inappropriately adopted out of cultural or psychological confusion. But the overwhelming evidence of the scriptures and modern revelation (and, I think, common sense) is that though perhaps 10 percent of men and a lesser number of women are affected by the genetic and embryonic forces that produce same-sex orientation, that mortal condition is not a viable alternative to celestial marriage.

What then are we to say to homosexuals who are asking, "Why did God make me this way?" I think we should say about the same things we have to say to many, perhaps all the rest, of us human beings who also ask, "Why did God make me this way?" The Mormon answer is "God didn't. Natural processes created you, along with your particular crosses, which will be removed in the afterlife and must meanwhile be endured."

The longer I live the more I'm convinced that every human being has at least one cross to bear that he or she did not "choose," and though some, perhaps most, such crosses are not as difficult to bear as homosexuality, some are more difficult. Because of accidents, physical appearance, or handicaps, many more than 10 percent of humans in our culture are unable to enjoy normal sexual expression and marriage and have to settle for a life devoid of sexual intimacy, even affection. Many others who are able to marry are afflicted with frigidity, impotence, excessive sexual desire, accident, disease, or other conditions which make compatible and satisfying sexual relations impossible. Are they to be freed from the moral responsibility, sealed by solemn temple covenants, to endure in fidelity to their companions simply because nature has "played a trick" on them?

Mormonism is unique in claiming that we all chose, with some knowledge of what we faced, to come into a world where many genuine choices could be made, despite natural restrictions, and thus crucial moral growth could occur. We did this even though we knew that the freedom from God's control necessary for such purposeful development would also result in many conditions and "accidents" according to natural law that would result in genuine handicaps for all of us to bear. But Mormonism is also unique in promising that all such crosses will be removed as we leave mortality and that our final judgment and eternal progression will be free from their effects. For instance, I believe we will each be provided, in that long period of continued probation after death when we are no longer limited by the genetic, developmental, and psychological burdens of mortality, a time and way to work out (if we have not already) a fully satisfying one-to-one relationship that is the basis for celestial marriage. We will finally be "judged" only according to our response to opportunities there that are the same for all of us.

A believable case for celibacy should, of course, offer more than a hope for rewards and compensations in the life to come—pie in the sky bye and bye. What about right now? What can those with same-sex orientation but desiring to be faithful to their testimony of the restored gospel and its prophetic leadership do in mortality, while they still have bodies and bodily affections?

Perhaps, despite our uneasiness about the apparent rejection of the body, particularly sexuality, in the great tradition of celibacy in Catholicism and some other religions, we can take some courage and inspiration from the best of that tradition. The vow of life-long celibacy has been, for many, a form of personal discipline and a source of spiritual power that has energized lives of remarkable service. I recommend a similar vow to Mormons of same-sex orientation, not as a self-punishment or rejection of the body, but as a heroic decision, based in devotion to Christ—and confident in his response and assistance. By such a vow you can be freed from the distractions and difficulties of sexual relationship during this life and devote yourself to a focused kind of development and service that many of us who are married will have to achieve in the next life.

I firmly believe that, though it is centrally important to our eternal salvation eventually to learn love through opposition in heterosexual marriage, there are many other dimensions to saving love which all of us must learn—and which all will have opportunity eventually to learn. Some of us, heterosexuals, may learn one kind of love in mortality through marriage and have to neglect other kinds that involve undistracted service; those with same-sex orientation may have to neglect one form of love but can cultivate those other kinds of saving love.

Alma taught his son to "bridle all your passions, that ye may be filled with love" (Alma 38:12). Each of us must learn to do that, in our own particular circumstances, including heterosexual marriage. If we do so, none of our individual crosses will prevent us either from joyful reunion with our heavenly parents or joyful relationship with them in this life. Such bridling, such celibacy, can also, as it has in countless lives that include St. Francis of Assisi and Mother Teresa but also thousands of unheralded single men and women, focus the energies and imaginations of those who choose it on the needs and opportunities for service and creativity that they may uniquely be able to perceive and attend to.

We in the church must learn better how to understand and fully accept homosexuals as fellow mortals with opportunities and burdens like our own. Recent scholarship on homosexuality can help Mormon heterosexuals improve in Christian empathy and response and can perhaps help homosexuals increase in self-respect and thus better endure the prejudice and fear that their orientation still engenders. But to encourage homosexuals to think that the range of acceptable expression of feeling includes extra-marital sexual activity or even monogamous homosexual marriage is, I believe (unless and until there is further revelation), to do them a disservice. On the other hand, celibacy can be a positive choice for those with same-sex orientation who wish to retain the principles and blessings of the restored gospel and church.

THIRTY-THREE

In Favor of Families

▼

Marvin Rytting

The sexual revolution officially ended in 1984—not with authoritarian edicts reminiscent of the novel *1984* but with research reports and news articles. It was reported in books such as *American Couples* and articles in professional journals and then heralded on the cover of *Time* magazine and confirmed by NBC news. It had of course been happening for some time. When the infamous baby boomers reached their mid-thirties, they started having second thoughts about the joys of being swinging singles. Commitment and family life became fashionable as a new profamily sentiment swept the country.

Because the profamily perspective of my generation is based on our experience in sexual and familial experiments, it is more honest than the position of the conservative politicians and ministers who use the "profamily" label as a way of mandating a particular version of family life rather than supporting the concept of good family life in general. The dominant theme of the new profamily movement is to recognize and support the entire spectrum of families, including single-parent, dual-career, and blended families. Recognizing that only a small minority of Americans live in the idealized traditional family of a father who works and a mother who stays at home with two adorable children, the new profamily advocates push for policies which will make a variety of families viable instead of promoting only the traditional pattern.

Contrary to a common perception that there has been a steady deterioration in family values in our society, I see the new profamily perspective as the latest improvement in a progression of increasingly enlightened values about relationships and families. Being more concerned with the welfare of people and the quality of family life than we are about adherence to rigid norms, the new profamily proponents seek to make healthy family life as accessible as possible to as many people as possible. The basic value judgment is that marital unions should be freely chosen and characterized by commitment, responsibility, stability, and a mutual loving care that provides a nurturing and secure environment for personal growth and the expression of physical and emotional intimacy.

Traditional societal norms, on the other hand, emphasize demographic criteria of form and appearance in evaluating families at the expense of these human values and in so doing often make it more difficult for people to succeed in establishing good family relationships. In the past there were many such demographic restrictions, and they were enforced with a vengeance. Over time as our concern has changed to the more qualitative criteria, these have decreased in both number and in the intensity of their enforcement. Bi-racial marriages, for example, are now legally permitted and have at least some measure of social recognition.

There is one demographic variable that is still used to disqualify couples from being married—gender. We have declared that no matter how deep the love, how strong the commitment, how pure the intentions, how stable the relationship, and how positive the consequences, two people of the same gender may not marry, may not establish a recognized family. In spite of all qualitative criteria, this one factor disqualifies them from an approved expression of physical and emotional intimacy, even if the results of this denial are unquestionably negative. This is, I suggest, an antifamily position—one that denies the blessings of family life to a significant segment of our population irrespective of the merits of the relationship. Those who seriously value the family would not want to deny these blessings to anyone who fervently and sincerely seeks them.

But our society does deny them, and this denial of legitimate family relationships to gays and lesbians has both direct and indirect negative consequences. In our society marriage is an important symbol of adulthood. Thus when we tell several million people that they must be forever single, there is also the hidden message that they should remain adolescent. The headlined promiscuity of the gay single scene, which many use as a justification for continued repression, is at least partly a function of the lack of a viable marriage option and of other societal impediments to establishing permanent adult intimate relationships.

The cruel irony of marriage norms which simultaneously encourage and condemn promiscuity for gays gains tragic proportions when this leads to AIDS with its double dose of death and discrimination. It is now clear that AIDS is not caused by homosexuality but is spread by indiscriminate sexual relationships. The answer to the AIDS crisis is safe sex, not heterosexual sex. In addition to the medical research to discover a cure for AIDS, there should be a national effort to promote responsible sex, the cornerstone of which must be the legitimation of marital relationships for gay couples. We cannot demand responsible sexual behavior if we continue to impede it.

A large segment of the gay community has already transcended societal norms by establishing families without our permission. There may be as many as five million lesbian and gay couples in America who are doing so and many million more who would like to. Our reluctance to accept these couples makes it more difficult for them to succeed. According to a recent study, it takes an average of about three years for these couples to both begin receiving support from a broader network and to start developing the kind of family traditions which provide marital stability for heterosexual marriages from the start. This includes being recognized as a couple by their respective families and by friends and co-workers and thus being invited together to family gatherings or social affairs. It also involves starting holiday traditions such as spending Christmas together with their own celebration. The difficulty is that they have to survive two or three intense and unstable years together with very little support before they reach this stage, and even then the support is much less than heterosexual marriages can expect. We do not even give them toasters and blenders.

An honest profamily position would suggest that we help these lesbian and gay couples achieve a stable long-term relationship by respecting their decision to love each other with caring and commitment and by symbolizing their union with ritual and fortifying it with social support. Some religious groups are beginning to grapple with the hypocrisy of the traditional antifamily attitudes toward gay relationships. The Presbyterians are looking for ways to avoid the "sin of homophobia." In submitting a recommendation to the Episcopal Church that they should recognize and bless committed homosexual relationships, a task force on changing patterns of sexuality and family life observed that it is "difficult to believe that a church that blesses dogs in a Virginia fox hunt can't find a way to bless life-giving, lasting relationships between human beings." The prototype of this profamily position is that taken by the Unitarian Church, which has the courage to go beyond merely refraining from discrimination and actively provides support by celebrating the union of gay and lesbian couples and welcoming them into their congregations. [See Statements of Professional and Religious Organizations.]

Some people fear, however, that by allowing gay marriages, we may be encouraging people to become gay. In answer to that fear, first let it be noted that even though bi-racial marriages are now legal, they account for less than 2 percent of all marriages. There has hardly been a flood of them. Those who are not inclined to marry interracially do not feel compelled to do so. Likewise it seems incredible to assume that making gay marriages legal would encourage anybody who is not gay to enter into one. The fear of gay marriages becoming rampant suggests an uncertainty about the value of heterosexual relationships.

Still some people may be concerned that even if allowing lesbian and gay unions does not encourage them, it would appear to condone them. I suggest that it is not hypocritical to say, "Our preference is for heterosexual relationships, but if you discover that you are gay and that you love someone of the same gender, please establish a loving, caring, committed, long-term relationship because that is better than cruising bars and having casual sex with many partners—*and* better than living alone forever. And if you find a loving partner with whom to spend your life, we shall rejoice with you and support your union (and give you toasters and blenders)." The true hypocrisy is to pretend to favor family life while denying it to some people solely because of their choice of partner.

The new profamily perspective does not advocate any particular kind of family. It supports loving, committed relationships over either unhappy relationships, promiscuity, or loneliness. At an individual level it recommends the family model (whether legal or not) as the most likely path to satisfying intimacy. At the societal level it pleads that we make our society more hospitable to the variety of families that can exist by making marriage more accessible and by providing support for quality family life.

THIRTY-FOUR

I Do Not Believe
Homosexuality a Sin

▼

Melvin E. Wheatley, Jr.

I am an enthusiastically heterosexual male. Is my heterosexuality a virtue? A sign of righteousness? Either an accomplishment or a victory of some kind on my part? Of course not. I had nothing whatsoever to do with my being heterosexual. It is a mysterious gift of God's grace communicated through an exceedingly complex set of chemical, biological, chromosomal, hormonal, environmental, developmental factors—totally outside my control. My hetero-sexuality is a gift—neither a virtue nor a sin.

What I do with my heterosexuality, however, is my personal, moral, and spiritual responsibility.

My behavior as a heterosexual may be, therefore, very sinful—brutal, exploitative, selfish, promiscuous, superficial. My behavior as a heterosexual, on the other hand, may be beautiful—tender, considerate, loyal, other-centered, profound.

Precisely this distinction between being a heterosexual and behaving as a heterosexual applies to homosexual persons as well, unless you and I are to be guilty of that lowest blow of all, and that

---

Melvin E. Wheatley, Jr., is Bishop of the United Methodist Church (retired). He currently resides in Laguna Hills, California.

is to work by double standards.

Homosexuality, quite like heterosexuality, is neither a virtue nor an accomplishment. It is a mysterious gift of God's grace communicated through an exceedingly complex set of chemical, biological, chromosomal, hormonal, environmental, developmental factors totally outside my homosexual friend's control. His or her homosexuality is a gift—neither a virtue nor a sin. What she or he does with their homosexuality, however, is their personal, moral, and spiritual responsibility.

Their behavior as a homosexual may, therefore, be very sinful—brutal, exploitative, selfish, promiscuous, superficial. Their behavior as a homosexual, on the other hand, may be beautiful—tender, considerate, loyal, other-centered, profound.

With this interpretation of the mystery that must be attributed to sexual orientation, both heterosexual and homosexual, I clearly do not believe that homosexuality is a sin.

THIRTY-FIVE

Sexuality as Spiritual

▼

Adonna Schow

The spiritual aspects of sexuality are too frequently overlooked. However, Mormonism traditionally accepts sexuality as part of the eternal plan. Indeed, sexuality is at the heart of spirituality. This can be seen by recognizing that sexuality is fundamental to creation. For biological life this is abundantly displayed. Yet sexuality is also necessary and essential to the creation of life in a spiritual sense. Spiritual life is more than birth of spirit. It involves the continual creation of a person spiritually throughout life. Spirituality is sensitizing oneself more fully to the divine in one's existence, directing one's intellect and higher endowments of mind, teaching one's emotions, developing moral feelings and thus exercising agency for oneself. In the ongoing creation of life, sexuality and spirituality are vitally connected: they espouse each other.

God, who is at the center of spirituality, is also the creator of life. He created persons as sexual beings. He "created man in his own image, in the image of God created he him; male and female

Adonna Schow holds B.S. and M.S. degrees in mechanical engineering. She currently resides in Pocatello, Idaho.

created he them" (Gen. 1:27). The apparent human, physical sexuality is but one dimension of a deeper, all-pervading reality of sexuality. All things were created "spiritually, before they were naturally upon the face of the earth" (Moses 3:5). This implies that sexuality, maleness and femaleness, are intrinsic spiritual as well as physical attributes of humans.

To expand understanding of this reality, we may ask, What is male and what is female? In the physical realm, the answer seems obvious. Yet even here a problem arises in the case of intersexes. Concerning the spiritual life of people, this question is vital but challenging. One way to probe this question is through a personal ontological viewpoint. In search for essence of maleness and femaleness, we might be guided by considering the physical sex act. The intent here is not to define and limit maleness and femaleness on the basis of the sex of one's body, but to use the obvious and commonly experienced physical biology as a springboard to project our thinking toward greater awareness. We are searching beyond the physical manifestations to the essences, the archetypes, the spiritual realities of sexual gender. As we expand to such illuminations, we can then create other more sensitive ways of dealing with ourselves and each other as sexual spiritual beings. So, let us consider the physical sex act. The male is the penetrator, the infuser, the scatterer, the one bursting forth from himself. The female is the receiver, the gatherer, the gestator, the one holding close to herself. If we contemplate the physical sexual act carefully, it becomes clear that these aspects of femaleness and maleness extend beyond physiological processes. We see that all human beings involve themselves in both what we could call maleness and femaleness all the time. In manifesting ourselves as persons, we vibrate in both modes, rhythmically.

For example, verbal expression of oneself is an outpouring of words and thoughts, which we could call maleness. When one teaches, expounds, writes, or calls to repentence, one manifests oneself outwardly in what might be considered maleness. When one dances or sings or demonstrates other skills or talents from sports to culinary arts, one gives oneself toward others in a male mode. When one gently probes into the heart of another, stimulating another to perceive with greater vision or to rise to higher levels of love or to uncover personal fulfillments, that may be seen as maleness. On the negative side, destructive interference, force, and inauthentic advice or pressure are actions debasing and perverting maleness. Similarly, spewing out anger, hatred, or violence is destructive.

Complementally, when a person hears another, this is a receptive experience, a femaleness. When one observes, reads, reflects, ponders, one dwells inwardly in femaleness. When one abides in humility, turning within to assess oneself and others accurately; when one searches for direction, for answers, for infusion from on high; when one waits expectantly and hopefully; when one is silent and still; when one receives the Holy Ghost, then one opens oneself and participates in female receptivity. Femaleness can also be used and experienced destructively. When one places one's hope on another who "rewardeth you no good thing" (Alma 34:39), waiting interminably, submitting not to the pregnancy of fruitfulness but to the void of unfulfilled expectations and tyrannical manipulations, then one distorts and desecrates femaleness. Similarly, degrading oneself or accepting others' judgments which violate oneself is participation in destructive femaleness.

All individuals always think and act in both modes, sometimes separately, sometimes simultaneously, in creative or destructive ways, and to varying extents. Thus we see a limited usefulness in defining females and males based entirely on physical attributes. Likewise, differentiation by stereotypical role assignment, dress, or gender behavior is inaccurate. Such biologically and traditionally imposed rigidity tends to perpetuate sexual inequalities, phobias, and dysfunctions which plague our culture. The resulting conflict concerning sexual identities does not help us see the androgyny in all of us.

This concept of the essence of sexuality allows us to perceive that both maleness and femaleness are involved in processes and acts that are traditionally ascribed to one or the other gender. Even in the sexual act itself, both partners experience waves of rising anticipation, intensified inner feelings, outward bursts of joy, stimulating and accepting stimulation, release, yielding to a higher power, receiving energizing renewal deposited deep in one's psyche, immersion in calm, bestowing tenderness, infusing and being infused, alternately and rhythmically. In the gestation and birth of a baby, there is likewise a combination of sexualities. For example, the delivering of new life into the world by a woman is analogous to male emission, a bursting forth in joy that cannot be contained.

In delineating between maleness and femaleness, we then perceive that creation of spiritual as well as physical life involves the conjoining of femaleness and maleness. Indeed, we cannot be created, cannot achieve wholeness in a spiritual sense, without the presence of both. Spiritual life involves personal fulfillment, progression, salvation, redemption. Thus infusion/reception, giving/receiving, expression/impression, penetrating/being penetrated, are necessary *in each person* to have life and live it more abundantly. These creative, spiritual male and female sexualities are essential for conception, gestation, and maturation of soul life, for probing the divine, receiving the divine, and becoming divine.

In the sanctity in which the Godhead creates diversity, the ratio of maleness to femaleness in each person varies widely. Each person has (is) one's own appropriate, divinely-given-and-developing union of both aspects. When a person dwells in the dynamic harmony of maleness and femaleness that is one's very own, then that authentic combination of spiritual sexualities creates a person.

On the other hand, when the proportion and rhythms between one's sexual facets are out of balance, a person experiences frustration, negative tension, and destruction of oneself. Such inauthenticity can give rise to confusion, perverting physically and spiritually one's own enlivening ways of being. For example, heterosexualities, whether biological, emotional, or spiritual, may be misapplied and become corrupting. The same can be said for homosexualities. Conversely, all sexual orientations may not be deviations from the personal truth of each individual.

People's appropriate combinations manifest themselves in various sexual attractions and desires, in varying emotional bondings, and in differing psychological patterns. These diversities in physical/spiritual sexuality are many-faceted and complex. Yet even in a person whose sexual orientation is a 6 or a 0 on the Kinsey Scale, and regardless of that person's gender, there exists a unique joining of the essences of maleness and femaleness. A homosexual or heterosexual or any other kind of sexual person may dwell in creative sexuality and thereby has abundant life through finding what is "right" for him or for her and living accordingly, always in consonance with one's own spiritual and physical sexuality.

Sexual harmony within a person provides the foundation for life to be created between people. Regardless of where one fits on the spectrum of physical sexual orientation, spiritual life is created and enhanced by being with other people. Inherited by persons is a divine yearning for union with others. "It is not good that the man should be alone" (Gen. 2:18), declared the creator who created and magnified femaleness and maleness in man, in the image of God. Physical and emotional sexual urges are manifestations of these intrinsic spiritual realities. Here again, diversity among us is a "beautifying of the earth"; desires for union vary and so do the kinds of unions.

Individual inauthenticity prohibits creative interpersonal relationships. It is impossible to mesh one's sexuality creatively with another when discordance exists in oneself. In seeking sexual authenticity and fulfillment in relationship with another, we must be aware of possible destructions of life, particularly spiritual, through physical and spiritual raping and being raped. Hence we need to esteem the divine commands/advice concerning sexuality: that we will not adulterate ourselves or each other through violence, through sinful giving up of ourselves, through desire for power over others, through spiritual and physical promiscuity, through lustful thinking, through intolerance of diversity. Unions and interactions attempted under such spiritual deficiencies are sterile at best, annihilative at worst.

Jesus Christ, the exemplar of spirituality, embodies these aspects of life in his creative work. He frequently referred to himself as the bridegroom—he comes, with desire, to imbue the world with his conceptions of life. Yet his receptivity is evidenced in his learning obedience by the things which he suffered, his willingness to be constantly prepared from the foundation of the world, his readiness to accept the terrible imposition on his person of the crucifixion, and his humility to fill himself with and follow his father.

As we envision and pursue divine harmony and union, as we seek to relate the expression of physical sexuality to deeper spiritual sensitivity, we will find that "cures" for variant sexualities become irrelevant. Coming to dwell in the awareness of the spiritual nature of sexuality and the sexual realities of spirituality will infuse us with life and the more abundant life of personal meaning, fulfillment, peace, joy, and love.

THIRTY-SIX

Religious and Moral Issues in Working with Homosexual Clients

▼

James B. Nelson

At the outset, let me offer a linguistic comment. I consider "homosexuality" an abstraction. There is no such thing as "homosexuality" *per se*. When we use the term we are speaking about people—people who happen to be more or less erotically oriented to their own sex; people who are more or less comfortable with this orientation; and people who experience more or fewer difficulties, personal and social, because of their orientation. Always we are speaking of concrete persons, in spite of the limitations of language (see Nugent 1980).

Can a Therapist be Neutral? Can a therapist, whatever her or his own sexual orientation, be neutral when working with "homosexual" clients? Quite apart from the question of sexual orientation, when the general issue of religious and moral neutrality in

"Religious and Moral Issues in Working with Homosexual Clients," by James B. Nelson, originally appeared in *Homosexuality & Psychotherapy* (New York: Haworth Press, 1982). Dr. Nelson is professor of Christian ethics at United Theological Seminary of the Twin Cities, New Brighton, Minnesota, where he has taught since 1963. He is an ordained minister of the United Church of Christ and has served parishes in Connecticut and South Dakota.

counseling is considered, a distinction is sometimes made between "pastoral counseling" and "secular psychotherapy." The former is assumed to be interlaced with normative values and religious beliefs, since clergy are expected in all of their ministerial functions to represent and interpret the meanings of the religious group. In contrast, many people assume that the "secular psychotherapist" (whether or not committed to a religious tradition) will take an educative counseling approach. As such, the therapist will not attempt to impose solutions but, maintaining a neutral standpoint, will attempt to educe both emotional and moral solutions from the client.

This neat division, however, is highly misleading. In recent decades many clergy have moved toward substantially psycho-therapeutic models of counseling, attempting to keep their own religious and moral convictions very much in the background. At the same time, it is increasingly recognized that the professional psychotherapist is not dealing with a religiously or morally neutral process. Psychotherapy, like religion, tries to help people change their lives. In assisting clients to alleviate their emotional distress, the therapist necessarily operates with certain images of "sin" (the causative factors and dynamics of the distress), certain images of "salvation" (the dynamics of change, the hoped-for cure or pattern of growth), and some general interpretation of human fulfillment and life's meaning (see Browning 1976).

If these observations are true of counseling in general, it is even clearer that religious and moral neutrality are impossible when one is working with homosexual clients. Although counselors will vary in the extent to which they allow their own convictions to enter the process, I believe it neither possible nor desirable for them to escape altogether a whole series of moral and religious questions, the answers to which will critically affect the pattern and course of the counseling or therapy: Is homosexuality as such good, bad, or neutral? Are certain difficulties frequently encountered by gay men and lesbians intrinsic to their sexual orientation, or are they rooted in the dynamics of social oppression? What are the ethics of genital expression; and are these criteria the same for both homosexual and heterosexual persons, or are they different? What are the purposes of human sexuality? How does one assess the varied Western religious traditions on the issue of homosexuality? Are clients likely to be helped or hindered by their particular religious belief systems and involvements? As these questions—and others—will be answered in one way or another by the therapist, it is important that the counselor be clear about her or his own commitments and knowledgeably sensitive to particular issues commonly faced by gay men and lesbians.

The following discussion will reflect a number of my own convictions which I have attempted to elaborate elsewhere: that homosexuality is a Christianly valid orientation; that homosexual genital expression should be guided by the same general ethical criteria as are appropriate for heterosexual expression, though with sensitivity to the special situation of an oppressed minority; that the church, while too frequently a participant in oppression, does have important healing resources for gay men and lesbians; and that the church deeply needs the gay and lesbian presence and witness (see Nelson 1978). Although I shall address these issues out of my own Protestant Christian context, I believe that much of what I write is applicable to Catholic and Jewish positions as well.

Understanding the Religious Tradition. No gay or lesbian person in our society can escape responding in some manner to the ways in which the Judeo-Christian tradition has dealt with homosexuality. Likewise, it is predictable that numerous gay and lesbian clients will be working on issues of self-worth and self-esteem stemming from preconceived condemnation by organized religion. Whether the biblical and theological arguments are of personal interest to the therapist is beside the point. They *do* matter to many gay and lesbian clients. Accordingly, it can be enormously helpful if the counselor is able to respond knowledgeably to the question "But doesn't the Bible say homosexuality is a sin?" with "No, not as I understand it." Fortunately, a number of books and articles now available afford reliable, detailed treatment of the biblical and theological issues. My purpose here is limited to a summary overview.

Any specific biblical passage relating to homosexuality must, I believe, be interpreted with several things in mind. First, homosexuality as a *psychosexual* orientation is not dealt with in the Bible. The concept of sexual orientation is distinctly modern. The Bible's references are, without exception, statements about certain types of same-sex *acts.* In all probability, the biblical writers assumed all persons to be "naturally" heterosexual; hence, those who engaged in homosexual activity were doing so in willful and conscious violation of their own (heterosexual) natures.

Second, the strong link between sex and procreation, particularly in the Old Testament, must be understood in a particular historical context. A small Hebrew tribe in a hostile environment indeed needed children for its survival.

Third, both Old and New Testaments (though I believe they also contain a doctrine of radical human equality) were admittedly written in the context of male-dominated societies. The issue of *male* homosexual activity receives virtually all the attention, for lesbian activity hardly constitutes the same threat to the patriarchal mind-set.

Fourth, coupled with the procreative emphasis and patriarchal assumptions, there was a biological misunderstanding. The prescientific (male) mind, knowing nothing of eggs and ovulation, and assuming a special life-transmitting power for the semen alone, frequently concluded that deliberate nonprocreative expulsion of semen was a serious life-destroying act.

Fifth, biblical references to homosexual acts almost always reflect a genuine anxiety about idolatrous religious practices. In the ancient Mid-East, idolatry frequently found sexual expression. In such practices (both heterosexual and homosexual), sex was depersonalized and seen as a mysterious power which one must dedicate to the deity out of fear.

Given these contextual factors, what might we make of the specific biblical passages? The answer, in short, is: not very much. In the vast spectrum of biblical material there are surprisingly few references to homosexual acts and almost all of these speak to religious and social conditions significantly different from our own. Consider, briefly, the most frequently cited texts (and those with which most gay and lesbian clients have had personally to deal).

The destruction of Sodom and Gomorrah (Genesis 19), though often believed to show God's condemnation of homosexual activity, cannot fairly be interpreted in this manner. In recent decades, many noted biblical scholars have concluded that "the sin of Sodom" actually was the general violation of Hebraic standards of social justice, including the violation of the norm of hospitality to the stranger. Even if one grants a primarily sexual focus to the story, the only reasonable conclusion is that here are condemnations of sexual intercourse with divine messengers and of violent gang rape—but not condemnations of other forms of homosexual genital activity or of homosexuality as an orientation.

In two other Old Testament passages, however, there are unmistakable denunciations of homosexual acts, both explicitly male in reference. Leviticus 18:23 and 20:13, part of the "Holiness Code," reflect an overriding concern for the separateness and purity of God's chosen people in contrast to the surrounding tribes with their idolatrous practices, including the use of female and male temple prostitutes. Selective literalists today frequently single out these texts, forget (or are unaware of) their historical context, and ignore the numerous other proscriptions in the same code, such as those against eating rare meat, having marital intercourse during menstruation, and wearing clothing of mixed fabrics.

The New Testament contains no recorded words of Jesus on the subject. Its principal references are those of Paul in Romans I and First Corinthians 6, and of the "Pauline" writer in I Timothy 1. The latter two texts deal with types of activity which, it was believed, warrant excluding persons from the Kingdom of God. Both passages, however, need careful linguistic interpretation and when given such appear not to be directed toward all homosexual persons but rather to specific kinds of homosexual acts, namely exploitation, homosexual prostitution, and the sexual use of boys by adult males.

Paul's words in Romans I are usually taken as the strongest New Testament rejection of homosexuality. (Here is the one and only biblical reference to female as well as male same-sex activity.) Paul, however, speaks specifically of same-sex acts that express idolatry and acts undertaken in lust (not tenderness or mutual respect) by "heterosexuals" who willfully act contrary to their own sexual natures. I am not inferring that the Apostle necessarily would have approved of other kinds of same-sex acts. I am simply arguing that it is inaccurate and unfair to interpret his words as directed to non-exploitive and loving acts by same-sex couples for whom mutual homosexual attraction is part of the given of *their* natures.

Clients and their counselors, therefore, need to be aware that careful examination of the biblical material renders no definitive scriptural word on homosexuality as a sexual orientation or upon homosexual genital expression in a relationship of respect and love. Specifically, what the Bible gives us is several references to certain kinds of same-sex acts in quite different religious and cultural contexts from those faced by gay men and lesbians today. Often forgotten, too, is the manner in which scripture celebrates instances of genuine love between two men or two women—David and Jonathan, Ruth and Naomi, Jesus and the Beloved Disciple. Beyond all this, a Christian approach counsels its adherents to assess every moral judgment (whether made by ancient Hebrews or later by Christians) in terms of the spirit of love and to recognize that the central question is not what constitutes a breach of divine moral law as understood in certain historical periods but rather what constitutes responsive faithfulness to God, the Cosmic Lover, who is revealed in Jesus the Christ. The Bible conveys the message that human sexuality is one of the Creator's great and good gifts, to be integrated fully into one's personhood and expressed in ways that honor both God and the human partner.

Dealing with Current Theological Opinion and Church Practice. The scriptural questions by themselves do not exhaust the theological issues with which many gay men and lesbians must deal. The church has a long and unfortunate history of homosexual oppression, which continues into the present. As John Boswell's (1980a) impressive scholarship has recently demonstrated, Christianity's opposition to homosexuality was not original but derived from non-Christian sources. Nor has it always been consistent. There were centuries of Christian tolerance. Nevertheless, most of today's gay men and lesbians have met with enormously more rejection than affirmation by the church.

Two theological issues in particular frequently surface in counseling. One is the claim that the homosexual orientation itself is contrary to "nature," or to "natural law," or to God's intention in creation. To the extent that this is internalized, the individual will likely regard her- or himself as freakish and unnatural in this very fundamental way. Frequently, of course, the "unnatural" label is coupled with psychological notions of illness, perversion, and arrested development, or even with religious notions of idolatry.

The religiously-sensitive therapist can assist the client on several levels: for example, the cognitive process of sorting out the natural-law argument. Several points deserve attention. One is the grounding of this argument in a static metaphysical world view that appeared appropriate to the Middle Ages but is quite inappropriate today. There is no fixed human nature which can be read off the structure of human biology. Because human beings are constantly in the process of becoming, the definition of what is "naturally" human is forever being modified and changed. Numerous theologians now recognize this, even within the Roman Catholic Church, which has been most heavily committed to the tradition of natural law. Thus, Father Gregory Baum (1974) argues that what is normative for "normal life" is the human nature toward which we are divinely summoned—the life of mutuality, in terms of which homosexual love is not to be excluded or seen as contradictory.

Related to the above are the biological assertions that procreation is the primary purpose of sex and that, since homosexual intercourse is by definition nonprocreative, it is unnatural and contrary to creation. Mainstream Protestant thought began to move away from the primacy-of-procreation position three centuries ago; more recently much Roman Catholic thought has done likewise. Indeed, the church has always recognized the validity of the marriage in which sterility made procreation impossible, and since 1931 the Catholic Church has officially endorsed love-making without baby-making through approval of the rhythm method. If the primary purpose of sexual expression is communion or love, then it is difficult to exclude any type of love-making, heterosexual or homosexual, which is either intrinsically or deliberately nonprocreative. The central question is thus the inescapable one: What is the fundamental meaning of our sexuality?

Finally, it should be remembered by both counselor and client that most natural-law arguments against homosexuality, whether they articulate it or not, rest upon an assumption of "gender complementarity." It is assumed that men and women are naturally constituted with essentially different personality configurations (e.g., men are cognitive, women are intuitive, etc.), so that one sex is incomplete until finding its complement in the other. But this notion is based upon disproven sex-role stereotypes, covertly supports an unjust dominance-submission relation between the sexes, and allows neither sex to develop its androgynous possibilities. What the argument misses, in short, is the uniqueness of human personality. We are, indeed, destined for communion with others. We do, indeed, find our loneliness assuaged and our deficiencies met with another's strengths. But such can be the case in the homosexual couple just as fully as in the heterosexual. It is not biologically destined. The gay or lesbian client can be encouraged to tap personal experience to verify this.

Closely related to and overlapping the above natural-law arguments is a position officially subscribed to by several major church bodies today. It holds that while homosexuality as an *orientation* is contrary to God's created intention, the homosexual *person* ought not be adversely judged or rejected by the church. Often this position carries the acknowledgment that sexual orientation is seldom if ever the result of voluntary choice and that constitutional homosexuality appears largely unsusceptible to psychotherapeutic reorientation. While some church people see this as a more tolerant and compassionate view than outright condemnation, it places gay men and lesbians in at least two impossible binds.

One, of course, is the individual's recognition that her or his own sexual orientation is as natural and as fundamental to identity as is the color of the skin. It is both naive and cruel to tell the lesbian or gay man, "Your sexual orientation is still unnatural and a perversion, but this is no judgment upon you as a person." The individual knows otherwise.

The other bind concerns churchly pressure toward celibacy. When the church presumes to be non-judgmental toward orientation but then draws the line against any genital expression, it is difficult to understand how the sense of guilt—even in the celibate— will be significantly alleviated. In most lesbians and gay men it is likely and understandable that anger will increase.

In the face of this, both client and counselor can recognize two important things. One is that there are both intellectual and psychological contradictions in any position which is based upon an outmoded version of natural law or which attempts to make sharp distinctions between orientation and genital expression.

The second recognition is equally important: there is a significant and increasing pluralism within organized Christianity with regard to these issues. Theologians and churches, both Protestant and Catholic, simply do not have a unified mind, and the client needs to know this. In spite of the official Vatican position, there are distinguished Catholic theologians who publicly proclaim homosexuality as Christianly valid, and there are creative and affirming Catholic ministries to gay and lesbian communities. Within Protestantism, the spectrum is even greater. Here, too, one can find an increasing number of significant theological voices giving full affirmation to lesbians and gay men—not only among "liberal" theologians but now also among those who identify themselves as "evangelical."

There have been ordinations of publicly affirmed gay and lesbian persons in at least two major Protestant churches (the United Church of Christ and the Protestant Episcopal Church) and pressures in other denominations for similar openness. In recent years, several denominations have undertaken major studies of human sexuality, occasioning considerable reassessment of traditional Christian attitudes about homosexuality. Further, since 1968 there have arisen gay-lesbian organizations within virtually every American denomination (Gearhart and Johnson 1974). And a new movement, the Metropolitan Community Churches, with ministries and congregations organized primarily by and for gay men and lesbians, has become a rapidly expanding urban religious phenomenon in this country and abroad (Perry 1972).

The point is this: Particularly within the last dozen years there has been a vigorous ferment about homosexual issues within American church life. In every case except the most conservative and fundamentalist groups, this ferment has produced new openness toward and affirmation of lesbians and gay men. If, as is sadly true, the legacy of rejection is still alive, it is also true that changes are occurring within the churches as never before within recent centuries. It would be a mistake for any therapist or client to assume that the church is a monolithic, condemning entity.

Questions Surrounding Gay-Lesbian Spirituality and Life-Style. It is probable that proportionately fewer lesbians than gay men are still attempting to find their spiritual home in the organized church. After all, in spite of some encouraging progress on feminist issues, the churches are still unquestionably male-dominated. Hence, lesbians have two strikes against them—their sex as well as their sexual orientation—and feeling their powerlessness in the church, a number have voted with their feet. Yet, for those lesbians and gay men who still seek a religious life within organized Christian communions, what are the important resources for their wholeness and mental health?

One resource is the experience of community. It is imperfectly present in some churches, sadly absent in others, but genuinely available in some congregations and in all of the specifically gay-lesbian Christian groups. The internalization of such labels as "sinner," "sick," and "unnatural" inevitably leads to shame and guilt, and thence to social withdrawal. The need for a community of acceptance and affirmation more personally inclusive than can be found in the bars and baths is real. That this enormously important resource does exist for gay men and lesbians—at least in some religious groups—ought not to be overlooked by therapists and clients. When the religious community can assist the coming-out process, help to mitigate its pain, and help the individual to celebrate new openness, the rewards are particularly great, inasmuch as the energy drain and heightened possibility of self-hatred in the closeted person forced to live the double life can take a heavy toll.

Feelings of guilt over homosexuality can be exacerbated to a point of moral scrupulosity by the internalization of negative attitudes toward sexuality itself. A positive, indeed celebrative, religious attitude toward human sexuality, then, is another resource possible within the church. Even though much of the church throughout much of its history has been remiss on this score, the foundations for sexual affirmation are central to Christianity's theological tenets.

Christianity is a religion of incarnation. At the core of its belief system is the affirmation that the Word has become flesh and has dwelt among us, full of grace and truth. This is a radical proposition. It claims that the most decisive experience of God is not in doctrine or creed or other-worldly mystical experience, but *in flesh.* Insofar as this is taken seriously, the embodiment of God is not limited to the critical manifestation in the historical Jesus but continues in our human flesh now. Against any Greek dualism dividing spirit from body, proclaiming the eternal spirit good and the temporal body corrupt, suspect, even evil, an incarnationalist faith sees the body as good. We can be both fully spiritual and fully sexual—indeed, that is our destiny.

Christian faith at its core is not only incarnationalist, it is also a religion of grace. In contemporary terms, grace means radical, unconditional acceptance. This means (even if some elements of the church have little understood it) that we are accepted and affirmed as sexual selves. Our bodies, our sexual feelings and fantasies, our ascetic attempts at self-purification, our hedonistic flights from authentic relationship, our femininity and our masculinity, our homosexuality and our heterosexuality—all are accepted by God.

The dynamics of grace, of God's radical acceptance, afford a whole range of possibilities in sexual growth. One is growth in self-acceptance. Such positive self-love personalizes the body and puts us more in touch with the roots of our emotions. Another possibility is growth in sensuousness, in the self's ability to experience the erotic throughout the entire body (not only in the genitals), and in the self's increased capacity to give and receive pleasure. Still another arena of growth is that of androgyny, for grace aims at the fullest possible development of each unique individual beyond all of the constructions of sex-role or sexual-orientation stereotypes. Perhaps all of these possibilities of growth are summarized in one word—love. For love means the increasing ability to integrate fully our sexuality and our capacity for caring and intimacy.

If the majority of Christians have internalized some sex-negative attitudes from their religion, lesbians and gay men have been susceptible to an even heavier dose than have heterosexual men and women. Forced by a hostile majority to focus more attention and energy upon defending their own sexual orientation, gay people are forced to deal more constantly with their sexuality in general. Hence, the likelihood of internalizing shameful feelings simply because of *being sexual* is all the greater. Given this, I cannot overestimate the importance of the therapist's awareness of the need for positive religious approaches to sexuality. To be sure, our salvation (or "health" or "wholeness"—the words all have the same root) is always incomplete. Because none of us is whole, the unhealed parts of our sexuality will continue to hurt us and others. But the religiously concerned client needs to know that the first and last word of the Christian message is incarnate grace: grace as acceptance and grace as empowerment for new growth and life as a body-self. The Word is made flesh, and our flesh is confirmed.

What does all this mean for a moral life-style for the religiously sensitive gay or lesbian? Celibacy is one option. It is an option to be honored when voluntarily chosen for positive rather than negative reasons. If celibacy is embraced not from a belief that homosexual genital expression is intrinsically wrong, nor out of generalized fear of sex and intimacy, nor because celibacy is believed to be religiously more meritorious, but rather is embraced because celibacy best expresses the person's own sense of integrity or vocational commitments, it is to be celebrated. The celibate is still "a sexual celibate" for whom her or his positively affirmed sexuality, while not genitally expressed with another, is the grounding of emotional richness and interpersonal intimacy (Goergen 1975; Gustafson 1978).

But celibacy ought not to be considered the only Christianly valid life-style for the gay man or lesbian. Against the biologism that sex and erotic love are moral only when they are potentially procreative, there is a second major Christian tradition. It might be called "the transcendent approach" to sexuality, for it strives to transcend biological determinations of eroticism and love (Boswell 1980b). Though it will surprise many, this latter approach has more New Testament grounding and was, in fact, dominant in theology for several centuries in the early Christian era (a time when, significantly, ecclesiastical opposition to homosexuality was very rare). If current secular society is now ahead of the church in its tolerance of "non-biological" love, the church needs to reclaim its earlier tradition and not capitulate to the fears of ultra-conservative Christians who would move us back into an even more stringent biological determinism.

Human sexuality, for all of its similarity to animal sexuality, is different. It is not under the tyranny of biology. Our sexuality is highly symbolic in its meanings and capable of expressing the depths of human self-understanding and desires for relatedness. Our sexuality is capable of expressing and sharing a total personal relationship that contributes immeasurably toward our intended destiny as human beings—that of lovers after the image of the Cosmic Lover.

Hence, the core issue for sexual ethics is not the assessment of certain types of physical acts as right or wrong. Abnormality or deviance ought not to be defined statistically, but rather in reference to the Christian norm—authentic humanity as revealed in Jesus the Christ. Gay men and lesbians desire and need deep, lasting relationships no less than do heterosexual people, and appropriate genital expression should be denied to neither.

Thus, the appropriate ethical question is this: What sexual behavior will serve and enhance, rather than inhibit and damage the fuller realization of our divinely intended humanity? The answer, I believe, is sexual behavior in accordance with love. This means commitment, trust, tenderness, respect for the other, and the desire for responsible communion. On the negative side it means resisting cruelty, utterly impersonal sex, obsession with sexual gratification, and actions that display no willingness to take responsibility for their consequences in human lives. This kind of ethic is equally appropriate to both heterosexual and homosexual Christians.

But this statement deserves a word of qualification. The social and religious oppression experienced by most gay men and lesbians has driven many—especially men—to rely heavily upon the satisfactions of impersonal sex associated with cruising, the baths, and "tea rooms." While such impersonal sex is by no means a homosexual monopoly, it is understandably more of a temptation when the majority society does all in its power to discourage lasting homosexual unions and when most of the church refuses to bless and support the covenants of gay and lesbian couples. Given the realities of social oppression, it is insensitive and unfair to judge gay men and lesbians simply by a heterosexual ideal of the monogamous relationship. What can be said to all persons regardless of orientation is that genital expression can find its greatest fulfillment within a relationship of ongoing commitment and communion. That other sexual encounters and experiences can have elements of genuine good in them even while falling short of the optimum remains an open possibility.

For the gay male or lesbian couple who intend a covenant of indefinite duration, will "fidelity" always mean "genital exclusivity"? Some such couples (as is true of some heterosexual couples) have explored relationships that admit the possibility of sexual intimacy with secondary partners. For these couples, "infidelity" does not have a simple biological meaning (sex with someone other than the permanent partner). Rather, infidelity means the rupture of the bonds of faithfulness, trust, honesty, and commitment between the partners. On the positive side, fidelity is seen as the enduring commitment to the partner's well-being and growth, a commitment to the primacy of this covenant over any other relationship. While there are undoubted risks for such a course of action, and while the weight of Christian tradition is on the side of sexual exclusivity, there are also risks when a couple's relationship becomes marked by possessiveness.

These, then, are guidelines and ideals that can assist the religiously sensitive individual in deciding about appropriate genital expression. They are guidelines, however, and not legalisms. They respect the necessity of personal decision, and they function within a Christian understanding of forgiveness and new beginnings when our sexual expression has become more destructive than creative of our destined humanness (see Nelson 1978, chaps. 5 and 6).

Homophobia and the Church's Need for Gay and Lesbian Christians. Thus far my emphasis has been upon the resources which gay men and lesbians might find within Christian faith. What remains to be emphasized is the need of other Christians to have homosexual brothers and sisters within the religious community. In a word, churches and society both desperately need release from homophobia, that irrational fear of same-sex orientation and expression.

While some resistance to homosexuality is, to be sure, based upon calm and reasoned religious belief (though my own disagreements with its major arguments have already been indicated), undoubtedly much is based upon unreasoned, ill-understood emotional reactions. Without the presence of homophobia it is difficult to understand the persistence of selective biblical literalism and long-disproven homosexual stereotypes among so many church members.

While homophobia can be accounted for by a variety of psychodynamics, importantly including the projection of fears about homosexual feelings in the self, its deep roots in the twin forms of alienating sexual dualism need also to be recognized. Spiritualistic dualism (spirit over body) is likely to be present. Virtually everyone in our society suffers from the internally divisive effects of spiritualism and longs for (in unconscious as well as conscious ways) the essential reunion of the body-self. And, since stereotypes insist that gay men and lesbians are more sexually defined and simply "more sexual" than heterosexual men and women, they become the targets of subconscious envy. Hence, the stereotype bears its curiously unintended harvest, but one which gives a powerful dynamic to homophobia.

The dynamic of sexist dualism may be even stronger in Western society, as witnessed by the predominance of biblical concern with male homosexuality as compared to lesbianism. Male homosexuality appears to threaten "normal" masculine gender identity. It calls into question the dominance-submission patterns of any patriarchal society as well as the myths of super-masculinism by which that society lives. And, unconsciously, the heterosexual male seems to fear that an acceptance of male homosexuality in others would open him to the risk of being "womanized," losing his power, and becoming the same sort of sex object into which he has made women.

Thus, not only gay men and lesbians, but surely also heterosexual people within the church and in society generally, have enormous benefits to gain by being released from the destructive dynamics of homophobia. Insofar as this occurs there will be release from dehumanizing sex-role stereotypes and liberation from fears about the continuum of sexual feelings within the self. There will be more genuine self-acceptance and self-affirmation, and with this greater relational equality. There will be enriched possibilities for intimate friendships with fewer debilitating sexual fears between the sexes, as well as in same-sex friendship patterns. We can expect a diminution of male-biased social violence in its myriad forms. There will be more permission for each individual to develop her or his own human uniqueness. And the churches will learn more of the heart of the Christian message, including the freedom, inclusiveness, and justice which come from taking incarnate grace seriously. In a word, gay men and lesbians need to know how much everyone in society will benefit from the gains in their own struggle for liberation. While it is grossly unfair to place the burden of liberating the oppressors upon the oppressed, it may be that the latter can find reason for augmented self-assurance in knowing how deeply they are needed by the former. And such knowledge can be therapeutic.

References

Baum, G. *Catholic Homosexuals.* 99 (1974): 479-482.

Boswell, J. E. *Christianity, Social Tolerance and Homosexuality.* Chicago: University of Chicago, 1980.

————. "A Crucial Juncture." *Integrity Forum* 6 (1980):1-6.

Browning, D. S. *The Moral Context of Pastoral Care.* Philadelphia: Westminster, 1976.

Gearhart, S., and W. Johnson. *Loving Women/Loving Men.* San Francisco: Glide, 1974.

Goergen, D. *The Sexual Celibate.* New York: Seabury Press, 1975.

Gustafson, J. *Celibate Passion.* San Francisco: Harper and Row, 1978.

Nelsen, J. B. *Embodiment: An Approach to Sexuality and Christian Theology.* Minneapolis: Augsburg, 1978.

Nugent, R. "Gay Ministry." *Ministries,* Nov. 1980, 6-27.

Perry, T. *The Lord is My Shepherd and He Knows I'm Gay.* Plainview, NY: Nash, 1972.

THIRTY-SEVEN

Statements of Professional and Religious Organizations on Homosexuality

▼

Professional Organizations

American Bar Association, House of Deputies, 1973

RESOLVED that the legislatures of the several states are urged to repeal all laws which classify as criminal conduct any form of non-commercial *sex conduct between consenting adults in private,* saving only those portions which protect minors or public decorum.

American Medical Association, Action of the Trustees, 1973

Passed a resolution urging the endorsement of the Model Penal Code of the American Law Institute, which recommends to legislators that private sexual behavior between consenting adults should be removed from the list of crimes and thereby legalized.

American Psychiatric Association, Board of Trustees, 1973

Unanimously voted for a resolution urging "the repeal of all legislation making criminal offenses of sexual acts performed by consenting adults in private," and another resolution urged sexual practices (including homosexuality) between consenting adults in private should be removed from the list of crimes. In another resolution, the Board of Trustees voted to remove homosexuality, per se, from its official list of mental disorders.

The Trustees also approved the following resolution:

Whereas homosexuality *per se* implies no impairment in judgment, stability, reliability, or general social or vocational capabilities, therefore, be it resolved that the American Psychiatric Association deplores all public and private discrimination against homosexuals in such areas as employment, housing, public accommodation, and licensing, and declares that no burden of proof of such judgment, capacity, or reliability shall be placed upon homosexuals greater than that imposed on any other persons. Further, the American Psychiatric Association supports and urges the enactment of civil rights legislation at the local, state, and federal level that would offer homosexual persons the same protections now guaranteed to others on the basis of race, creed, color, etc. Further, the American Psychiatric Association supports and urges the repeal of all discriminatory legislation singling out homosexual acts by consenting adults.

American Psychological Association, Board of Directors, 1975

The American Psychological Association supports the action taken on 15 December 1973 by the American Psychiatric Association removing homosexuality from the Association's official list of mental disorders. The American Psychological Association therefore adopts the following resolution:

Homosexuality *per se* implies no impairment in judgment, stability, reliability, or general social or vocational responsibilities;

Further, the American Psychological Association urges all mental health professionals to take the lead in removing the stigma of mental illness that has long been associated with homosexual orientations.

Religious Organizations

American Baptist Churches

We, as Christians, recognize that radical changes are taking place in sex concepts and practices. We are committed to seeking

God's guidance in our efforts to understand faithfully and deal honestly with these changes and related issues. We recognize that there are many traditional problems of family and personal life for which the church's ministries have not been adequate, but we are committed to be used by God to strengthen and broaden these ministries. In this spirit we call upon our churches to engage in worship, study, fellowship and action to provide for meaningful ministries to all persons as members of the "Family of God" including those who are homosexuals.

Christian Church (Disciples of Christ), General Assembly, Study Document, 1977

Acknowledging . . . the wide differences of opinion, there does seem to be a minimal consensus to which the church can strive: homosexuals are persons whom God created, loves and redeems and seeks to set within the fellowship of faith communities to be ministered to and to minister. The church can affirm that God's grace does not exclude persons of differing life styles or sexual preferences, nor does the church which is enlightened by the Holy Spirit. Homosexuals may be included in the fellowship and membership of the community of faith where they are to love and be loved and where their gifts of ministry are to be welcomed.

The General Assembly *disapproved* this resolution noting the following statement by the General Board: "In light of the General Board's recommended action [on other resolutions] . . . it is premature at this time to take action on this resolution. Homosexuality is a very important issue in our time. Every congregation is urged to pray about it, and attempt to have compassion for the persons who are touched by it directly or indirectly. It ought not be inferred that homosexuality is a topic Christians should not talk about. It should not be inferred that anyone has all the answers about this complex matter."

The Church of Jesus Christ of Latter-day Saints (Mormon), *Priesthood Bulletin,* **Feb. 1973, 2-3; July 1977 (Press Release); reissued April 1991.**

A homosexual relationship is viewed by the Church of Jesus Christ of Latter-day Saints as sin in the same degree as adultery and fornication.

In summarizing the intended destiny of man, the Lord has declared: "For behold, this is my work and my glory—to bring to pass the immortality and eternal life of man." (Moses 1:39) Eternal life means returning to the Lord's exalted presence and enjoying the privilege of eternal increase. According to his revealed word, the only acceptable sexual relationship occurs within the family between a husband and a wife.

Homosexuality in men and women runs counter to these divine objectives and, therefore, is to be avoided and forsaken. Church members involved to any degree must repent. "By this ye may know if a man repenteth of his sins—behold, he will confess them and forsake them" (Doctrine and Covenants 59:43). Failure to work closely with one's bishop or stake president in cases involving homosexual behavior will require prompt Church court action.

For the Strength of Youth, 1990, 14-15:

The Lord specifically forbids certain behaviors, including all sexual relations before marriage, petting, sex perversion (such as homosexuality, rape, and incest), masturbation, or preoccupation with sex in thought, speech, or action. . . .

Homosexual and lesbian activities are sinful and an abomination to the Lord (see Romans 1:26-27, 31). Unnatural affections including those toward persons of the same gender are counter to God's eternal plan for his children. You are responsible to make right choices. Whether directed toward those of the same or opposite gender, lustful feelings and desires may lead to more serious sins. All Latter-day Saints must learn to control and discipline themselves. . . .

Friends, Philadelphia Yearly Meeting of Friends, 1973

We should be aware that there is a great diversity in the relationships that people develop with one another. Although we neither approve nor disapprove of homosexuality, the same standards under the law which we apply to heterosexual activities should also be applied to homosexual activities. As persons who engage in homosexual activities suffer serious discrimination in employment, housing and the right to worship, we believe that civil rights laws should protect them. In particular we advocate the revision of all legislation imposing disabilities and penalties upon homosexual activities.

Lutheran Church in America, Biennial Convention, 1970

Human sexuality is a gift of God for the expression of love and the generation of life. As with every good gift, it is subject to abuses which cause suffering and debasement. In the expression of man's sexuality, it is the integrity of his relationships which determines the meaning of his actions. Man does not merely have sexual relations; he demonstrates his true humanity in personal relationships, the most intimate of which are sexual.

Scientific research has not been able to provide conclusive evidence regarding the causes of homosexuality. Nevertheless, homosexuality is viewed biblically as a departure from the heterosexual structure of God's creation. Persons who engage in homosexual behavior are sinners only as are all other persons—alienated from God and neighbor. However, they are often the special and undeserving victims of prejudice and discrimination in law, law enforcement, cultural mores, and congregational life. In relation to this area of concern, the sexual behavior of freely consenting adults in private is not an appropriate subject for legislation or police action. It is essential to see such persons as entitled to understanding justice in church and community.

Moravian Church, Synod, 1974

. . . whereas the Christian Church has the responsibility of reexamining its own traditional sexual stance in the light of more recent interpretation and scientific evidence . . . for the benefit of both youth and adults, and

whereas the basic policies of the Moravian Church . . . "oppose discrimination based on race, culture or any other barrier and its own life will demonstrate that we are brothers and sisters in Christ. This includes open membership in our own congregations and working toward open structures and situations in society"; and

whereas the homosexual has too often felt excluded from and persecuted by society; therefore be it

resolved that the Moravian Church reaffirms its open welcome to all people by specifically recognizing that the homosexual is also under God's care; and be it further

resolved that Moravian congregations will extend an invitation to all persons to join us in a common search for wholeness before God and persons; and be it further

resolved that as Christians, recognizing our common sinfulness and the miracle of God's grace, accepting God's pardon, and together striving to help free each other from bonds of fear, despair, and meaninglessness, fitting us for lives of commitment, responsibility, witness, service, and celebration in God's Kingdom, we will share in this venture as children of God and brothers and sisters in Christ toward wholeness.

Protestant Episcopal Church in the USA, General Convention, 1976.

Resolved, that it is the sense of this General Convention that homosexual persons are children of God, who have a full and equal claim with all other persons upon the love, acceptance, and pastoral concern and care of the Church.

Resolved, this General Council expresses its conviction that homosexual persons are entitled to equal protection of the law with all other citizens, and calls upon our society to see such protection is provided in actuality.

Roman Catholic, Vatican Congregation for the Doctrine of the Faith, 1977

At the present time there are those who, basing themselves on observations in the psychological order, have begun to judge indulgently, and even to excuse completely, homosexual relations between certain people. This they do in opposition to the constant teaching of the magisterium and to the moral sense of the Christian people.

A distinction is drawn, and it seems with some reason, between homosexuals whose tendency comes from a false education, from a lack of normal sexual development, from habit, from bad example or from other causes, and is transitory or at least not incurable; and homosexuals who are definitely such because of some kind of innate instinct or a pathological constitution judged to be incurable.

In regard to this second category of subjects, some people conclude that their tendency is so natural that it justifies in their case homosexual relations within a sincere communion of life and love analagous to marriage insofar as such homosexuals feel incapable of enduring a solitary life.

In the pastoral field, these homosexuals must certainly be treated with understanding and sustained in the hope of overcoming their personal difficulties and their inability to fit into society.

Their culpability will be judged with prudence. But no pastoral method can be employed which would give moral justification to these acts on the grounds that would be consonant with the conditions of such people. For according to the objective moral order homosexual relations are acts which lack an essential and indispensable finality.

Union of American Hebrew Congregations, General Assembly, 1977

Whereas the UAHC has consistently supported the civil rights and civil liberties of all persons, and

Whereas the Constitution guarantees civil rights to all individuals,

Be it therefore resolved that homosexual persons are entitled to equal protection under the law. We oppose discrimination against homosexuals in areas of opportunity, including employment and housing. We call upon our society to see that such protection is provided in actuality.

Be it further resolved that we affirm our belief that private sexual acts between consenting adults are not the proper province of government and law enforcement agencies.

Unitarian Universalist Association of Churches in North America, General Assembly, 1970

Discrimination Against Homosexuals and Bisexuals: Recognizing that

1. A significant minority in this country are either homosexual or bisexual in their feelings and/or behavior;

2. Homosexuality has been the target of severe discrimination by society and in particular by the police and other arms of government;

3. A growing number of authorities on the subject now see homosexuality as an inevitable sociological phenomenon and not

as a mental illness;

4. There are Unitarian Universalists, clergy and laity, who are homosexuals and bisexuals;

THEREFORE BE IT RESOLVED: That the 1970 General Assembly of the Unitarian Universalist Association:

1) Urges all people immediately to bring an end to all discrimination against homosexuals, homosexuality, bisexuals, and bisexuality, with spec-ific immediate attention to the following issues:

a. private consensual behavior between persons over the age of consent shall be the business only of those persons and not subject to legal regulations. . . .

3) Urges all churches and fellowships, in keeping with our changing social patterns, to initiate meaningful programs of sex education aimed at providing a more open and healthier understanding of sexuality in all parts of the United States and Canada, and with the particular aim to end all discrimination against homosexuals and bisexuals.

Gay and Lesbian Services of Union, 1984:

WHEREAS, the Unitarian Universalist Association has repeatedly taken stands to affirm the rights of gay and lesbian persons over the past decade; and

WHEREAS, legal marriages are currently denied gay and lesbian couples by state and provincial governments of North America; and

WHEREAS, freedom of the pulpit is a historic tradition in Unitarian Universalist Societies;

BE IT RESOLVED: That the 1984 General Assembly of the Unitarian Universalist Association:

1. Affirms the growing practice of some of its ministers of conducting services of union of gay and lesbian couples and urges member societies to support their ministers in this important aspect of our movement's ministry to the gay and lesbian community. . . .

Proposals of the Common Vision Planning Committee, 1989

WHEREAS the survey conducted by the Common Vision Planning Committee has shown that, despite a long and luminous tradition of leadership toward an era of wider justice, inclusion, and recognition of the dignity and worth of all, still the fear of same-sex love runs deep among Unitarian Universalists; and

WHEREAS the persistence in our midst of homophobia and heterosexism sorely tests our commitment to our Principles and Purposes;

WHEREAS Unitarian Universalists have consistently committed ourselves through the General Assembly to the dignity and rights of gay, lesbian, and bisexual persons and to their full inclusion in our movement; and

WHEREAS the Welcoming Congregation program has been proposed by the Common Vision Planning Committee and approved by the UUA Board of Trustees as an effective response to the aforementioned concerns and as a model for training in the practice of inclusive community;

THEREFORE BE IT RESOLVED that the 1989 General Assembly of the Unitarian Universalist Association adopts the recommendation of the Common Vision Planning Committee that the Welcoming Congregation Program be established as set forth in the attachment hereto . . . and

BE IT FURTHER RESOLVED that the 1989 General Assembly urges the Unitarian Universalist Association Administration to implement this Program through its Office of Lesbian and Gay Concerns.

The Welcoming Congregation Program:

Definition

1. A Welcoming Congregation is inclusive and expressive of the concerns of gay, lesbian, and bisexual persons at every level of congregational life, in worship, in program, and in social occasions welcoming not only their presence but the unique gifts and particularities of their lives as well.

a. A Welcoming Congregation does not assume that everyone is heterosexual. Vocabulary of worship reflects this perception; worship celebrates the diversity of its people by inclusivity of language and content.

b. An understanding of the experience of lesbian, gay and

bisexual persons will be fully incorporated throughout all programs. It will be fairly represented in Religious Education.

2. The bylaws and other official documents of a Welcoming Congregation include an affirmation and non-discrimination clause affecting all dimensions of congregational life, including membership, hiring practices, and calling of religious professionals.

3. The Welcoming Congregation engages in outreach into the gay, lesbian, and bisexual communities both through its advertising and by supporting actively other lesbian, gay, and bisexual affirmative groups.

4. A Welcoming Congregation offers congregational and ministerial support for services of union and memorial services for gay, lesbian, and bisexual persons, and celebrations of evolving definitions of family.

5. A Welcoming Congregation celebrates the lives of all people and welcomes same-sex couples, recognizing their committed relationships; and equally affirms displays of caring and affection without regard for sexual orientation.

6. A Welcoming Congregation seeks to nurture ongoing dialogue between gay, lesbian, bisexual, and heterosexual persons, and to create deeper trust and sharing.

7. A Welcoming Congregation encourages the presence of a chapter of Unitarian Universalists for Lesbian and Gay Concerns.

8. A Welcoming Congregation observes and celebrates lesbian, gay, and bisexual pride as part of its congregational life.

9. A Welcoming Congregation, as an advocate for gay, lesbian, and bisexual people, attends to legislative developments and works to promote justice, freedom and equality in the larger society. It speaks out when the rights and dignity of lesbian, gay, and bisexual people are at stake.

United Church of Christ, Tenth General Synod, 1975

Therefore, without considering in this document the rightness or wrongness of same-gender relationships, but recognizing that a person's affectional or sexual preference is not legitimate grounds on which to deny her or his civil liberties, the Tenth General Synod of the United Church of Christ proclaims the Christian conviction that all persons are entitled to full civil liberties and equal protection under the law.

Further, the Tenth General Synod declares its support for the enactment of legislation that would guarantee the liberties of all persons without discrimination related to affectional or sexual preference.

United Methodist Church, *Book of Discipline,* 1988

E) Single Person.—We affirm the integrity of single persons, and we reject all social practices that discriminate or social attitudes that are prejudicial against persons because they are unmarried.

F) Human Sexuality.—We recognize that sexuality is God's good gift to all persons. We believe persons may be fully human only when that gift is acknowledged and affirmed by themselves, the Church, and society. We call all persons to the disciplined, responsible fulfillment of themselves, others, and society in the stewardship of this gift. We also recognize our limited understanding of this complex gift and encourage the medical, theological, and social science disciplines to combine in a determined effort to understand human sexuality more completely. We call the Church to take the leadership role in bringing together these disciplines to address this most complex issue. Further, within the context of our understanding of this gift of God, we recognize that God challenges us to find responsible, committed, and loving forms of expression.

Although all persons are sexual beings whether or not they are married, sexual relations are only clearly affirmed in the marriage bond. Sex may become exploitative within as well as outside marriage. We reject all sexual expressions which damage or destroy the humanity God has given us as birthright, and we affirm only that sexual expression which enhances that same humanity, in the midst of diverse opinion as to what constitutes that enhancement. . . .

Homosexual persons no less than heterosexual persons are individuals of sacred worth. All persons need the ministry and guidance of the Church in their struggles for human fulfillment, as well as the spiritual and emotional care of a fellowship which enables reconciling relationships with God, with others, and with self. Although we do not condone the practice of homosexuality and consider this practice incompatible with Christian teaching, we affirm that God's grace is available to all. We commit ourselves to be in ministry for and with all persons.

THIRTY-EIGHT

Resources

▼

Affirmation/Gay and Lesbian Mormons
Support group for lesbian and gay Mormons. Publishes *Affinity* monthly.

> P.O. Box 46022
> Los Angeles, CA 90046
> (213) 255-7251

> P.O. Box 26302
> San Francisco, CA 94126
> (415) 641-4554

> P.O. Box 510751
> Salt Lake City, UT 84151-0751
> (801) 534-8693

AIDS Hotline National Public Health Service

> (800) 342-2437 (information line)

The Book Service
The source for gay and lesbian Christian materials.

> P.O. Box 5760
> Woodland Park, CO 80866

Delta Institute
Sponsors "Beyond Stonewall," annual gay and lesbian retreat.

(801) 531-6846

Department of LDS Social Services (Homosexual Concerns)
Therapy services for those dealing with homosexual issues.

625 East 8400 South
Salt Lake City, UT 84070
(800) 453-3860 or (801) 566-2556

Desert and Mountain States Lesbian and Gay Conference

P.O. Box 1221
Salt Lake City, UT 84147-1221
(801) 355-0854

The Family Fellowship
A group of caring LDS families and individuals formed to help overcome the pain, isolation, and divisiveness associated with same-sex orientation.

P.O. Box 3930
Salt Lake City, UT 84110
(801) 582-2348

GALA (RLDS Gays and Lesbians Acceptance)

262 South Mansfield Avenue
Los Angeles, CA 90036
(213) 939-7611

Gay and Lesbian Alliance of Cache Valley

P.O. Box 1761
Logan, UT 84322
(801) 752-1129

Gay and Lesbian Community Council of Utah

770 South 300 West
Salt Lake City, UT 84101
(801) 534-8989

Gay and Lesbian Historical Society and Archives of Utah
Gathers, preserves, and presents historical information about lesbian and gay Utahns.

P.O. Box 510121
Salt Lake City, UT 84151-0121 .

Homosexual Education for Latter-day Saint Parents (HELP)
Quarterly newsletter.

P.O. Box 3315
San Ramon, CA 94583
(510) 829-8528

Lambda Rising
Gay and lesbian bookstore and mail order outlet; publishes *Lambda Rising Book Report.*

1625 Connecticut Avenue NW
Washington, D.C. 20009
(202) 462-6969 or (800) 621-6969

Legacy Foundation
Utah County support groups.

(801) 373-0515

Cornerstone (affiliated support group)
(801) 768-9537

Lesbian and Gay Student Union
Social support group for students, staff, and interested friends.

Lesbian and Gay Student Union
University of Utah
Salt Lake City, UT 84112
(801) 581-6866

Lesbian Task Force of Salt Lake City
Part of the National Organization for Women (NOW); educates people about issues affecting lesbians and all women; sponsors monthly forums and special events.

(801) 483-5188

Parents, Family and Friends of Lesbians and Gays (P-FLAG)

P-FLAG National Headquarters
1012 14th Street NW, Suite 700
Washington, DC 20005
(202) 638-4200

P-FLAG (Salt Lake City Chapter)

Hank Carlson
(801) 942-0157

People Who Care
For families, wives, former wives, husbands, former husbands, etc., of gay men and lesbians.

P.O. Box 520785
Salt Lake City, UT 84152-0785
(801) 568-1141

Carol Bickmore (Utah County)
(801) 373-5980

The Pillar
Monthly magazine for Utah's lesbian and gay community.

637 East 400 South, Suite H
Salt Lake City, UT 84102
(801) 466-4062

Reconciliation: Gays, Lesbians, and Mormon Families
Scripture discussion group for Mormon lesbians and gays, family, and friends.

P.O. Box 1501
Salt Lake City, UT 84110-1501
(801) 596-8315

P.O. Box 3246
Idaho Falls, ID 83403
(208) 523-3786

The Second Stone
National newspaper for lesbian and gay Christians.

> P.O. Box 8340
> New Orleans, LA 70182

Unconditional Support of Ogden

> P.O. Box 12302
> Ogden, UT 84312
> (801) 399-4270

Utah AIDS Foundation

> 1408 South 1100 East
> Salt Lake City, UT 84105
> (801) 487-2323 or (800) 366-2347

Utah Gay and Lesbian Youth
Social and support group for lesbians and gays from fourteen to twenty-three years old.

> c/o Stonewall Center
> 770 South 300 West
> Salt Lake City, UT 84101
> (801) 539-8800

Utah Stonewall Center
Gay and lesbian community center.

> 770 South 300 West
> Salt Lake City, UT 84101
> (801) 539-8800

Womyn's Community News (WCN)

> P.O. Box 65102
> Salt Lake City, UT 84165
> (801) 484-6325

THIRTY-NINE

Annotated Bibliography

▼

According to the current listings under gay, lesbian, and homosexual headings in the 1990-91 *Books in Print,* approximately 1,000 books are currently available, not counting those out of print but obtainable in libraries. In addition, there are available in the United States many articles in popular magazines and professional journals, as well as information on videos and tapes. We have chosen to include here books that Mormons or those interested in Mormon issues can read easily and books pertinent to Mormonism and homosexuality. Our list represents many vantage points: religious, secular, sources advocating change, those advocating a healthy acceptance of homosexuality, and those that provide practical advice.

Most of these books have bibliographies of their own. Readers should also be aware that mainstream Christian churches and religious presses often have extensive booklists on homosexuality and spirituality. Characteristically such works advocate a basic position, pro or con. Many of these pamphlets and shorter works will not be listed in *Books in Print* but may be obtained from organizations in the list of Resources which appears just prior to these annotated references.

Anonymous. *Prologue: An Examination of the Mormon Attitude Towards Homosexuality.* Los Angeles: Affirmation, 1978.

This pamphlet was first published anonymously in 1978 and has been re-issued several times. It was written primarily by Cloy Jenkins, a former student at Brigham Young University. Although the tone is occasionally strident, it nevertheless describes vividly the treatment of homosexuals at BYU and within the Mormon church. It lays out several of the arguments raised by church leaders against homosexuality and presents counter-arguments. It became a rallying cry for many gays who formed the support group Affirmation.

Back, Gloria G. *Are You Still My Mother? Are You Still My Family?* New York: Warner Books, 1985.

The author describes reactions to the revelation of homosexuality from the perspective of gay children and their parents. Additionally she describes her workshops for families with gay members. Many personal and relationship issues are discussed. This book does not investigate causes; rather it emphasizes understanding and building relationships.

Barrett, Martha Barron. *Invisible Lives: The Truth About Millions of Women Loving Women.* New York: William Morrow, 1989.

In an attempt to dispel common myths about lesbian women and culture, Barrett relies on research, interviews, and previously printed material. Her stance is positive but not idealistic as she strives to outline an inside view for these women. The chapters consider the developmental process of becoming aware of one's sexual orientation, the secrecy of and discrimination against lesbian women, the many facets of temporary and permanent relationships, lesbian culture, religion, sexuality, older lesbians, efforts for change in American society. She portrays lesbians as women who have complex, intricate lives in which their gender orientation is often a minor part.

Bell, Alan, and Martin Weinberg. *Homosexualities: A Study of Diversity Among Men and Women.* New York: Simon and Schuster, 1978.

–And–

Bell, Alan, Martin Weinberg, and Sue Hammersmith. *Sexual Preference: Its Development in Men and Women.* Bloomington: Indiana

University Press, 1981.

These two books report an extensive study of homosexual men and women. They are based on data from approximately 1,000 people with homosexual orientation and 500 heterosexual control subjects. The findings of this study have helped to dispel many of the myths and stereotypes associated with homosexuality. For instance, the idea that homosexual orientation is caused by weak fathers and domineering mothers was clearly shown to lack support. Likewise, the common myth that homosexuality is caused by a history of sexual abuse in the formative years was dispelled, since such same-sex abuse was found to be more common in the heterosexual controls than it was in the homosexuals. One important finding from this work was that there are at least five different patterns of homosexual adaptations common in the gay and lesbian community, including a close-coupled pattern much like that found in the heterosexual monogamous relationship.

Berzon, Betty. *Permanent Partners: Building Gay and Lesbian Relationships That Last.* New York: E. P. Dutton, 1988.

Berzon outlines the relationship factors needed for permanently committed partners in this well-written, practical book. She covers many emotional and practical concerns, similar to those found in a manual for married couples, with useful perspectives on the needs of homosexual partners. Some of the topics considered are compatibility, conflict, power, jealousy, money, in-laws, children, interfacing with the world, legal issues, and sexual relations. All chapters include information about the topic, her personal position as a therapist, and detailed practical advice about how to achieve the goals she advocates. This book will help parents and friends of gay persons dismantle the myth that all gay unions are temporary and promiscuous.

Blumstein, Philip, and Pepper Schwartz. *American Couples: Money, Work, Sex.* New York: William Morrow, 1983.

This book reports on a survey conducted among large numbers of heterosexual married couples, heterosexual unmarried couples living together, gay couples, and lesbian couples. The total sample was over 10,000 couples for all four groups, and the comparisons on sexual, money and work issues are revealing. For those who believe that homosexuality arises from a standard set of conditions and manifests predictable behavior patterns, it shows that remarkable differences in sexual practices and stability are evident when gay and lesbian relationships are compared. Differences are also evident in money and work issues.

Borhek, Mary V. *Coming Out to Parents: A Two-Way Survival Guide for Lesbians and Gay Men and Their Parents.* New York: Pilgrim Press, 1983.

This is an easily readable, step-by-step guide for gay people about the process of coming out to parents. The author covers each stage of disclosure and subsequent reactions in a warm, friendly tone. She also weaves in her awareness of important psychological factors and family interaction dynamics. One particularly helpful chapter is titled, "Grief Often Does Not Look Like Grief." She also discusses religious issues and parents' "coming out" to others about their children's homosexuality.

Boswell, John E. *Christianity, Social Tolerance and Homosexuality.* Chicago: University of Chicago, 1980.

According to Boswell, Christianity's opposition to homosexuality was not unique but can be traced to non-Christian sources. Nor has the Christian church always been consistent in its condemnation. In fact, for centuries the church tolerated homosexuality among its members.

Brown, Victor L., Jr. *Fred's Story.* Sacramento: H. R. Associates, 1985.

Brown presents a fictional account of a young homosexual man named Fred who seeks therapy. The narrative assumes that homosexuality is learned and later reinforced by erroneous habits. Brown maintains that homosexuality can be changed through three principles: self-understanding, self-mastery, self-definition. He lists several techniques of change, including the learning of "manly" skills in order to be better accepted in the male world. Three appendices are included: a bibliography and two outlines for the change program. The book falls into the trap of stereotyping homosexuals.

Buxton, Amity Pierce, *The Other Side of the Closet: The Coming Out Crisis for Straight Spouses*. Santa Monica, CA: IBS Press, Inc., 1991.

The author, an educator and lecturer for PFLAG, bases the contents of this volume on five years of research and interviews with straight and gay spouses. The major topics include: the damaged sexuality of the straight spouse, the range of marital styles chosen to accomodate gayness, conflicting roles as parent and spouse, the identity crisis of the straight spouse, the power of the lies about homosexuality for both spouses, and salvaging shattered belief systems. The book contains personal stories and practical guidelines for people "on both sides of the closet."

Carl, Douglas. *Counseling Same-Sex Couples*. New York: W. W. Norton, 1990.

A marriage and family therapist who is on the faculty of the Atlanta Institute for Family Studies, Carl interweaves family therapy theory and techniques with the particular issues gay and lesbian couples face. He reviews briefly the three theories of etiology: psychoanalytic, biological, and social learning theory and concludes we do not know enough to answer the question of what causes homosexuality. He discusses appropriate therapy interventions for same-sex couples facing parenting, AIDS, alcohol, drugs, and ending relationships—in addition to the common concerns all couples face, heterosexual or homosexual. Each topic is treated only briefly, and more material on each subject area is needed.

Fairchild, Betty, and Nancy Hayward. *Now That You Know: What Every Parent Should Know About Homosexuality*. New York: Harcourt Brace Jovanovich, 1989.

A primer about homosexuality for people seeking information. It includes definitions of basic terms and answers questions most parents ask: what is being gay like for their children, how did it happen, what about love relationships, religion, and AIDS, and most importantly, what about their relationship now with their child? Numerous life experiences of a variety of people are included. The stance of the authors is one of positive acceptance.

Feliz, Antonio A. *Out of the Bishop's Closet: A Call to Heal*

Ourselves, Each Other, and Our World. San Francisco: Aurora Press, 1988.

Feliz shares his own story of committed Mormon church service as a church leader and employee, while slowly coming to terms with his homosexuality. The book describes his coming out, including his activity in Affirmation and his attempts to help other people. He describes the suicides of a number of homosexuals whose experiences he saw judged in church courts.

Fishbein, John R. *Homosexuality.* San Jose, CA: the author, 1989.

This pamphlet, third in a series titled "Emotional First Aid: A Practical Approach to Common Concerns," was written by a Brigham Young University graduate and a marriage and family therapist. He outlines a program for change based on behavioral techniques. His premise is that homosexuality is learned, but he does not develop a theory of defective development. Upbeat and simply written, the pamphlet portrays change as difficult but possible. No research or bibliographic material is listed.

Gonsiorek, John C., ed. *A Guide to Psychotherapy with Gay and Lesbian Clients.* New York: Harington Park Press, 1985.

Written for therapists, this book is nonetheless accessible to lay readers. Chapters by various authors cover diverse therapeutic issues, including the developmental stages of the coming out process, relationship therapy with gay couples, how the sexual orientation of the therapist affects therapy, bisexual and gay men in heterosexual marriage, religious and moral issues in therapy, and victims of sexual assault. Written to be supportive of gay people, there are no articles on techniques for changing sexual orientation.

Griffin, Carolyn Welch, Marian J. Wirth and Arthur G. Wirth. *Beyond Acceptance: Parents of Lesbians and Gays Talk About Their Experiences.* Englewood Cliffs, NJ: Prentice-Hall, 1986.

This is an easy-to-read, well-organized book about the personal reactions of parents who have discovered that their child is gay. Various aspects of their experience are covered in different chapters: finding out, personal reactions, communicating with others including other family members, AIDS, resources for understanding and support.

Johnson, Barbara. *Where Does A Mother Go to Resign?* Minneapolis: Bethany House Publishers, 1979.

Described by one mother as the book that got her through the shock and anger that followed her son's coming out, this autobiographical book will appeal to those who want religious faith woven into the discussion of adjustment to homosexuality within the family.

Kinsey, Alfred, Wardell Pomeroy, and Clyde Martin. Chapter 21: "Homosexual Outlet" In *Sexual Behavior in the Human Male.* Philadelphia: W. B. Saunders, 1948. See Appendix I.

—And—

Kinsey, Alfred, Wardell Pomeroy, Clyde Martin, and Paul Gebhard. Chapter 11: "Homosexual Responses and Contacts." In *Sexual Behavior in the Human Female.* Philadelphia: W. B. Saunders, 1953.

These two major reports showed homosexuality to be more prevalent than many had thought. The interview and descriptive techniques introduced in the 1948 study on males were new and brought significant changes in the understanding of homosexuality.

Konrad, J. A. *You Don't Have to be Gay.* Newport Beach, CA: Pacific Publishing House, 1987.

This book is a series of easy-to-read letters to a young man with homosexual orientation based on the Elizabeth Moberly theory (see annotation in this bibliography), which is presented as fact. It also relies on stereotyped descriptions of gays and promises a universal cure for anyone who tries hard enough. It ignores considerable scientific evidence and mis-quotes specialists, including John Money. It is an enthusiastic testimonial but is heavy-handed in suggesting that everyone's situation is alike. The book addresses neither female homosexuality nor how gays develop heterosexual relationships; rather it describes the transition to what may be termed a celibate homoemotional person.

Livingood, John, ed. *National Institute of Mental Health Task Force on Homosexuality: Final Report and Background Papers.* Rockville, MD: National Institute of Mental Health, 1972.

This report represented the thinking of a broadly-based scientific group in the early 1970s. It contains statistics on the success of treatment programs for homosexuals, showing that position on the Kinsey Scale makes a major difference in prognosis for change. For example, bisexuals were found to be much more amenable to accommodational changes than #6 homosexuals.

MacPike, Loralee, ed. *There's Something I've Been Meaning to Tell You.* Tallahassee, FL: Naiad Press, 1989.

This is an anthology of personal stories by gay parents coming out to their children. A variety of perspectives are shared: from parents who were open to their children from early youth to parents who have experienced ongoing turmoil or emotional alienation from their children. MacPike gives little direct advice and takes no formal professional stance on how to direct the process of coming out. One section addresses the political and legal issues of coming out to children.

McWhirter, David, Stephanie Sanders, and June Reinisch. *Homosexuality/Heterosexuality: Concepts of Sexual Orientation.* New York: Oxford University Press, 1990.

This book grew out of a 1986 conference at the Kinsey Institute to evaluate current knowledge on homosexuality in connection with the AIDS crisis. Among other things the essays address the Kinsey Scale and sexual orientation in a historical and scientific context. Many of the foremost authorities on research in homosexuality participated in the writing of this book, including Vern Bullough, who was reared in Utah and has ties to Mormonism.

The book has seven major sections: historical and religious, psychobiological, evolutionary, cultural and sociological, identity development, relational, and conceptual and theoretical. Throughout the book the Kinsey Scale is recognized as having played a crucial role in the understanding of sexual orientation. At the same time it is shown to be a limited instrument for dealing with an extremely complex, multifaceted issue. Some researchers now wish to deemphasize scaling as they focus on self-identification by individuals, on questions related to a core identity, on discontinuities in sexual orientation, and on the importance of relationships in determining sexual orientation patterns. There is a considerable diversity of opinion in this book, but fascinating new findings are presented. Researchers are observing levels of success among gays in relationships that many had not anticipated. Also the gay and lesbian communities are evolving in response to many forces. These changes are creating ever more diversity and proving assumptions about a stereotypical homosexual identity untenable. Apparently even though the Kinsey Scale still has utility, we will increasingly move beyond the elementary level of the scale continuum in seeking to understand this complex topic.

Masters, William, and Virginia Johnson. *Homosexuality in Perspective.* Boston: Little Brown & Company, 1977.

This book summarizes a series of studies on homosexuals completed at the Masters and Johnson Institute. It reports on efforts to treat homosexual couples with dysfunctional sexual interaction. Similar success rates were found as compared to heterosexual couples. It also compared sexual techniques of heterosexuals compared to homosexual couples. The few differences noted generally showed the homosexual couples to be more caring and tender than the heterosexual couples, probably because same-sex couples have a same body response to each other. Finally, they reported reasonably successful efforts (low rates of failure) in working to reverse sexual orientation among dissatisfied homosexuals. The major problem with their therapy is that it requires homosexuals to bring with them a willing opposite-sex partner to practice love-making during the two-week therapy program. Persons with homosexual orientation who are in heterosexual marriages, however, may find this feasible. This report on conversion and reversion therapy, based on fewer than 100 individuals who were followed for five years, has a number of critics.

Miller, Neil. *In Search of Gay America.* New York: Harper and Row, 1989.

This book provides a look at the diversity of homosexuals in the U.S. The author discusses the variety of occupations gay people pursue, including mainstream farmers, miners, and so on. He searches out gays in rural as well as urban locations and discusses racial and religious issues. Included as well are overviews of political and civil rights concerns.

Moberly, Elizabeth R. *Homosexuality: A New Christian Ethic.* Cambridge, England: James Clarke and Co., 1983.

In four chapters Moberly analyzes the biblical sources commonly associated with homosexuality, details a "new" Christian position, and offers psychoanalytic ideas for therapy.

This small book contains Moberly's basic theory about defective male attachment to father and thus insufficient male bonding as the cause of homosexuality. A restatement of previous psychoanalytic theories on homosexuality, it consititutes the basis for some current experimental programs for change of sexual orientation. Her theory is not accepted within the mainstream of psychological thought or therapeutic practice. It does not seem to fit the facts in many cases of homosexual orientation.

Therapeutic efforts encouraged by this book focus on nonsexual aspects of relationships with same-sex individuals rather than directly moving to opposite-sex interdynamics. The therapeutic gains attributed to it may occur as a by-product of a more tolerant view of such orientations and the positive benefits from acknowledging such feelings and allowing them expression in group therapy with other like individuals.

Money, John. *Gay, Straight, and In-Between: The Sexology of Erotic Orientation.* New York: Oxford University Press, 1988.

Written by one of the most eminent sexologists in the world, this book is a complex biological/genetic analysis of the development of gender orientation. Money's thesis is important: sexual orientation develops in a complex yet dimly understood interplay between both genetic predisposition and early childhood learning. He does not take a value stance relative to the preferred course of development. One chapter, easy for the lay person to understand, is titled "Lovemaps and Paraphilia." It details the process through which sexual interaction patterns develop and, once developed, remain constant and persistent for both heterosexuals and homosexuals. Money also considers the development and perpetuation of what has in the past been called perversions, currently professionally labeled "paraphilias" or in lay terms "sexual addictions." Interestingly, Money asserts that a too-rigid religious stance can create a strong split between spirituality and sexuality, which may lead to increased risk for sexual addictions.

Nicolosi, Joseph. *Reparative Therapy of Male Homosexuality: A New Clinical Approach.* Northvale, NJ: James Aronson, Inc., 1991.

The approach that Dr. Nicolosi advocates is identical in theory and technique to that of Elizabeth Moberly and other proponents of the re-education approach. He states that homosexuality is a result of conflicts arising from developmental problems, particularly defective father-son bonding. The therapy involves exploring and healing this wounded relationship. Woven throughout the book are counter-arguments to the premise that homosexuality is a normal developmental pattern. Unfortunately, some of the quotes from other researchers and authorities are taken out of context or are misrepresentative of the original intent of the author. The treatment program, which focuses on male-male relationships, is clearly outlined and transcripts of individual and group sessions are given. An extensive reference section is included.

Paul, William, James Weinrich, John Gonsiorek, and Mary Hotvedt. *Homosexuality: Social, Psychological, and Biological Issues.* Beverly Hills: Sage Publications, 1982.

A series of papers by prominent scientists. For the first time, scholars from the gay and lesbian communities helped in the writing and editing of such a scientific book.

Pearson, Carol Lynn. *Goodbye, I Love You.* New York: Random House, 1986.

An autobiographical account of Pearson's marriage to a homosexual husband. She chronicles her experience from the beginning of their relationship to his death from AIDS. This book, widely read by Mormons (and others), greatly extended awareness of human issues in the lives of homosexuals.

Presbyterian Church Education Services. *Breaking the Silence, Overcoming the Fear: Homophobia Education.* New York; undated.

A manual developed by the Presbyterian church to provide information, both practical and theological, to church members wanting to decrease stereotyping and fear about homosexuality. Several programs and lesson plans are outlined for action within the church for both gays and the general laity.

Pritt, Thomas, and Ann Pritt. "Homosexuality: Getting Beyond the Therapeutic Impasse." *AMCAP Journal* 13 (1987): 37-65.

This article relies heavily on the Moberly theory but is written from a Mormon perspective. The Pritts do not provide supportive data, only testimonials. Homosexuals are stereotyped, and therapy is aimed at helping those with addictive patterns of sexual behavior, not necessarily at changing homosexual orientation.

Reinisch, June M. *The Kinsey Institute New Report on Sex.* New York: St. Martin's Press, 1990.

A new summary of information from the Kinsey Institute on its continuing sexual research projects. Homosexuality is one of many topics covered. Commentary on homosexuality addresses causes, behavior, treatment approaches, and family attitudes. Easy to read, the book largely follows a question and answer format. A good general reference guide.

Smedes, Lewis B. *Forgive and Forget: Healing the Hurts We Don't Deserve.* New York: Guideposts, 1984.

Although not a book about homosexuality, the author provides a well-written model for forgiveness and for dealing with pain, anger, and resentment. He writes from a religious viewpoint and makes recommendations for action as well as recognition of feelings in the "letting go" process.

Spong, John Shelby. *Living in Sin: A Bishop Rethinks Human Sexuality.* San Francisco, Harper and Row, 1989.

In three important chapters this Episcopal bishop offers new interpretations and suggestions on how the church should respond to homosexuality. He explicates biblical passages on homosexuality and promotes church-sanctioned homosexual marriage.

Weltge, Ralph W. *The Same Sex: An Appraisal of Homosexuality.* Philadelphia: United Church Press, 1964.

Although dated, this book includes several chapters on Christian thought and homosexuality. Considered are topics within Christianity such as history, ethics, and relationship to church organization. This treatise advocates a positive rethinking of homosexuality within a religious context.

Appendix I

Homosexual Outlet

(Excerpts from pp. 623-27, 629-31, 636-39, 641, 647, 651, 659-63, 666, Alfred Kinsey, Wardell Pomeroy, and Clyde Martin, *Sexual Behavior in the Human Male,* Chap. 21 [W. B. Saunders, 1948])

[*Editors' note:* Figures, together with most tables and references to figures and tables, have been deleted.]

... The statistics given throughout this volume on the incidence of homosexual activity, and the statistics to be given in the present section of this chapter, are based on those persons who have had physical contacts with other males, and who were brought to orgasm as a result of such contacts. By any strict definition such contacts are homosexual, irrespective of the extent of the psychic stimulation involved, of the techniques employed, or of the relative importance of the homosexual and the heterosexual in the history of such an individual. These are not data on the number of persons who are "homosexual," but on the number of persons who have had at least some homosexual experience—even though sometimes not more than one experience—up to the ages shown in the tables and curves. The incidences of persons who have had various amounts of homosexual experience are presented in a

---

Reprinted by permission of the Kinsey Institute for Research in Sex, Gender, and Reproduction, Inc.

later section . . .

An individual who engages in a sexual relation with another male without, however, coming to climax, or an individual who is erotically aroused by a homosexual stimulus without ever having overt relations, has certainly had a homosexual experience. Such relations and reactions are, however, not included in the incidence data given here nor in most other places in this volume, because the volume as a whole has been concerned with the number and sources of male orgasms. On the other hand, the data on the heterosexual-homosexual ratings, which are presented later in the present chapter, do take into account these homosexual contacts in which the subject fails to reach climax. Accumulative incidence curves based upon heterosexual-homosexual ratings may, therefore, be somewhat higher than the accumulative incidence curves based upon overt contacts carried through to the point of actual orgasm.

Data on the homosexual activity of the pre-adolescent boy have been presented in another chapter (Chapter 5) and no male is included in any of the calculations shown in the present chapter unless he has had homosexual experience beyond the onset of adolescence.

In these terms (of physical contact to the point of orgasm), the data in the present study indicate that at least 37 per cent of the male population has some homosexual experience between the beginning of adolescence and old age (U.S. Corrections. See Table 139 . . .). This is more than one male in three of the persons that one may meet as he passes along a city street. Among the males who remain unmarried until the age of 35, almost exactly 50 per cent have homosexual experience between the beginning of adolescence and that age. Some of these persons have but a single experience, and some of them have much more or even a lifetime of experience; but all of them have at least some experience to the point of orgasm.

These figures are, of course, considerably higher than any which have previously been estimated; but as already shown they must be understatements, if they are anything other than the fact.

We ourselves were totally unprepared to find such incidence data when this research was originally undertaken. Over a period of several years we were repeatedly assailed with doubts as to

AGE	TOTAL POP. U.S. Corrections		EDUC. LEVEL 0-8		EDUC. LEVEL 9-12		EDUC. LEVEL 13+	
	Cases	% with Exper.	Cases	% with Exper.	Cases	% with Exper.	Cases	% with Exper.
8	3969	0.0	662	0.0	490	0.0	2817	0.0
9	3969	0.1	662	0.0	490	0.2	2817	0.1
10	3969	0.5	662	0.2	490	0.6	2817	0.5
11	3968	1.7	661	1.2	490	2.0	2817	1.8
12	3968	6.1	661	5.6	490	6.3	2817	6.2
13	3968	12.6	661	11.0	490	13.7	2817	11.6
14	3965	21.3	658	17.8	490	24.1	2817	18.0
15	3957	27.7	652	24.8	488	31.1	2817	21.1
16	3934	31.6	635	27.7	483	36.0	2816	23.0
17	3874	34.5	598	27.8	462	40.9	2814	24.1
18	3738	36.7	574	29.3	426	43.7	2738	25.6
19	3507	37.5	544	29.0	389	45.0	2574	26.7
20	3203	36.7	516	28.9	348	43.4	2339	27.6
21	2830	37.0	492	29.1	305	43.6	2033	28.6
22	2428	37.1	473	29.0	283	43.5	1672	29.8
23	2113	37.3	458	29.0	258	43.4	1397	31.5
24	1822	36.5	438	29.2	232	41.8	1152	32.1
25	1636	35.4	418	28.0	216	42.1	1002	33.0
26	1493	35.6	407	28.0	202	42.6	884	32.9
27	1358	35.6	393	28.5	191	41.9	774	33.7
28	1252	35.5	379	28.2	174	42.0	699	33.9
29	1143	33.7	355	27.3	154	39.0	634	33.6
30	1049	32.4	339	26.5	137	38.7	573	33.7
31	973	31.3	319	25.4	125	36.8	529	34.2
32	915	30.5	307	26.1	116	34.5	492	32.9
33	856	31.0	295	25.4	113	36.3	448	33.9
34	804	29.9	287	23.7	105	35.2	412	34.7
35	747	27.5	273	22.3	92	33.7	382	34.0
36	703	27.2	260	22.7	87	32.2	356	33.7
37	641	26.1	242	21.9	76	30.3	323	33.4
38	611	25.4	234	20.9	70	30.0	307	33.2
39	556	25.3	212	20.8	64	29.7	280	33.6
40	509	25.0	194	21.6	58	29.3	257	32.7
41	474	23.3	183	20.2	53	26.4	238	31.9
42	445	23.3	174	19.5	50	28.0	221	31.2
43	399	22.9	159	20.1			192	32.8
44	369	23.5	146	21.9			177	31.1
45	340	22.9	135	21.5			161	32.9

Table 139. Accumulative incidence data on total homosexual outlet covering the life span, including premarital, extra-marital, and post-marital experience. In three educational levels, and in the total population corrected for the U.S. Census of 1940.

whether we were getting a fair cross section of the total population or whether a selection of cases was biasing the results. It has been our experience, however, that each new group into which we have gone has provided substantially the same data. Whether the histories were taken in one large city or another, whether they were taken in large cities, in small towns, or in rural areas, whether they came from one college or from another, a church school or a state university or some private institution, whether they came from one part of the country or from another, the incidence data on the homosexual have been more or less the same. . . .

Those who have been best acquainted with the extent of homosexual activity in the population, whether through clinical contacts with homosexual patients, through homosexual acquaintances, or through their own firsthand homosexual experience, will not find it too difficult to accept the accumulative incidence figures which are arrived at here. There are many who have been aware of the fact that persons with homosexual histories are to be found in every age group, in every social level, in every conceivable occupation, in cities and on farms, and in the most remote areas in the country. They have known the homosexual in young adolescents and in persons of every other age. They have known it in single persons and in the histories of males who were married. In large city communities they know that an experienced observer may identify hundreds of persons in a day whose homosexual interests are certain. They have known the homosexuality of many persons whose histories were utterly unknown to most of their friends and acquaintances. They have repeatedly had the experience of discovering homosexual histories among persons whom they had known for years before they realized that they had had anything except heterosexual experience.

On the other hand, the incidence of the homosexual is not 100 per cent, as some persons would have it. There is no doubt that there are males who have never been involved in any sexual contact with any other male, and who have never been conscious of any erotic arousal by another male. For while some of the psychoanalysts will contend to the contrary, it is to be pointed out that there are several dozen psychoanalysts who have contributed histories to this study who have insisted that they have never identified homosexual experience or reactions in their own histories. . . .

The drop in the active incidence figures between 21 and 25 appears so consistently through all of the calculations, that there is reason for believing that it represents an actual fact in the behavior of the population. During their late teens, many males experience considerable personal conflict over their homosexual activities, because they have become more conscious of social reactions to such contacts. Particularly in that period, many individuals attempt to stop their homosexual relations, and try to make the heterosexual adjustments which society demands. Some of these individuals are, of course, successful, but in a certain number of cases they finally reach the point, somewhere in their middle twenties, where they conclude that it is too costly to attempt to avoid the homosexual, and consciously, deliberately and sometimes publicly decide to renew such activities. Another factor which certainly contributes to the decrease in active incidence in the early twenties is the fact that heterosexually oriented males are then marrying in great numbers, and this leaves an increasingly select group at older ages in the single population. . . .

Homosexual activities occur in a much higher percentage of the males who became adolescent at an early age; and in a definitely smaller percentage of those who became adolescent at later ages. For instance, at the college level, during early adolescence about 28 percent of the early-adolescent boys are involved, and only 14 per cent of the boys who were late in becoming adolescent. This difference is narrowed in successive age periods, but the boys who became adolescent first are more often involved even ten and fifteen years later. It is to be recalled . . . that these early-adolescent boys are the same ones who have the highest incidences and frequencies in masturbation and in heterosexual contacts. It is the group which possesses on the whole the greatest sex drive, both in early adolescence and throughout most of the subsequent periods of their lives.

Homosexual activities occur less frequently among rural groups and more frequently among those who live in towns or cities. On the other hand, it has already been pointed out . . . that this is a product not only of the greater opportunity which the city may provide for certain types of homosexual contacts, but also of the generally lower rate of total outlet among males raised on the farm. It has also been pointed out that in certain of the most remote rural areas there is considerable homosexual activity among lumbermen, cattlemen, prospectors, miners, hunters, and others engaged in out-of-door occupations. The homosexual activity rarely conflicts with their heterosexual relations, and is quite without the argot, physical manifestations, and other affectations so often found in urban groups. There is a minimum of personal disturbance or social conflict over such activity. It is the type of homosexual experience which the explorer and pioneer may have had in their histories.

On the whole, homosexual contacts occur most frequently among the males who are not particularly active in their church connections. They occur less frequently among devout Catholics, Orthodox Jewish groups, and Protestants who are active in the church. The differences are not always great, but lie constantly in the same direction.

Among married males the highest incidences of homosexual activity appear to occur between the ages of 16 and 25, when nearly 10 per cent of the total population of married males . . . is involved. The available data seem to indicate that the percentage steadily drops with advancing age, but we have already suggested that these figures are probably unreliable. Younger, unmarried males have regularly given us some record of sexual contacts with older, married males.

Many married males with homosexual experience currently in their histories have, undoubtedly, avoided us, and it has usually been impossible to secure hundred per cent groups of older married males, especially from males of assured social position, primarily because of the extra-marital intercourse which they often have, and sometimes because some of them have active homosexual histories. About 10 per cent of the lower level married males have admitted homosexual experience between the ages of 16 and 20. About 13 per cent of the high school level has admitted such experience after marriage and between the ages of 21 and 25. Only 3 per cent of the married males of college level have admitted homosexual experience after marriage—mostly between the ages of 31 and 35. It has been impossible to calculate accumulative incidence figures for these several groups, but they must lie well above the active incidence figures just cited.

Finally, it should be noted that there is no evidence that the homosexual involves more males or, for that matter, fewer males today than it did among older generations, at least as far back as the specific record in the present study goes.

The Heterosexual-Homosexual Balance

Concerning patterns of sexual behavior, a great deal of the thinking done by scientists and laymen alike stems from the assumption that there are persons who are "heterosexual" and persons who are "homosexual," that these two types represent antitheses in the sexual world, and that there is only an insignificant class of "bisexuals" who occupy an intermediate position between the other groups. It is implied that every individual is innately—inherently—either heterosexual or homosexual. It is further implied that from the time of birth one is fated to be one thing or the other, and that there is little chance for one to change his pattern in the course of a lifetime.

It is quite generally believed that one's preference for a sexual partner of one or the other sex is correlated with various physical and mental qualities, and with the total personality which makes a homosexual male or female physically, psychically, and perhaps spiritually distinct from a heterosexual individual. It is generally thought that these qualities make a homosexual person obvious and recognizable to any one who has a sufficient understanding of such matters. Even psychiatrists discuss "the homosexual personality" and many of them believe that preferences for sexual partners of a particular sex are merely secondary manifestations of something that lies much deeper in the totality of that intangible which they call the personality. . . .

It should be pointed out that scientific judgments on this point have been based on little more than the same sorts of impressions which the general public has had concerning homosexual persons. But before any sufficient study can be made of such possible correlations between patterns of sexual behavior and other qualities in the individual, it is necessary to understand the incidences and frequencies of the homosexual in the population as a whole, and the relation of the homosexual activity to the rest of the sexual pattern in each individual's history.

The histories which have been available in the present study make it apparent that the heterosexuality or homosexuality of many individuals is not an all-or-none proposition. It is true that there are persons in the population whose histories are exclusively heterosexual, both in regard to their overt experience and in regard to their psychic reactions. And there are individuals in the population whose histories are exclusively homosexual, both in experience and in psychic reactions. But the record also shows that there is a considerable portion of the population whose members have combined, within their individual histories, both homosexual and heterosexual experience and/or psychic responses. There are some whose heterosexual experiences predominate, there are some whose homosexual experiences predominate, there are some who have had quite equal amounts of both types of experience.

Some of the males who are involved in one type of relation at one period in their lives, may have only the other type of relation at some later period. There may be considerable fluctuation of patterns from time to time. Some males may be involved in both heterosexual and homosexual activities within the same period of time. For instance, there are some who engage in both heterosexual and homosexual activities in the same year, or in the same month or week, or even in the same day. There are not a few individuals who engage in group activities in which they may make simultaneous contact with partners of both sexes.

Males do not represent two discrete populations, heterosexual and homosexual. The world is not to be divided into sheep and goats. Not all things are black nor all things white. It is a fundamental of taxonomy that nature rarely deals with discrete categories. Only the human mind invents categories and tries to force facts into separated pigeon-holes. The living world is a continuum in each and every one of its aspects. The sooner we learn this concerning human sexual behavior the sooner we shall reach a sound understanding of the realities of sex.

While emphasizing the continuity of the gradations between exclusively heterosexual and exclusively homosexual histories, it has seemed desirable to develop some sort of classification which could be based on the relative amounts of heterosexual and of homosexual experience or response in each history. . . . An

RATINGS :   0   1   2   3   4   5   6

Based on both psychologic reactions and overt experience,
individuals rate as follows:

0. Exclusively heterosexual with no homosexual
1. Predominantly heterosexual, only incidentally homosexual
2. Predominantly heterosexual, but more than incidentally homosexual
3. Equally heterosexual and homosexual
4. Predominantly homosexual, but more than incidentally heterosexual
5. Predominantly homosexual, but incidentally heterosexual
6. Exclusively homosexual

Adapted from Figure 161. **Heterosexual-Homosexual rating scale.**

individual may be assigned a position on this scale, for each age period in his life, in accordance with the following definitions of the various points on the scale:

0. Individuals are rated as 0's if they make no physical contacts which result in erotic arousal or orgasm, and make no psychic responses to individuals of their own sex. Their socio-sexual contacts and responses are exclusively with individuals of the opposite sex.

1. Individuals are rated as 1's if they have only incidental homosexual contacts which have involved physical or psychic response, or incidental psychic responses without physical contact. The great preponderance of their socio-sexual experience and reactions is directed toward individuals of the opposite sex. Such homosexual experiences as these individuals have may occur only a single time or two, or at least infrequently in comparison to the amount of their heterosexual experience. Their homosexual experiences never involve as specific psychic reactions as they make to heterosexual stimuli. Sometimes the homosexual activities in which they engage may be inspired by curiosity, or may be more

or less forced upon them by other individuals, perhaps when they are asleep or when they are drunk, or under some other peculiar circumstance.

2. Individuals are rated as 2's if they have more than incidental homosexual experience, and/or if they respond rather definitely to homosexual stimuli. Their heterosexual experiences and/or reactions still surpass their homosexual experiences and/or reactions. These individuals may have only a small amount of homosexual experience or they may have a considerable amount of it, but in every case it is surpassed by the amount of heterosexual experience that they have within the same period of time. They usually recognize their quite specific arousal by homosexual stimuli, but their responses to the opposite sex are still stronger. A few of these individuals may even have all of their overt experience in the homosexual, but their psychic reactions to persons of the opposite sex indicate that they are still predominantly heterosexual. This latter situation is most often found among younger males who have not yet ventured to have actual intercourse with girls, while their orientation is definitely heterosexual. On the other hand, there are some males who should be rated as 2's because of their strong reactions to individuals of their own sex, even though they have never had overt relations with them.

3. Individuals who are rated 3's stand midway on the heterosexual-homosexual scale. They are about equally homosexual and heterosexual in their overt experience and/or their psychic reactions. In general, they accept and equally enjoy both types of contacts, and have no strong preferences for one or the other. Some persons are rated 3's, even though they may have a larger amount of experience of one sort, because they respond psychically to partners of both sexes, and it is only a matter of circumstance that brings them into more frequent contact with one of the sexes. Such a situation is not unusual among single males, for male contacts are often more available to them than female contacts. Married males, on the other hand, find it simpler to secure a sexual outlet through intercourse with their wives, even though some of them may be as interested in males as they are in females.

4. Individuals are rated as 4's if they have more overt activity and/or psychic reactions in the homosexual, while still maintaining

a fair amount of heterosexual activity and/or responding rather definitely to heterosexual stimuli.

5. Individuals are rated 5's if they are almost entirely homosexual in their overt activities and/or reactions. They do have incidental experience with the opposite sex and sometimes react psychically to individuals of the opposite sex.

6. Individuals are rated as 6's if they are exclusively homosexual, both in regard to their overt experience and in regard to their psychic reactions.

It will be observed that this is a seven-point scale, with 0 and 6 as the extreme points, and with 3 as the midpoint in the classification. . . .

It will be observed that the rating which an individual receives has a dual basis. It takes into account his overt sexual experience and/or his psychosexual reactions. In the majority of instances the two aspects of the history parallel, but sometimes they are not in accord. In the latter case, the rating of an individual must be based upon an evaluation of the relative importance of the overt and the psychic in his history.

In each classification there are persons who have had no experience or a minimum of overt sexual experience, but in the same classification there may also be persons who have had hundreds of sexual contacts. In every case, however, all of the individuals in each classification show the same balance between the heterosexual and homosexual elements in their histories. The position of an individual on this scale is always based upon the relation of the heterosexual to the homosexual in his history, rather than upon the actual amount of overt experience or psychic reaction.

Finally, it should be emphasized again that the reality is a continuum, with individuals in the population occupying not only the seven categories which are recognized here, but every gradation between each of the categories, as well. Nevertheless, it does no great injustice to the fact to group the population as indicated above.

From all of this, it should be evident that one is not warranted in recognizing merely two types of individuals, heterosexual and homosexual, and that the characterization of the homosexual as a third sex fails to describe any actuality.

It is imperative that one understand the relative amounts of the heterosexual and homosexual in an individual's history if one is to make any significant analysis of him. Army and Navy officials and administrators in schools, prisons, and other institutions should be more concerned with the degree of heterosexuality or homosexuality in an individual than they are with the question of whether he has ever had an experience of either sort. It is obvious that the clinician must determine the balance that exists between the heterosexual and homosexual experience and reactions of his patient, before he can begin to help him. Even courts of law might well consider the totality of the individual's history, before passing judgment on the particular instance that has brought him into the hands of the law.

Everywhere in our society there is a tendency to consider an individual "homosexual" if he is known to have had a single experience with another individual of his own sex. Under the law an individual may receive the same penalty for a single homosexual experience that he would for a continuous record of experiences. In penal and mental institutions a male is likely to be rated "homosexual" if he is discovered to have had a single contact with another male. In society at large, a male who has worked out a highly successful marital adjustment is likely to be rated "homosexual" if the community learns about a single contact that he has had with another male. All such misjudgments are the product of the tendency to categorize sexual activities under only two heads, and of a failure to recognize the endless gradations that actually exist.

From all of this, it becomes obvious that any question as to the number of persons in the world who are homosexual and the number who are heterosexual is unanswerable. It is only possible to record the number of those who belong to each of the positions on such a heterosexual-homosexual scale as is given above. Summarizing our data on the incidence of overt homosexual experience in the white male population . . . and the distribution of various degrees of heterosexual/homosexual balance in that population (Table 147), the following generalizations may be made:

37 per cent of the total male population has at least some overt homosexual experience to the point of orgasm between adolescence and old age. . . . This accounts for nearly 2 males out of every

that one may meet.

50 per cent of the males who remain single until age 35 have had overt homosexual experience to the point of orgasm, since the onset of adolescence. . . .

63 per cent of all males never have overt homosexual experience to the point of orgasm after the onset of adolescence.

50 per cent of all males (approximately) have neither overt nor psychic experience in the homosexual after the onset of adolescence.

13 per cent of the males (approximately) react erotically to other males without having overt homosexual contacts after the onset of adolescence.

30 per cent of all males have at least incidental homosexual experience or reactions (i.e., rate 1 to 6) over at least a three-year period between the ages of 16 and 55. This accounts for one male out of every three in the population who is past the early years of adolescence.

25 per cent of the male population has more than incidental homosexual experience or reactions (i.e., rates 2-6) for at least three years between the ages of 16 and 55. In terms of averages, one male out of approximately every four has had or will have such distinct and continued homosexual experience.

18 per cent of the males have at least as much of the homosexual as the heterosexual in their histories (i.e., rate 3-6) for at least three years between the ages of 16 and 55. This is more than one in six of the white male population.

13 per cent of the population has more of the homosexual than the heterosexual (i.e., rates 4-6) for at least three years between the ages of 16 and 55. This is one in eight of the white male population.

10 per cent of the males are more or less exclusively homosexual (i.e., rate 5 or 6) for at least three years between the ages of 16 and 55. This is one male in ten in the white male population.

8 per cent of the males are exclusively homosexual (i.e., rate a 6) for at least three years between the ages of 16 and 55. This is one male in every 13.

4 per cent of the white males are exclusively homosexual throughout their lives, after the onset of adolescence.

None of those who have previously attempted to estimate the incidence of the homosexual have made any clear-cut definition of

Homosexual-Heterosexual Rating: Active Incidence

AGE	CASES	X %	0 %	TOTAL POPULATION—U.S. CORRECTIONS					
				1 %	2 %	3 %	4 %	5 %	6 %
5	4297	90.6	4.2	0.2	0.3	1.2	0.3	0.2	3.0
10	4296	61.1	10.8	1.7	3.6	5.6	1.3	0.5	15.4
15	4284	23.6	48.4	3.6	6.0	4.7	3.7	2.6	7.4
20	3467	3.3	69.3	4.4	7.4	4.4	2.9	3.4	4.9
25	1835	1.0	79.2	3.9	5.1	3.2	2.4	2.3	2.9
30	1192	0.5	83.1	4.0	3.4	2.1	3.0	1.3	2.6
35	844	0.4	86.7	2.4	3.4	1.9	1.7	0.9	2.6
40	576	1.3	86.8	3.0	3.6	2.0	0.7	0.3	2.3
45	382	2.7	88.8	2.3	2.0	1.3	0.9	0.2	1.8

Table 147. Heterosexual-homosexual ratings for all white males. These are active incidence figures for the entire white male population, including single, married, and post-marital histories, the final figure corrected for the distribution of the population in the U.S. Census of 1940. . . .

the degree of homosexuality which they were including in their statistics. As a matter of fact, it seems fairly certain that none of them had any clear-cut conception of what they intended, other than their assurance that they were including only those "who were really homosexual." . . .

Scientific and Social Implications

In view of the data which we now have on the incidence and frequency of the homosexual, and in particular on its co-existence with the heterosexual in the lives of a considerable portion of the male population, it is difficult to maintain the view that psychosexual reactions between individuals of the same sex are rare and therefore abnormal or unnatural, or that they constitute within themselves evidence of neuroses or even psychoses. . . .

Factors Accounting for the Homosexual. Attempts to identify the biologic bases of homosexual activity, must take into account the large number of males who have demonstrated their capacity to respond to stimuli provided by other persons of the same sex. It must also be taken into account that many males combine in their single histories, and very often in exactly the same period of time, or even simultaneously in the same moment, reactions to both heterosexual and homosexual stimuli. They must take into account that in these combinations of heterosexual and homosexual experience, there is every conceivable gradation between exclusively heterosexual histories and exclusively homosexual histories. It must be shown that the fluctuations in preferences for female or male partners are related to fluctuations in the hormones, the genes, or the other biologic factors which are assumed to be operating (Kinsey 1941). It must be shown that there is a definite correlation between the degree in which the biologic factor operates, and the degree of the heterosexual-homosexual balance in the history of each individual.

If psychologic or social forces are considered as agents in the origin of the homosexual, the same sorts of correlations must be shown before any causal relationship is established. An infrequent phenomenon might be accounted for by factors of one sort, but the factors which account for the homosexual must be of such an order as the incidence and frequency data show this phenomenon to be in our culture. Moreover, it should be emphasized that it is one thing to account for an all-or-none proposition, as heterosexuality and homosexuality have ordinarily been taken to be. But it is a totally different matter to recognize factors which will account for the continuum which we find existing between the exclusively heterosexual and the exclusively homosexual history. . . .

Hereditary Bases of Homosexuality. . . . In order to prove that homosexual patterns of behavior are inherited in the human animal, the following conditions would need to be fulfilled:

1. It would be necessary to define strictly what is meant in the study by the term homosexual. The term should be limited to persons of particular position on the heterosexual-homosexual scale; but whatever the restrictions of the original study the conclusions should finally be applicable to all persons who have ever had any homosexual experience.

2. There should be a determination of the incidence of the phenomenon in groups of siblings in which the complete sexual history of every individual in each family is known. It would be very desirable to secure complete histories of all the siblings in each family for at least two successive generations. . . .

8. Whatever the hereditary mechanisms which are proposed, they must allow for the fact that some individuals change from exclusively heterosexual to exclusively homosexual patterns in the course of their lives, or vice versa, and they must allow for frequent changes in ratings of individuals on the heterosexual-homosexual scale.

Social Applications. It is obvious that social interpretations of the homosexual behavior of any individual may be materially affected by a consideration of what is now known about the behavior of the population as a whole. Social reactions to the homosexual have obviously been based on the general belief that a deviant individual is unique and as such needs special consideration. When it is recognized that the particular boy who is discovered in homosexual relations in school, the business man who is having such activity, and the institutional inmate with a homosexual record, are involved in behavior that is not fundamentally different from that had by a fourth to a third of all of the rest of the population, the activity of the single individual acquires a somewhat different social significance. . . .

The difficulty of the situation becomes still more apparent when it is realized that these generalizations concerning the incidence and frequency of homosexual activity apply in varying degrees to every social level, to persons in every occupation, and of every age in the community. The police force and court officials who attempt to enforce the sex laws, the clergymen and business men and every other group in the city which periodically calls for enforcement of the laws—particularly the laws against sexual "perversion"—have given a record of incidences and frequencies in the homosexual which are as high as those of the rest of the social level to which they belong. It is not a matter of individual hypocrisy which leads officials with homosexual histories to become prosecutors of the homosexual activity in the community. They themselves are the victims of the mores, and the public demand that they protect those mores. As long as there are such gaps between the traditional custom and the actual behavior of the population, such inconsistencies will continue to exist.

There are those who will contend that the immorality of homosexual behavior calls for its suppression no matter what the facts are concerning the incidence and frequency of such activity in the population. Some have demanded that homosexuality be completely eliminated from society by a concentrated attack upon it at every point, and the "treatment" or isolation of all individuals with any homosexual tendencies. Whether such a program is morally desirable is a matter on which a scientist is not qualified to pass judgment; but whether such a program is physically feasible is a matter for scientific determination.

The evidence that we now have on the incidence and frequency of homosexual activity indicates that at least a third of the male population would have to be isolated from the rest of the community, if all those with any homosexual capacities were to be so treated. It means that at least 13 per cent of the male population (rating 4 to 6 on the heterosexual-homosexual scale), would have to be institutionalized and isolated, if all persons who were predominantly homosexual were to be handled in that way. Since about 34 per cent of the total population of the United States are adult males, this means that there are about six and a third million males in the country who would need such isolation.

If all persons with any trace of homosexual history, or those who were predominantly homosexual, were eliminated from the population today, there is no reason for believing that the incidence of the homosexual in the next generation would be materially reduced. The homosexual has been a significant part of human sexual activity ever since the dawn of history, primarily because it is an expression of capacities that are basic in the human animal.

Appendix II

1970 Kinsey Institute Survey
summary and analysis by Ron Schow

(based on Albert D. Klassen, Colin J. Williams, and Eugene E. Levitt, *Sex and Morality in the U.S.: An Empirical Enquiry under the Auspices of the Kinsey Institute* [1989])

[*Editors' note:* Rather than include excerpts from the 1953 Kinsey study on females, which would be somewhat repetitive of the male report, we have chosen to include a more recent report comparing females and males.]

Through the use of a national population probability sample, both males and females were asked a series of questions about their homosexual experience and feeling. The total male sample involved an N=1,465, while the female sample had a slightly larger N=1,553. Respondents were asked a large number of questions about their sex play as children, about other males and females they had known who had engaged in sexual activities with the same sex, about the first time they engaged in sexual experience with someone of the same sex, about the possibility of enjoyment of sex with same-sex persons, and finally about thoughts that they might be homosexual.

The results revealed differences between males and females and interesting patterns of non-response. Although nearly all respondents were willing to answer questions about sex play as a child, several hundred did not answer on each of several other questions about homosexual conduct and feeling. The failure to respond cannot be assumed to be an admission of homosexual participation, but it is interesting to consider that possibility.

When asked about same-sex play as children (sexual parts touched) only 23 males and 39 females failed to respond. Similar high percentages of response were recorded when respondents were asked about males and females they knew who engaged in sex acts with other same-sex individuals. However, when asked for their age the first time they had experience with same-sex individuals leading to sexual climax of one or the other or both, there were 273 males and 265 females who did not answer. If these non-responders were included as participants in such activity, the male percentage for such behavior rises from 18 percent to 33 percent and the female from 9 percent to 25 percent. If even half of these non-responders were included the male percentage is 23 percent and the female 16 percent. One analysis of these data used a conservative interpretation which assumed almost half of the non-responders were hiding participation (Turner, Miller, and Moses, 1989).

For a substantial portion of the respondents, this homosexual activity occurred not only early in life; neither was it limited to a single episode. Of those 18 percent of males and 9 percent of females who acknowledge this activity (N=1,192 males and 1,288 females answering this question) there were 7/18 of the males and 7/9 of the females who admit such activity first at age sixteen or older, and for 3/18 of the males and 3/9 of the females this first happened in their twenties and later. There were 77 percent of these participating males and 63 percent of the participating females who reported having the experience more than once, and most participated more than twice. There were 59 males (5 percent of 1,192) and 14 females (1 percent of 1,288) who had the experience with more than 3 partners. If a portion of the non-responders were included as participants in such activity this would, of course, increase these percentages.

More respondents were evident when the survey asked: "If there was no question of right or wrong would same-sex activity offer any possibility of enjoyment?" Only 128 men and 98 women did not respond. Among the respondents 14 percent of the men and 10 percent of the women said yes. These percentages would change to 22 percent of the men and 16 percent of the women if the non-respondents had said yes. There were 151 men and 106 women who reported the possibility of sexual enjoyment with both sexes; however, most of these said opposite-sex enjoyment would be greater. These numbers suggest about 10 percent of men and 7 percent of women acknowledge some degree of bisexuality, so apparently a large portion of those enjoying same-sex activity would be bisexual.

Despite the above indications of homosexual or bisexual inclination, only 3 percent of the males (N=1,370) and 2 percent of the females (N=1,473) directly acknowledged that they had ever thought they might be gay or lesbian.

These numbers suggest at least 18 percent of the men and 9 percent of the women have had homosexual activity leading to orgasm at some time in life. When the non-responders are considered, these numbers could easily increase to the one-quarter to one-third proportion in males reported by Kinsey et al. (1948) and by Gebhard (1972) and to a higher number in females as well. The number of persons with homosexual or bisexual feelings seems to be at least 14 percent in males and 10 percent in females, but again when non-responders are considered, these numbers could increase so they would be closer to the nearly 30 percent in males and 20 percent in females as reported for the original Kinsey studies. While those admitting enjoyment with same-sex activity was 10-14 percent, those thinking they are homosexual or lesbian and admitting it involved only 3 percent for men and 2 percent for women. These latter numbers fall below the 4-5 percent of males considered to be strictly homosexual (6's) and the 8-10 percent usually considered to be predominantly homosexual (5's and 6's). Also this understates the percentages for females which are usually about one-half those for males. Consideration of the non-responders again may be the key to the discrepancy here.

It is predictable that the percentages as found with a written questionnaire in this study would not be as high as those deriving from the interview format of Kinsey's early work. An alternate interpretation is that the original Kinsey reports were biased and overstated with regard to homosexuality. If so, perhaps the percentages reported originally should be halved. Even with this more conservative view, however, the number of people involved is still on the order of 10-17 percent who have various degrees of homosexuality and bisexuality. Consideration of non-responders and bias may suggest that the truth lies somewhere in between the original Kinsey findings and the newer data from more careful samples which nevertheless have non-respondent bias. (Full citations for references noted above are found on page 162.)

Selected Data from the 1970 Kinsey Survey
(Excerpted from *Sex and Morality in the U.S.*
Appendix F, pages 396-420)

A. When you were a child, before your body developed sexually, did you ever have playmates, brothers or sisters, or anyone else who had any kind of sex play or sex games with you? This idea of "sex play" does not require that sexual parts of one child touched the sexual parts of another; it *does mean* that sexual parts of one child were touched by another child.

	Males (N=1442)	Females (N=1514)
No	53.3%	65.1%
Yes	46.7	34.9

[If yes:]
A(1). Was the sex play with children of your own sex, of the opposite sex, or of both sexes?

	(N=673)	(N=528)
Only of my own sex	6.8%	21.6%
Only of the opposite sex	42.2	35.6
Of both sexes	51.0	42.8

Excerpts reprinted by permission of the Kinsey Institute for Research in Sex, Gender, and Reproduction, Inc.

66. The way people feel about these things is sometimes influenced by people they may have known. Have you ever been personally acquainted with any men or boys—not necessarily as friends—who engaged in sex acts with other males?

	(N=1447)	(N=1553)
No, or don't know	55.5%	69.8%
Yes	44.5	30.2

66F. About how many is that altogether?

	(N=653)	(N=472)
One or two	27.1%	45.3%
Three to five	24.0	29.0
Six to ten	24.0	13.6
11 to 25	12.4	8.1
More than 25	12.4	4.0

67. And have you ever been personally acquainted with any women or girls—not necessarily as friends—who engaged in sex acts with other females?

	(N=1455)	(N=1543)
No, or don't know	75.9%	76.2%
Yes	24.1	23.8

67F. About how many is that altogether?

	(N=352)	(N=371)
One or two	31.5%	56.6%
Three to five	26.1	23.5
Six to ten	19.9	11.9
11 to 25	14.5	7.3
More than 25	8.0	0.8

I. What was your age the first time you had sexual experience with someone of the *same sex,* when either you or your partner came to a sexual climax? This includes persons of the same sex helping each other masturbate.

	(N=1192)	(N=1288)
7 or younger	0.8%	0.7%
8 to 10	2.2	0.9
11 to 15	7.6	1.1
16 to 19	3.9	3.3
20 to 24	2.0	2.8
25 to 29	0.7	0.4
30 or older	0.3	0.1
Never	82.6	90.8

J(2)a. Did you have this experience only once?

	(N=184)	(N=88)
No—more than once	76.6%	62.5%
Yes, only once	23.4	37.5

[If more than one homosexual experience:]

J(3). Was there a period of time when you had this experience fairly often, occasionally, or rarely, or did it happen only twice?

	(N=137)	(N=48)
Only twice	19.0%	25.0%
Rarely	27.7	20.8
Occasionally	35.0	22.9
Fairly often	18.2	31.2

J(4). Altogether, with about how many persons did you have this experience?

	(N=126)	(N=49)
Always the same partner	17.5%	51.0%
Two different partners	35.7	20.4
Three partners	14.3	12.2
Four to six partners	18.3	6.1
Seven to nine partners	2.4	6.1
10 to 20 partners	9.5	2.0
More than 20 partners	2.4	2.0

L. If there was no question of right or wrong, would you say that sex with a person of the *same sex* offers you any possibility of enjoyment?

	(N=1337)	(N=1455)
No	85.8%	90.2%
Yes	14.2	9.8

M. Does sex with a person of the *opposite sex* offer you any possibility of enjoyment? Any possibility of enjoyment, including love, affection, marriage, should be counted as "yes" here.

	(N=1352)	(N=1452)
No	11.8%	14.3%
Yes	88.2	85.7

[If yes to both:]

N. Does sex with a person of the opposite sex offer you more, less, or about the same amount of enjoyment as sex with a person of the same sex?

	(N=151)	(N=106)
Opposite sex more enjoyable	80.1%	85.8%
About the same	9.3	8.5
Same sex more enjoyable	10.6	5.7

P. Have you ever thought that you might be homosexual or lesbian?

	(N=1370)	(N=1473)
No	96.9%	98.0%
Yes	3.1	2.0

Index

ABOUT THE EDITORS

RON SCHOW is Professor of Audiology in the College of Health-Related Professions at Idaho State University in Pocatello. He draws on his training and interests in zoology, genetics, psychology, and counseling in attempting to reconcile various professional and religious perspectives on homosexuality.

WAYNE SCHOW is Professor of English and chairs the Department of English and Philosophy at Idaho State University. Having confronted homosexuality through the experiences of his oldest son, he has seen directly the alienation and ostracism experienced by Mormon homosexuals and their families.

MARYBETH RAYNES is a licensed clinical social worker and marriage and family therapist in Salt Lake City, Utah, as well as an adjunct assistant professor in the Graduate School of Social Work at the University of Utah. She has long been aware through her professional and clinical experiences of the challenges facing homosexual Mormons.